THE SECRETARY

THE SECRETARY

A JOURNEY WITH

HILLARY CLINTON

FROM BEIRUT TO

THE HEART OF

AMERICAN POWER

KIM GHATTAS

Times Books
Henry Holt and Company
New York

Times Books
Henry Holt and Company, LLC
Publishers since 1866
175 Fifth Avenue
New York, New York 10010
www.henryholt.com

Henry Holt® is a registered trademark of Henry Holt and Company, LLC.

Library of Congress Cataloging-in-Publication Data

Ghattas, Kim.
  The secretary : a journey with Hillary Clinton from Beirut to the heart of American power / Kim Ghattas.—First edition.
    pages cm
  Includes bibliographical references and index.
  ISBN 978-0-8050-9868-6
  1. Clinton, Hillary Rodham.   2. United States—Foreign relations—2009–
3. Cabinet officers—United States—Biography.   4. Women cabinet officers—United
States—Biography.   I. Title.
  E887.C55G53 2013
  327.730092—dc23
  [B]   2012043835

Henry Holt books are available for special promotions and premiums.
For details contact: Director, Special Markets.

First International Edition 2013

Designed by Meryl Sussman Levavi

10 9 8 7 6 5 4 3 2 1

For Lebanon and for my family,

they made me who I am.

CONTENTS

PART III

INTRODUCTION

War is a force that gives us meaning.

—Chris Hedges, 2002

grew up in Beirut, on the front lines of a civil war. My father always said, "If America wanted the fighting to end, the war would be over tomorrow." He waited fifteen years for the guns to fall silent. From 1975 to 1990, everybody waited while 150,000 people died. Did America not care that people were being killed? Did it not have the power to stop the bloodshed? Were we just a pawn in the hands of the neocolonial imperial power? And why were we all blaming this distant land for our war, anyway?

As a child, I never imagined I would one day live in that distant land and would be able to put some of those questions to the American secretary of state Hillary Clinton. As a reporter, in the State Department press corps, I would even fly from Washington to Beirut with her, on an aging American government plane, which contrasted somewhat with my image of an omnipotent superpower.

During the war in Lebanon, America received the most calls for help and the biggest share of blame in a conflict so complicated that even the Lebanese sometimes lost the plot. The United States was one of many countries playing a role, though there were those who believed only the United States could save Lebanon from its descent into a seemingly bottomless hell. Others were convinced America was the reason for our suffering. People who disagreed about everything, who either loved or resented the United States, shared one conviction: America was omnipotent; its power knew no bounds.

My own family was liberal and secular, and with a Dutch mother, we felt attached to Lebanon yet also connected to the West. Although we often felt ambivalent about U.S. foreign policy in the Middle East, Europe and America symbolized hope, a chance for a better life if we decided to leave Lebanon. We did not identify with the Soviet Union, Iran, or Syria, though many of our compatriots did. Ours is a country with multiple political identities and a multitude of religious communities.

War is a maturing experience; at the age of thirteen, I decided I would be a journalist. I was tired of explaining to friends and relatives abroad that Lebanon was not flattened by bombs, that I still went to school— though there were long periods where the shelling was too intense—that we still went out for family lunch on Sundays when the snipers took some time off. I was tired of the raised eyebrows when we presented our passports at airports during the days when Lebanon and Beirut were associated with plane hijackings and bloodthirsty gunmen. I just wanted the world to understand what was really going on in my country.

One day, we woke up and peace had arrived. Or at least a semblance of peace—postwar societies are rarely stable. We were in fact under the military occupation of Syria, our neighbor to the east. I was just a teenager, but war was all I had known and I had trouble adjusting to life without adrenaline. Bombardments had been replaced with a deafening silence, and fireworks made me jump. I still hoped for an outburst of fighting that would shut down the road to school as an excuse not to do my homework. The army was still on the move often, its tanks rumbling on city streets, checkpoints manned by trigger-happy Syrian soldiers terrified us at all hours of the day, and scores were still being settled with gruesome political assassinations. After high school, many of my friends left Lebanon and enrolled in universities in Europe and the United States, hoping to build a better, more sane future. I followed my childhood dream and stayed in Beirut.

I reported on my country for American and European newspapers and then became a radio and television journalist for the British Broadcasting Corporation. After covering political unrest, assassinations, uprisings, and more wars in Lebanon, as well as the invasion of Iraq and repression across the Middle East, I finally left the city that had made me a journalist and moved from Beirut to Washington in 2008, at the age of thirty-two, to be the BBC's State Department correspondent. I had over-dosed on instability and uncertainty and felt only relief as I arrived in the United States. I did sometimes wake up in Washington wondering about the meaning of life now that it didn't involve a daily struggle. Could it really be just a steady stream of days in the office, dinner with friends, and weekends puttering at home? I got my adrenaline fix from a new, much healthier source. I had become part of the small group of journalists, known as the traveling press corps, covering the secretary of state in Washington and on international diplomatic missions—last-minute plans for frenzied jaunts around the globe on a U.S. government plane, motorcades racing through world capitals at breakneck speed, and high-wire diplomatic talks about war and peace.

My BBC predecessors had all been British; I was also the only non-Western journalist in the group. My background informed and enriched my reporting—I had lived on the receiving end of American foreign policy my whole life; I knew the very real-life consequences of decisions made at the White House, the State Department, or the Pentagon. Now I had a front-row seat to watch that policy unfold, succeed, and often fail.

On my travels, from London to Kabul and Beijing, I heard countless echoes of my own frustrations and hopes about the United States. Even today, while America is deeply in debt again, exhausted by two wars, its influence challenged by rivals big and small, millions of people around the world still believe that the United States can snap its fingers to make things happen, for good or bad, just as I had believed as a child. But in Washington, I found American officials frustrated and exhausted by the heavy lifting required to advance their country's interests or to get any-thing done around the globe. America really did seem to be in decline. Or was this just the reality of a complex and fast-changing world?

As I prodded for answers and dug deeper, I began to feel that news reports for television and radio were no longer enough to share every-thing I was learning—it was time to write a book. I didn't want to simply record observations from my travels and reflect on my feelings along the way; I wanted to enrich my perspective on the events I saw unfolding in public with the points of view of those at the heart of action, working behind closed doors. Those untold moments rarely make it into short news stories or big headlines but they provide valuable context that tells a fuller story. Over the course of a year, I interviewed several dozen senior American officials, junior officials, foreign ministers of other countries and their advisors, in Washington and abroad, sometimes immediately after a diplomatic crisis, other times with hindsight. Many of them spoke to me more than once, often for several hours, in person or by phone. I conducted the interviews on a "deep background" basis, a journalistic term that means I would use the anecdotes, observations, or analyses shared with me during the interviews, but I would not identify the source. The promise of anonymity often allows people to be more open in their descriptions, in their retelling of events, and in sharing their emotions and thoughts. Dialogue in quotation marks has been retold to me by the speaker or someone in the room; I have paraphrased occasionally to condense long conversations or because my sources were uncertain about the precise wording used, but the context or content was never in doubt.

The result is a rich canvas of different points of view, American and foreign: a multidimensional look at some of the issues and crises that have marked the Obama administration over the last four years, from the Arab Spring to the Asian pivot. It's a journey across hundreds of thousands of miles, from the Elysée Palace in Paris to the Saudi king's desert retreat. It's a journey in the company of the real people behind American power, the fallible human beings who devise American foreign policy in an increasingly complicated world and the foreign officials with whom they cooperate, jostle, and clash on a daily basis.

It's also my own journey from Beirut to Washington, as I try to come to terms with my personal misgivings about American power and look for answers to the questions that haunted my childhood: Did America not care that the Lebanese were dying? Does America still matter in today's world where China, Turkey, Brazil, India, and others are all competing for a bigger say in how the world is run?

I look at the bigger picture of American power on the world stage through the eyes of the woman who came to symbolize America, almost as much if not more than President Barack Obama. For four years I traveled on a plane with Hillary Clinton, scrutinizing her every word and move to determine what the essence of American power and influence may be. And I watched her make her own journey during that time, from defeated presidential candidate and polarizing politician to a rock star diplomat, admired and respected around the world, at an all-time high in the polls in her own country. I've observed Clinton, the secretary of state, grow into her role and establish her own brand of diplomacy. But I also saw Hillary, the woman, in action, close-up, with and without makeup. In the spotlight for decades, Hillary Rodham Clinton is often referred to simply as Hillary and I have chosen to refer to her as Hillary occasionally in the book, not out of any familiarity but to highlight more private moments as the public rediscovers a woman it has known for years.

When she took on the challenge of restoring America's reputation, the United States was at a crossroads, its influence shunned by others after eight years of the Bush administration. As President Barack Obama's envoy to the world, Clinton set out to make her country a wanted partner once more, finding new spheres of influence and exploring the new frontiers of twenty-first-century diplomacy from her very first day at the State Department.

PART I

You are the agents of innocence. That is why you make so much mischief. You come into a place like Lebanon as if you were missionaries. You convince people to put aside their old customs and allegiances and to break the bonds that hold the country together. With your money and your schools and your cigarettes and music, you convince us that we can be like you. But we can't. And when the real trouble begins, you are gone. And you leave your friends, the ones who trusted you the most, to die. I will tell you what it is. You urge us to open up the windows of heaven. But you do not realize that the downpour will come rushing and drown us all.

—Fuad, Palestinian CIA informant,
in David Ignatius, *Agents of Innocence*

1

WHO DO YOU CALL?

The armored black Cadillac stood waiting in the horseshoe driveway outside 3067 Whitehaven Street, in northwest Washington. Inside the three-story Georgian house, last-minute preparations were under way ahead of a first day at work. Two women talked through their schedule, checked that their BlackBerries were in their handbags, applied a last dab of lipstick. For the umpteenth time, Fred Ketchem went over the route for his package in his head. In his left ear, he could hear the chatter of his team along the way: the road was still clear. He checked alternative routes again, just in case. Until just a few weeks ago, he had been responsible for the safety of three thousand people implementing American foreign policy in one of the world's most dangerous diplomatic missions— Baghdad. Now, he was charged with the security of America's top diplomat. He had to remind himself that this wasn't Iraq. There would be no hair-trigger checkpoints, no bearded gunmen, no roadside bombs planted along the way; the only hazards here were fire trucks and car accidents. Even so, he wanted the first day, the first drive, to be as smooth as possible. Standing in the crisp January cold, Fred kept his eyes on the portico. A few miles away, in a building that looked like a remnant of Soviet architecture, the crowd was gathering.

It was just a few minutes past nine in the morning on January 22, 2009, when the dark door between the two white columns swung open and a middle-aged woman with short ash-blond hair, wearing a coffee-brown woven wool pantsuit and kitten heels, emerged. She walked down the steps to the car, a young statuesque woman with flowing jet-black hair following closely behind her.

"Good morning, Fred!" said Hillary Clinton.

"Good morning, Madame Secretary."

"Thank you for being here on our first day. We're going to be very busy in the coming few years."

Fred opened the rear right door for his new boss before getting into the front passenger seat. Huma Abedin, Hillary's longtime aide, got in on the other side. Otis, the trusted government driver who had ferried Condoleezza Rice and Colin Powell around the city, was at the wheel. The package, the now-full Cadillac sandwiched between a black SUV leading in front and two following, headed down the hill to Foggy Bottom. When the Department of State chose the area as its home in 1947, the swampy fog had long since dissipated from the banks of the Potomac. As the government redeveloped the area, the industrial slum, smoke stacks, and tenement dwellings at the southwestern edge of the nation's capital gradually gave way to more government offices, luxury residential buildings such as the curved Watergate complex, and the boxlike white marble Kennedy Center for the Performing Arts. But the area's name had stuck, an inadvertent reminder of the fog of information that American diplomats often had to swim through to make their decisions.

That morning, the skies were a bright blue, and Hillary's mind was clear. She felt excited about her new job, expectant about the contribution she could make to her country, and determined to tackle the daunting challenges facing America around the world. The chatter of National Public Radio's *Morning Edition* news program provided a background hum as she went over the day's schedule with Huma one more time.

Clinton had spent the past few weeks preparing for her Senate confirmation hearing as secretary of state in Barack Obama's cabinet. She had to lay out her vision for American diplomacy and leadership around the world while demonstrating her loyalty to the new president, her former rival. But she also had to absorb vast amounts of information to prove she knew all the issues. It was like preparing for the bar exam again. On the campaign trail, Obama had reduced her foreign policy experience to sipping tea with foreign leaders as a First Lady. She was not exactly a neophyte but neither was she a seasoned diplomat, so the learning curve was steep. But Hillary had always known how to be a star pupil. She nailed questions about the more obscure, dry pet subjects of her former Senate colleagues and brought them to life as though she'd spent years thinking about Arctic policy and mineral-rich countries. She talked about cruise ships sailing past Point Barrow because of melting ice and Botswana's great stewardship of its diamond riches. She outwonked all the wonks in the Senate room by mastering all the details. Clinton also explained how she envisaged the exercise of American power: it had to be "smart." Not just soft diplomacy, with a focus on development or just hard military power, but a combination—an updated, global version of the Marshall Plan. "Smart power" was a concept coined by political scientists like Joseph Nye but had never been implemented methodically before.

Hillary couldn't remember the last time she'd had some real time off. She had gone from being First Lady to running for senator, then jumped from the daily business of the Senate to the campaign trail to her new, unexpected job. The race for the Democratic nomination had been bruising, hurtful, and ugly. She had been defeated and discredited by her loss despite the millions of loyal voters who had backed her. Campaigning for Barack Obama on the shoulders of such loss had just added to her exhaustion. Obama had urged her to accept the job with unusual candor, telling Clinton he needed her, but serving her former nemesis involved a bracing lesson in humility. Clinton didn't know how the relationship with Obama would work out, but she knew what a president needed—team players. Her Girl Scout instincts kicked in. She was on the team and she wanted the whole team to look good. She wanted America to look good again. Hillary was ready to play, but she was also ready for some red-carpet treatment, some respect, and some camera attention to soothe her campaign wounds. New challenges invigorated her. The adrenaline had kicked in, and she felt and looked energized, ready for her grand entrance.

The package pulled up outside the main entrance of the State Department. Fred opened the car door for the secretary of state. The crowd erupted in cheers.

"Hello, hello," she said in her booming voice as she stepped out of the limousine. She held her hands above her head, clapping, smiling, and began to shake hands with the senior officials who stood on the red carpet to welcome her. Clinton walked the rope line, greeting her new staff, shaking hands with some of them. One man screamed "Yeah, Yeah!" as though he'd just won something. She shook hands with the two guards standing by the glass doors before walking into the Harry S. Truman building and being engulfed in a crowd of hundreds of State Department employees. Colin Powell, a deeply respected and personable former general, had been greeted with applause in the State Department lobby when he arrived in 2001, and even Condoleezza Rice had received an unexpectedly warm welcome in the midst of the Iraq debacle in 2005.

But no one could pack a room almost half the size of a soccer field like Hillary. A polarizing, controversial politician, she was also a celebrity with the ability to elicit fervent support and admiration. The three-story-high lobby of the State Department echoed with rapturous applause, punctuated with cries of "We love you, Hillary!" Across the whole floor and the steps leading to the mezzanine on either side, dozens of people craned their necks, stood on their toes, or leaned over the glass-and-aluminum railing to catch a glimpse of her. People waved their cell phones to snap pictures, and camera crews beamed the event to television networks around the country and beyond. Hillary waded through the human mass pressed against thirty-foot-tall marble and granite columns. Three diplomatic security agents cleared the way in front of her, Fred and another agent following behind. Even a friendly crowd of overexcited Foreign Service officers could crush the secretary. She smiled, excited but poised, shook hands, paused to speak to those who didn't let go quickly enough.

In the State Department lobby, there were young women who had voted for her in the primaries and older women who'd always admired her as a trailblazer for women's rights and a fighter who had defied the odds and overcome adversity in her personal life. There were those who always voted for a Democrat. And then there were all the others too—American diplomats and civil servants, men and women, who had felt sidelined during almost eight years of war in Iraq and Afghanistan and were demoralized by the damage that the Bush administration's high-handed foreign policy had inflicted upon America's image. When Clinton made it to the landing of the steps leading to the mezzanine, Steve Kaskent, a representative of the Foreign Service union, introduced her to some of her twenty thousand new employees, joking that it looked like they were all crammed in the space below them. No one even tried to hide their relief that the country was moving on.

"Both you and the president have decried the neglect that the Foreign Service and the State Department have suffered in recent years," he said. "No one knows better than the people in this room and our colleagues around the world how true that is. We are thrilled to have you here."

In the crowd below, Lissa Muscatine looked around her and smiled, pleased to see her longtime friend bathed in affection and appreciation, a welcome change after almost two years of searing battles and disappointments. Muscatine had been Hillary's speechwriter at the White House when she was First Lady, and she had once again agreed to craft Hillary's speeches to the world.

Clinton waved and bowed her head, smiling. Fred, with a long, serious face and round cheeks, stood guard behind her, his dark hair parted neatly to the side, his eyes darting around.

"I believe with all my heart that this is a new era for America," Clinton said into the microphone. In front of her, the northern glass wall of the lobby was lined with the flags of all the countries where the United States had an embassy and where she would deliver the Obama administration's message of engagement with the world over the coming four years. She warned the crowd that it wasn't going to be easy. She asked her new staff to think creatively about old problems. She said she welcomed debate, and she waved her right hand to emphasize each point. It sounded like a political stump speech, but this was a new campaign to lift the spirits of those who kept the American foreign policy machine running. She announced to wild cheers that President Obama and Vice President Joe Biden would be visiting the State Department, or as Clinton called it, "this organic, living creature called the Building."

"This is a team, and you are the members of that team. There isn't anything that I can get done from the seventh floor or that the president can get done from the Oval Office, unless we make clear we are all on the American team. We are not any longer going to tolerate the kind of divisiveness that has paralyzed and undermined our ability to get things done for America."

Then it was time to get down to work. Hillary had been in the building many times before, as a First Lady during her husband's presidency and, more recently, during the transition period between Bush and Obama. Like everybody else, she rode in one of the main elevators. But now, as secretary of state, she had access to a private, wood-paneled elevator that took her straight to the foyer of her quarters on the seventh floor. She walked down Mahogany Row, a carpeted hallway that was home to the top tier of State Department officials, one of the rare plush hallways in a building that otherwise reminded some of its occupants of a psychiatric institution, all stark white corridors, white fluorescent lights, and linoleum floors. Though it was her first day at work, it was a normal workday in the building and Hillary stopped in each office along the way, shaking hands and meeting her staff. Then she walked into her light-flooded outer office with its elegant living room furniture and fireplace, and stepped into her darker, smaller study. In a drawer of the desk, a welcome note awaited her. Signed "Condoleezza Rice," it had almost been thrown out the day before by staffers clearing the office of all things Condi, saved at the last minute by a staffer who noticed the name on the envelope in the drawer. Neither Rice nor Clinton ever revealed what the note said.

The two women had first met in August 1996, when Rice was provost of Stanford University. Hillary's daughter, Chelsea, was deciding which university to attend, and Rice welcomed mother and daughter at the start of their tour of the university campus. The two women had spoken occasionally during the eight years and three weeks that Clinton spent in the Senate, but they were backing different teams. Clinton, like most Democrats, was a harsh critic of the Republican administration. Now Clinton found herself in Rice's position, occupying her old office. There may have been a new president inside the White House who was all about change, but outside, it was the same unruly world that Rice had faced. Clinton had consulted all her living predecessors, but it was over a long dinner at Rice's Watergate apartment in Washington a few weeks after the presidential election that she got the most up-to-date information about all the players on the international scene and the lowdown on every issue in her in-box. It would be the first of many conversations between the two women over the next four years.

On the second floor of the Building, around the corner from the mezzanine, Fred settled into his professional quarters. His job guarding the secretary put him in charge of a large team of Diplomatic Security agents who would protect Clinton during every move she made, both in the United States and around the world. A thin-built, meticulous man with an aquiline nose, he looked more like a banker than a security official. He kept his surroundings uncluttered—on one wall, a world map; on another, a flat-screen television; on a table, his parting gift from Iraq, the flag that had flown over the Iraqi Republican palace that had housed America's diplomats before the new embassy was inaugurated. The flag was now folded into a triangle, resting in a flag box with a plaque thanking him for his services.

On the other side of the mezzanine, down a hallway with blue linoleum floors and a picture of Tanzania's Mount Kilimanjaro, the occupants of Room 2206 were eagerly awaiting their first conversation with the woman who was the new subject of their reportage. Room 2206 housed the permanent State Department press corps: all of the major American newspapers, radio stations, and television networks had desks here (and a seat on the secretary of state's Boeing 757). International news agencies like the Associated Press (AP), Reuters, and Agence France-Presse (AFP) were also part of the pack, telegraphing news from the American capital to the outside world. Thanks to its international reach, the BBC was admitted into this exclusive travel circle in 1993. The room was a large rectangular space overlooking a 1960s bronze sculpture—*Man and the Expanding Universe*—that presided over one of the department's two inner courtyards. Cubicles lined the walls and occupied the center of the room. A couple of us were lucky enough to have windows. The rest typed away in semidarkness surrounded by gray walls and gray carpets. With only a few minutes' notice on a drab, cold Tuesday morning, a few days after her grand entrance in the Building, the secretary arrived at our threshold, and we scurried out of our holes to shake her hand.

We were all seasoned reporters—some of us had covered several secretaries of state—so no one applauded, though most of us couldn't help feeling slightly starstruck, grinning widely and trying to think of something clever to say other than hello to make a lasting impression. But we were also wary, unsure about how the political machine Hillary had brought with her from the Senate and her campaign would coexist with the content and detail-obsessed world of foreign policy. The national media had clobbered Hillary during the primary race, ready to pounce on her at every corner. Americans loved her or hated her with equal passion. She said she'd felt like a piñata. Now, she slowly sized up her new press pack, about fifteen of us, probably wondering how we would treat her, whether we'd continue the battering. We introduced ourselves, and she repeated each of our names, shaking our hands, nodding mechanically with a semi-smile. She was guarded and seemed cold behind her smile, a politician on duty. She looked around at our grim quarters and said, with no trace of irony, "Your digs are better than those of the press at the White House." Ouch. We had been hoping for an upgrade.

Clinton sat down at the head of the large conference table on one end of the room in between two rows of cubicles and faced a torrent of questions.

"Madame Secretary, what about North Korea?"

"Madame Secretary, what about Iran?"

"What about Middle East peace?"

Everything was a priority, but one task mattered most to Clinton and Obama.

"There's a great exhalation of breath going on around the world as people express their appreciation for the new direction that's being set," Clinton said. "We have a lot of damage to repair."

This had been a key message of Obama's campaign but hearing it from Clinton's mouth at such proximity made it real, as if it could happen. But I also wondered how different things could actually be under a new administration.

Obama's campaign rhetoric made it sound like America had lost its way and would now return to the right path. But it wasn't as though the United States had been a virtuous force for good or a perfect superpower for decades that had suddenly and inexplicably taken a turn for the worse during the Bush administration. The reality was more complex. The misgivings of America's critics around the world had only been exacerbated by the hubris that the Bush administration had displayed. My own ambivalence about America had started well before the election of George W. Bush. I was a liberal, moderate secular Lebanese woman with a Dutch mother. In a country where many looked to Iran or Syria for guidance, I was more at home in the other half of the country, the pro-Western, pro-American camp. Yet I had often felt let down by the United States, whether the president was a Democrat or a Republican.

As a young woman living in Beirut, I couldn't quite explain why and I didn't know where to look for the answers amid the uncertainty that seemed to permeate all aspects of life in the Arab world. Now, I enjoyed living in the United States away from that chaos, though I struggled to reconcile my positive impression of this country, its people, and its diplomats, with the confusion and frustration I often felt in the face of American foreign policy. After eight years of the Bush administration, with its two wars and its "You're with us or against us" approach to the world, I wondered if the United States would ever understand the rest of the planet. I was ready to give up for good. "Maybe America should just stay home" was a common refrain around me.

But I was willing to give the United States another chance and find out what the new president would bring to the world. And judging from the headlines around the world on November 7, 2008, and the parties celebrating his victory from France to Kenya, people everywhere expected Obama to deliver for them. Now Clinton was his envoy to the world.

An assembly line of problems was making its way through the Building, bursting into people's offices at all hours of the day. Every issue was urgent, every crisis a priority, like triage in a hospital emergency room. There was also pressure of another kind. At the White House, when a new president moves in, he finds a mostly empty shell that he then fills with his team—advisors from the campaign, die-hard loyalists who yearn to serve, policy experts who share his vision. But at the State Department, when a secretary of state leaves, he or she takes only a couple hundred political appointees, leaving a steady cadre of twenty thousand career Foreign Service officers and civil servants at their desks in Foggy Bottom and at State Department offices across town. Inevitably, there is friction between the old and the new. With Clinton's arrival, it was of a wholly different order.

In the Building, most were willing to overlook Clinton's faults, forget the acrimony of the campaign, and embrace her as a rock star because she was now the emissary of the president of change. But Clinton didn't arrive alone. There was far less forgiveness for Hillaryland, Hillary's often chaotic, chronically late, and occasionally dysfunctional political machine made up of fiercely loyal friends, campaign advisors, and Senate staffers, people like Huma, Lissa, or Philippe Reines, Hillary's gatekeeper and media advisor. Their job was to serve her as Hillary the woman as much as the secretary of state, to make sure she had everything she needed to do her job, to make sure she looked good. But Hillary's close aides were met with skepticism, suspicion, and occasional disdain. *What do they really know about foreign policy*, people thought. "Hillaryland" originated from Hillary's days in the White House, the first time a First Lady occupied her own offices in the West Wing. The term described Hillary's staff, and the name stuck, though the size and lay of the land had changed over the years. Once again Hillaryland would grow and morph into something new.

When he gave her the job, Obama had agreed that Clinton could choose the political appointees who would fill the vacant seats in the Building to help her implement American foreign policy. The president's team bristled at such latitude: no other cabinet member was being given such freedom in this administration. Why should a woman who had wrestled him for the Democratic nomination be allowed to reward her friends with plummy jobs? Presidential campaigns are divisive, all consuming, and emotional—and the fighting for the Democratic nomination had been drawn out, malicious, and messy. Obama too was surrounded by loyalists, and some were never able to lay the campaign mind-set aside. These key policy positions, they felt, should go to Obama supporters, to those who had sided with Obama and with change from the beginning, not to the woman who had challenged him.

Although he had belittled her foreign policy experience during the campaign, Obama knew that only Clinton came with the built-in international stature and credibility that allowed her to instantly board a plane and stand in for him while he fixed the economy at home. He had decided to ask her to do the job well before the election of November 4. She had not expected the offer, but the call of public service was strong, and she agreed to support his mission to restore America's lost face in the world. You don't say no when the president asks you to serve, she kept telling her friends. There were also more narrow political considerations. Obama didn't want to risk having her as a critic in the Senate, and she was uncertain how much more she could rise as a senator. Obama and Clinton decided to trust each other. It would take them some time to find their groove, but they saw themselves as teammates, even if their respective squads did not share this vision.

Obama's advisors formed a close bubble around him in the confines of the West Wing. The newcomers in the Building were quickly swallowed up by a massive, unwieldy bureaucracy. It was hard to maintain a coterie around Hillary when the political appointees she brought with her weren't in the office next door but housed somewhere in the Building's 4,975 rooms, down one of the eighty-four hallways, on one of the eight floors, connected by twelve elevators. Hillary and her team had always worked in small, agile offices where staffers devoted more time to substance than process. She had never worked in an office where she didn't know everyone's name, and now she was in charge of thousands. Every paper her team wrote, every memo they issued, seemed to zing around the building for hours, up and down the hallways and elevators to various floors, before it would finally be approved. The Building was a place, but it was also a massive operation that groaned under the weight of dated habits. Dozens of copies of the *New York Post* arrived every morning because this paper had been Colin Powell's favorite, never mind that his last day on the job had been in January 2005. Clinton started her workday at 8:00 in the morning, but her special assistant, left over from the Rice era, had been showing up every day at the predawn hour of 4:30. That's how it had worked under Rice, who showed up at work at 5:00 on most days. Working hours were promptly adjusted.

Hillary's team had to figure out how best to serve Hillary in her new role, how to find their way to the cafeteria on the first floor and make it back to their desks again in the labyrinthine building, how to fit into the system or bend it to their needs. And every day, they had to ask, "Who do you call?" Who did you call if you wanted to translate an opinion piece by the secretary of state into dozens of languages and have it published in 139 newspapers and on websites in sixty countries? Who did you call if you wanted to plan media coverage of her next speech? Who did you call if you needed a printer? Who did you call if you wanted to get anything done?

Jake Sullivan wasn't even certain what needed to be done or where to start. A pale, blue-eyed, young Minnesotan lawyer, he was a newcomer, arriving at the State Department a few hours after Clinton's raucous welcome. He rode the elevator to his new cubbyhole office on the seventh floor and turned on his computer. Hillaryland was new territory for him. He had met her only two years earlier, when he joined Clinton's campaign as a deputy policy advisor. It sounded like a grand title, but he was just one of the many players in the massive campaign machine. After Clinton lost the Democratic nomination, he jumped to the Obama team, helping with the presidential debate preparations and later working on the transition team. Jake had been planning to head back to Minnesota when Cheryl Mills, a key figure in the Clinton White House who was going to be Hillary's chief of staff, called to say Clinton wanted him with her at the State Department. He didn't know Hillary well, but he had liked her instantly when they met for his job interview at her campaign headquarters on Seventeenth and K Streets in Washington in March 2007. He found her impressive but down-to-earth, as keen to connect with people as she was to discuss ideas—a real, three-dimensional person. "Holy cow," Jake thought to himself that day. "You make a joke, she laughs; she asks you a question, she listens to the answer; she makes eye contact." He did not expect an exalted figure to behave this way.

Most of all, Jake had loved the way she talked about America on the campaign trail, and about how and why she wanted to be president of the United States. If there was one reason why he had ever wanted to serve in government, it was because Jake believed in America's ability to be a force for good. The pull of home was strong, Jake was not a fan of Washington, but when Cheryl, and later Hillary, told him he would regret not serving at a time of historic change in America, he agreed to be Clinton's deputy chief of staff. He didn't really know what that would involve, precisely. It was a new position in the building, and he didn't know how the State Department worked either. But on this first day, here he was, sitting across the hall from the secretary of state's office on Mahogany Row, his e-mail in-box already overflowing.

The phones were ringing incessantly. The world was calling. Countries around the world had always obsessively and irrationally craved attention from America, but now it seemed that everybody wanted to be touched by Obama and his secretary of state. European countries competed for an audience with Clinton at the State Department. The British and German foreign ministers both arrived for visits on the same day, February 2. David Miliband got to go first. After the talks, he declared before the cameras that the United Kingdom admired and respected

Clinton as an ambassador of America and "everything good it stood for." She lunched with the Germans. Then came the French. They all pleaded for her to visit the Old Continent on her first visit abroad. The Europeans believed that a quick visit from Clinton would perfectly seal the reconciliation with America that had only just started toward the end of the Bush administration after the deep rift caused by the Iraq War. The reconciliation could only feel real with a proper visit from the new Democratic administration. No promises were made and most visitors left with a signed copy of Hillary's autobiography, *Living History*. Clinton spoke to the Italian foreign minister, Franco Frattini, on the phone.

"Hi, this is Hillary, how are you, Mr. Minister?" she began. They talked about the close ties between Italy and the United States, and by the time the call ended, she was calling him by his first name.

"I look forward to seeing you in Washington, Franco," she ended. On the other side of the Atlantic, the minister was startled by the rapid transition in tone and by the unexpected warmth of this woman who had always seemed cold and distant on television.

In her first few months in office, Clinton took all the calls and welcomed all the visitors her schedule could accommodate from South Africa to Brazil, Lithuania, and Afghanistan. She believed that part of repairing America's standing in the world meant both reaching out to leaders she had known for years as well as making new connections, to ensure they knew they had access to her. She was making a very conscious investment for the future, when she would need these leaders. And for days on end, grown men would gush and beam at the cameras as they stood next to the politician turned diplomat. If there was one thing Hillary didn't need to learn, it was how to be in the limelight: she slid seamlessly into the role of a popular secretary of state, reveling in the attention of her foreign counterparts, attention that came with none of the bitter sniping of American politics.

The world was nearing a state of hysteria as governments everywhere waited for Washington to announce which country Clinton would visit on her maiden voyage as secretary of state. Newspapers around the world were full of speculation and advice about where Secretary Clinton should go first.

On the seventh floor, Jake Sullivan, Huma Abedin, Philippe Reines, Cheryl Mills, and the deputy secretary of state Jim Steinberg were drawing up a list of options. Europe was a traditional destination for the first visit, but the new administration wanted to signal change. The Middle East was still roiled by the Israeli military campaign code named "Cast Lead" against the radical militant group Hamas in the Palestinian territory of Gaza. The war had erupted in December 2008, right after the American presidential election, and had stopped just before the inauguration. Obama had signaled his commitment to the Middle East on his second day in office, but there was no reason to plunge Clinton into the quagmire of this conflict so quickly when all the talk was still of hope. The options were narrowed down to Afghanistan and Pakistan. Afghanistan was going to be "Obama's war," and having its neighbor Pakistan on board to tackle al-Qaeda and the Taliban would be key to any progress. In a town where everyone's favorite pastime is to speculate about who's up and who's down in the administration and in the political world, people were already murmuring about how much power Clinton really had on Obama's team. Her old friend Richard Holbrooke had just been appointed special representative for Afghanistan and Pakistan, and the Middle East file had been handed over to the quiet former senator from Maine George Mitchell, at Clinton's own suggestion. A trip to Afghanistan and Pakistan would show the world that Clinton had a say on the big issues. But for some on her team, even these choices were too traditional. The twenty-first century was taking shape in the East. If America wanted to be part of the future, the country needed to up its game in Asia.

The world was still reeling from the 2008 financial crisis. In her many phone calls to leaders around the world, Hillary had picked up on a strange combination of hope and anxiety. People still wanted American leadership, but the economic crisis had further tarnished the veneer of American invincibility.

"What is America going to do? What are you going to do about your own economy? If your economy goes down, how many more are you going to take down?" they asked her. Their questions implied more troubling concerns: "What do you stand for? Who are you?"[1]

Clinton believed deeply in American leadership. She was pained by the questions, and the world's perception of her country.

What better way to signal confidence and try to get the world economy back on track than by sending the chief diplomat of the biggest economy in the world to visit the countries with economy number two, China, and economy number three, Japan? Suddenly, Asia moved to the top of the list. Jeffrey Bader, the man in charge of Asia at the National Security Council at the White House, had been advocating for this as well, and Hillary needed no further convincing; the choice resonated with her own priorities. During her presidential campaign, she had said America's ties with China would be the most important bilateral relationship in the world in the twenty-first century. Huma, Jake, Cheryl, and the rest of the team started to painstakingly put together the itinerary. Japan, neglected by the Bush administration, forgotten even by Bill Clinton on his last presidential trip to the region, won top honors: the golden first visit. Indonesia was to be the second stop, followed by South Korea and China. Not since Dean Rusk in 1961 had an American secretary of state chosen Asia for a first trip. Rusk had gone to Thailand.

The Japanese were ecstatic though surprised, and the foreign ministry was flooded with media inquiries about why Clinton had chosen Tokyo as her first stop. What did it mean? They pored through their records to find out if an American secretary of state had ever chosen to visit Japan first but found nothing. There was no precedent. The Japanese foreign minister then declared the new U.S. administration clearly prioritized the Japan-U.S. alliance, and the visit was a "significant move." Every country on the itinerary made the exact same declaration. If showing up is half the battle, this battle had already been won before takeoff.

The detailed schedule still had to be fleshed out. What would happen on arrival; whom would she meet; where would she go? Huma and Philippe, the guardians of Hillary's image, wanted her trips to be different from anything the world had seen before. In the first two years of her tenure, Condoleezza Rice had indulged in town hall meetings with young people and cultural diplomacy events, but overall she conducted her trips like one might conduct business meetings: short jaunts, quick stops, mostly formal talks with officials. But Hillary wasn't simply a secretary of state: she was Hillary Rodham Clinton. She was a political powerhouse in her own right, and she was bigger than the job of secretary of state—the job would have to fit her, not the other way around.

The Asian visit was also a key moment for American leadership and the country's status as a superpower. The world had become allergic to

U.S. leadership by the end of the Bush administration. America's influence was waning, and without relentless work, the new beginning ushered in by Obama's election would quickly be wasted. The country needed to repair old alliances and build new partnerships around the globe that would help position America once again as a sought-after partner. But in a world deeply interconnected by technology, where popular opinion had increasingly more impact on national policy—even in countries that were not democracies—it was no longer enough to talk to governments. Hillary's team wanted America to connect with everyday people using twenty-first-century technology, and they were going to deploy their best asset to make that connection: the secretary of state.

Clinton already had her own style on the road, developed during her tenure as First Lady. She had visited clinics, villages, schools, sat down with women and girls, talked about education, human rights, empowering the disenfranchised. As secretary of state, she wanted to continue engaging with people on a personal level: connecting was what she did best and what she loved doing most. Clinton particularly wanted to use her new position to advance the rights of women and children everywhere, a project that stemmed from her deep belief that the world would never be a better place until half the population was no longer neglected. No matter how many wars, peace efforts, missile launches, or nuclear crises lay ahead, women's rights had to be part of the agenda. There would be much eye rolling at the State Department for four years, but the men on the team would eventually buy into Hillary's vision about American smart power.

Jake, the thirty-two-year-old Yale graduate from Minnesota, was thinking big thoughts with big words, long-term strategies and abstract concepts. He was a brain. His sixty-one-year-old boss was a brain too, but she added her gut instincts and heart. She knew how to translate dry concepts into a language that made sense to real people. Huma and Philippe began to search for the right mix of events for this new campaign for America, a combination of public diplomacy and traditional foreign policy that would ensure Hillary did not appear as though she was slipping back into the soft role of a First Lady. Together, with Jake, they were going to expand the frontiers of American power and beam Hillary into living rooms, computer screens, and Twitter feeds everywhere. They were going to make the discussion about American foreign policy accessible to everyone.

A few weeks after Clinton's arrival in the Building, it was time for her team to consult the occupants of Room 6205. The Asia experts, the bureau deputies, the desk directors for each country on the itinerary were taken aback when they were asked to contribute ideas for the agenda and schedule of the trip. Where should Clinton hold a town hall in Seoul? Who should she meet in Tokyo? Which television show was most popular in Indonesia? No one had consulted them for a while, it seemed. The final word on foreign policy decisions has always come from the White House, but the decision-making process can include varying levels of input from the State Department. Rice, a former national security advisor, had relied little on the Building, and Colin Powell had often been left out of the process.

When she had stood in the mezzanine on the day of her arrival, Clinton had promised to look for everyone's input, but no one had really expected she would tap them all. Clinton wanted to use the Building's considerable brain power and years of experience to inform her own decision making, and—perhaps learning from her past mistakes—she wanted to be inclusive. Just as they had expected her to be a prima donna in the Senate, so too people at the State Department were bracing for a diva. Instead, she was the one pouring the coffee.

The meetings under the new leadership were yet another surprise. After eight years out of office, Democrats seemed out of practice when it came to the daily business of government. Rice and Powell ran meetings with military precision; schedules were final unless a crisis erupted and plans were set well in advance. The newcomers ran their meetings like cocktail parties—filled with lots of air kissing and talking, the gatherings often ran overtime, and there was not always a clear action plan at the end.

The Democrats had also arrived en masse in Washington. America was proud to have elected its first African American president, but it was also divided: just over half the population had voted for Obama. But as the Obama'ites descended onto the capital, they found a city that seemed in the grip of the same euphoria that had swept the world on election night. Around town, folks excitedly reported sightings of Obama administration officials who had attained mythical status. David Axelrod, the brain behind the campaign, was seen having brunch at Commissary, a popular restaurant just east of Dupont Circle. BlackBerries beeped and vibrated everywhere as the news spread like wildfire. The White House chief of staff Rahm Emanuel was swimming at the YMCA at five in the morning. Or was it Timothy Geithner? Was that Obama's speechwriter Jon Favreau moving in next door? Was he really only twenty-seven? How many profiles of the Obama team could you run in a week in the *New York Times*?

Washington is a quiet, provincial town with Parisian-like avenues lined with trees, hundreds of federal employees in ill-fitting suits, and barely a handful of memorable restaurants. But with the arrival of Obama and his entourage, the capital of the world's superpower was suddenly the new capital of cool. Everyone wanted to move to the District and be part of history. Every evening, anxious journalists watched their in-boxes for the e-mails sent out by the White House with the schedule of the president for the next day. He was going to attend a service at the National Cathedral; he was going to sign an executive order to close the detention facility at Guantánamo Bay; he was going to visit members of Congress on Capitol Hill. For months, every Daily Guidance e-mail sent reporters around the city into a tizzy.

The second week of February rolled around, and in the Building Hillary's Asia schedule was finalized. Well, almost. Either way, a plane with a State Department seal attached to its door with Velcro was waiting on the tarmac of the Andrews Air Force Base in Maryland for a Special Air Mission.

2

HILLARY RECONQUERS
THE WORLD

Around midmorning on the Sunday after Valentine's Day 2009, the Building stood deserted. But unlike most Sundays, there was some quiet activity inside a windowless office on the seventh floor behind a heavy, cream-colored door that looked as if it should open a bank vault. Two young people in suits were stacking up thick white binders of papers and making sure their black rolling cases were stocked with all the highlighters, staplers, and pens they might need.

Outside the Building's empty lobby, several dozen people chatted, standing next to suitcases. Six hulking black vans waited at the curb. A woman ticked the names of those present off her list and distributed yellow cabin-bag tags. Forty passports were packed into a shiny metal case, in the safe hands of Lew Lukens, the logistics guru. Something about the preparations felt like a guided bus trip around the capital, but there were no tourists snapping photos here. This was how the State Department officials and the contingent of reporters who followed the secretary on her trips abroad traveled—in a pack, or, as we called it, the Bubble. We did have guides at all times, Caroline Adler, Ashley Yehl, and Nick Merrill, and they were waiting for us outside the Building already. They worked with Philippe to make sure that we had everything we needed to write our stories about American foreign policy and Clinton. Detailed schedules included mentions of where we could get access to Wi-Fi Internet, and for endless days of diplomacy in faraway lands there were even mentions of where our best or last chance was for a restroom visit.

Matthew Lee, from the Associated Press, had started covering the beat under Secretary Madeleine Albright nine years ago. With blue slanting eyes and thinning light brown hair, he towered over the rest of us and represented a dying breed of reporter—he smoked, he drank, and he grilled officials ruthlessly and relentlessly before cracking jokes with them over a beer. Mark Landler, the diplomatic correspondent for the *New York Times*, was a bespectacled, conscientious father of two, recently transplanted to Washington from Berlin. Glenn Kessler from the *Washington Post* had a round face and big dark eyes; like me, he had Dutch roots, but he had been on the secretary's plane for nine years and had written a book about Condoleezza Rice. They all wore khaki trench coats. The news agencies were always present as well: the Associated Press, Agence France-Presse, and Reuters. Their wires were the first to grab people's attention across the world whenever something important happened. Even in the age of twenty-four-hour television news and Twitter, the wires had correspondents everywhere. They were reliable and indispensable. Without them, trees could fall in forests and no one would hear about it. The celebrity correspondents of the American television networks had stopped traveling with Rice as the Bush administration entered its final year. But now, Andrea Mitchell from NBC, Martha Raddatz from ABC, as well as correspondents from CBS and CNN were all back for the Hillary-on-the-road show.

Suitcases disappeared into the black vans, and we squeezed, laptops and handbags in hand, into the three rows of seats in each of the press vans in the back of the convoy. The officials in the staff vans led at the front, and we set off for the forty-minute drive to Andrews Air Force Base (AAFB) in Maryland. The base was home to Air Force One, the plane of the president of the United States, sometimes referred to as POTUS by people in D.C. Queens, presidents, and prime ministers flew into the United States through AAFB, and its runways were also used by the planes carrying American distinguished visitors, or DVs as the air force referred to them—the secretary of state, secretary of defense, the vice president, and members of Congress. They shared a fleet of four aging 757 Boeing planes that flew them on Special Air Missions (SAMs) around the world.

While we waited for Clinton to arrive, we spread out in the VIP lounge off the tarmac and munched on the chewy chocolate chip cookies that were a staple of American air force bases. When the dogs were done sniffing our carry-on bags and suitcases, the belly of thirteen-year-old SAM started filling up with luggage, a large metal trunk carrying gifts from the secretary for her hosts, and dozens of black cases of security equipment.

We used an empty white paper cup with the air force golden stamp for our lottery. This was a trip with no tickets, no boarding passes, and no assigned seating. It offered many luxuries: someone else sorted out your visas, you never had to go through passport control anywhere, your luggage was delivered straight to your hotel, and you mingled in a VIP lounge with top American officials who loved to talk. But the trip also had its downsides: the traveling press was squeezed in the back of the secretary's reconfigured, no-frills plane. The section had eight comfortable business-size seats and twelve cramped coach seats. Some of the business seats went to Diplomatic Security agents and to Caroline, Ashley, and Nick. We got whatever seats were left. The lotteries took place only once, at the start of each trip, and they could get surprisingly emotional, especially when there were only six "good" seats and the handwritten 9 looked like a 6. On an eight-day trip with seven flights just like the one we were embarking on, drawing 13 felt like being dispatched for a root canal procedure.

When it was time to board, we walked the short distance on the tarmac to the steps up the plane. A Raven, a member of specially trained U.S. Air Force Security Forces, who guard SAM at all times, checked our names off a list before we were allowed to settle into our little capsule. The litany of the roll call shouted over the deafening roar of the plane's engines punctuated every departure at every stop.

On our seats, we found red tin boxes with heart-shaped ginger crisps, "hand rolled with love" by Mrs. Hanes in her factory of Moravian cookies somewhere in North Carolina. The air force wanted to mark Hillary's first trip with a special gesture. From my seat, I could see the activity farther up the plane, beyond the lavatory that marked the Line of Death—an imaginary barrier between us, mere mortal journalists, and the officials who had started to pore over the big white binders of documents that had traveled over from the vault on the seventh floor in one of the staff vans, intently guarded by the two young Foreign Service officers. The vault was known as the Line, once an actual physical line of desks where classified policy papers and statements were edited, improved, and passed up the chain until final approval. The Line now snaked through computers, into BlackBerries, and out of printers, but the line officers' job remained unchanged—they produced all the background information documents, talking points, and briefing notes that the secretary and her team needed. For trips, it was all gathered into the trip Book, with a big, red "CLASSIFIED" stamp across the front, just above the seal of the secretary of state. The Book was the reason we were not allowed beyond the lavatory without explicit permission. Instead, we waited for visits back to our quarters on the plane.

Hillary had emerged from her private cabin and was chatting to her staff in the front section, a conference-like area where four big leather seats, for her closest aides, faced each other on either side of the aisle. She then stopped in the middle section, with three rows of seats reserved for officials from the State Department, the NSC, and the Pentagon officials who accompanied her, and of course Fred and his agents. Then she crossed the Line of Death.

"Hello, everyone, nice to see you," Clinton began. She asked us if we were excited about the trip and then introduced Jake and Huma, who had walked down with her along with a few of her other aides. It was our first opportunity to meet the new team of the secretary, or "S," the department's abbreviation. I didn't know what to make of Jake. On paper he was impressive: a Yale graduate, Rhodes scholar, Supreme Court clerk. But he just looked so young. Was he really helping to shape American foreign policy? Would the future of my home country, Lebanon, be affected by his thoughts and advice?

Huma, Hillary's deputy chief of staff at the State Department, had first worked for her as an intern in the White House in 1996. Over the years, Hillary had taken Huma under her wing. In the small Senate office and then on the grueling primary campaign trail, the two women had developed an increasingly tight bond. Born in Kalamazoo, Michigan, to an Indian father and Pakistani mother, Huma had moved to Saudi Arabia with her family at the age of two and returned to the United States to attend George Washington University in D.C. During the campaign, as Hillary's traveling chief of staff, Huma had an almost mythical reputation for her unflappable calm and endless energy, her cool manners and impeccably styled jet-black hair, and, perhaps most of all, for her wardrobe full of designer clothes, including those from her personal friend Oscar de la Renta.

Huma was probably the coolest thing on the secretary's plane, which lacked all the high-tech gadgetry and plush feel of Air Force One. The blue and gray leather seats were from another era, the walls had taken on a gray tinge, and the tiny overhead screens creaked loudly whenever they opened up for the start of in-flight entertainment. We did get toothpaste, mouthwash, shaving cream, combs, and antacids in the lavatory. But the plane was not modern or impressive enough to reflect American power. But at least the secretary of state had a plane at her disposal, which was more than most foreign ministers around the world could say.

What mattered was that we were on the same plane as her, and this was worth the bill our news organizations had to foot to get us a seat on those trips. On presidential travels, only a handful of reporters fly on board Air Force One; the rest of the press follow in a separate plane and rarely see the president while on the road. We were, at all times, in a Bubble with Clinton, from the plane to the motorcade, to our hotel, to the next event or meeting, back to the motorcade, back onto SAM. It limited our ability to connect with the countries we visited but it was priceless access to the heart of the U.S. foreign policy machine.

And here was Clinton, standing in the aisle of our section. For twenty minutes, she answered our questions about the impact of the financial crisis on America's relationship with Asia, questions about how she would address the human rights agenda in China, and questions about North Korea's nuclear program. She said she wanted to listen more than talk, but mostly she wanted to make clear to us that the Obama administration was reaching out to the world, to Asia—not only to suit-wearing officials sitting in ministries but to people as well.

"We do see Asia as part of America's future," Clinton told us. "We are both a transatlantic and a transpacific power. And part of what I hope we can do is better understand and create the kind of future that will benefit both Asians and Americans."

She spoke in a slow, deliberate tone, with little inflection, sounding like the briefing notes she must have been reading in preparation for the trip. There was no smiling; this was serious diplomacy. She seemed to be treading carefully (Jake was listening intently from behind her). She was dealing with a group of foreign policy junkies who were going to dissect her every word.

For more than two decades, Hillary had had a checkered relationship with the American media. She had been hailed and demonized, scrutinized and lauded. She had never known what was coming and understandably kept her guard fairly high, encased in a protective shell. She related comfortably to individual reporters, and she could grow to trust a traveling press corps accompanying her on the campaign trail. She had once even phoned the partner of a reporter who was stuck on the road with her on Valentine's Day to apologize. But she looked at us and saw a faceless group of hacks of indeterminate nature and unknown intentions.

Finally, the grilling was over. Hillary walked up front to the conference area and relaxed, surrounded by people she knew were on her side. Rice, who was much warmer and gracious in person than she appeared on television, was still very reserved and had spent most of her time in her private cabin. But Hillary was curious about other human beings and enjoyed chitchat. She sat down in one of the empty seats as the air force flight attendants started to serve refreshments. From then on, the seat would be kept free for her on every trip and became known as the "Hillary seat." Shocked staffers, who had been on S trips before, fidgeted nervously, uncertain about the protocol.

"Why does she want to know my name?" one of them thought. She had never before had to explain to a secretary of state where she was from, whether she had a family, or what her career path had been like so far. The real shock came later, when Hillary remembered her name.

Jake hungrily finished the lunch of spaghetti, meatballs, and salad, one of the few proper meals he'd had in weeks. Back at the State Department, he had been at his desk from eight in the morning until well past midnight every day, charting out the contours of his job and trying to work through the reams of paperwork that the bureaucracy of the department seemed to produce every second. Lunch and dinner were courtesy of the vending machine down the hall, a healthy combination of Cheetos and Doritos and Pop-Tarts, washed down with a Diet Dr. Pepper. He drove everyone in the Building slightly mad as he scrutinized every word on every single piece of paper, every policy talking point, every memo destined to reach Clinton, until he felt it was perfect. The already lengthy clearance process for documents became a few hours longer under Jake's hand. Only months later would he come to accept that even in the capital of the world's superpower, sometimes "good enough" had to suffice.

But in those first few months and especially on this trip, everything still had to be perfect. This was Hillary Clinton's debut on the world stage as secretary of state, her latest incarnation. All those papers were going into the trip Book, a version of which awaited the secretary in her private cabin. The Book contained an extra layer of classified documents about issues beyond the focus of the trip and copies of all the speeches and public statements she would be making. These statements were crafted by Lissa Muscatine, the speechwriter.

Every evening in Washington, Clinton also received a daily Book, a cordovan leather binder with all the briefing material required to prepare for the following day.

Preparing the first Book for Clinton, line officers had asked how she liked her information presented to her—some officials like oral reports; others preferred bullet-point briefings. Some needed it all condensed into the basics. Hillary wanted all the details, all the angles, all the background. She was a voracious reader and could extract what she needed from the tome and let the rest lie in the back of her mind to inform her general approach to a subject. Her instincts honed as a lawyer had also taught her to stay nimbly ahead of the brief—whatever question came her way, she wanted to have an answer. But mostly she wanted to have all the information in front of her so she could slowly learn to transform the pile of dry diplomatic statements into lively sentences that matched her personality and sounded like something she would actually say, something that her audience outside of government buildings would understand.

For four years prior, the trip Book had contained the basics and sat mostly untouched on the narrow desk in the cabin during long overseas flights, next to the communications equipment that enabled the secretary to call the president or any world leader. Rice had come to the State Department from the NSC, where she had devised policy. She knew what the policy was, and she knew the talking points. She would react to her environment and change course accordingly, but she still followed a tight script. She didn't need a binder.

But on the long flight to Tokyo, Clinton's cabin kept spitting out papers with annotations, requests for more information, questions about sites she was going to visit, and changes to the language used in speeches she would be making the following day. Sitting on the leather foldout couch in her cabin, a humidifier in one corner, a *National Geographic* map of the world on the wall behind, the new secretary of state had been reading the Book cover to cover. Armed with the office supplies in their black rolling cases, the line officers got to work. On every trip, there would be two of them—the plane team. And at each stop an advance line officer was preparing the ground for S's arrival. They were among the brightest of the Foreign Service cadre and helped to keep the wheels of the foreign policy machine spinning. But on the trips they were interchangeable.

When we landed at Haneda Airport at eleven that night, twenty-two hours after walking out of our homes in Washington, Lissa the speechwriter realized her job was only just starting. In the coming months, she would often find herself rewriting speeches till five in the morning. When the departure for the day's first event was only a couple of hours away, she would give up on sleep and just go to the gym. The Book had become a living thing. It was going to need feeding, day and night, throughout our trips.

Hillary too was only getting started, but her energy was bubbling. She loved being back on the road. She had always enjoyed her overseas travel as First Lady; no matter how polarizing or vilified she was at home, the rest of the world was mostly fascinated by her and treated her with respect. As a senator, she had traveled abroad a dozen times with colleagues like Republican senator John McCain. She had enjoyed those trips, but now this was her show again. And she arrived in Asia not just as a former First Lady and senator, or the wife of Bill Clinton and a woman who had reinvented herself over the years. She now came in a new, even bigger role: as America's chief diplomat, the emissary of Barack Obama, the new, promising face of America. She emerged from the plane with a wide smile and perfect hair, her eyes ever so slightly red from the journey. Huma followed with one of her designer handbags.

Inside the VIP terminal, the first group of excited fans waited at the rendezvous—a welcome committee of young athletes from the Special Olympics and Japanese women astronauts who had all just been to the

United States. The camera crews were there to beam out the images of her arrival, and for the traveling press this was the start of a long night. We were all on the phone, calling our editors with the news: she's arrived, she's landed, she's here!

We piled into the vans outside the VIP terminal, typing on our laptops, talking on the phone, the motorcade sirens wailing in the background of our live interviews with our radio and television stations. Late into the night, sitting in the filing center set up for the traveling press in the hotel, I continued broadcasting: She's still here! She's still saying the Obama administration is reaching out to Asia and the world! In the wee hours of the morning, on the various floors of the Okura hotel, with its dated 1960s decor, members of the State Department delegation, their work finally done, collapsed into bed one after the other. In her suite on the tenth floor, Hillary woke up at four thirty in the morning, feeling like she was in a vibrating bed and someone had accidentally just dropped in some quarters.[2] Just another, minor Japanese earthquake.

The dawn jolt didn't stop Hillary from being out the door at eight in the morning for her first event—a display of respect for Japanese history and traditions. The Meiji Shrine, a religious Shinto shrine dedicated to Emperor Meiji, who ruled Japan for forty-five years, until 1912, was a large, green sanctuary amid the soaring towers and concrete blocks of Tokyo's Shibuya business district. Clinton and her retinue walked on foot into a forest of one hundred thousand trees toward the shrines made of cypress and copper. The sound of the city faded. Fred, always two steps behind Clinton, found himself walking into an oasis that mirrored his internal oasis: no matter the traffic, noise, or danger around him and the chaos within the big Bubble, Fred's mind and demeanor remained focused and calm. He savored this rare moment where his mind was at one with his environment. He and his team formed their own small, serene bubble around the secretary and helped her glide through her day.

The packed schedule demonstrated the combined power of America and of Hillary. A one-two punch. Unlike most foreign ministers who travel to meet fellow foreign ministers, an American secretary of state is rarely restricted by protocol to rank: presidents fling open the doors of their palaces and kings grant them audiences. Clinton had a business lunch with foreign minister Hirofumi Nakasone, but the two were old friends, so they reminisced over a picture of the two of them meeting eighteen years ago, when he was a member of parliament delighted to meet an up-and-coming Arkansas governor named Bill. Hillary was also afforded the rare honor of tea with the imperial couple. Emperor Akihito and his wife, Michiko, emerged from their cloistered palace to greet her, and the seventy-four-year-old empress, in a cream-colored skirt suit, embraced Hillary like an old friend. They held hands and posed for photographs. Hillary and Bill had hosted the imperial couple at the White House in 1994 for the Clinton presidency's first state dinner. At the time, President Clinton had declared that the "ties that bind our two nations have never been stronger." And in Tokyo, at the prime minister's office, Clinton invited Taro Aso to be the first foreign leader to visit President Obama in Washington.

The mood was buoyant and the ceremonies elegant. But even close friends have disagreements. Japan had been home to ten American military bases for more than six decades. These bases were one of the many building blocks for America's surging world power in the aftermath of World War II and a continued source of influence in Asia. They were both a testament to the alliance that developed between the two countries after Japan surrendered to the Allies and also a reminder of that same surrender. Over time, the bases grated increasingly on the proud Japanese, who wanted to strike a more independent course and felt America was always dictating the terms of the friendship. Incidents like the rape of a twelve-year-old Japanese girl by three American marines in 1995 fed the resentment and the debate about the U.S. military presence in Japan. One of the bases in particular, the Futenma Marine Corps Air Station, was a constant source of friction. It sat in the middle of Ginowan city on the island of Okinawa, surrounded by stunning coral reefs. Washington and Tokyo had signed an agreement to relocate the noisy base away from population centers. But islanders wanted it off Okinawa completely. Sure, Japan worried about the eccentric, unpredictable leader of nearby North Korea, was anxious about China's rise, and fretted it might no longer be America's best friend in Asia. But every now and then, the Japanese people rebelled and their leaders protested. After all, America was a superpower, and it could take a bit of poking.

Prime Minister Aso was sinking in the polls and would be defeated in the upcoming general elections in September of that year. So although she had invited Aso to visit Obama, Clinton broke protocol rules in a different way and sought to make contact with the leader of the opposition, Ichiro Ozawa, from the Democratic Party of Japan. Ozawa thought the Futenma base should be exiled to a disused airport on a distant island at the very southern tip of the Japanese archipelago. His office said the meeting with Clinton couldn't be scheduled. Ozawa hemmed and hawed and kept everybody waiting, his way of showing he didn't kowtow to America. But he eventually agreed to a meeting. On his way out, he offered his terse views on the U.S.-Japan relationship. "Both sides must be on an equal footing, and one should not be subordinated to the other."

Hillary also encountered resentment toward America in Indonesia, the world's third-largest democracy. Outside the presidential palace, protestors greeted her with placards reading "America is a rubbish civilization" and "America is the real terrorist."

The world's largest Muslim country, Indonesia once held the United States in high esteem. In 2000, 75 percent of Indonesians had a positive view of America. But in the aftermath of the attacks of September 11, the Bush administration's war on terror and invasions of Afghanistan and Iraq looked like a war against Islam to many Muslims around the world. Superpowers are never universally loved, of course, but under George W. Bush anti-Americanism only increased. By 2007, only 29 percent[3] of Indonesians liked America. But like many countries around the world, Indonesia had cheered the election of President Obama, who had spent four years of his childhood in Jakarta. The Obama administration saw an opportunity to work with Indonesia and reach out to the Muslim world.

Clinton was also here for a serving of alphabet soup. The State Department had its own love affair with acronyms. This was an EAP trip—East Asia Pacific region. We had an EAP-AS (assistant secretary) with us on the plane, but the EAP-DAS (deputy assistant secretary) had stayed in Washington. Looking after the journalists were the overworked officers from the PA—Public Affairs office. The new S team was absorbing all this as quickly as it could. Now Clinton was going to visit ASEAN to sign a TAC, which she'd never heard of before, but which would help with the United States' accession to the EAS.

Once again delighted shrieks greeted Hillary as she entered the Secretariat of ASEAN, the Association of Southeast Asian Nations in Jakarta. She was the first American secretary of state ever to visit the headquarters. It was a symbolic gesture of support for an organization that had received virtually no attention from the Bush administration, which spent as little time as possible on the seemingly inconsequential acronyms. But this symbolism went a long way toward showing countries in the region that when the Obama administration looked at Asia on a map, it didn't just see China and the Pacific Ocean. It was all thrilling to Surin Pitsuwan, the ASEAN secretary-general, who offered Clinton effusive compliments and thirty-two perfect yellow roses. The number stood for the thirty-two years of cooperation between the United States and ASEAN, while the yellow symbolized a new beginning under the Obama administration. Standing next to Clinton, Pitsuwan told her, "Your visit shows the seriousness of the United States to end its diplomatic absenteeism in the region."

ASEAN countries had long tried to cajole the United States into signing the Treaty of Amity and Cooperation (TAC) a feel-good agreement with no binding obligations that promoted peace and cooperation between its signatories. It was a necessary step if the United States wanted to be part of the more important East Asia Summit (EAS), a regional political and economic forum that included ASEAN and all the key Pacific countries, from India to Australia. All countries, that is, except the United States and Russia. Almost every day on the trip, Clinton had said the United States was not just a transatlantic power but also a transpacific power. To prove it, she announced that the United States would sign the treaty.

Trailing behind Clinton, across time zones, in and out of motorcades, I had a hard time getting excited about all these treaties and diplomatic hooplas. It all sounded tedious—death by acronyms. I would eventually come to understand the careful thinking that had gone into this.

The Obama administration believed that power through military might alone was too expensive and no longer sufficient to remain relevant in a world that was changing so quickly. Rising countries, big and small alike, all wanted their say on the global podium. These countries were testing the limits and possibilities of their power. America had to be needed. It had to draw others close and sit at the center of a vast diplomatic web, an essential connector. For the proponents of smart power, this was another, essential way in which the United States could maintain its edge as a superpower in the twenty-first century. Anne-Marie Slaughter, a Princeton University professor, had developed much of the thinking about this edge. Clinton hired her to run the Building's policy planning department to develop the blueprint of this style of diplomacy. The big multilateral organizations like the United Nations were important but also stood as relics of a previous era. The United States was going to latch on to what was already there and create new initiatives and treaties everywhere—a large sticky web of diplomacy. TAC was just the beginning.[4]

From Indonesia, we retraced our steps and flew due north again for just over six hours. This time we turned left instead of right, and on Friday morning, we woke up in snowy Seoul. Once an American-backed dictatorship, South Korea was now a democracy and a steadfast ally of the United States.

The highlight of this stop was the seventh event of the day—a town hall at the Ewha Womans university. Founded in 1886 by the American Methodist Episcopal missionary Mary Scranton, the university was the sister college of Wellesley, where Hillary had studied.

Inside a massive auditorium with a futuristic concrete exterior, the audience waited for Hillary to come onstage while listening to the Christian hymn "Amazing Grace." Huge banners hung all around the stage welcoming "Secretary of State Hillary Rodham Clinton" and large television screens were on the walls to beam Hillary's performance to the back of the room. On our large press passes, a picture of a younger Hillary dwarfed the written details of the time and place of the event. In the audience, a woman was proudly showing her friends a picture of herself with Hillary and Bill Clinton in the 1990s.

The secretary was running late. Everything on this trip had run late, every day, all day. If it was a hallmark of the Clinton administration to be an hour late, this was the Hillary-at-the-State-Department version. The tardiness was deeply frustrating for everybody, the traveling press corps who had to hurry up and wait and then miss their deadlines, the State Department staffers running the show, the local officials trying to keep to their own schedules, the local journalists who had to show up early for events to be screened for security and then wait and wait some more for Hillary to actually arrive.

But Hillary was in a back room meeting the university's president and some of its alumni. As she always did, she gave the people she was talking to her full attention and listened closely to their stories, head tilted, eyes focused. She didn't rush, didn't cut anyone off. She made them feel like she had traveled all the way from Washington just for them. The crowds could wait. And when she finally walked onto the stage, the two thousand women in the audience leapt to their feet, clapping excitedly like groupies. And when she told them, speaking into a microphone from behind a lectern, how delighted she was to be with them, they felt so special that they forgave her instantly for being late. In her red jacket and black trousers, Clinton began by saying that women's rights weren't just a "moral issue" but a "security issue."

"[No democracy] can exist without women's full participation," she told the crowd. "No economy can be truly a free market without women involved." That's why she was putting women's rights at the center of her agenda. The women listened intently as she moved on to discuss North Korea, the nuclear Non-Proliferation Treaty, and climate change. And then it was time for questions.

When the line officers had been told to organize the town hall, they asked how free-flowing the secretary liked the exchange to be. The answer had been: "Very." Looking for raised hands in the dark auditorium, she picked at random, acting as her own master of ceremonies, walking up and down the stage and trying to be equitable between the different sides of the auditorium.

"Do you have a microphone? Here, I'll take one over there. Okay. Oh, too many hands. Too many hands," she said laughing.

How did she balance work and marriage?

Be true to yourself and make your own choices.

What was it like being at Wellesley College?

She loved it.

How did you know Bill was the one for you?

"I'm very lucky because my husband is my best friend, and he and I have been together for a very long time, longer than most of you have been alive. We are—we have an endless conversation. We never get bored. We get deeply involved in all of the work that we do, and we talk about it constantly. And I just feel very fortunate that I have a relationship that has been so meaningful to me over my adult life."

How special is Chelsea to you?

We could be here forever, she replied.

She answered each question with enthusiasm and candor, as though she were sitting in a café with friends having a cup of coffee. She told them she felt right at home and drew rousing applause. She spoke about the discipline of gratitude—the need to be grateful about at least one thing a day, regardless of how difficult your problems were. I suddenly thought that Ewha sounded rather like Iowa, and that this felt and sounded like the primary campaign trail where voters wanted to know what the candidate was really all about—only here, unlike in Iowa, there was no sniping.

Hillary's autobiography had been a huge best seller in South Korea; the audience had clearly read it and wanted to dig deeper. She obliged graciously. It was hard to tell where Hillary Rodham Clinton—wife of Bill, former First Lady, political icon, and best-selling author—ended and where the American secretary of state began. The women in the audience looked at her and saw America.

The crowd listened intently. The seats were filled with politicians, movie stars, designers, the crème de la crème of Korean society, and they were all floored. No official of theirs had ever spoken to them with such candor or made herself so accessible and human. And in a deeply patriarchal society, with still-formal notions of how a senior official should behave, a woman with Hillary's power, speaking in such a manner, was nothing short of extraordinary.

"I feel more like an advice columnist than secretary of state today," Clinton said with a giggle. She answered questions until her anxious staff signaled she was running over schedule again. It was hard to imagine any other secretary of state responding to an audience's expectations with such passion.

This was part of the grand experiment to find Hillary's new public persona as secretary of state. For eight years, she had watched Bill Clinton execute American foreign policy; she had been his eyes and ears when he wasn't in the room. She had met countless heads of state, sat next to them and their wives for hours at dinners and lunches. She had held her own meetings, attended summits, and delivered speeches in various capitals. She had been on the Senate Armed Services committee. She knew the world and all the issues, even if she didn't yet know all the details and nuances. She was as comfortable on the world stage as in her own dining room, and here she was, redefining the job at the same time as she was redefining herself. Every day, every meeting, and every public event was an opportunity to test and learn. But Clinton didn't just use her plain talk to discuss her personal life. She also made news—real, unexpected news.

After World War II, the United States and the Soviet Union had split up Korea between the two of them. The two Koreas forged very different destinies. The North was ruled repressively for decades by Kim Il Sung. When he died in 1994, his son Kim Jong Il took over and ruled with the same principles: starve the people, build up the army and a nuclear program. Kim Jong Il was now sixty-eight years old, frail and sick, and Seoul and Beijing worried about what would happen when he died. Would the country collapse? What would happen to the nuclear weapons? Would millions of refugees flood South Korea and China?

No one said a word in public. The Chinese even refused to discuss contingency planning in private with American officials for fear it would end up on the front page of the *New York Times*. American officials, respectful of their allies' sensitivities, did not discuss the succession in public either. Erratic Kim Jong Il could go into one of his missile-firing fits just to prove he was strong and going nowhere.

During a briefing given to the traveling press, Clinton broke the diplomatic taboo. She not only mentioned the word "succession," but she also discussed South Korea's concerns about the day after Kim Jong Il. Her words ricocheted from Seoul to Beijing, to Pyongyang, Washington, and back as Asia experts and Asian officials gasped.

Standing next to Clinton at a press conference, the South Korean foreign minister was asked for his reaction to her comment. He ventured only that his country had an eye on the situation. Clinton seemed amused. She may have sounded bookish at the start of her trip, but she had quickly translated diplomatic facts into her own language.

"I think that to worry about saying something that is so obvious is an impediment to clear thinking," she said when we asked her what she thought of the reaction to her very public reference to Kim Jong Il's frail health. "And I don't think it should be viewed as particularly extraordinary that someone in my position would say what's obvious . . . The open press is filled with such conversations. This is not some kind of a classified matter that is not being discussed in many circles."

Kim Jong Il's life expectancy was not the only obvious conversation to Clinton. The global economic crisis had left the United States and the world reeling. China held more than a trillion dollars in U.S. Treasury bills, and its economy was still growing at the astounding rate of 8 percent a year. For years, American officials had been forceful in their public criticism of China's human rights records. In 2008, a State Department report had listed China as one of the world's worst abusers of human rights, and Hillary herself had urged the Bush administration to boycott the opening of the Beijing Olympics in the authoritarian state. Talking to the traveling press ahead of the flight to Beijing, she indicated that human rights had to be part of the whole range of issues on the agenda, not a focus of the talks. The economic crisis had to be the heart of the conversation.

"We pretty much know what they're going to say. We know that we're going to press them to reconsider their position about Tibetan religious and cultural freedom and autonomy for the Tibetans and some kind of recognition or acknowledgment of the Dalai Lama. And we know what they're going to say, because I've had those conversations for more than a decade with Chinese leaders."

The secretary of state sounded as though she didn't want to harangue America's banker, and the reaction was vociferous. Headlines on front pages everywhere in the United States and Europe screamed treason—the Obama administration was going soft on Chinese human rights, cowering in the face of the rising Asian giant. American congressmen accused Clinton of pandering to Beijing. Human rights organizations called on her to make clear human rights in China were a priority for the Obama administration.

Clinton was trying to say she didn't want to bang her head against the wall on the issue of human rights with a government that wasn't listening anyway. She found this approach counterproductive and wanted to advance the human rights agenda in new ways: by connecting with grassroots organizations, by using the Internet—anything to bypass the government. It was part of the strategy devised on the seventh floor of the Building by her team to connect American diplomacy with people around the world.

Clinton's statement, however, was not part of the traditional diplomatic script, and the world was not ready for her new style of diplomacy. The White House was annoyed by the criticism that her off-script comments had unleashed about the administration's approach to human rights. Hillary's team was somewhat taken aback. They knew her bluntness would likely displease some quarters, but they weren't ready for the all-out onslaught. Hillary was no longer just a presidential candidate expressing her opinion on the campaign trail when she opened her mouth; now, it was America speaking. Every word was weighed, examined, parsed. People read between the lines, below them, above them; they read into commas and pauses.

Fifty years ago, even twenty years ago, secretaries of state came out on specific, often orchestrated, occasions to make a statement or a speech or take the occasional question from a reporter. Their words were the definitive position of the United States of America. When Henry Kissinger traveled to Lusaka, Zambia, in 1976, he attacked the apartheid regime in what was then Rhodesia, today's Zimbabwe, spelling out America's support for racial equality and black self-determination on the continent. The *New York Times* reprinted his speech in full—over a whole page. No one got that kind of newspaper coverage anymore, except perhaps lifelong presidents of developing countries where the state controlled the media.

Words now also traveled around the globe at lightning speed. Social media, cable news television, and the Internet were all accelerating the news cycle, forcing American officials, including the president, to react more frequently and swiftly in public. The secretaries of state and defense gave more press conferences and spoke in different forums, more casually. Their utterances were no longer scripted down to a comma. Yet the world's expectations had not evolved in parallel; every word spoken had the same value and weight as ever. There should have been a discount rate for words, Jake thought.

Hillary waved away the controversy over her comments; she was used to being excoriated. Jeffrey Bader from the NSC gave her a yellow sheet with a few scribbled points[5] that she could use as an aid to make her point next time she mentioned human rights, mainly that the United States raises concerns about human rights privately and publicly and that she had done so on this trip as well. Though she rarely admitted she had been wrong, Hillary would often then try to adjust course. But this comment left a permanent stain on her record, in the eyes of the human rights community.

Chinese officials too were surprised. They religiously stuck to the script, especially about human rights. Say it once in private; repeat it once in private; move on. They didn't know what to make of Clinton's statement. How did her words fit into the bigger picture? What did this statement say about America? This was the woman who had infuriated them in 1995 at the UN conference about women's rights in Beijing when she famously said that human rights are women's rights and women's rights are human rights. Her hosts had dismissed her at the time, saying "some people from some countries" had made "unwarranted remarks and criticisms." The foreign ministry added that "these people had to pay more attention to the problem within their own countries." The Chinese government had blacked out her speech from the closed-circuit TV in the conference hall, and the only reference to her speech in the Chinese media was one line in the official *People's Daily*: "American Mrs. Clinton made a speech."

Now, "American Mrs. Clinton" was back. She was no longer just a First Lady with a soft agenda of human rights; she was secretary of state of the United States of America, and she was coming to do business. This was also what she had been trying to telegraph to Beijing with her comment about a comprehensive relationship with China. There was a method to Hillary's off-script comments, even though it wasn't always immediately apparent to others and could come at a high cost.

SAM landed at the Beijing airport on a cold night. The day had started in South Korea and was finally coming to an end in China. In a black belted coat and red scarf, Clinton walked out of the plane and down steps lined with red lights. The ice and snow had kept away the marching bands and guard of honor, and Clinton was escorted to her waiting limousine on the tarmac by China's assistant foreign minister.

The non-newsworthy passengers quietly got out of the back door of the plane down the steps lined with blue lights. Jake had slept an average of two hours a night since leaving Washington six days earlier. The biting cold on the tarmac reinvigorated him briefly before he sunk into his seat on the overheated staff minibus. Jake had been to China once before, as a teenager, when his parents had packed him, his three brothers, and his sister on one of the first nonstop flights to Beijing from the United States in the spring of 1996. His parents liked to explore; Jake learned the world capitals on the globe that lived on their kitchen table.

On the tarmac, staffers from the U.S. embassy guided us to our vehicles. "Press! This way! Press! Vans at the back of the motorcade!" Three vans were usually assigned for the traveling press corps. As we drove into the city, U.S. embassy staff handed out the usual press packs with city maps, embassy information, and a hand-sized binder booklet with the number 30 written on the cover in black, the Chinese and American flags sharing the empty space inside the zero. The People's Republic of China and the United States had established diplomatic relations thirty years ago. The booklet contained cultural tips and useful Chinese phrases, information about tourist sites and China's economy and legal system ("China does not have an independent judiciary. Corruption and conflicts of interests are acknowledged problems"), in addition to some peculiar extras. The booklet included a biography of the secretary and her delegation members (she was a best-selling author and resided in New York), and several unusual biographies of the Chinese officials she would be meeting. The Chinese president Hu Jintao, for example, was sixty-seven and hadn't intended to go into politics. He had wanted to become a hydropower expert. He was a member of the dance team at his university and occasionally "danced solo at parties. He also plays tennis fairly well."

The press booklets were often assembled with information provided by the host country, and this biography seemed to originate from the Communist Party's official newspaper, the *People's Daily*.

The Chinese were perfect hosts. They viewed hospitality, ceremony, and carefully cultivated personal relationships as tools of statecraft. They treated Clinton to a crescendo of official meetings, from the foreign minister all the way up to the president. The Chinese took it all very seriously— this wasn't just a series of pleasant get-to-know-you meetings. There were official talks to be had, inside the Diaoyutai State Guesthouse, in the middle of a one-hundred-acre compound of ancient villas scattered between ginkgo trees and frozen lakes. Kissinger had stayed here in 1971 when he had established the first direct contact with Communist China in over twenty years. Before the age of Twitter and the twenty-four-hour news cycle, Kissinger had slipped out of Pakistan unnoticed, leaving reporters behind, to make his secret trip and pull off his diplomatic coup.

If the Chinese art of feng shui is meant to reflect the flow of energies and purpose of a space, then the room where Clinton and foreign minister Yang Jiechi met showed a great deal about how the Chinese viewed their position. In a long rectangular room with small crystal chandeliers, two long tables faced each other, separated by three large potted azaleas. A small Chinese flag marked Yang's seat at the left table; an American one marked Clinton's on the right. Officials from both sides sat facing one another; the Chinese delegation was larger than the American one. The setup was decidedly strange. Diplomatic talks usually take place on either side of one wide rectangular table, not two tables, five feet apart. The Chinese seemed to want to evoke their growing sense of importance, emphasizing the gulf between them and their counterpart.

The agenda for the talks had been set in advance, as always, and the two sides went through the script. There would be no surprises in Beijing, especially not in a first meeting. The Chinese presented their points. Clinton followed. The economy, climate change, North Korea. Yang spoke English so they were able to cover a lot of ground, without wasting any time in translation. The Chinese recited their usual "one-China principle." Taiwan, the rebellious, separatist island that claimed the title of Republic of China, was a sensitive issue, a key interest for mainland China. Clinton assured them that this administration would continue to abide by the thirty-year-old U.S. policy toward Taiwan. Washington did not support independence for Taiwan but at the same time it did not recognize China's claim of sovereignty over the island. The Chinese knew that Washington would maintain strong ties with Taiwan and sell them fighter jets, just as the United States knew that China would protest loudly when it happened.

But the power balance between the United States and China had been slowly changing over the last few years, and this shift grew even more perceptible in the months preceding Obama's inauguration. While America's economy was grinding to a halt and the international financial system imploded, China had put on a breathtaking display of its culture and riches. The opening ceremony of the Beijing Olympics was conceived as an expression of China's resurgence and was broadcast to a global audience for all to see.[6] China's economy continued to grow at a clipping pace. Real estate was booming, and though the world was buying less, Chinese goods were still being flown out to the four corners of the globe. The grand old economies of the West were gutted by recession, and the Chinese saw the financial crisis of 2008 as America's comeuppance. The Chinese had a new swagger to their step, flying around the world, their large delegations walking confidently through the lobby of the State Department, filling up rooms in meetings with officials, and confidently asserting their wishes. American officials saw the swagger and thought, I guess that's what it looked like all these years when we walked into a room.

Obama had been careful to minimize the China bashing that seemed an intrinsic part of American presidential campaigns, and the Chinese had noticed. They'd heard all the talk about America reaching out to foes. And then there was Clinton speaking softly about human rights. It all fed the perception that the new American administration was being overly deferential to the Chinese. They saw a picture with "decline" written all over it. But as eager as China was to show off its new ascendance on the world stage, the country's continued growth was still linked to the United States. If the Chinese wanted to enact their plans—to push back against American hegemony and assert their authority in the Pacific—the country needed a smooth beginning with the Obama administration. They were keen to get off on the right foot with Clinton while they studied her more closely.

Yang, the square-faced foreign minister with a large forehead and gold-rimmed glasses who sat facing Clinton across the potted azaleas, had lived through the changes in both countries. In the late 1970s and early 1980s, he had been an English interpreter for Deng Xiaoping, the man who rose out of Communist Party purges and the repression of the Cultural Revolution to lead China into modernity. Deng served as China's top leader from 1978 to the early 1990s, and his policies set his country on the path that had led to its current status as an economic superpower. Yang had risen through the ranks steadily, and at the age of fifty-seven he became China's youngest foreign minister. He was also a graduate of the London School of Economics and had served at the Chinese embassy in Washington twice, once in the mid-1980s and then as ambassador from 2001 to 2005. Yang had walked on the streets of the American capital as the United States went from budget surplus to crippling debt.

Clinton's own swagger and persona helped to mellow the often stilted diplomatic exchanges with Chinese officials. Dai Bingguo, the energetic smiling state councilor who was China's top foreign policy official, outranking Yang, hosted Clinton to lunch. Dai looked much younger than his sixty-eight years and told Clinton she looked younger and more beautiful than on television. Hillary blushed. "Well, we will get along very well," she said, a hint of flirtatiousness in her voice. Soon they were talking about their children, and Dai was showing her pictures of his grandchildren.

Later that evening, Yang hosted Clinton at a magnificent dinner at the Diaoyutai. Ten Chinese and ten American officials sat around two large tables. Waiters delivered food simultaneously to each diner in an elegant dance. Hors d'oeuvres of "prawn ball with Thai sauce" and "laver and fish ball" arrived on the table in an elaborate dry-ice presentation as a dense foglike vapor rose from the plates.

Throughout the visit, Clinton charmed her impassive hosts with her knowledge of Chinese proverbs. "When you are in a common boat, you need to cross the river peacefully together" was her way of saying that China and the United States had to work together to prop up the world economy. Premier Wen Jiabao reciprocated with his own proverb, also from Sun Tzu's *The Art of War*. "Progress together, hand in hand." This proverb diplomacy would become a constant in Clinton's exchange with China.

Unlike in democracies like Japan or South Korea, public diplomacy events in tightly controlled Communist China made the country's officials nervous, and they tried to manage Clinton's schedule as much as they could, so she tried to find ways to deliver her message. She gave a web-chat interview hosted by the government-controlled *China Daily* newspaper and went beyond just answering the questions, weaving her message about cooperation into the answers. Ten million Chinese later accessed the interview. She told women's rights activists meeting with her inside the U.S. embassy that change only comes when people stand up and say, "I am not going to be quiet." On Sunday, before leaving, she attended a service at a state-approved church in Beijing. But none of Clinton's actions alarmed the Chinese: this was not the same shrill woman who had issued her rallying cry about human rights and women's rights all those years ago. She was not going to harangue them at every instance. And she was also no Condoleezza Rice, who could be gracious and warm in public and then shockingly tough and curt in private. Handling Clinton and America would be easy. It would take the Chinese more than a year to realize how wrong their reading had been.

By the end of the seven-day trip, Jake, Huma, and the others around Hillary felt the trip had been a resounding success. Asia had weathered fifteen speeches, eleven media interviews, six town halls and round tables, and seven press conferences, and Hillary had started to find her voice as secretary of state. It was time to go home, to go to sleep. Almost.

SAM couldn't fly more than nine hours without refueling; Washington and even Alaska were too far for a direct flight home. So after three hours in the air, the secretary was back in Japan, at the Yokota Air Base for an hour-long pit stop. Instead of staying on the plane, Clinton walked into a hangar where more than three hundred soldiers and their families were eagerly waiting to shake hands and take pictures with her. She looked tired, but a pink scarf lifted her complexion. Ever the politician, Hillary tapped into the energy of the crowd.

Bedraggled and exhausted, a few of the senior officials had lumbered out of the plane to stretch their legs before the next seven-hour flight. They stood in the back of the hangar to shelter from the freezing cold outside and watched the show.

"If every one of her trips is going to be run like a campaign stop, we're all going to fall apart," one of them complained.

The Asia whirlwind became the template for every trip Clinton took in her four years as secretary of state.

3

FROM WASHINGTON
TO BEIRUT

There were, naturally, trips that were exceptions to the Hillary template, where protocol and pomp had no place—war-ravaged countries where tanks were part of the urban landscape, where America was a sworn enemy for many, where marines got blown up. Countries where the arrival of an American secretary of state was kept tightly concealed until landing, and Fred had final approval on the secretary's minute movements.

One spring evening in April, the State Department sent out an e-mail for wide distribution to all journalists around town with guidance for the next day's schedule.

Friday, April 24, 2009
SECRETARY OF STATE CLINTON: NO PUBLIC APPOINTMENTS
THERE WILL BE A DAILY PRESS BRIEFING: At approximately 12:30 p.m. with Robert A. Wood

But that morning, SAM was waiting at Andrews Air Force Base to take us overseas. The State Department traveling press corps had received another e-mail, a couple of days earlier, with a heading in screaming capitals.

STRICTLY EMBARGOED—NOT FOR BROADCAST—FOR PLANNING PURPOSES ONLY.

The secretary was going on the road again. We were given our destination and told to prepare in secret. The unspoken rule was that we couldn't share our plans with anyone except with an editor or two at our organizations to help with setting up what was needed for coverage of her visit once we arrived at our destination. Gaps in the schedules of the president and vice president, the secretary of defense and secretary of state always sent Washington buzzing with speculation. Gaps could mean a surprise visit to an undisclosed location. Only a handful of countries fit into that category. Journalists traveling with American officials always respected the embargo. On this particular Friday, no one thought much of the fact that Clinton had no appointments. After all, everyone was entitled to a quiet end of the week once in a while.

By the time Clinton was seen in public again, it was Saturday morning and she was in Baghdad. We had spent the night incognito in neighboring Kuwait and traveled to Iraq on a military aircraft. Our motorcade was now driving into an enclave on the banks of the Tigris River in Baghdad—the Green Zone, where Saddam Hussein's former palaces now housed Iraq's American masters, the country's newly elected leaders struggled to lead, and a new parliament was clumsily experimenting with democracy. Nestled in a bend of the river, the Green Zone was protected on its northwest side by concrete blast walls, barbed wire, and checkpoints. Humvees and Abrams tanks stood guard. Outside was the "red zone"—the rest of Iraq, where 240 people had just been killed in four suicide bombs over two days.

Since 2003, the violence in Iraq had ebbed and flowed; mostly it flowed, and recently it was surging. Obama had openly opposed this war as a senator, and now as president he wanted out. At the end of 2008, the Bush administration and the Iraqis had agreed on a plan for U.S. troops to withdraw from the center of cities, retreating to their bases by summer 2009. By the end of 2011, all U.S. soldiers were to leave Iraq. The Bush administration thought there would be time to finagle a way to stay. Obama wanted to make sure the departure would happen.

This war had torn at the fabric of the United States, soured international alliances, and caused a deep schism between the United States and Europe. The war continued to siphon off America's wealth—the direct cost of the invasion and the occupation hovered around $800 billion.

Over the eight years since the invasion, this meant a spending rate of $3,000 per second. Together with the operations in Afghanistan, America's wars had cost the country more than a trillion dollars. The toll on the economy and the people went even deeper: America's debt was ballooning and the long-term impact on soldiers and their families was felt across the country. The world perceived America as chastened and weakened. Pundits invoked Vietnam daily. There was talk of imperial overstretch. America's foes and friendly rivals were inordinately, smugly pleased.

This was some of the damage that Obama and Clinton were looking to repair.

The U.S. invasion of Iraq had overthrown a dictator but the war and the subsequent years of occupation had killed more than 100,000 Iraqis. Although the United States had rustled up a coalition of the willing, it had gone to war on its own terms, without the UN, charging into the region with little planning for the day after. The war unleashed all of Iraq's internal demons. Saddam Hussein's weapons of mass destruction, the motive for the war, were never found, further feeding the deep mistrust in Iraq and the region of America's motives. Now, Iraqis were still suffering, not only from military roadblocks and night raids from occupying forces but also from the militants fighting the occupation—their violence killed civilians too. People screamed daily in newspapers, at checkpoints, on television that they'd had enough of being trampled on. Iraqis and their leaders had pushed hard for the troop withdrawal plan, but suddenly, when the moment of withdrawal crept up, many sounded wary. Though it was hard to imagine, they worried that their lives would become more dangerous. What if America neglected them completely once all U.S. troops had left, leaving them alone to face the militants who still planted car bombs and the politicians who were already turning into authoritarian feudal lords, with an army that was barely holding together?

After the invasion in March 2003, those who welcomed the removal of Saddam Hussein—and even those who hadn't—expected that almighty America would transform their country into a well-ordered, prosperous Switzerland-like bastion on the Euphrates. Exhausted by decades of dictatorship, an eight-year war with neighboring Iran, and years of international sanctions, Iraqis were impatient for a decent life. Just weeks after Iraqis had toppled Saddam Hussein's statues across Baghdad and stood in front of cameras hitting posters of his image with their shoes, my conversations with people in Baghdad revealed swells of frustration and disbelief: Where was the water? Why was the city power not on? Where were the jobs? The salary raises? The truck loads of medication?

The expectations were beyond what any country could have realistically delivered, let alone a U.S. administration that naively thought things would simply fall into place after the invasion because it had brought freedom to the people. But no one in Iraq wanted to believe that a superpower which could, in just a few weeks of war, remove a dictator as entrenched as the earth itself didn't have a detailed plan for what was to follow, as well as foolproof means to implement it. Iraqis had lived in fear of Saddam for more than two decades; a whole generation had known only him as a leader. He and his intelligence services instilled widespread fear, spying on everybody and sowing distrust within families. A Sunni ruler, he had crushed Shiite dissent and rebellion ruthlessly. He didn't spare Sunnis who stood up to him either. But even the Shiites, who had suffered the most and were expected to welcome American soldiers with rose petals, quickly turned against the U.S. occupation. America's swift removal of their dictator confirmed to them that the United States was evil and all-powerful. The looting and burning of government buildings in the days after the fall of Baghdad, the destruction of the national museum, the power cuts, the chaos—it must have all been part of the plan. Washington wanted to destroy Iraq. It wanted the chaos, they clamored. Now, they were asking what Obama's plan was. Sure, he wanted to leave, but before that, could he please improve their living conditions? Maybe now American companies could come and rebuild the country?

We had driven into the compound of the U.S. embassy inside the Green Zone—a sand-colored fortress within a fortified enclave that had cost $700 million to build. The size of Vatican City, with twenty-seven buildings, a swimming pool, outdoor tennis courts, and neatly paved walkways with yellowing grass on either side, it was the largest U.S. embassy in the world. No wonder Iraqis thought America was staying forever. But the United States often harbored grand ambitions and wanted quick results; it tried one thing after another, changed course and strategies, hoping something would stick. And then it got tired with the project and started to downsize.

Inside the enclave of the embassy, we walked around freely. Fred reconnected with colleagues he had worked with just a few months earlier. There was even a town hall, always Hillary's favorite event of the day. Iraqi NGO workers, teachers, and legislators, all known to the U.S. embassy, had been invited to attend and told they were meeting a VIP guest. A human rights activist named William went first. Was America going to abandon Iraq? Others followed: What was America going to do to help modernize Iraq's agricultural sector? What was America going to do to empower women in Iraq? Could she send more American NGOs to Iraq?

There was a deluge of requests, and, unusually, Clinton seemed to grow weary of the questions. America was the occupier and it had responsibilities toward the country, but the questions carried an abdication of initiative and an undertone of fatalism. After years of being told what to do and think by Saddam, Iraqis were now looking for definitive answers and solutions from someone else. Because of the security restrictions in organizing the town hall, Clinton was facing a soft audience. The participants still believed America had something to offer them, but their anger and despair did not bode well for the day after America's withdrawal. Across the country, others saw the United States as a hegemonic power preying on their country's riches, imposing its will and offering nothing in return. Those two worldviews collided every day in Iraq and across the Middle East.

A long day of meetings followed with Iraq's president, prime minister, and foreign minister, as well as a press conference. We had left Kuwait at 7:30 in the morning and expected to return by early evening. But we were on "Hillary Time." It was 11:00 in the evening when we landed in Kuwait. We were going to spend the night at the Bayan Palace state guesthouse, which afforded the delegation some privacy to keep Clinton's next stop, Beirut, under wraps.

My home country was also on that exclusive list of troubled countries where U.S. officials made unannounced, "surprise visits," because of a bloody event that had permanently altered how America saw Lebanon.

In 1983, a few years into Lebanon's civil war, a suicide bomber drove his truck into the U.S. Marine barracks near the Beirut airport, killing 241 troops. Shiite Muslim militants were blamed for the carnage, and they coalesced into a group that called itself Hezbollah, Party of God. For them, America was the Great Satan. Israel, which was often referred to as the Little Satan, had occupied south Lebanon since 1978. Hezbollah strived to liberate the swath of occupied land until Israel withdrew in 2000. An ally of Iran and Syria, the Party of God was also working its way into Lebanese national politics while holding on to its arsenal. Though the State Department listed Hezbollah as a terrorist organization, it formed a part of the country's social and political fabric: it represented the country's long downtrodden Shiites. The group now had allies in the coalition cabinet, Lebanon's mostly pro-Western government. New elections were around the corner, and Hezbollah was always looking for ways to tighten its grip. Clinton was going to Beirut to check in on the state of affairs.

We had spent the whole day on the move, filing our stories in the heat of Baghdad and fading in our chairs waiting for Clinton. We were desperate for some rest before the next day's packed schedule. But our Kuwaiti hosts had laid out a lavish buffet dinner for the secretary and her whole delegation. We freshened up and took our seats at the tables under the garden tent surrounded by grass and hibiscus and oleander trees. Hillary held court at the middle table, surrounded by Jake, Huma, Philippe Reines, and Jeffrey Feltman, a former ambassador to Lebanon and the assistant secretary of state for Near Eastern Affairs—the Middle East expert in the Building.

I was helping myself to some of the food from the buffet, scooping up some of my favorite dessert, Umm Ali, when Mark Landler from the *New York Times* asked how it felt to be going home. I had tried not to think about it till now. I hadn't been able to tell my family that I was coming because of the security rules. I continued piling up the soft, milky pastry with pine nuts and almonds, staring blankly at Mark, smiling. I didn't tell him that I felt like an Iraqi would have, sitting on top of an American tank advancing into Baghdad in April 2003, though I wasn't sure whether the tanks were liberating or occupying. What was I doing on Clinton's plane? I was a journalist doing a job, but did I want my friends in Lebanon to know I was flying in with the American secretary of state? Or was I going to keep it quiet upon arrival? I was ambivalent about Clinton. I still found it hard to read her, and because of that, I found it difficult to get a feel for America's intentions toward my country.

At the end of the dinner, Clinton walked around to the different tables to chat. It was the first time we were in a social setting with her. The mood was slightly tense. She tried to appear informal but she wasn't relaxed; she was still very much the politician on duty. We had regular spats with her gatekeepers, who were intent on protecting her while we pushed for access. She came to a stop behind me, one hand on the shoulder of Matt Lee from the AP, one hand on mine. I stared at my plate, trying to come up with some smart comment about the state of world affairs.

Instead, I turned around, looked up, and said, "Madame Secretary, when I was growing up in Lebanon during the civil war, I never for a second imagined I would one day fly back to Lebanon on the plane of the American secretary of state."

I blurted it out because it neatly summarized the situation and all my emotions and because obviously it was true. As a kid I'd had my share of wild dreams about my future, but SAM and Hillary Clinton had not even featured. Hillary said she recalled watching the horror of my country's civil war on television with Bill. She said Lebanon had suffered so much, and that's why she was going, to show support. I was uncertain what that actually meant.

The next morning, we checked out of the guesthouse of the Kuwaiti emir with its outdated stuffy brown furniture from the 1980s. We loaded into the vans, almost leaving behind Arshad Mohammed from Reuters, who had overslept, and made our way to the airport.

I was nervous during the two-hour flight to the Beirut–Rafic Hariri International Airport, named after the billionaire prime minister who ran the country during much of the 1990s and again from 2000 until he resigned in 2004. A Sunni politician with broad appeal beyond Lebanon's borders he had had an international Rolodex that could rival Hillary's, and had helped rebuild Lebanon after the destruction of fifteen years of civil war, with all that it entailed of corruption, blind capitalism, and deal making with Lebanon's masters in Damascus. (Syria had occupied part or all of Lebanon since 1975.) Hariri was blown up by two thousand pounds of explosive as his motorcade drove along the city's seaside promenade on Valentine's Day in 2005.

Hundreds of thousands of demonstrators took to the street, accusing Damascus of killing him. He had started to push back against Syria's influence, and it was widely reported that Syria's president, Bashar al-Assad, had promised to "break Lebanon on his head." The demonstrators not only demanded justice; they wanted Syria's thirty thousand troops out of the country. It was the Beirut Spring. In April 2005, after thirty years of military occupation, fear, and humiliation, the Syrians finally left. Their Lebanese allies, Hezbollah and others, felt exposed. The country was deeply divided between those who had wanted Syria out and those for whom Damascus and Tehran represented a worldview they could connect with: anti-Western and anti-imperialist. Lebanon was a mosaic of faiths and had often split along religious lines during the war. But the divide this time was ideological and partisan: I had Shiite, Sunni, and Christian friends who despised Syria and Hezbollah, and I had other friends, also Shiite, Sunni, and Christian, who either liked Syria and Hezbollah or at least preferred them to the West.

The Mediterranean was in sight. I could see the tip of Beirut jutting into the dark blue sea. SAM had barely landed when my colleagues' chatter began to fill the air. They were all on the phone to their editors breaking the news of their arrival while frantically typing on their computers.

I made a very different kind of phone call, to my eldest sister.

"Ingrid, it's me. I'm in Beirut with Hillary," I said.

"I thought you might be coming—we heard rumors about her visit early this morning," Ingrid replied. "Why is she here? Will it be good for us?"

We had been asking ourselves these kinds of questions since we were children. But I didn't have answers for my sister, not yet.

I walked onto the tarmac and into an armored four-wheel-drive Suburban for the ride to the presidential palace. Along the highway leading out of the airport, yellow Hezbollah flags with a green fist raising a Kalashnikov were hanging from lampposts, and billboards were covered with the election campaign banners of members of the party running for parliament in June. The airport was in a Shiite Muslim area, and this was

Hezbollah territory. The palace was a fifteen-minute drive away, in Baabda, a hilly Christian suburb overlooking the capital.

The Bubble, always familiar, felt alien in Beirut. I was a stranger in my own country, separated from the Lebanese by tinted windows, armor, Fred and his team of Diplomatic Security agents, a Lebanese police escort. I was in the motorcade that irritated the hell out of me when I was living in Beirut, stuck in a traffic jam because roads had been blocked off for the American ambassador. For years after the civil war, even as Beirut reclaimed its title as glitzy party town of the Middle East, American embassy motorcades remained an elaborate affair, with machine gun turrets mounted on massive white SUVs. Today the U.S. embassy still has the most visible diplomatic motorcades. We rolled our eyes every time they drove past. In January 2008, an explosion targeted the embassy convoy, but it was a decoy, and the ambassador, Jeffrey Feltman, was unharmed. I was now in his convoy. He was in my convoy.

It was a surreal homecoming; an emotional moment at the end of a tortuous journey from Beirut war child to Washington State Department correspondent. Only much later did I realize that on that day I had embarked on another journey, within myself, as I tried to come to terms with my misgivings about American power. For now, all I really wanted was to go for a walk on the Corniche, the city seaside promenade. I didn't miss Lebanon now that I was living in Washington: too many painful memories. But I missed the Mediterranean, the sea breeze, the endless horizon that made me feel free even during the darkest days of fighting.

We had called it the war of others on our land: America sent in the marines. Israel invaded a few times, as did Syria, which was a client state of the Soviet Union. Palestinian militants hoping to reclaim what they saw as their lost land, now the State of Israel, used Lebanon as their launchpad, and Iran's Islamic revolutionaries set up shop on the Mediterranean by helping to form Hezbollah. From 1975 to 1990, at the height of the Cold War, all the different players and countries were fighting out their battles on our streets. America was just one of them, but as the superpower, it received the most attention, the most blame. We were convinced it was pulling all the strings—the war was a plot devised in the Oval Office, on a Sunday afternoon, with people poking pins into maps to divide the city between warring factions, President Ronald Reagan and Soviet leader Leonid Brezhnev discussing war spoils over the phone, deciding our fate. Growing up, that was my favorite image, and it was every Lebanese's favorite explanation to make sense of the chaos and killing surrounding us. The war didn't make sense to us, but it made sense to someone. We took strange comfort in that thought; it made our own powerlessness easier to bear; we were too busy trying to stay alive. The blame also allowed our warlords to abdicate their own responsibility to end the war. And just like millions of other people in fragile countries, repressive states, and dictatorships, my two sisters and I, my parents, our friends—we all lived and breathed politics every day: politics happened outside our front door; politics could be loud and dangerous; politics could kill you. My family was lucky to survive unscathed.

I was only thirteen when the war ended in 1990, but I remember so much of it, so vividly. I remember the nights cowering in the underground shelter, sleeping on mattresses we had brought down with us from our third-floor apartment, and the screaming as our building shook from the impact of bombs falling nearby. In the morning, my father would take my two sisters and me to school. At one point in the war, we would say good-bye to him at a checkpoint, walk for ten interminable minutes through a no-man's-land, then past some gunmen to get onto the blue bus that would take us to our school on the other side of our divided city. Every afternoon, we made the return journey, hoping our father had survived the day and was waiting for us. He would be sitting in his car, listening to the radio for reports of any shelling or sniper attacks as he waited for three girls with backpacks to appear from behind the barricades. We drove home and, if the shelling permitted, we stopped for some groceries at Abu Moussa's shop, mostly fruit and vegetables that my father loved to pick by hand, one by one.

Clinton's convoy was speeding up the hill, the roads cleared of all traffic. We cut across a large boulevard that led back into a different part of Beirut. I could see the intersection less than half a mile away below which had been a crossing point between East and West Beirut during the war and was named after the furniture shop on one corner— Galerie Semaan. With sand barriers and tall buildings overlooking it, it had been a favorite sniper outpost. My family and I had lived just off that intersection. During the war, radio announcers kept citizens informed with news flashes about where fighting had erupted and "Galerie Semaan" was in the news often. Whenever I tried to explain to people where I lived, all I had to say was Galerie Semaan—their eyes widened, their reaction ranging from disbelief to pity. Needless to say, we never had any visitors. Sometimes we referred to the area by its original name—Hay el Amerkan, the neighborhood of the Americans. When my family had settled there before the start of the war, it was a charming middle-class area, favored by expatriates and surrounded by orange groves. A year into the violence, the only expatriates were my mother and invading armies who all chose to set up their headquarters in our small cluster of buildings. Galerie Semaan didn't just sit on the dividing line between the Muslim West and Christian East sides of the capital, it was on the southern edge of the city. North of us was Christian Beirut and beyond it the mostly Christian north of Lebanon. South of us was dominantly Muslim territory, Sunni and then Shiite in the deep south, along the border with Israel.

Israel, which already invaded southern Lebanon once in 1978, invaded again on June 6, 1982. Palestinian guerrilla fighters, using Lebanon as their staging post to liberate the Holy Land, were all over south Lebanon and the western part of Beirut, and some of their gunmen had set up positions in our building. As Israeli tanks started advancing toward Beirut and Galerie Semaan, we fled farther north, deep into Christian territory, to escape the ferocious fighting. When we returned in the early fall, the Palestinian guerrillas and their ragtag Mercedes cars had been replaced by Israeli soldiers rounding up blindfolded men and driving them away in tanks. In our apartment on the third floor, I found my bedroom gutted by a shell, curtains torn, shrapnel holes on every wall, my toys and clothes covered by grime and dust. I was only five but intensely aware of my surroundings and the reality of war, yet unable to comprehend why I was being punished in such a fashion and by whom. I also didn't understand why they couldn't instead have destroyed the awful green carpet and orange bed frame, which survived the whole war.

Now, I was home again. This time I felt strange, like a traitor, as if I had crossed to the other side. I was in a big American convoy, and I had become part of the American press pack that I had once perceived as arrogant, pushy, and entitled. (The traveling press corps was in fact one of the most collegial group of journalists I had ever worked with.) Unlike local reporters, those of us in the Bubble didn't have to show up hours in advance to go through security; we could usually just waltz in a few minutes before the press conference started. We didn't have to hustle for seats because two rows were always reserved for us. We always got a turn to ask a question.

Around the country, families sitting down for Sunday lunch or driving to their favorite restaurant were turning on the television or radio for their midday fix of politics. Depending on their political leaning, they tuned in to the Lebanese Broadcasting Corporation (LBC), a Christian right-wing television station; Al-Manar television, Hezbollah's outfit; or Voice of Lebanon, for something in between the two. Each station presented its own, often wildly diverging, version of the truth. Most of them would carry Clinton's press conference live.

In her bright blue pantsuit, Clinton stood in the wood-paneled press conference room smiling for the television cameras, a gold Lebanese cedar stamped on the lectern in front of her, the top of a Roman column affixed to the walls on either side. She talked about the need for Lebanon to have a fair election, free of outside influence.

On Al-Manar television, she was being excoriated for interfering in Lebanon's affairs before the summer elections—an irony since Hezbollah of course had its own foreign backers. On LBC, they were talking about Clinton's show of support for the country as it prepared for the vote. It was my turn to ask a question.

"Madame Secretary, welcome to Lebanon. I know you don't want to speculate about the results of the elections, but it does look likely that Syria's allies, including Hezbollah, will make a strong comeback. How will that affect your support for the Lebanese army that you just discussed? You said it was a pillar of cooperation between the two countries. Would you reevaluate that cooperation with the Lebanese army?"

"Well, Kim, first let me say that it's a great delight to have you with me on this trip. As some of you know, Kim is Lebanese and has been so excited about coming back to a country that she loves, and I am pleased that I could be the reason she got to come back at this particular time."

I felt flattered: she remembered me and our conversation. But she had also made my feelings known in public on national Lebanese television, in front of all the local press. I knew it was a small moment, but I felt she used me to make a connection with the Lebanese people at a time of tension in the country, when the United States was trying to shore up support for Western-friendly politicians.

Much later, she would tell me that she had made the comment on the spur of the moment because she was deeply moved to see me return to Lebanon with her after all I had lived through. She had looked at me standing there with a microphone and seen someone who symbolized what Lebanon could be. But in that moment, long before I would ask her about it, the interaction left me feeling deeply unsettled. In Lebanon, as a journalist or a politician or anyone with even the tiniest bit of a profile or influence, you were considered either a stooge of the United States or an agent of its local opponents: Hezbollah, Iran, and Syria. Clinton's casual comment meant I had just been tainted by an American stamp—or graced, depending on who was judging.

We drove back toward the Mediterranean, into the center of the city. Ottoman Empire and French Mandate–era buildings gutted by the civil war fighting had been painstakingly restored to their ancient glory. Whatever could not be saved had been razed to the ground. Empty plots of land and cranes dotted the landscape. Clinton was going to pay her respects at the tomb of Hariri, buried in the heart of the capital, near the mosque he had helped build, the largest in Lebanon. He had been prime minister during all the years that she had been a First Lady. Bill called him a personal friend. Once out of power, the two men had stayed in touch and had met at length just two months before Hariri was killed. Hariri's son Saad had taken on the political mantle and stood by Hillary's side as she laid a wreath.

We had arrived barely two hours before, and it was already time to leave. But I was exiting the Bubble and staying behind in Beirut to see my family. Lew Lukens had given me my passport back. I took my suitcase out of the press van. My colleagues, the secretary, Jake, Jeff, Huma, and all the others got into the armored motorcade. One by one, the black cars took off, police sirens wailed. I watched the convoy drive up the road toward the airport and disappear beyond the small hill.

Suddenly I felt strangely vulnerable, abandoned by the side of the road with my luggage. I wanted to wave good-bye like a child, but everybody was off, going back home. And I was home.

Was I?

I was standing on a patch of gravel, a shrine to a dead politician to my right, a statue to Lebanon's many martyrs since the Ottoman Empire to my left, and a six- or eight-story-high banner hanging from a building behind me, stamped with the face of Gebran Tueni, a prominent journalist watching me from beyond the grave. Like Hariri, he had been killed by a targeted car bomb in 2005. He was the husband of a close friend. His death was also blamed on Syria. Nine political and public figures had been killed in explosions between 2005 and 2008, and an international investigation was under way to look into the connection between the murders and find the culprits. Syria's friends, like Hezbollah, saw the investigation as an international machination to destroy Damascus. But the West had also long wanted Syria to make peace with Israel. In Lebanon, Syria's opponents worried that justice would fall victim to wider geopolitical considerations.

During the press conference, Clinton had been asked whether the United States was going to strike a deal with Syria at the expense of Lebanon. She said justice was overdue in Lebanon—the age of impunity had to end.

"So, I want to assure any Lebanese citizens that the United States will never make any deal with Syria that sells out Lebanon and the Lebanese people," she said, becoming animated, softly banging her hand on the lectern, emphasizing every other word.

"You have been through too much, and it is only right that you are given a chance to make your own decisions, however they turn out, amongst the people who call Lebanon home, who love this country, who are committed to it, who have stayed here and done what you can to navigate through these difficult years. It's a complicated neighborhood you live in, and you have a right to have your own future. And we believe that very strongly."

I had heard that before. Or at least I had wanted to believe it was what I had heard, back in September 1990. I was becoming politically aware and sitting in the back of my parents' olive-green Peugeot one sunny September

Sunday morning, listening to President George H. W. Bush on the radio. We were driving to a restaurant in the hills east of Beirut for Sunday lunch on a rare quiet day during one of the darkest periods of the war. My sisters, Ingrid and Audrey, both older than me, had been sent to universities abroad, away from the madness. Michel Aoun, an army general who had recently been appointed interim prime minister, had declared a war of liberation against Syria, which occupied most of Lebanon with forty thousand troops. The rebel general ruled only over the Christian enclave where I lived and the army he commanded was just a small remnant of the country's divided national army. But his soldiers were conducting a ferocious assault against Syria's occupation, making some gains or at least fighting the Syrians to a stalemate. Aoun was greatly helped by the supplies of weapons he was receiving from Saddam Hussein in Iraq. The world had grown tired of watching the televised gory images of our internecine clashes, except when, like now, moving battle lines in Beirut reflected the shifting balance of world power.

Iraq had just invaded Kuwait. Oil fields were burning. The Berlin Wall had fallen a year earlier. The Soviet Union was trying to keep itself together while the U.S. eagle puffed its chest and spread its wings. On the radio, the voice of President Bush was telling us he stood with the Lebanese.

"America is finally listening," I thought with relief. "They're going to help; all will be well."

I thought it meant he stood by me and what I thought was best for Lebanon. Just a few weeks later, on October 13, 1990, Syrian troops invaded the Christian enclave of Lebanon, looting and raping on their way in and arresting scores of soldiers and Aoun sympathizers or shooting them at close range execution style. We were convinced a deal had been struck: the United States had given Syria the green light to take over the rebellious but prized part of Lebanon that had so far remained outside its control. In exchange, Hafez al-Assad, the dictator in Damascus, a bastion of anti-Americanism, agreed to participate in the American-led coalition against Iraq to liberate Kuwait. America wanted the broadest possible coalition and Arab participation was key.

I felt betrayed, devastated, and furious at the United States for selling us out, for lying to me about their support for my country. I couldn't fathom that elsewhere in Lebanon, in a different community, another neighborhood, someone listening to a different radio station but hearing the same words of the American president had understood them very differently. For them, the Syrian invasion was a sign that America had supported their version of what was best for Lebanon. Either way, it seemed clear that there was a plan, that America did pull the strings and could end wars if it wanted to. I didn't understand the intricacies of the geopolitical ballet the United States had had to perform, the work it had required to make everybody's positions align from Russia to Israel to Syria. But the guns fell silent, and we found ourselves under Syrian occupation.

If America was the source of all our trouble, we also believed it had the answer to our problems, and this elicited hope and disappointment in people like a roller coaster. And if we believed America pulled all the strings or could save us, it was probably because the United States had once intervened in Lebanon with great success.

I n 1958, Operation Blue Bat brought fourteen thousand U.S. troops to the shores of Beirut. President Dwight Eisenhower had sent them to help prevent the overthrow of the Christian president by a rebellious, dominantly Muslim opposition backed by the nationalist Egyptian leader Gamal Abdel Nasser. It was a time when "international communism" preoccupied Washington, and Nasser's links with the Soviet Union were a good enough reason to back the pro-Western president of Lebanon.

The opposition was intimidated, another more widely accepted president was elected, and the Americans left three months later with barely a shot fired. It was a successful projection of American power etched in the memories of the Lebanese and many others who had watched around the world. America was a reliable, powerful friend that got things done or, for its enemies, a power to be feared. The Soviet Union and Communism appealed to many as well, but America had better, bigger, shinier toys.

The next time a Lebanese president asked for help, in 1982, after the Israeli invasion and our escape from Galerie Semaan, we were a different country, seven years into a savage civil war. Everybody still thought it was 1958. When we heard the marines were coming, my sister Audrey was ecstatic. She was thirteen years old at the time, I was five, and our exposure to the war's raw images was limited by power cuts and curfews.

The only way my sister could picture what an American marine landing could look like was to imagine an endless supply of bubble gum.

The marines arrived with French, Italian, and British troops ostensibly as a neutral force to help bring peace back to Lebanon, separate warring Christian and Muslim militias, and keep the Israelis in check, away from the Syrians, who had also invaded. These forces were going to make sure that the Palestinian guerrilla fighters left the country as had been agreed. In the process, America would strengthen the central authority— the president and the Lebanese army, the good guys. But the lines had become murky—the good guys were bastards too, though they spoke English and wore ties. The president, a Christian, roped the smiling, optimistic marines into his feud against his Muslim opponents. America believed in good and evil, black and white, but Lebanon was now full of gray. By the summer of 1983, the marines were increasingly drawn into the fighting as they tried to shore up the president and his army against the Muslim militias—they had picked sides, de facto. The leftist, pro-Syrian newspaper *As-Safir* started referring to the Western troops as the international militia. It ended in blood and tears on October 23, 1983, with the smoldering marine barracks, hit by a suicide truck packed with twelve thousand pounds of TNT at 6:20 a.m.

After the attack, the single deadliest day for the U.S. Marine Corps since the Battle of Iwo Jima in World War II, President Reagan swore his commitment to Lebanon. There would be no run for the exits, he said, because America would not be cowed by terrorists. Four months later, the marines left. Those who had carried out the attacks and saw America as the enemy cried victory. But thousands of others felt utterly abandoned. And Audrey still wanted her bubble gum.

The sacrifice for America had been great, but we couldn't grasp the enormity of it. We were still living in hell and we still wanted the world to help. To us, it looked like America had made promises, raised our hopes, and then cut its losses, leaving us in the downpour—a deluge that would eventually catch up with the United States too.

The marine barracks bombing was the first salvo in the war between radical Islamic militants and the West, America in particular. Warning shots had been fired a few years earlier, in 1979, in revolutionary Shiite Iran when Islamists had overthrown the country's secular monarch, Shah

Mohammed Reza Pahlavi, a friend of the United States and an enlight-ened despot. Later that year, still seething with anger at American inter-ference in their country, students and militants took over the U.S. embassy in Tehran and kept fifty-two Americans hostage for 444 days. Iran's new ruler, Ayatollah Ruhollah Khomeini, wanted to push America even farther out of the region, and with his allies in Beirut, he delivered a deadly mes-sage to Washington on that October morning. Combined with the Viet-nam War debacle, still fresh in the collective memory, the events in Iran, and the Beirut bombing, the headlines were all about American decline. Politicians, pundits, and grocers emphatically declared that America was over.

In Lebanon, the war continued until that day in October 1990 when Syria imposed its peace on us. The tanks were retired and the snipers went home. But Lebanon was still a troubled country in a difficult neigh-borhood where the stakes for America remained high, and peacetime brought its share of crises. As a journalist, my stories were about our power plants being bombed by Israel, Hezbollah kidnapping Israeli sol-diers, Syria imposing presidents on us, politicians and journalists getting blown up; and with each crisis, journalists, friends, and family waited to hear what Washington had to say or what it was planning to do about the situation. As ever, interpretation of any statement depended on your political leanings: you were either looking for a sign that help was on its way or looking for a clue about America's nefarious designs. More often than not, the news anchor, speaking in Arabic, would start the evening news bulletin with "The spokesperson for the American foreign minis-try today said the situation in Lebanon was . . ."

Now I was living in Washington, and I knew the current spokesper-son, P. J. Crowley. A jovial man with the gift of gab, probably due to his Irish ancestry, P. J. was a retired air force colonel who had served in the Clinton administration. Sharing a drink with him and other journalists in Washington, at the beginning of my time in the United States, I still wondered what he knew that I didn't. I knew that America had changed, that the world had changed. China was looking more and more like a rival to the United States, Turkey was vying for a regional role, Brazil was becoming a superpower in Latin America, and Moscow was slowly recov-ering from the breakup of the Soviet Union. Yet people's vision of America as omnipotent remained.

Were we stuck in the past, holding on to the image of America as a superpower because it was simply what we knew? What was twenty-first-century American power made of, anyway? Was it smart? Or would it end up being more of the same, just better than the last eight years? Lebanon wasn't the only country in the Middle East that hung on Washington's every word looking for a clue about its intentions and about the future.

4

NO NATURAL GROWTH

A few weeks before the trip to Beirut, Clinton had faced a crowded, chaotic room full of hostile Arab journalists and a smattering of equally skeptical American and European reporters. She had just pledged $300 million in aid for the Palestinians during an international conference in the Egyptian seaside resort of Sharm el-Sheikh. Cast Lead, the Israel military assault against the Gaza Strip which had ended just as Obama was inaugurated, had killed up to 1,400 Palestinians, including 300 children, and left an already bleak economy in ruins. The Israeli army had pounded the territory to stop rocket fire into Israel and was keeping the strip under blockade. The Arab journalists didn't care so much about the aid: America had made many promises before, but life as a Palestinian under Israeli occupation was still miserable. The money was just a Band-Aid.

The journalists had a very simple question for Clinton: Would an independent Palestinian state come into existence within a year?

This was Hillary's first foray into the decades-old conflict as secretary of state, but she had a long history with the region, as did her husband, who had tried until his last minute in office to get the Palestinians and the Israelis to make peace. Overall, Arabs did not trust America when it came to resolving conflict. They accused the United States of siding with Israel, always and without reservations. They were not wrong, but they were not entirely right either. The conflict was about so much more than land and elicited deep emotions, unrealistic hopes, and bursts of anger on all sides. American officials expressed empathy with Israel more often, leaving Palestinians living under the humiliation of occupation feeling like lesser humans, but Arabs still pleaded with the United States to help broker peace, perhaps precisely because they knew no one else could deliver Israel to the negotiating table. There were still fond memories in the region of Bill Clinton, of his rare ability to empathize with Palestinians and his desperate efforts to broker peace. Discussing the conflict with Arab leaders, including Egypt's president Hosni Mubarak, Hillary referenced the long days and nights her husband had spent working for peace. Then she reached out to her skeptical audience. A viable Palestinian state was the goal.

"You all know that this is a very difficult and complex set of issues. You also know that I personally am very committed to this. And I know that it can be done. I believe that with all my heart. I feel passionately about this. This is something that is in my heart, not just in my portfolio," said the secretary.

In 1998, as First Lady, Hillary spoke to a group of young Palestinians, Israelis, Jordanians, Egyptians, and Americans, who were holding an unprecedented joint youth summit in Switzerland. She spelled out exactly how she thought the outcome of peace talks should look: the Palestinians should have their own state. She was ahead of White House policy. No American official had mentioned a Palestinian state yet, though some had been thinking it and the Palestinians had been calling for it. Since the creation of Israel in 1948, Palestinians had lived either as refugees in neighboring states or under occupation in two separate pieces of territory: the Gaza Strip, in the Mediterranean, and inland, on the border with Jordan, the West Bank, and East Jerusalem. The two territories had first been annexed by Egypt and Jordan in 1948 but then captured by Israel during the 1967 Six-Day War. Tens of thousands of Palestinians also became Israeli citizens and today make up 20 percent of the country's population. American presidents who labored for peace between Israel and the Palestinians had so far never spelled out in detail what the outcome should look like. But Hillary had said it aloud; it seemed obvious to her.

The Israeli prime minister was apoplectic—the country's leadership openly opposed the idea of a Palestinian state and was unable yet to envisage giving the Palestinians anything more than an amorphous nationlet made up of cantons with little or no geographical connection between them. The White House quickly put out a disclaimer, saying Hillary's statement was not official U.S. policy. As a U.S. senator from New York, Hillary was less public about her views on Palestinian hardship and more in tune with the many Jewish voters in her constituency. Now, as a secretary of state, she told the Arab journalists before her that Palestinian children deserved a better future and that Palestinian parents had the right to expect such a future for their children. She promised that the Obama administration was going to work hard for peace and for a Palestinian state.

"You will see the amount of effort that the United States puts into this. I wish it could happen tomorrow. I wish it could happen certainly by the end of this year. But I will not give up. We will make progress."

Arab journalists, most of them Egyptians, were taken aback by her show of emotion. During the eight years of the Bush administration, there had been little or no empathy. Emoting wasn't Condoleezza Rice's strong suit, and it was never part of her talking points. Suddenly the room erupted into applause. American officials standing along the wall listening were stunned, especially those who were steeped in Middle East affairs and protected themselves from the vagaries of the warring parties with layers of cynicism. Journalists never applauded at the end of a press conference, and in the Arab world no one ever cheered for American officials. The applause wasn't just the result of Hillary's ability to charm when she spoke from the heart; it was a reflection of the deep yearning, both in the room and in the region, for renewed hope about an intractable conflict, a reflection of the inexplicable continued desire among Arabs to see America take their side—preferably unconditionally. Despite their wariness about the United States, the Arabs in the region had welcomed President Obama's election, and so far they liked what they were hearing.

On his second day in office, Obama had declared that seeking a solution to the sixty-year-long conflict between Arabs and Israelis was in America's national security interest. From Washington to Ramallah, ears perked up. American presidents rarely tackled Middle East peace at the start of their administrations. Even more striking was the new language. For the past forty years, every American president had tried to broker peace: peace would be good for the people of the region and pulling

it off would make everyone look good. Only two presidents had succeeded in bringing Arabs and Israeli leaders together for a handshake on
the White House lawn: Bill Clinton and Jimmy Carter. The others tried
their best to produce the same photo opportunity. But to seek peace
because it was a matter of national security for the United States, as
Obama had said, elevated this to an essential and urgent goal.

Obama's first phone call to a foreign leader on January 21 was to the
Palestinian president Mahmoud Abbas—an unprecedented, symbolic,
and powerful gesture. Because 78 percent of American Jews had voted for
Obama, he felt strong, convinced that his persona alone could deliver a
breakthrough. Looking at the region, he saw elements he could build on.

Just before Obama's election, the Israeli military onslaught against
the Palestinian territory of Gaza had deepened the political divide
between Palestinians and further weakened Abbas. Since 2007, Abbas had
ruled over only part of the Palestinian territories, the West Bank. Hamas,
the Sunni Islamist political party and armed militant group listed as a
terror group by the United States, ruled over Gaza. Wars often create diplomatic momentum: they focus everybody's minds on the need to find
a solution. Obama saw an opportunity. There were also signs that an
agreement could be within reach. The Israeli prime minister Ehud Olmert,
from the centrist Kadima Party, had been negotiating on and off for two
years with Abbas, both with the help of the United States and also alone.
They had been making real progress on all the issues, from the borders of
a future Palestinian state to the status of Jerusalem, which both Israelis
and Palestinians claimed as their capital. Olmert claimed they were "very
close"[7] to a deal. But progress was stalled when the Israeli leader faced
corruption charges; he was on his way out and his foreign minister, Tzipi
Livni, also from Kadima, was running for office. She was in a dead heat
race with the leader of the right-wing Likud Party. At the State Department, many officials were secretly rooting for Kadima. On February 10,
Livni and her party won the greatest number of seats but she had such
a narrow majority, she struggled to form a coalition. The Likud party
leader, the other contender for power, was more successful in wooing small
parties, and at the end of March he became the prime minister. Benjamin
Netanyahu was back, and that wasn't part of anyone's plan.

Netanyahu, or Bibi, as he was known, was the Israeli prime minister
who had reacted with such fury to Hillary's statement about a Palestinian

state back in 1998. He had also driven Bill crazy. After a lecture from Netanyahu about the Arab-Israeli conflict during one of their first meetings in 1996, President Clinton had exploded. "Who the fuck does he think he is? Who's the fucking superpower here?"[8]

Then secretary of state Madeleine Albright had described Bibi as "pugnacious, partisan and very smooth," a man who could be both "disarming and somewhat disingenuous"[9] and constantly played games in the negotiations. He had spent years in the United States, had studied at the Massachusetts Institute of Technology, and he used his familiarity with America both to make friends and to game the system, pitting Congress against the president.

The contrast with his predecessor Yitzhak Rabin was stark. Rabin had been assassinated by a right-wing Israeli in 1995 because of concessions he made for peace. President Clinton and Rabin had been great friends. The Israeli statesman had shaken hands with then Palestinian leader Yasser Arafat on the White House lawn and signed a peace treaty with Jordan. Mostly, he was a man who stuck to his words and acted on them. Bibi constantly reneged on his promises. Rahm Emanuel, one of President Clinton's senior advisors, said little in public but watched with dismay as Bibi frustrated Clinton's efforts to reach a lasting deal. Now Rahm was back in power too, this time as Obama's chief of staff.

Bibi probably did not have the best of memories from the Clinton administration. When his government coalition had collapsed at the end of 1998, early elections were called, and in Washington top administration officials were hoping that Bibi's opponent, Labor leader Ehud Barak, would win. The Israeli press speculated that Clinton was actively trying to bring about Bibi's defeat, a narrative that was fed by the presence in Israel of a handful of Democratic political strategists who were close to Clinton and helped Barak on the path to victory.

Two years after Hillary's 1998 off-script comment, Bill Clinton himself called for a Palestinian state and the position became official U.S. policy. But the details, Washington insisted again, would have to be decided by Israel and the Palestinians: the borders of the state, the status of Palestinian refugees, security agreements. But once again Bibi was dragging his feet—he could not even utter the words "Palestinian state." He and previous Israeli leaders had tried to alter the contours of the territory that they occupied in Israel's favor. They built more and more settlements for Israelis on land that would make up the future Palestinian state and erected a barrier separating Israel from the West Bank. Supporters of the barrier argued that it was essential to protect Israelis from Palestinian militant attacks. But already, Palestinian territory was not contiguous; the Gaza Strip was separated from the West Bank by Israel proper—land that Palestinians were not allowed on without Israeli permission. Palestinians complained they were negotiating about how to split a pizza while the Israelis were busy eating it.

Bibi and his right-wing maximalist views threatened Obama's hopes for Middle East peace. Emanuel advised Obama to be tough on Netanyahu and show him, immediately, who the superpower was. Senator George Mitchell, Obama's new Middle East peace envoy, had tackled this all before too. At the end of the Clinton administration, when peace failed and violence erupted, he had been tasked with finding a way forward for the parties. One of the items on the long list of recommendations was a settlement freeze. Obama appointed Mitchell at the behest of Hillary, who, although she could speak with passion about a Palestinian state, was wary of associating herself too closely too soon with the thankless task of Mideast peace. Mitchell, a seventy-six-year-old man with a calm demeanor, had negotiated peace in Northern Ireland and believed in details and small steps. He brought the settlement issue to the front again. Although he was not formally in charge of the Mideast file, Emanuel was keen to show Bibi who was boss, and he actively pushed for the freeze to top the agenda. When Netanyahu came for his first meeting at the White House on May 18, President Obama established his position.

"Settlements have to be stopped in order for us to move forward," Obama said. "That's a difficult issue. I recognize that. But it's an important one, and it has to be addressed."

In public, Bibi said he was willing to consider refraining from new construction, but if a school needed a new playground, if a building was still under construction, if a family needed an extension to their house—all that construction had to continue. Daily life had to grow, he insisted, it was natural. There were more than 300,000 settlers living in the Israeli occupied territory of the West Bank in between Palestinian towns and, even though settlements were illegal under international law, they kept growing. Like a game of rope pulling, Palestinians and Arabs had felt

America leaning toward them. Israel was now pulling hard on the other side, and tension was settling in.

On May 27, Clinton met with the Egyptian foreign minister Ahmed Aboul Gheit at the State Department. She was asked what she thought of Bibi's offer to continue building what was already under way but not allow any new construction.

"The president was very clear when Prime Minister Netanyahu was here. He wants to see a stop to settlements," said Clinton. Then, with the sleeve of her electric-blue pantsuit going back and forth for emphasis, she continued with a faint indignant smile, detailing exactly what she believed Obama had meant.

"Not some settlements, not outposts, not natural growth exceptions. We think it is in the best interests of the effort that we are engaged in that settlement expansion cease. That is our position."

Standing next to her, Aboul Gheit, one hand in his pocket, smiled smugly. He knew the Obama administration wanted to push for a stop in settlement construction, and he didn't necessarily agree. He thought it was a short-term tactic when what was needed was a comprehensive long-term strategy—ideally America should put a detailed plan on the table and get to the finish line quickly. But he liked Clinton's firm tone of voice. This was a strong, powerful, and very public statement, and it boded well for tough negotiations with the Israelis.

Finally, the Palestinians thought. Finally, the United States has seen the light and was showing Israel who was boss. Clinton's firmness was beyond just a general call for a stop in settlement activity. No natural growth meant drop all your cinder blocks, immobilize your cranes, park your trucks. The Palestinian president and his advisors adopted it as their new mantra. They certainly couldn't ask less than what Washington was setting as a standard. America had spoken, it was the will of the American president, and all they had to do now was wait for the Israelis to comply. They would get their house in order, continue fixing up the economy, and build state institutions, and America would make peace talks happen. The radical group Hamas was more cynical. Words, all words, they said. Nothing will change.

In Washington, analysts and activists were coming forward with suggestions about how the administration should punish Bibi if he didn't halt settlement construction: link elements of aid to a stop in settlement construction, announce a review of the strategic relationship between the two countries, or even boycott a settlement products. Obama's and Clinton's statements were taken as a sign that the administration was ready to go to the mat with Bibi. Previous presidents, like Richard Nixon, Gerald Ford, and George H. W. Bush, had gone that route with Israeli leaders—if America stood its ground, it could pay off.

The Israelis were livid. Bibi didn't like to be told what to do, especially not in public. He wasn't going to let an American administration push him around again. He was convinced that Hillary and Rahm wanted to throw him under the bus and had turned Obama against him.[10] But a few days later, Obama called for settlements to stop, and this time he used Clinton's more elaborate wording.

"I've said very clearly to the Israelis both privately and publicly that a freeze on settlements, including natural growth, is part of those obligations [that Israel will have to meet]," he told NPR in Washington.

But, as in 1998, Hillary had been ever so slightly ahead of the White House—and this time of herself. She had spoken more forcefully than the president, and it had taken the White House by surprise. A nascent policy on settlements was crystallized with a statement: "No natural growth."

A few days after his NPR interview, Obama flew to Riyadh and then on to Cairo, where his prose enchanted the crowds. He promised again to work hard for peace, telling the crowds that "all of us have a responsibility to work for the day when the mothers of Israelis and Palestinians can see their children grow up without fear." And he promised a new beginning with the Muslim world, which had grown weary of being lumped together in the same group as Osama bin Laden. With every lofty line, expectations rose higher and higher, in the halls of the American University of Cairo and across the region. There was only one way to go from there: down. But it was a question of how hard and fast the fall would be and how damaging to American interests.

5

THE SHRINK WILL
SEE YOU NOW

Nine months into her job and Hillary had already flown 140,000 miles crisscrossing the world. She had honed her voice and style as secretary of state with friendly audiences in Asia, Africa, and Europe. She had made a few more missteps along the way, tripping over names of officials and mistakenly saying the United States had no diplomatic ties with Burma. She had reconnected with allies, reset relations with rivals like Russia, and started spinning her web of diplomatic connections and initiatives. It was time for the frying pan.

On the morning of Tuesday, October 27, when the State Department sent another one of its cryptic e-mails announcing that the secretary had no public appointments, we were already on a plane. It was a seventeen-hour journey to another country that warranted surprise visits: prickly Pakistan. A nuclear power as well as India's neighbor and archenemy, Pakistan had helped prop up the Taliban government in Afghanistan on its western border during the 1990s, and the Taliban sheltered al-Qaeda.

The Obama administration's policy toward Pakistan was still in flux, and Clinton's team was still shaping the contours of the trip as we boarded the plane. The trip Book was an untamed mess. Schedules were never final with Hillary, and there didn't ever seem to be enough reading material in the Book to satisfy her voracious appetite. In Pakistan, the advance teams from the Line were still negotiating the content of the agenda of her talks, the exact look and location of her town halls, which shrines she would visit, and what security arrangements would be needed. Just like Lebanon and Iraq, Pakistan was one of those countries where security concerns kept American officials from fully engaging with the local population, but the State Department was still planning a Hillary template trip.

The relationship with Islamabad was broken, and attempting to fix it required a bold approach, such as having the secretary connect with average people as she had done so well in other countries. None of her predecessors had bothered with public diplomacy in Pakistan; they instead focused on meetings with the country's generals. Rice only once spent the night in the country. Pakistani officials were a slippery bunch and the people often openly hostile to the United States. Over three days, in two cities, Clinton would face a battery of town halls with students; meetings with tribal leaders, women's groups, and businessmen; and interviews with feisty journalists. She had essentially agreed to be a punching bag. The idea was to help Pakistan release some of its anger toward the United States by allowing people to vent their frustrations and disappointments at the secretary. Jake, Huma, and Philippe were nervous about putting their boss in this position: it was a gamble with no guarantee of success. But even the tiniest bump in the dismal 19 percent approval ratings of the United States in Pakistan would be welcome.

President Obama and his National Security team were exploring a new strategy for the war; American soldiers were still fighting against al-Qaeda and the Taliban across the border in Afghanistan. Obama had already increased troop numbers and was considering sending in even more soldiers, but if he wanted to make progress in Afghanistan, Islamabad's help was crucial. Even after agreeing to help fight al-Qaeda in 2001, Pakistan was still a base for radical militants. The administration was still determining how to handle Pakistan: Clinton's trip was in large part a live test of nascent policy.

Pakistan was not exactly an American ally nor was it an enemy. Pakistan wanted strong ties with America, but the relationship between the two countries was long and fraught. Each distrusted the other equally. The United States was one of the first countries to recognize an independent Pakistan in 1947. The new country was born from the partition of British India, which gave birth to Muslim Pakistan and secular India. Washington provided Pakistan with generous aid. But when the young nation sent 30,000 soldiers into the contested border territory of Kashmir in 1965 and provoked a war with India, the United States cut off military and economic aid to both countries. By 1975, American military aid flowed into Pakistan again but then stopped in 1979 because of concerns that Pakistan was trying to build a nuclear weapon. When the Soviet Union invaded neighboring Afghanistan on Christmas Eve 1979, America's priorities in the area shifted. Now concerned with fighting the advance of Communism, Washington turned a blind eye to Pakistan's nuclear program, cozied up with its leaders, and in the 1980s the aid started up again. The two countries and their intelligence agencies started working together to fund and arm the anti-Soviet Afghan guerrillas. Many of them had strong Islamic militant views and wanted the Communist unbelievers out of their land—their war was a jihad. Millions of Afghan refugees fled into Pakistan, and America sent $5.6 billion of military, economic, and food aid to support Pakistan. In 1989, the jihadi guerrillas defeated the Soviets and forced them to withdraw from Afghanistan.

The job was done, Communism had been dealt a blow, the United States forgot about Afghanistan, and Pakistan was left to deal with the collapsing country next door, where civil war raged. Afghan refugees continued to cross the border, fleeing the fighting in their villages and towns. Pakistan was still hard at work on its nuclear program, despite warnings from Washington. In 1990, the United States became concerned enough that it once more stopped all military aid and drastically cut back economic assistance to Pakistan. A decade later, the September 11 attacks put this fraught relationship under unprecedented strain. When Washington asked President Pervez Musharraf to show whether his country was with the United States or against it, Pakistan chose the cash cow. Military aid flowed again. The Pakistanis were getting seasick from the on-again, off-again relationship.

But it was a lucrative one. Plagued by years of unchecked military power, corruption, rampant tax evasion, ballooning debt, extremism, and an all-consuming rivalry with India, Pakistan's economy had become addicted to outside aid, its generals avid recipients of military assistance. The Pakistanis wanted the money with no strings attached. Just a few weeks before Clinton's trip, Congress had approved the Kerry-Lugar-Berman bill, a new package of aid for Pakistan—$7.5 billion over five years in nonmilitary assistance. The idea was to help shore up the civilian government and state institutions, after years of military dictatorship—if the Pakistanis could show that they were really building a civilian state. Though Pakistan complained that this was interference in its internal affairs, the government still took the money. The contradictions were giving America a headache, and though the relationship was a drain and a nuisance, no one dared contemplate the risk of letting go of Pakistan again.

Flying across the Atlantic, Hillary was in her cabin being briefed by the top man in charge of Afghanistan and Pakistan policy, Richard Holbrooke, a longtime diplomat, and by his deputy Vali Nasr, the expert outsider. An acclaimed academic and author, Vali had never been in government before and had not yet traveled on Hillary's plane. An authority on the Islamic world and a professor of international politics at the Fletcher School of Law and Diplomacy of Tufts University, Vali was born in Tehran. Although he left Iran after the 1979 revolution to settle in the United States with his family, Vali's background enriched his perspective, allowing him to see the world from a non-Western point of view. He had spent a year living in Pakistan in 1989 while researching his PhD thesis about Islamic fundamentalism in Pakistan, and he knew the country intimately. Back then, American embassy staffers traveled around the country, went on trips to the idyllic Swat valley, and held glamorous cocktail parties where they mingled freely with Pakistanis. How things had changed.

Almost exactly thirty years ago, as the United States was emerging from the trauma of the Vietnam War and the Soviets were plotting their invasion of Afghanistan, the Iranian revolution that deposed the U.S.-backed shah was still in full swing. On November 4, 1979, Americans started watching television every evening for news about the hostages held at the U.S. embassy in Tehran. On November 20, in Saudi Arabia, gunmen stunned the world when they seized the Grand Mosque in Mecca, the holiest site in Islam. The following day in Iran and in Pakistan, conspiracy-driven news reports claimed America was behind the desecration of Mecca in a plot to take over the Gulf region. American diplomatic missions and schools in Pakistan were mobbed by angry anti-American crowds across the country. The U.S. embassy in Islamabad was torched and besieged for a whole day; three people were killed, and four hundred Americans were evacuated out of Pakistan. It had taken four hours for Pakistani forces to react to the pleas for help from the embassy and control the mob. Pakistani officials then complained that the American evacuation was an overreaction. Washington was preoccupied with Communism and fighting the Cold War and saw the violence in Pakistan as an aberration. Few connected the dots of the events from Iran to Saudi Arabia, Islamabad, and later to Beirut, dots that signaled the swell of militant, political Islam that would eventually lead to the attacks of September 11. Soon, life at the embassy returned to normal, and American diplomats resumed drinking cocktails with Pakistanis at fancy parties in Islamabad or Lahore.

In 2009 the American diplomatic mission in Pakistan still occupied the same thirty-two acres of rolling hills but was now shielded from the dangers of the outside world by several layers of security, a walled-off compound within a larger diplomatic enclave with checkpoints at every turn. Almost all the embassy staff lived within the compound. As in so many other countries where Americans were targets, life in a fortress deprived diplomats of real encounters with average Pakistanis. American diplomats saw Pakistan mostly through the prism of the liberal elite, the English speakers who seemed open to the West and were very much Western in lifestyle. But they were often also nationalists who held grudges against America. The lack of contact fed the mistrust that the general population felt toward the United States, so Vali was enthused by the decision that Hillary and her team had taken to leave the fortress and reach out more widely to the people.

Fred Ketchem was less happy. He had been to Pakistan once before, in 1992. He always found it helpful to have a mental image of the country where he was about to deploy his agents and protect the secretary, but Pakistan had only become more dangerous since his last visit. American diplomatic missions continued to be attacked; an American journalist, Daniel Pearl, had been kidnapped and beheaded in 2002, and others had been gunned down in the street. Since that first trip to Asia, Fred had started to adapt to the secretary's elastic concept of the Bubble, but his can-do attitude didn't stop him from pushing back as much as he could against what he saw as risky exposure. In a way, it was easier for him to feel in control of security in a country like Iraq or Afghanistan with thousands of American troops. In Pakistan, there was not enough trust and too many unknowns. But Hillary's team was determined that she would go beyond government buildings and embassy compounds and into everyday Pakistan.

In Washington, at every planning meeting, Fred would bring with him a list of all the new threats that had emerged. Every time someone put forward a proposal for a visit to a shrine or a mosque, the Diplomatic Security's first reaction was: "No." Huma understood the concerns, but she was exasperated.

"Maybe your answer should be 'maybe' until you've checked on the ground," she snapped.

The planning had been shrouded in secrecy, and our printed schedules were stamped all over with "CLOSE HOLD—CONFIDENTIAL." We were going to spend two nights in Islamabad, maybe three, then would end up in Marrakesh in Morocco, by the weekend, but there was a gap in the middle. Where were we going? On the plane ride out of the United States, the traveling press corps speculated endlessly. Next door to Afghanistan? Perhaps back to Iraq? Someone heard Addis Ababa. Or was that Abu Dhabi? The Palestinian president was apparently touring the Gulf. Maybe Clinton was about to announce major progress between the Israelis and the Palestinians.

Oblivious to the building anticipation, Jake couldn't think beyond Islamabad. He was exhausted from the preparations for the high-stakes trip and from finally moving his life in boxes from Minnesota into his new apartment in Washington, D.C., just a couple of weeks before our departure.

From my seat, I could see incessant activity behind the Line of Death. Thanks to communication equipment on SAM, officials were calling both "post"—the embassy in Islamabad—and the Building in Washington to tee up last-minute details. The printer was overheating, pieces of paper were going around, and Paul Narain, the solo line officer on the plane for this trip, was typing away furiously on his laptop. Vali, Paul, Jake, Holbrooke—they were all defining and refining policy on the fly. Literally. Sitting in Beirut or Islamabad, it was easy to forget that the foreign policy of the world's superpower was being devised not by superhumans but by real people, tired, fallible human beings working in imperfect conditions, faced with imperfect choices, who didn't have all the answers. They didn't even have a finished Book.

Jake was excited about the possibilities and nervous about the diplomatic dangers on this trip. His job was to focus on the substance: what the secretary had to say, what she needed to know, how her message was being received, how it had to be fine-tuned for the next appearance. Engrossed in his thoughts, his papers, his e-mails, he generally paid scant attention to his surroundings and followed people in front of him off the plane, into the motorcade, into buildings, and out of rooms. His awareness of his surroundings had never been as low as on this trip: he didn't notice Fred and his agents putting on bulletproof vests before getting off the plane, didn't feel the searing heat that greeted us on the tarmac of Chaklala military air base outside Islamabad on Wednesday morning, didn't lift his head from his BlackBerry in the staff van to see the security officers posted along the wide streets as Clinton's motorcade made its way into Islamabad.

Now that we had arrived and the veil of secrecy had been lifted, I called my mother in Beirut to tell her I was in Pakistan. She was not pleased.

"Why do you have to go to all these dangerous places? What if someone tries to kill her or bring down her plane? She's a target, and you'll be in the middle of it. I'm not sure this is such a good idea."

The thought had crossed my mind before. Back in Beirut when American embassy convoys drove through the streets, we didn't simply roll our eyes. We also stayed far behind: you didn't want to be too close in case someone tried to blow them up. But my mother even worried about me living in Washington, D.C. Years ago, she had heard it was the crime capital of the United States, and when I first moved there, she asked whether I would be safe. I'm not sure she realized the irony of her question. After living through the war in Lebanon, surely I could fend for myself in a country where tanks weren't part of the urban landscape. When I once told her I was going on a beach holiday to Mexico, she called me every morning until my departure to tell me I was crazy and that I should come on holiday to Lebanon where we had the best sun and sea and no violent drug cartels. No, we didn't have drug cartels, just wars.

But that was a danger we had grown to understand instinctively in Lebanon: we knew where the sniper bullets might be coming from, where to take shelter if bombs were coming toward us from the east or the west. More recently, we knew where to be safe if there was an Israeli air raid, and we knew to stay away from motorcades of Lebanese politicians who were also being targeted for assassination. In Washington, Pakistan, or Mexico, my mother worried I would lose my bearings and lack the adequate survival reflexes. My senses were certainly dulled by the hours on the plane, the heavy air force food, the jetlag, and the baking heat. I was starting to learn to trust Diplomatic Security and Fred. His task wasn't to protect us journalists but to protect the whole package in which the secretary traveled, and that included me. There had never been an assassination attempt on foreign soil against an American secretary of state or even the president as far as I could tell, so I was probably safer inside the Bubble than outside. There was still plenty of violence to greet us.

A few hours before we landed in Pakistan that Wednesday morning, a bomb had exploded in Peshawar, a two-hour drive from the capital. The bomb tore through a women's market, killing more than a hundred people. It was the kind of attack that often stupefied American diplomats—there were no demands, no clear agenda. The violence barely cast a shadow over the country, which seemed to simply pause for a second and move on. The logic of it all escaped Hillary's team: What good did it do to anyone? What goals did it advance? But the perpetrators had their own logic defined by spite and obstructionism.

On Pakistani television, split screens showed the aftermath of the bombing and Clinton's arrival side by side, as if the two were linked. In the minds of many Pakistanis, they were. They saw the violence as a result of American pressure on their country to tackle militants. Hundreds of soldiers had died in the fighting and scores of civilians killed in bomb attacks. Pakistanis felt they were fighting America's war and paying a heavy price for it. And Pakistan's sensationalist media fed that narrative.

In the Middle East, the devising of conspiracy theories is an art form, but rarely before had I seen this level of unsubstantiated reporting. Even by Middle East standards, the Pakistani media were shameless. The *Nation*, Pakistan's leading daily, published a front-page article claiming that America funded and supported the Pakistani Taliban in a bid to weaken Pakistan and bolster India. The article offered no proof, no supporting documents, no logic; it was seemingly just speculation by one author. But there it was, in black and white for millions of readers to see.

Clearly, it must have been "the Truth." The article was a fairly typical example of Pakistani sensationalist journalism—little care for the facts, no attribution to sources, and often focused on stoking anti-American sentiments. At its best, the Pakistani media were rambunctious and feisty; reporters asked the most unexpected questions. At Clinton's press conference with the foreign minister, one earnest journalist asked whether President Obama would return his Nobel Peace Prize if he didn't bring peace to Afghanistan. Hillary couldn't resist laughing.

Pakistani journalists were a key target of her public diplomacy. On all her trips, Clinton gave a couple of interviews to local journalists, and in Pakistan, she wanted to take over the airwaves and fill the newspapers. She started with two television interviews with Pakistani journalists based in Washington that were to be aired the day of her arrival. In Pakistan over the course of three days, she was going to hold four separate group interviews, with seven television presenters, eight radio journalists, and six newspaper editors. She was also planning a town hall with five women journalists.

The questions they all asked were really just a long recitation of their grievances.

The wording of the Kerry-Lugar-Berman bill was humiliating, they said, and there was a hidden agenda. Why wasn't the money completely unconditional? They claimed American diplomats were breaking the law, walking around with arms in Islamabad at three in the morning. They said there was a secret marine barracks being built inside the embassy. Why wasn't the United States helping Pakistan regain the territory of Kashmir? The Pakistani parliament had voted unanimously to condemn U.S. drone attacks against Pakistan, and yet the attacks only intensified. Obviously, the United States did not respect the Pakistani parliament.

Over and over, the journalists mentioned the Kerry-Lugar-Berman bill and used the words "respect" and "trust." Hillary smiled and patiently answered question after question. Every now and then, she whipped out her plain talk.

"Pakistan doesn't have to take this money," she said. The group of television journalists who had sat down with her for this interview in the U.S. ambassador's residence were startled. Not take the money? It hadn't even occurred to them.

"Let me be very clear: You do not have to take this money. You do not have to take any aid from us. Nobody is saying you must take this money so that we can help you rebuild your energy sector or put more kids in school or provide better maternal and child health. You don't have to take the money."

Undaunted, the journalist now argued that the $7.5 billion promised in the bill was but a pittance. Half defiant, half mocking, Talat Hussain from Aaj TV set out to prove the United States was not serious with its aid to Pakistan.

"Let me give you numbers. You talked about the civilian aid and the military aid [for Pakistan]. Your one base in Kyrgyzstan—you know how much Kyrgyzstan charges you? Seven hundred million U.S. dollars!" Wagging his finger, Hussain was referring to the Manas Air Base, opened in 2001 to support the transit of American military personnel in and out of Afghanistan.

Eyebrows arched, her head tilting to the right, Hillary smiled calmly.

"That is wrong."

"Seven hundred!"

"That's wrong. We negotiated the contract. I'm sorry, that is not right."

"You negotiated it down."

"No, no."

The question was turning into a ping-pong match. Sitting in the back of the room, Vali couldn't believe that the Pakistani journalist was trying to correct Hillary's facts.

"They are charging you seven hundred million U.S. dollars. Give us a figure on that," Hussain demanded, his hand raised, wielding a pen.

"Fifty million dollars."

"Just one air base! Do you know how many air bases the U.S. uses in Pakistan?"

"And do you know how many billions of dollars we've provided to Pakistan?" Hillary asked with the faintest of scoffs but still smiling.

Hussain now complained that the aid to Pakistan during Pervez Musharraf's seven-year rule had been all swallowed up by the military and American contracting agencies.

"Well, okay, but let me just stop you here," Hillary interjected, leaning forward in her dark-emerald pantsuit and holding out her arm. "The United States did not install Musharraf."

"You backed him. You supported him. George W. Bush lionized him."

"Well, George Bush is not my president right now."

"But he did it with the U.S."

"Musharraf and Bush are gone. I'm very happy about Bush being gone. You're apparently happy about Musharraf being gone."

"But Musharraf is lecturing around in your country about democracy. Okay, let's—" Hussain wanted the last word, but Hillary cut him off.

"Look, we can either argue about the past—which is always fun to do, but can't be changed—or we can decide we're going to shape a different future. Now, I vote that we shape a different future. And I cannot take responsibility for everything that was done in your country, just like you can't take responsibility for everything that's done in our country. But we can certainly try to chart a different course."

D riving from one interview to the next, to meetings with officials, we watched Islamabad roll past our windows, a colorless administrative city on a grid system that appeared under siege. There were military checkpoints every few blocks, barricades surrounded official buildings, even people's homes seemed to have unusually high walls topped with barbed wire.

When we finally made our way to the presidential palace for Clinton's final meeting of the day, the sun had long set over the Margalla Hills that rim the northwest of the capital. The tiered palace looked like a wedding cake and, like all government buildings in Pakistan, gave off the air of a country much more well-off and stable than it had been for a while. Clinton walked through the lobby with her retinue, past glass displays of gifts given to the country's rulers from Saudi Arabia, Qatar, and the United Arab Emirates. The golden doors of the elevator closed, and up they went to meet President Asif Ali Zardari and Prime Minister Yousuf Raza Gilani. We had been told to wait on the bus.

A Pakistani guard boarded and asked to check our IDs. Our State Department media handler pushed back. We were part of a "secure package." There was no reason to screen us. The guard didn't speak English, and the handler didn't speak Urdu. They stood there, facing off tensely. The rest of us were too tired to argue, but these were the moments when

American might and arrogance came face to face with the defiance of smaller powers. I could almost hear their silent thoughts.

We are here with the American secretary of state, she represents the world's top superpower, we give you billions of dollars, without us you would be nothing. Who do you think you are?

I am guarding the Pakistani president, Pakistan is a great country with an ancient civilization, we developed our own nukes, we've tricked you for years into giving us money, and we don't even really like you, who do you think YOU are?

The Pakistani guard eventually backed down, and we got off the bus. Our phones and recorders were taken away. In most countries traveling with the American secretary of state meant you were waved through security but not in Pakistan. It wasn't clear whether they didn't trust that her guards had done their job right or whether they just didn't trust us.

Clinton had insisted that her whole delegation, including the traveling press, be invited to the dinner that the president was throwing in her honor. Ministers, journalists, politicians, and members of parliament were also attending. Our invitations said eight thirty, and we waited in a one-hundred-foot-long rectangular room with wooden floors and crystal chandeliers in the company of some of the dinner guests. We were back on Hillary time—or perhaps it was Pakistan time.

"Sit down; tea will be served shortly," the servants kept telling us as we paced the room and tried to walk around the palace. Just outside the door, in the marble-floored foyer, the walls were lined with portraits of Pakistan's presidents starting with the founder of the country, Mohammad Ali Jinnah, who was holding a cigarette in one hand. An abstract sculpture by Pakistani artist Amin Gulgee, *The Message*, stood in the middle, engraved with the words "God taught man what he knew not."

Around ten o'clock, Hillary finally emerged, looking remarkably fresh in her white blazer, Huma by her side. We all walked into the dining room on the other side of the foyer. In between four pistachio-green walls, twenty-one round tables were set for dinner for two hundred people. The large main table stood in the middle, between the entrance and a lectern below a white gazebo on the opposite wall.

We sat down for a fifteen-course curry meal starting with a strange-tasting "creamy pasta sausage salad appetizer," according to our menu. Sandwiched between the president and the prime minister, Clinton looked around the table to where her aides sat between the foreign minister and the top military brass, from the head of intelligence, Ahmad Shuja Pasha, to the army chief, Ashfaq Kayani, and the head of the air force. They were wearing civilian clothes, an unusual break from tradition, and it was a feat just to have them all around the same table.

The civilians and the military in Pakistan rarely spoke to one another, and they had barely acknowledged one another's presence so far. Since Pervez Musharraf's military dictatorship ended in 2008, Washington had spent a lot of time managing the relationship between the two sides. The military and the civilians distrusted each other deeply, and each vied for the upper hand in a constant political struggle. Hillary kept the conversation light, talking about her day, about how much she loved Pakistani mangoes. Out of her earshot, two of the military men were discussing the current military operations in the North West Frontier targeting the Taliban. Clamping down on militants in Pakistan was essential to stem the flow of fighters and supplies for al-Qaeda and the Taliban in Afghanistan, and Washington had been pushing Pakistan to act more forcefully. But the military chiefs weren't discussing how much of a blow the operations were to the militants—rather, how training to maneuver helicopters over the region's glaciers in the winter was a skill transferrable to the country's border with India. Members of the American delegation listened, partly amused, partly annoyed.

Wearing glasses, his black hair slicked back, President Zardari got up for his speech, and, standing under the white wooden lattice gazebo, he spoke about the "healing touch" that the world and his country needed. Addressing Clinton, he added that together they could make a difference. Zardari, in his midfifties, had been thrust into politics after the assassination of his wife, Benazir Bhutto, in December 2007. He was known as "Mr. 10%" for allegedly skimming 10 percent off lucrative contracts while his wife was in power in the 1990s. Zardari spent several years in jail facing various accusations, including money laundering, but always denied the charges. After a decade in self-imposed exile because of corruption charges she herself faced, Bhutto had returned to Pakistan to run in elections as Musharraf's grip on power waned. When she was killed, her widower stepped in and became president after their party, the Pakistan Peoples Party, won the elections in February 2008. For years, Pakistan had slumbered in and out of military dictatorships that couldn't provide long-term stability because of the consistent exclusion of civilians from the system. When civilians took over, weak and disorganized, they blamed the army for all the country's problems and lived with constant fear of another military coup. In a country where the military and intelligence agencies had become kings, the Americans wanted Zardari to succeed if only because he was a civilian.

It was Clinton's turn to speak. Vali had gone over the speech with her earlier, emphasizing the key points she had to make as part of the general message of engagement and support she was bringing to Pakistan. But before the dinner, Zardari had taken out a picture of Clinton and Bhutto from 1995, when, as First Lady, Hillary had visited Pakistan with Chelsea. She had spent time with Bhutto and met her children and Zardari. The picture and the memory of a woman killed so violently had brought tears to Hillary's eyes. She tossed the script and spoke from her gut.

"The reason why we do what we do, serve in public life, is to allow for our children to reach their God-given potential. . . . Our message is simple. The U.S. is ready and willing to work with you and support you."

At the Gujranwala table, where I was seated, two ministers and three journalists smiled politely as they helped themselves to prawn biryani and harees, a hearty meat stew with wheat. Hillary was really wonderful, they told me, but they didn't buy a word she said. The minute the United States won or lost in Afghanistan, they said, Washington would only talk to India.

"If the U.S. wins in Afghanistan, Pakistan will be left out of the game; we can't have that," offered one as he explained why the Pakistani army was withholding help on Afghanistan. Pakistan was playing a long-term game: it was in the country's best interest to maintain a foothold in Afghanistan thanks to militant groups. I thought about how difficult it was for Americans to fully grasp the state of mind of people living in constant fear of their neighbor. Americans left the United States, invaded or liberated countries overseas, and then went home to their own country between two oceans, with a northern and southern neighbor that would never invade them.

When we finally returned to the embassy, well past midnight, our day had lasted thirty-two hours from the moment we had loaded into the vans outside the State Department in Washington that Tuesday morning. When Hillary was here in 1995, she had stayed at the Marriott Hotel in town. No American official delegations stayed outside the compound anymore, and the Marriott itself had been bombed in 2008 in an explosion that killed fifty-six people and wounded more than two hundred. The hotel was now protected by concrete barriers, barbed wire, and checkpoints. So Hillary was spending the night at the ambassador's residence. Before retiring to her quarters, she went over the day with Jake, Vali, Huma, and Richard. Jake was going through her statements of the day, studying how to adjust the message for the rest of the visit.

In a nearby brown-brick building, Paul, the line officer, was getting the secretary's daily briefing book ready. He had been flying solo to free a seat for someone in the large pack of journalists who wanted to accompany Clinton on this trip. His plane teammate would hop ahead on a commercial flight to each stop on our yet-to-be-determined itinerary. The daily briefing folder was a smaller version of the trip Book—a cordovan leather binder stamped in gold letters with "Secretary of State Hillary Rodham Clinton" that was delivered by Huma to the secretary every evening while on the road. The book contained Clinton's speeches for the following day; briefing checklists with talking points for her meetings, both on paper and on cards she could refer to during meetings; truncated briefing checklists, detailed instructions for how events or meetings would unfold. There were ten events on the next day's schedule in Lahore.

The traveling press headed over to the "pods," the spartan rooms for two housed in two-level prefabricated visitors quarters by the football field at the bottom of the hilly compound. On the plane, Caroline Adler had distributed earplugs in blue transparent plastic containers, apologizing for making us bunk "à deux."

SAM was sleeping across the border in Kyrgyzstan, at the Manas U.S. military base. The Ravens were better able to protect him there. In the morning, he would come back and pick us up for the one-hour flight north to the capital of Punjab.

A vibrant cultural city of eleven million people, Lahore looked depopulated on Thursday morning. In the front seat of the armored limousine carrying Clinton, Fred listened to his agents chatter in his left ear, watching for the security assets dotting the road, visible only to his expert eyes. We had been briefed by a DS agent before leaving Washington about what to do if our convoy got hit. It wasn't going to happen, they insisted, but they wanted us to be prepared just in case. The priority would be to get the secretary safe, but we shouldn't panic if we were separated from the main motorcade. Other cars and agents placed along the road would come to our rescue.

At every cross street, huge black curtains hung between buildings, blocking the view. The Pakistani population at large seemed to have been pushed back several blocks from the route of the motorcade. There was not a car in sight. Pakistani soldiers stood along the way, their backs to the road.

In 1995, Hillary had visited a village near Lahore and walked into people's homes. The closest she could get to real people now was an auditorium packed full of students at the Government College University of Lahore. She stood on stage behind a lectern and delivered her opening remarks with a gentle smile and a soft tone to several hundred Pakistani students.

"As someone with a deep respect for Islam, visiting Pakistan is a special honor. And I have several members of my staff, Muslim Americans, who accompanied me on this trip, and I know I can speak for them and say that we are all very pleased to be here," she said. She told them about her visit to the Badshahi mosque in the morning, a stunning reminder of the grandeur of the Mughal Empire and the fifth-largest mosque in the world.

"One cannot stand in the midst of the mosque without appreciating the contributions to human thought and cultural expression that emanate from Pakistan."

She worked hard to mollify her audience, show respect for their culture and their religion, and promised them that the United States stood by their side. Mostly, she was trying to impress on them that the battle against militants wasn't a war for America; it was a battle for Pakistani democracy.

When she was finished speaking, Clinton took questions from the audience and, as usual, picked at random.

"What can the Americans give Pakistan that we can now trust you and believe this time in your sincerity and that the Obama administration is not going to use us like the Americans did in the past when they wanted to destabilize the Russians in Afghanistan?"

The audience erupted in wild applause. Thinking back to my own disappointments in Beirut, I couldn't help but relate.

Hillary had learned the art of saying, "I've learned from my mistakes." It was how she transformed what had been a weakness during her days as First Lady into a strong point during her campaign for the presidency. It was a magic, disarming utterance, and she put it to work on a bigger scale. America, she told the Pakistanis, had made a mistake when it shifted its attention away from the region after the Soviets withdrew from Afghanistan. She then tried to explain why this time it really was different, that America was there for the long term.

The world had rarely heard an American official apologize for past mistakes. This approach didn't go down well with Republicans back in the United States; but around the globe, it went a long way to buy goodwill. And yet, Clinton could not hide that all the issues high on America's agenda—finding bin Laden, fighting the Taliban, al-Qaeda, making it possible for American soldiers to eventually leave Afghanistan—were short-term concerns. Vali knew that the only way the Pakistanis would be convinced this was really a long-term relationship was if it indeed became a long-term relationship. But if America could create a small opening, perhaps Pakistan would walk through it.

The questions continued. If Clinton thought the Pakistani journalists had been a feisty bunch, she found the students—those who had rarely or perhaps never had a chance to speak to a politician, let alone a high-ranking American official—even more passionate.

"I wanted to say that why American government always support Indians as compared with Pakistan, although Pakistan always standing with Americans in every battle?"

Rapturous clapping.

The U.S. Agency for International Development attracted the students' wrath as well.

"USAID did betray us, and this is a fact. Even back when you were just an intern in Ford Administration back in the seventies, and later on when you became First Lady, even in the eighties, they did that. My main question is: What is the difference that we will see between Obama administration and Bush administration toward Pakistan?"

It was relentless. Even I was starting to feel under attack.

"I can't believe we're putting her through this," Jake thought, standing at the very top of the auditorium, looking down at the rows of students.

For more than an hour, the students pounded Hillary, letting out their frustrations, fears, and disappointments. It was akin to national therapy for a country in a perpetual state of insecurity. After that first session, Hillary went to a small room nearby for a round-table interview with Pakistani newspaper editors and another intense round of ping-pong. There was no pause.

Half an hour later, we made our way to the motorcade. Vali, who had sat in on the interview, filled in Jake and Philippe, both of whom had stayed outside to catch up on e-mails. The world didn't stop turning during those trips. It was good to get away from Washington and immerse oneself in the issues of each country visited, but there were still urgent problems to solve around the globe and other trips to plan. Philippe and Jake were half listening, typing away on their BlackBerries, a skill every Washingtonian had mastered.

"Oh, by the way," Vali suddenly added as an afterthought. "She also said she doesn't believe that no one in Pakistan knows where bin Laden is."

Jake and Philippe almost dropped their BlackBerries on the floor. This was big. Jake called the White House and spoke to the deputy national security advisor Denis McDonough. This was going to make news, Jake said, in a good way—her statement would help move the dial with the Pakistanis.

"Good, own it, run with it," came the reply. Clinton's answer was consistent with the administration's overall take that Osama bin Laden was somewhere in Pakistan. There was no point skirting the issue anymore.

After lunch, we made our way to the Governor's House of Punjab. A huge white building left over from British colonial rule, with columned arcades, perfect green lawns, and palm trees, it was home to Salman Taseer. An outspoken liberal and self-made business tycoon, the governor's ties to the Bhutto family and the Peoples Party of Pakistan went back to the late 1970s. He had struggled under the dictatorship of General Zia-ul-Haq, spending six months in solitary confinement in the Lahore Fort, but it had strengthened his resolve to fight against the darkness of dictatorship rule. Now, he was fighting religious extremism.

Taseer's wife, Aamna, was a bit nervous about hosting the former First

Lady. She had attended Hillary's speech at a women's college in Lahore in 1995 but had only seen her from afar. She seemed immediately at ease when Hillary addressed her by her first name. An odd thought crossed Aamna's mind: "She's a real human being."

Hillary also displayed her usual sense of humor to the delight of the Pakistani couple.

"Mrs. Clinton, I should probably let you know that when I lived in London I used to throw rocks at the American embassy in Grosvenor Square," said Taseer, who loved cracking jokes.

"Don't worry, Mr. Governor," she replied deadpan, "so did I."[11]

Aamna had asked for a selection of finger food to be served, mostly Pakistani, but had added some smoked salmon sandwiches just in case. Though she had had an elaborate Pakistani lunch after the town hall, Hillary ate the samosas presented to her by stiff servants wearing red tunics and starched turbans. On her way out, she complimented the beaming cooks who had lined up to greet her.

"The food was delicious; thank you!" Hillary made their day. It shouldn't have mattered, because she represented unpopular America, but somehow it did because it was a human moment that transcended the acrimony of politics and years of distrust.

"If only there were more of these moments," Aamna thought. "Maybe things could be different between us."

"Your aides said it wasn't possible but I was really hoping we could take a photograph with my children," she ventured. She couldn't resist.

"Oh, I love family photographs," exclaimed Hillary, posing for several of them with Salman and Aamna, their two sons, and their daughter-in-law. The couple's daughter, Shehrbano, was in the United States attending college in Massachusetts. Hillary told Shahbaz, the eldest son, she liked that his name meant "eagle" in Urdu. Bill Clinton's Secret Service name was Eagle. Hillary's name was still Evergreen.

Then, all smiles, Hillary headed with aplomb into her eighth event of the day—a roundtable with businessmen who were eager to know how their country's largest trading partner could facilitate trade even further and what additional aid their country would get. The businessmen had hit on a pet peeve of Hillary's—tax evasion by the elite in developing countries—and she had come prepared. In fact, this peeve was the whole reason behind the roundtable. Clinton wanted to know when they were going to start paying their taxes to help fill the coffers of the state instead of asking for the United States to help solve their problems. She always wondered why charming, educated, entrepreneurial Pakistanis were unwilling to give up an iota of their power or their money for the good of their country.

Clinton recognized that the United States and other donor countries had fostered that dependent attitude, helping to bail out Pakistan repeatedly over the years for fear it would collapse. It was a codependent relationship. But it was time for Pakistanis to decide what kind of country they wanted to live in.

In 1965, Pakistan was hailed as a remarkable example of postindependence nation building, and experts predicted great economic success. Today, barely 3 million of the country's 174 million people paid income taxes because of a combination of tax exemptions and endemic tax evasion, especially by businessmen and landowners. Only oil-rich countries collected so little taxes because they had enough revenue. But with a $55 billion debt, Pakistan could not afford to forgo all that income, spending all its money on the military while its people suffered through power outages and its infrastructure fell apart.

While Hillary pressed hard, her team and the traveling press slumped on the rigid upholstered wooden chairs, almost comatose in the fading daylight of the large wood-paneled basement reception room. The second day of any trip was always the worst: my body clock was stuck in limbo, not quite in the United States anymore but not yet adjusted to the new location. I was nauseous from the jetlag, from the heat, and from the heavy curry lunch. I fell asleep for an hour before we departed Punjab.

We landed back in Islamabad in the early evening. Clinton was going to the army headquarters to meet the generals: the head of the Inter-Services Intelligence agency Ashfaq Kayani and the army chief Ahmad Pasha. The press was not invited, so we were driven to the embassy compound, where a barbecue dinner was under way around the swimming pool.

Clinton preferred to meet the generals in a more informal atmosphere than their offices, so Kayani welcomed her at his house. He too asked for a picture with Hillary with his wife and children. He saw her as someone of substance who spoke for Obama and the United States. She saw him as someone with whom she could have a real conversation.

The meeting was businesslike but friendly. There was always an inherent tension in those exchanges—after all, America and Pakistan were indirectly fighting each other in Afghanistan. But the mood was positive because of her two days of outreach. She didn't pull out her briefing note cards. She had been briefed ad nauseam, and she knew the subject matter enough that she could cite detailed aid budget figures and discuss exactly how many CIA officers had to be allowed into the country to ramp up the hunt for Osama bin Laden.

But in all of her conversations, Pakistani officials had given evasive answers, and the generals were no different from the civilians. When she told them that the United States and Pakistan had a common interest in lowering tension with India, she received only partial answers. When she warned that if Pakistan didn't hold a serious trial for the suspects of the 2008 Mumbai attack it would give terrorists a signal that they could continue to operate out of Pakistan, they brushed her concerns aside with niceties. Clinton didn't necessarily doubt their intentions but, as she left the meeting, she worried about their ability to overcome history.

Our third day in Pakistan rolled around; everybody except Clinton was starting to flag. She soldiered on in meetings with tribal leaders and a town hall interview with women journalists. Her team had hoped for a repeat of the electrifying town hall meeting in Seoul with an all-women audience, a real moment of connection between women. But the Pakistani women were feisty, asking her repeatedly if she understood why the United States was being criticized. There was barely a question about women or education, and there were no softballs. They chided Hillary for drone attacks and wanted to know why the United States didn't just make India give Kashmir to Pakistan. Kashmir was an obsession here, and nationalism had such a strong hold on people's psyches that it seemed to leave no room for other feelings.

Some of the traveling journalists had stayed behind at the embassy compound, writing longer articles reflecting on Clinton's three days in Pakistan. The work space that was set up for us at each stop so we could write our stories was a refreshing change from the usual cramped, windowless hotel rooms that were commandeered for our purposes. The large airy hall that housed our filing center overlooked the compound's pool, and an assortment of finger food magically appeared in the evenings. Internet access, phone lines, printers, and multiple electrical outlets were always set up. We also used our time that morning to read up on the news for our next stop. We had just been told that we were indeed going to Abu Dhabi, and then on to Jerusalem.

By the end of the visit, the tone of the Pakistani media coverage had changed, and the newspaper headlines were less acerbic. It wasn't a lovefest, but Hillary's charm offensive had made a dent in the wall of mistrust.

The United States and Pakistan were de facto at war, with Islamabad using the proxy of militant groups. Everybody knew it, even if no one acknowledged it publicly. But the Obama administration wanted to believe that change was possible. Hillary didn't want to overestimate what had been achieved; this was a relationship that was going to require constant tending, and change would come five degrees at a time. But as the plane took off from Chaklala, she felt good: being a punching bag had been tough, but it had been worth it.

In the middle section of the plane, Vali was still high on adrenaline, eager to go over the trip with his colleagues. But there was no one to talk to. The Pakistan Books were shut and cast aside. Different books came out. Vali had been briefing the secretary almost nonstop since leaving Washington. Suddenly he was not the one they needed.

"Okay, guys, we need to brief her on the Mahmoud Abbas meeting this evening," said Jake. The Palestinian president was waiting to meet Clinton in the United Arab Emirates. It was a five-hour flight to a whole new set of complicated interactions and more countries with too much of a past.

Vali had been in government for only ten months, and he already knew that he would never again say: "The U.S. government should do this or that." He had come to appreciate how enormously complicated it was to be the world's only real superpower, to have to think about and react to every issue under the sun, and to get things done. This was a sobering moment—one book shut, one book opened, one country down, another to go—barely any time to think or reflect.

"If only people on the ground could see that," Vali thought as he watched the others passing around notes and making calls to Washington and Abu Dhabi to prepare for their arrival.

"Every country believes that the United States sleeps and wakes up thinking about them and just them. They're really just a tiny speck on the map." Just a few pages in a big book.

6

HALLOWEEN IN
JERUSALEM

As we flew east and back in time, Lew Lukens, the logistics guru, pried the classified phone handset out of its base on the plane's wall below his window. Sitting up in his leather seat, in the middle section of the plane, he called Abu Dhabi. He was dreading having to inform forty people that they would be sleeping on the plane. The whole world seemed to be descending on the small emirate for its first-ever Formula One Grand Prix that weekend, and the embassy was having trouble finding hotel rooms.

But there was good news: the secretary and her staff could be accommodated at the opulent Emirates Palace. Ground staff from the embassy were preparing to set up a secure floor with offices where Paul and his colleague could work on the next day's briefing book, and Hillary's aides would hold their morning meetings. Signs appeared on the walls with the State Department seal, and red arrows pointed to various rooms. A couple of marines would be standing guard. Lew would bring over the communication kit that traveled everywhere with the secretary so that she could hold secure conference calls with Washington on the road. There weren't enough rooms for everyone, but eventually the embassy found a brand-new hotel on the other side of town. It wasn't officially open yet, and the traveling press corps would be its first customers. Setting up a filing center would be too much for staff to handle, so we would be confined to our rooms.

Lew was a blue-eyed, unflappable, longtime Foreign Service officer in his early forties; he had lived abroad as the son of a diplomat. Now, as the head of the department's Executive Secretariat, Lew was in charge of all travel, communications, budget, and security for the secretary and all the other officials of the department. Without him, the secretary would be sitting in her office on a never-ending videoconference call to the world.

The unpredictable and punishing traveling schedule meant Lew, a father of two, had missed countless family events. But he did love the challenge the trips presented. They were like a puzzle with moving pieces, from the secretary's wish to visit as many countries as possible on a given trip, to the crew's required fifteen hours of rest in between twenty-four-hour days, to motorcades with insufficient vehicles for forty people, and nonexistent hotel rooms in desert countries. This particular trip had been quite the Rubik's Cube.

When he left Washington, Lew was not aware of any stops between Pakistan and Morocco. Huma, his main point of contact for planning the trips, had known that Abu Dhabi and Jerusalem were on the itinerary but had not shared the information. The meetings with Abbas and Netanyahu were not fully confirmed, and much depended still on whether the Middle East envoy, George Mitchell, would be able to extract a concession or even the promise of one from either side. Even nine months into this job, Huma still had political campaign reflexes—she wanted the flexibility of switching gears or directions at the last minute. If she'd told Lew about stops in the Middle East, he would have reached out to local U.S. embassies to make preparations, and calls to hotels and the hiring of buses for the motorcade would have given away their arrival, when the meetings with Abbas and Netanyahu had not been scheduled yet. Expectations would have been built up unnecessarily, and if the schedules had not aligned, or if nothing tangible emerged from the talks, the headlines would be about Clinton's failure as she flew back to Washington. But the secrecy and the sudden news of our Middle East stops had only fueled anticipation about what Clinton was going to do in the region. Perhaps it was true that there was a deal in the works between the Palestinians and the Israelis? Otherwise, why would Clinton suddenly fly to the region? In the Sisyphean endeavor of American peacemaking in the Middle East, hopes seemed to spike dramatically every time the

United States announced an initiative or a senior official made a visit, and the crash was only more painful.

Mitchell had been working hard to get the Israelis to agree to freeze settlement activity so that Abbas would sit down for talks. This was now the Palestinians' precondition; they refused to come to the table while the Israelis were putting up "facts on the ground" on occupied territory. They brandished Hillary's own words about "no exception, no natural growth" to justify their position. The Israelis were now suggesting to Mitchell that they could refrain from starting any new construction for only ten months, but they insisted that any work already under way would continue and had announced thousands of new constructions in the preceding weeks. The building was also part of the "natural growth," a loophole that Israel always used to justify continued construction on settlements. Crucially, occupied East Jerusalem was excluded from the deal. The Palestinians and the Israelis both claimed the divided city as their capital but only Israel had the means to enforce construction on the contested territory. The imperfect offer of a partial freeze of construction was the best that Mitchell had been able to get so far. It wasn't that different from what Bibi had suggested earlier in the year in his talks in Washington, but this was a somewhat firmer offer. Now Abbas had to accept this as sufficient to start talks, and Bibi had to stick to his word. Clinton was coming to play three-dimensional chess. She also had to get the Arab world to both acknowledge the Israeli gesture— never an easy feat—and support Abbas in his decision to start talks, an even more arduous task.

We landed midevening in Abu Dhabi, only half a motorcade awaiting us on the tarmac. The late notice of our arrival meant the embassy had not been able to rustle up all the cars needed to drive the whole delegation into town. Clinton and her closest aides sped off first while the rest of the delegation waited in the VIP lounge.

The second motorcade took us to our hotel, with no filing center, intermittent Internet in our rooms, and a barely operating restaurant. Lew was always the last to leave the airport. He handed over his shiny metal case with all our passports to the embassy staffer who got them stamped into the country. They then drove our luggage into town. Clinton was already well into her meeting with President Abbas.

n a large conference room with gold paneling and glittering crystal sconces, the secretary of state and her delegation sat at a table covered with white linen and a small bouquet of white and yellow lilies. Facing them, Abbas looked deflated and acted defeated.

The Palestinians were once again tangled up in a mess, partly of their own making. The Israeli military operation against Gaza in December 2008 had targeted Hamas, the radical militant Islamic group that ruled over the strip of Palestinian territories by the sea. They were Abbas's political rivals so he had mostly stood by, not unhappy to see them get a pounding. But his credibility as a Palestinian leader had suffered. A report commissioned by the UN criticized Hamas militants for taking cover behind civilians, but it had been harsher on Israel, accusing it of using excessive force. To make up for his tarnished image, Abbas wanted a vote at the UN Human Rights Council to endorse the report. Some Palestinians also hoped it would lead to Israeli officials being tried before international courts of justice. But if Abbas pushed for the vote now, the Israelis would be furious, and any progress Mitchell had made so far would come to an abrupt end. Washington pressed Abbas to reconsider. Before doing so, the Palestinian leader sought the support of Arab countries and when they winked he asked for the vote to be postponed, just a few weeks before our visit to the UAE. He was then promptly excoriated by the Arabs for betraying the Palestinian cause. Worse, he was being lambasted by his own people. In Gaza, posters went up on the walls, with the words: "To the dumps of history, you traitor, Mahmoud Abbas." He told Clinton that even his grandson's schoolmates asked why his grandfather was a traitor to Palestine. Abbas was deeply hurt; he believed in the Palestinian cause and in peace, and he felt he deserved better.

Hillary was moved by his story. With her interlocutors, Hillary always reacted first as a person, as a mother. Children often came up. Her empathy was real, and it was a feeling that was sorely missing between Israelis and Palestinians. They had long ago lost the ability to understand each other's suffering, past and present. Perhaps they'd never had it. When the new State of Israel was declared in 1948, on parts of what was then British Mandate Palestine, the Holocaust was a distant occurrence for Arabs. The Jewish push for a homeland had become both more urgent and aggressive in the wake of the Holocaust and there was little room to consider the pain this was inflicting on others, not least the creation of a quarter of a million Palestinian refugees. To this day, Palestinians often wonder why they are being made to pay for Europe's horrors.

Under Israeli shelling in Beirut in 1982, and then again in 1992 and in 1996, I had no ability to empathize with the "other" side. There was no other side. I was being bombed. Even in my Christian school in our liberal, Westernized enclave, where Christian warlords had once been staunch allies of Israel, my history lessons barely mentioned the Holocaust. I knew vaguely that Jews had been killed in Europe during the war, but mostly the Holocaust was a vague, distant event that those around me said was being used by Jews to justify their land grab. Growing up in Beirut, I'd never met a Jewish person. Lebanon's once thriving Jewish community had left the country in waves, either choosing to move to Israel or being pushed out by violence. Those who remained did not advertise that they were Jewish. For people who have lived all their life in the Arab Middle East, Israelis and Jews are faceless; they are the "other," the unknown.

In my twenties, my worldview was suddenly turned upside down when I fell in love. He was European and we were together for a few years. Three of his grandparents had died in concentration camps in Europe. When I met his parents, I finally understood that the Holocaust wasn't some distant historical event. It was real. His family still carried the trauma of its memory and lived with the emptiness the concentration camps had forced into their lives. His father liked me very much, but he was terrified of traveling to Lebanon and he never visited Beirut. For him, we were the "other."

Hillary's ability to empathize allowed each side to glimpse its "other," helping to defuse tensions or bring someone around. She rarely admonished, hectored, or gave orders but laid out the arguments in favor of the course of action she supported. She appealed to Abbas to see the opportunity in the Israeli offer. Every time a house is finished, a new one will not start, she said. The Palestinian leader only saw the gaps—construction would continue, cinder blocks would be making their way into Israeli settlements in the West Bank, cranes would be lifting stone after stone into place. The imagery was terrible. He would be branded a traitor again. Clinton emphasized to Abbas that without the partial freeze in settlement construction, the situation on the ground and his position would only get worse. Every now and then, she lowered her voice, taking

Abbas into her confidence. This was an opportunity; it had to be seized, she said. What was most important was to start moving forward. She appealed to his sense of pragmatism: once the talks started, progress could be made on the issues at the heart of the conflict, starting with the future borders of a Palestinian state.

Abbas said that excluding East Jerusalem from the offer was impossible; he couldn't take that back to his people, or the region for that matter. Jerusalem was sacred. The Arabs would pounce on him. The secretary promised that the United States would work hard to ensure Israel would behave and not make any provocative announcements about new construction in Jerusalem.

Abbas couldn't do it. The Israelis had to offer more.

The American delegation was frustrated and slightly perplexed. Everyone always overestimated America's ability to move others. Abbas had just refused Clinton's request that he take the Israeli offer and start negotiations. If the United States had no power to make him do something, why did he think the Americans had the power to the force the Israelis to do anything? It was true that the Palestinians were the weaker party, and the Americans often leaned on them when they couldn't make the Israelis budge, but what the Palestinians really wanted was a deus ex machina, an improbable God that would suddenly sweep in and deliver a solution without them having to do all the hard work. Yet they resented American power and didn't want to be seen as American lackeys.

Hillary, Jake, Jeff, and George Mitchell were drained by the two-hour-long conversation with the Palestinian leader, the six-hour flight, and the busy day they'd already had in Islamabad. When they returned to their hotel rooms, on each of their beds sat a big chocolate race car, in honor of the upcoming Formula One car race. Everything in the Emirates was flashy, down to the ATM that dispensed gold bars in the hotel lobby.

On Saturday, Clinton would meet the country's crown prince Mohammed bin Zayed, or MBZ, as our schedule referred to him. He wanted to show off his country and the example it could set for the region. He invited the secretary to lunch at Nautilus, a modern restaurant in the Yas Viceroy hotel. An elongated structure with a rounded roof, overlooking a marina with gleaming, oversized yachts, the hotel straddled the lower part of the racetrack loop that was modeled after the Monaco track. A Ferrari theme park sat just around the corner, and the whole lot was set on the man-made Yas Island. The restaurant was all white, with plastic molded furniture straight out of the *The Jetsons*. Dressed in a white flowing robe and headdress, MBZ sat across from Clinton in an alcove discussing everything from Iran to Lebanon, Syria, clean energy, and Gulf security. She lobbied for support for Abbas. Sitting slightly in retreat, Jake, Jeff, and the others strained to listen in to their boss's conversation while waiters served them multiple courses of seafood.

Vroooooooom, vroooooooooom—"and the peace process is"—vroooooooom, vroooooooooom—"but the Palestinians should"—vroooooooooooooooom.

The qualifying races ahead of the Grand Prix the following day had gotten under way, and the roar of the race cars drowned half the conversation as the vehicles looped around the track and its twenty-one twists. This modern, prosperous corner of the Middle East was attuned to the future.

Now it was time to get on a plane and travel to a land weighed down by history and conflict, to a city where the Sabbath was coming to an end and work could resume.

SAM landed in Tel Aviv at around eight in the evening, on Halloween night, and within minutes Clinton's motorcade left the Mediterranean behind and drove inland, heading east toward Jerusalem. The convoy split in two as it entered the holy city: the press would be going ahead to the prime minister's office to start going through extensive security checks. Wailing sirens followed the secretary's limousine and a couple of staff vans as they headed to the David Citadel Hotel, where in a basement room Israeli cabinet ministers awaited the American delegation.

Ehud Barak, a longtime fixture of Israeli politics who had vanquished Bibi Netanyahu in the 1999 election with the help of American political strategists, was now a defense minister in Netanyahu's cabinet. The short, ebullient man who was sometimes called Israel's Napoleon was telling everyone that Bibi had mellowed and was willing to make a deal. Hillary and the others wanted to believe him. But American officials were also anticipating a quick change at the top—Israeli politics shifted treacherously. During Bibi's first term in power, frustrated Clinton administration officials saw him as a "kind of speed bump that would have to be negoti-ated along the way until a new Israeli prime minister came along who was more serious about peace."[12]

Eight months into Netanyahu's second premiership, it was the same all over again. Any hope that Obama may have had coming into office of creating quick momentum toward serious peace talks was fading fast. Rahm Emanuel's advice to be tough on Netanyahu wasn't delivering any results so far. Washington would have to wait out Bibi.

"Bibi thinks he can just stick to his position and outlast us, but we're here for four years," one smiling official had told me that spring, soon after Bibi came to power. The official had also served in the Clinton administration. "And then we'll likely be here for another four years."

All the United States needed to do was coax him a bit further down the road he had already traveled to keep things moving forward. As it was so often with American officials, the strategy was hope and the time-table was hope. The Palestinians were hearing the same from Israeli poli-ticians in the center and on the left: "Bibi will be gone soon. We'll give you a better deal. Stick it out."

But the Democrats who were now back in power and thought they could handle Bibi like they had in the 1990s had misread the extent to which Israel itself had changed. The world might have celebrated Obama's election, but in Israel there was little fondness for him. He had traveled to Cairo but had not visited Jerusalem, and Israelis felt slighted. Obama had been elected with 78 percent of the Jewish vote in America, but Israel had been slowly veering to the right and it brought to power people like Avig-dor Lieberman, Israel's ultraconservative, Russian-born foreign minister.

Clinton was meeting with Lieberman as well as with Barak. Lieber-man lived in a settlement himself, though no one brought it up. The atmosphere was already stiflingly tense when he started complaining about Turkey, where a moderate Islamist party was in power. Hillary was developing a strong working relationship with her Turkish counterpart, Ahmet Davutoğlu. But Lieberman warned that the Turks were Muslim extremists. Clinton reminded him that Israel's own actions inflamed sentiments in the region.

While Clinton was sitting in a basement with the Israeli ministers, the traveling press were making their way, one by one, into the stone building housing the prime minister's offices, through the metal detector. Apart from Pakistan and Afghanistan, there was no other country where the delegation of the American secretary of state had to go through such thorough screening. The United States may have been Israel's top ally and biggest donor, but there was no preferential treatment here, even for senior and midlevel American officials on state business.

The wailing sirens signaled the arrival of Clinton's motorcade sometime after ten o'clock. The press conference would take place before the talks so the Israeli media could put something on air that evening. Netanyahu walked onto the slightly elevated stage, followed by Clinton. With two microphone stands and no lectern, it was an odd setting. Bibi stood so close to the edge of the stage that he loomed over the row of chairs where the journalists were waiting to ask their questions. The blue of his tie matched the blue of the Israeli flag behind him.

"We think we should sit around that negotiating table right away," Bibi said. "What we should do on the path to peace is to get on it and get with it." Standing along one wall to the side, American officials cringed. They knew he didn't mean it. It was a statement that cost him nothing and made him look like a noble, genuine peacemaker. He knew full well the Palestinians were not in a position to come straightaway to the table. He would look good, and the Palestinians would look like obstructionist fools. American officials described it as a well-honed Israeli trick. The settlement freeze before negotiations was a new demand by the Palestinians, Bibi added, and in the past they had always negotiated without it. It was true, but Abbas was politically weak, and he was clinging to the new American gospel about the settlement freeze.

Clinton kept a straight face, nodding mechanically, as she often did. As a politician, she understood the context that Bibi himself was operating in. She had just met his foreign minister, and understood that Bibi's right-wing coalition kept him boxed in. If she gave him some credit in public for his concessions, no matter how small they were, perhaps she could coax him a bit further out. After all, he had uttered the magic words "Palestinian state" for the first time in his life merely a few months ago. Crucially, there was no American plan B if Bibi remained obstinate in his refusal to give more on settlements. So in front of the world media, Clinton tried to lock him into the promise he had made in private.

"What the prime minister has offered in specifics of a restraint on the policy of settlements, which he has just described—no new starts, for example—is unprecedented in the context of the prior two negotiations," she said.

It was factually correct, but making peace in the Middle East often boils down to moving a comma here or a semicolon there. If you praise the Israelis for restraint on settlement construction, you have to add, "but they should do more and the U.S. position remains that continued settlement building is illegitimate"; otherwise, the Palestinians will sulk. If you talk about the suffering of the Palestinians under Israeli occupation, you have to say, "and the Israelis too suffer under Palestinian rocket attacks," or else the Israelis will go bonkers. But if you praise the Israelis for offering to refrain from any new construction while building continues in projects already under way, then you've just backed down from your own demand to stop all settlement activity.

It was past 11:00 p.m. in Jerusalem, and 2:00 a.m. in Pakistan, where we'd been just the day before. Somewhere it was breakfast time; we had been on the move for twelve hours. Clinton knew Netanyahu would talk forever, and the meeting would be intense. She wanted to get on with it. She omitted the "but."

"I know you're someone who is indefatigable," Clinton said smiling broadly, "so even though we're starting our meeting so late, I have no doubt that it will be intense and cover a lot of ground. And I'm very much eager to begin those discussions."

The press conference ended, and Netanyahu and Clinton went into their meeting. In the cramped room, journalists debated furiously what had just happened. What did this mean? Had the United States given in? Had Bibi won? Was this significant? The newswire agencies started sending urgent one-line stories called snaps.

"Clinton calls Netanyahu restraint unprecedented."

The statement had taken Hillary's own team by surprise. Praising Bibi's restraint hadn't exactly been part of the script. In fact, there wasn't a written script. Clinton was answering a question, and she had no notes in front of her. She often spoke from her gut, but the Middle East was not willing to let go of the accepted script, just like Asia hadn't on her maiden trip. The tiniest deviation provoked panic, anger, fear, depression, and feelings of betrayal. Mitchell, the peace envoy, and Jeff, the Building's

Middle East man, knew immediately that there would be some damage control needed to calm the Arab world. But sitting inside the meeting, they were not aware of the extent of the fury that was unfurling across the region. They were too busy, with Clinton, holding their ground in front of Netanyahu.

Sitting on either side of a rectangular table laid with finger food, the Israelis and the Americans talked and talked and talked. Bibi didn't move much. Neither did Hillary.

"We need something to hold Abbas's hand and bring him to the table," Clinton told Netanyahu. He didn't budge.

"The risk of not doing anything is greater than the risk involved in compromising," she went on. He didn't budge.

S itting in the press conference room, the traveling reporters wrote their stories until it was time to go. Everyone climbed into the black vans parked outside and waited some more in the parking lot. The vans started to drive but stopped just outside the gates. More waiting. Just after midnight, an e-mail arrived from Philippe:

> Senator Mitchell and his party aren't travelling on with us, so when we leave the PM's office shortly we're going to head back to the David Citadel hotel so the Secretary can huddle with him for a bit to discuss tonight's series of meetings.

Clearly, this was a crisis. It was starting to dawn on everyone that the delegation might be sleeping in Jerusalem. Maybe even in these vans, because no one had booked any hotel rooms. Lew was still at the airport in Tel Aviv with the delegation's passports and luggage. On quick stops like this, he stayed with SAM, awaiting our return and catching up on e-mails from Washington where he still had to run a whole a department of 100 people that looked after 750 top officials in the Building.

Twenty-two minutes after midnight, another e-mail from Philippe.

> We're going to fly to Marrakesh, arriving 6am. On the upside, we'll have 1AM pancakes and hot chocolate on the plane.

On the tarmac in Tel Aviv, the air force flight attendants were digging deep into their pantry.

The black vans headed to the David Citadel Hotel. Reporters and staffers settled in the lobby and begged for some food. The restaurant was closed, but the hotel managed to put out three salads for twenty people and some rolls of bread. Everyone spread out in the deserted mezzanine café area while Clinton and Mitchell huddled.

By two in the morning, the haggard travelers were all slouched on our chairs half asleep, still hungry, some browsing the Internet to find a restaurant for dinner in Marrakesh the following day. Suddenly, a booming perky voice echoed through the marble lobby.

"Hi, guys!" Hillary was walking up the stairs to the mezzanine where everyone had been waiting. "What have you been up to? Are you ready for Morocco?" She had just spent almost five hours in back-to-back meetings with hardheaded politicians on one of the thorniest issues on the agenda of a U.S. administration, but she seemed alive with the adrenaline that kicks in during crisis mode.

We arrived in Marrakesh at six in the morning on Sunday and went straight to breakfast by the pool of our hotel—the Palmeraie Golf Palace hotel. We felt like we had been propelled from a nightmare into a mirage. Clinton was here for a Forum for the Future conference. Traveling with the secretary of state sometimes meant an incongruous combination of deprivation, luxury resort accommodations, and explosive conflicts. (Once, in Thailand for an Asian regional meeting, we'd had to traipse across a sandy beach in our heels and suits, carrying laptop bags, to reach our rooms in ninety-degree heat and 80 percent humidity.)

The morning headlines in the region's newspapers revealed not only the damage done by Clinton's words but also the extent of the divide between Israelis and Palestinians. The Israeli press was jubilant. The Obama administration had finally seen the light. *Haaretz* wrote that Clinton had "demanded" that Abbas return to talks "immediately," and it was clear that the United States had accepted Israel's position about restarting peace negotiations. A "deal" had also been struck to allow Israel to continue building its three thousand units. Israel had won the rope-pulling contest.

The Arab press was despondent. Why did Clinton think the restraint was a concession worthy of praise? They accused her of trying to bully Abbas into entering peace talks. They saw her statement as the result of a clear decision made in Washington to drop the demand of a settlement freeze. Obama had made the decision and sent Clinton to deliver a message. It was part of the plan, they concluded. There was no room in anyone's reading of Hillary's comment for a politician's gut and an American administration feeling its way on the path to peace.

Later that afternoon, puffing on a cigar in the hotel's café, the secretary-general of the Arab League, Amr Moussa, lamented the dismal state of affairs. He said he hoped Obama would not accept this "slap in the face" by Israel. "I'm really afraid that we're about to see a failure," Moussa said, in English, holding up his cigar for dramatic effect. "Failure is in the atmosphere all over."

He ended the conversation by saying he still had a "reservoir of hope." Despite the outrage, Arabs didn't want to alienate an American president who seemed to be on their side and who spoke with empathy about their suffering. Keeping the Arabs on board was key to any progress, and Clinton wanted to make sure they wouldn't stab Abbas in the back again.

On Monday, Philippe had news for the traveling press.

This is for Your Planning Purposes ONLY—NOT for Reporting
    Want you all to know that we are considering stopping in Egypt after we leave Marrakesh tomorrow. This is by no means certain, the planning is fluid because we are trying to see if President Mubarak's schedule allows for a visit (he's currently not in Cairo, he's in Sharm El Sheikh). To reiterate, this is for your planning purposes ONLY, and NOT reportable.

Mubarak, Egypt's modern-day pharaoh, had been in power since 1981. He was Washington's reliable ally and often hosted peace summits; his backing would be crucial. Never mind that he was a dictator; this was just how things were done in the region.

With the secretary, Jake and Jeff labored for hours over a statement that would reassure the Arabs that the United States wasn't giving up on them. That Sunday, sitting next to the Moroccan foreign minister, Clinton read carefully from a piece of paper. Every comma, every "but," every caveat was scripted. The American position had not changed, she insisted. The United States did not accept the legitimacy of continued settlement construction.

"I will offer positive reinforcement to the parties when I believe they are taking steps that support the objective of reaching a two-state solution. I will also push them as I have in public and private to do even more."

Meanwhile, Lew was dealing with his own crisis, organizing another last-minute stop in yet another country—hotel rooms and motorcades could be arranged, but he couldn't do much about lunch on the plane; it would be a meager affair.

By now the flight attendants were rationing the food. All the meals were usually prepared on the plane and the air force crew always packed all the supplies they needed before departure, keeping perishables on dry ice or in cool storage on the plane. They rarely resupplied during the trip because they didn't want to risk serving anything that might give passengers an upset stomach. For very long trips, the crew made arrangements in advance to resupply in countries along the way—even American bases at some of our refueling stops were not necessarily equipped to provide meals for forty people on short notice.

When they had left Washington, the crew expected two country stops and five legs total. They had prepared for the exact number of lunches, dinners, and breakfasts on our route. We were now on our way to the fifth country, and there were going to be eight legs total until Washington. And all the times had been turned upside down—the snack and dinner on the way out of Islamabad had become a dinner and a breakfast. The breakfast on the way out of Morocco had become a lunch on the way to Egypt. The rest of the meals required ingenuity and serious forward planning. We still had two seven-hour flights before we arrived home. On our six-hour flight to Cairo, we were reduced to eating a thin cheese sandwich and about five tablespoons each of canned tomato soup. There was no more wine to lull our discontent. Clinton came to the back of our plane and handed out chocolates she had gotten from her hotel in Marrakesh.

Sitting in the front cabin, Paul, the plane team line officer with no team, was delirious with fatigue. When he had heard Cairo was next, he had reconciled himself to never going home. Marrakesh was a nine-hour flight across the Atlantic to Washington. Instead we were now flying five hours east to Egypt. "It's a good thing the earth is round," thought Paul. "Everything is always on the way to somewhere else."

Clinton spent a few hours speaking to President Hosni Mubarak and Foreign Minister Aboul Gheit, explaining why she believed that Bibi's offer was worth seizing upon. But mostly she pressed them to give Abbas the backing that he so needed to make the difficult choices on the road to peace.

On our sixteen-hour journey home, and in the following weeks in Washington, I pondered the drama I had seen unfold and the disappointment it had caused. I only learned later of the details of Clinton's conversations, but I still wondered whether one of the reasons countries and people were so often disappointed in the United States was their unrealistic expectations of what the United States should and could do. Governments everywhere that instinctively and narrowly pursued their national interest somehow expected the United States to suspend the pursuit of its own interests to please them. The Arabs wanted the United States to ditch the Israelis; the Israelis wanted the United States to bomb Iran; the Iranian president Mahmoud Ahmadinejad wanted Obama to wait with him for the Shiite messiah; Pakistan wanted to be given Afghanistan on a gold platter; India wanted the United States to say it could have Kashmir; Japan wanted Washington to make Beijing go away. Countries seemed to forget that the United States had different layers of overlapping interests it needed to align.

I also saw a clear dissonance between the reality of American power, whether hard, smart, or soft, and what people believed was in America's power to achieve. The sometimes bizarrely optimistic attitudes of American officials themselves and their belief in their own ability to get things done only fed that perception. It had always been so, but now American influence was being challenged in unprecedented ways in a world spinning faster than ever before.

Weeks later, I was sitting in my dark cubicle in the Building reading an interview with Obama by Joe Klein in *Time* magazine when one sentence about the stalled Middle East peace talks at the very end of the page caught my eye. "If we had anticipated some of these political problems on both sides earlier, we might not have raised expectations as high."[13]

I was perplexed. Even as a seasoned journalist walking the corridors of power in Washington, or seeing Hillary get skewered for her comments on China, or watching Jeff in full damage-control mode in Morocco, I still struggled sometimes to accept that American officials were just human beings. But it was astounding to me that the president of the United States had not expected that a sixty-year-old conflict would be difficult to resolve and that he had not appreciated the impact his words would have on the hopes of people in the region.

Obama was not the only president who had walked into the Oval Office convinced that the authority of his position combined with the power of his own persona were enough to move heaven and earth. Sometimes they could, when all the stars aligned, but often presidents left the White House more or less frustrated.

"The people can never understand why the president does not use his supposedly great power to make 'em behave," President Harry Truman had once complained. "Well, all the President is, is a glorified public relations man who spends his time flattering, kissing and kicking people to get them to do what they are supposed to do anyway."[14]

Around the world, people thought the same. They expected an American president to push a button and make things happen, because he wanted it, because they wanted it.

Washington's dilemmas in the Middle East date back to a chain of decisions made by President Truman starting in 1947. After the ailing president Franklin Roosevelt died in April 1945, Truman, his vice president, moved into the White House. He was facing an election in November 1948 and his ratings were dismal. Meanwhile, the British Mandate over Palestine was due to expire in May 1948 and Britain was going to turn over the territory to the UN. In the 1917 Balfour Declaration, the British had already promised the Jews a national home in Palestine, as long as nothing prejudiced the civil and religious rights of existing non-Jewish communities on the land. So, with a deadline looming, a UN plan was drawn up to partition the land into an Arab State and a Jewish state, by which Palestine would be divided between Arabs and Jews.

Truman's secretary of state, George Marshall, was opposed to the plan. He argued that the move would endanger supplies of Arab oil and jeopardize the Marshall Plan for the recovery of post–World War II Europe. The State Department's head of Near Eastern Affairs, Loy Henderson, Jeffrey Feltman's early predecessor, also repeatedly argued against support for a new Jewish state. The State Department received hundreds of letters requesting that Henderson be sacked for being too pro-Arab. The White House and the State Department were at odds. During a meeting at the White House, David Niles, Truman's political advisor, turned to Henderson, who was once again arguing against support for partition, and said: "Look here Loy, the most important thing for the United States is for the president to be re-elected."[15]

Truman was annoyed by the pressure that Zionist groups were putting on him but he needed their votes. And he had been blunt about it when he explained his position about the partition plan to American ambassadors posted in Saudi Arabia, Lebanon, and Syria. "I'm sorry, gentlemen, but I have to answer to hundreds of thousands who are anxious for the success of Zionism: I do not have hundreds of thousands of Arabs among my constituents."[16]

After much debate, the White House endorsed the UN partition plan during a UN Security Council meeting in November 1947. Jews everywhere were elated, Arabs warned partition was war. There was still another six months before the plan would be implemented and the State Department continued to look into other options, including the possibility of a temporary UN trusteeship of Palestine. Despite the domestic politics, Truman did not say whether, come the time, he would recognize the new Jewish state resulting from the partition plan. But on May 14, 1948, the day that the Jewish state was to be declared, there was still no alternative to partition or to recognition by the United States. So Truman signed a typed-up statement recognizing the new state. He crossed out the words "Jewish state" and instead wrote "State of Israel."

Ever since, America's relationship with Israel has been bumpy, evolving from mere sympathy to full support with billions in military aid, often tinged with annoyance or guilt. The two countries have clashed many times, particularly about the Israeli construction of settlements on occupied land. Some of the dynamics between the United States, Israel, and the Arabs that were established in the 1940s persist today, exacerbated by years of habit. As with family dynamics, the players struggle to find new ways to interact with one another.

In the Arab world, the impact of Jewish voters in the United States and the power of the pro-Israel lobby are often described in a sweeping statement as a conspiracy. Arabs raise their hands up in the air and accuse America of being unfair while despairing at their own powerlessness. But just like in 1948, raw politics are at work in a system susceptible to strong single-issue agendas, such as Israel, but also health care and guns. While liberal American Jews often dilute their energy to lobby for a wide range of issues from the environment to education, many right-wing Jews in the United States focus single-mindedly on shielding Israel from any criticism whatsoever, and they can lose track of the bigger picture—what does it mean not only for America's long-term national security interest but also for Israel's?

As I delved deeper into the fiasco of the Obama administration's efforts at peacemaking in the Middle East in 2009, I found there was more to it still than just American politics, an overconfident president, and complex dynamics between Arabs, Israelis, and America. Human interactions between players in Washington added a whole new layer of complication.

In May, when Hillary had stood in her blue pantsuit next to the Egyptian foreign minister at the State Department, she was unconvinced by her own tough words about the settlements. She knew settlements were a problem, but she didn't believe that making this the focus of the strategy for peace was wise. There was no plan B if Netanyahu said no. Inside the White House there was a belief that making Israel stop settlement construction was the quickest way to bring everybody to the negotiating table and then get to the finish line fast—after all, the rough outlines of a peace deal had long been known to all. This was why Obama made clear to Bibi, during their first meeting in May 2009, that a settlement freeze was imperative. Even the call for "no natural growth" wasn't new. Mitchell himself, in his report in 2000, had specifically mentioned it as an issue. While White House advisors like Rahm Emanuel were gung ho about pushing Bibi, the public tone was still subtle and the exact way forward had yet to be decided on. But Hillary picked up on the combative mood inside the White House and combined it with her own forceful speaking to overdeliver for her boss in public with a maximalist position.

She was focused on showing loyalty to the man whose advisors still doubted she was on their team. Her words tied Obama's hands. The president didn't want to undercut his own secretary of state, a former First Lady whose popularity matched his own and who was relentlessly campaigning for America on his behalf. After winning the election, winning Hillary over onto his team was Obama's second most satisfying victory and he couldn't undo that.

Both Obama and Clinton were also keen to project a united image to the world and avoid a repeat of the public sparring that had so marred the Bush administration. Powell was always watching his back while Condoleezza Rice and the defense secretary Donald Rumsfeld contradicted each other in public. The infighting further tarnished America's reputation and credibility.

So there were no retractions, no immediate public readjustment of the position that Hillary had stated so forcefully. Obama only reinforced her words when he next spoke about settlements, because deep down he believed it was time for Washington to show tough love toward Israel. The new standard stayed out there, taking on a life of its own, and crucially it provided a convenient cover for the two key protagonists in the drama. Abbas was the most moderate Palestinian leader Israel had ever had to deal with but he always worried he would be branded a traitor to the cause and didn't want his legacy to include the sin of signing away any bit of Palestinian land, even for peace. Bibi was risk averse as well, unable to accept that a Palestinian state could be created under his watch.

With an Israeli and a Palestinian leader who didn't want to make peace anyway, it's hard to tell whether a different approach from Washington would have produced a different outcome in the thankless, decades-long task of Mideast peacemaking, but the Obama administration's Middle East peace efforts would not recover from this false start. For months the administration tried to adjust the trajectory it was on, but even Hillary's statement in Jerusalem about Bibi's unprecedented offer wasn't enough to unblock the situation. When Abbas and Bibi finally agreed to sit down in the same room at the end of 2010, their positions were so far apart that the negotiations faltered within days.

Throughout 2009, Clinton and Obama were also learning to work together. All year, she had labored to gain the trust of the West Wing. Clinton wanted to erase the legacy of the bitter campaign by showing deference to the president and avoiding all impressions that she had her own agenda or was pushing her own policies onto the table. She kept her head down in Washington, developing her vision for her foreign policy as secretary of state, learning the details of the issues and the workings of the Building. In meetings at the White House, she was eager to sound supportive of the president, acting like a participant and not a leader.

Clinton's counterparts around the world were also impressed by the loyalty she showed her former rival. She had more experience and she was older than Obama, but there was never a hint of bitterness or any attempt to sound more important than the president. The seamless political reconciliation was unfathomable in many countries.

For a while, the subject of her failed bid for the presidency would still come up in town halls in world capitals. Hillary congratulated a woman who had just won the presidency of a leading NGO for women's rights in Mumbai and laughed heartily, telling her, "At least you won!"

It was hard to discern how much of the laughter was real and what residual bitterness still lingered. But Hillary also believed in what was meant to be: her presidency in 2009 was not. In public, on the world stage, Hillary was shining, reveling in the attention, as she worked to restore not only America's image but also her own, with careful stagecraft by her aides like Philippe. They laid the ground for her slow emergence from the shadows at home, and by the time she had gone to Pakistan in October, Hillary had found her footing and her voice.

Obama, meanwhile, was discovering that the world did not respond to his soaring speeches with immediate cooperation, that if other countries had stood against America over the last few years, it wasn't just because George W. Bush had been president but also because America was America. Clinton was not a fan of Obama's lofty addresses, and he in turn often didn't like her bluntness, but with Obama focused on the economy and the longer-term goal of reelection, Clinton's more pragmatic, deal-making approach to foreign policy came to the fore. Clinton was focused on diplomacy and development but never forgot that America's power was also military. She had allied herself with Secretary of Defense Robert Gates, and together they argued for a large surge of troops in Afghanistan. She pushed for tougher sanctions on Iran. She had spent the first year being a good soldier and a good listener, learning her brief and gaining the trust of the president and his aides. She had been mostly a participant. She would never become part of Obama's very tight inner circle; there was no chumminess. But now she was ready to lead and speak more forcefully.

By the end of the year, Obama and Clinton were easing into their alliance, and they bonded together against the chaotic rise of the world's emerging powers at a meeting in Copenhagen in December 2009. More than one hundred world leaders had come together to negotiate a new agreement on climate change at the Bella conference center, usually the stage for Copenhagen's Fashion Week every season. The summit was the most disorganized gathering Hillary had attended since her eighth-grade student council.[17] Chinese president Wen Jiabao kept deferring a meeting with Obama, claiming he wasn't ready, while he was in fact secretly conferring with the leaders of Brazil, India, and South Africa. Behind the scenes, Beijing was trying to block all efforts to impose standards for measuring, reporting, and verifying progress on carbon reduction. The emerging powers didn't understand why they were being asked to curb their carbon emissions at the risk of slowing their economic growth when climate change was the fault of rich nations that had spent the last few decades polluting the air and the world. (For years, the United States had flouted international agreements on climate change to protect its own economy.)

Obama and Clinton decided to crash the secret meeting. They pushed aside a Chinese protocol officer guarding the door of the Chinese delegation room and started shaking hands, smiling like candidates on a campaign trail, while everyone ignored the naked dummies left over from a fashion exhibit that were scattered around the room. With Obama doing most of the talking and Clinton sliding him pieces of paper, they negotiated with the developing world. Clinton had laid the groundwork two days earlier, and Obama closed the deal. They were developing a natural pas de deux, but they still mostly stayed out of each other's spotlight.

PART II

"You have come to visit our country, sir, at a season of great commercial depression," said the major.

"At an alarming crisis," said the colonel.

"At a period of unprecedented stagnation," said Mr Jefferson Brick.

"I am sorry to hear that," returned Martin. "It's not likely to last, I hope?"

Martin knew nothing about America, or he would have known perfectly well that if its individual citizens, to a man, are to be believed, it always IS depressed, and always IS stagnated, and always IS at an alarming crisis, and never was otherwise; though as a body they are ready to make oath upon the Evangelists at any hour of the day or night, that it is the most thriving and prosperous of all countries on the habitable globe.

—Charles Dickens, *The Life and Adventures of Martin Chuzzlewit*, 1844

7

CAMELS ARE UGLY

I t was Valentine's Day again, exactly a year after Clinton's maiden voyage to Asia, and we were going on the road once more. Snowmageddon had struck the U.S. East Coast, complicating everybody's preparations for the trip. The advance team from the Line and from Diplomatic Security had to drive six hours south to find an airport that was operating despite the snow. Embassies in Washington were shut, and the State Department employees who looked after visas for outgoing delegations—including the media—were struggling to get stamps into our passports. To make matters worse, there were no cookies on the plane.

But at the end of the journey, a king awaited us.

We left Washington wrapped in our coats, sweaters, and earmuffs and proceeded to take off a layer at each stop of our journey. SAM had to refuel at the Irish airport of Shannon, the westernmost part of Europe and the first bit of dry land after crossing the Atlantic. Airport officials regaled us with stories about their other VIP visitors: Ahmet Davutoğlu, the Turkish foreign minister, was a frequent visitor. We all ordered a drink to help us sleep on the next seven-hour flight. After a quick stop in Qatar, we stepped into the heat at the royal terminal of the King Khalid International Airport in Riyadh.

Hillary thought of her Bubble as a caravan going from place to place, which made her think of an old proverb: sometimes the dogs bark, but the caravan moves on. She called it a movable adventure. The caravan and the barking dogs with its imagery of a long majestic convoy of vehicles and camels snaking through the desert means one shouldn't pay attention to petty criticism. Hillary had long ago developed a thick skin. She moved on quickly and didn't take anything too personally, though her staff remained overprotective of her, even when she was literally in a caravan. On this occasion, she felt like was she was on a rock band tour.

The Saudi king had sent his personal bus to pick up the secretary and drive her to his private desert retreat in Rawdat Khuraim. It stood outside the VIP terminal at the head of the motorcade of heavy beige and black SUVs. Clinton's limousine was there too, just in case, but the foreign minister Saud al-Faisal escorted her onto the bus, Fred stepping in right behind her. Tea and plates of nuts and dates streamed out of the small kitchen at the back of the bus, behind the two thronelike chairs where the elderly Saudi official and Clinton sat facing each other. It was highly unusual for Diplomatic Security to agree for Clinton to travel in any vehicle other than an armored American embassy limousine. Huma's eyebrows had arched to the roof when she was told by the advance line officer in Riyadh that the king was sending a bus to pick up her boss. She asked for multiple pictures of the inside of the vehicle and checked with Hillary. Oh, come on, Hillary had said, Saud al-Faisal has asked for this. I'm going to do it. DS finally acquiesced. Both Clinton and the Saudis wanted this visit to be perfect. There was no room for more upsets: Obama's last meeting with King Abdullah had not gone well.

Much has been written about the chummy ties between the royal family and the Bush administration, but the king had greeted Obama's election with surprising relief.

"Thank God for bringing Obama to the presidency," the king had told visiting American officials in the following months.[18] He said it had created great hope in the Muslim world. America and the world needed such a president. He had only one request—that Obama restore America's credibility around the globe. The two men had first met in London in April; Obama had then stopped in Riyadh in early June 2009 on his way to Cairo for his speech to the Muslim world.

The Riyadh meeting with the king had been a last-minute addition to Obama's itinerary, hastily arranged and badly prepared. Obama was already frustrated with Bibi's lack of flexibility on the question of settlements. He and Clinton had just issued their forceful calls for a stop to Israeli settlement construction, and Bibi's recalcitrance was instantly obvious. Obama was planning to keep pushing the Israeli leader, but he wanted to create some momentum and was looking for an opening elsewhere. Clinton and Mitchell, the Middle East envoy, were meeting Obama in Cairo; he was surrounded in Riyadh by a team of close advisors, including Rahm Emanuel, his gung ho, abrasive chief of staff.

If the Israelis were not responding to pressure fast enough, perhaps the Arabs could be convinced to make peace offerings to Israel that the United States could then use to make Bibi budge. Such gestures were called CBMs, confidence-building measures, and whenever the parties to peace were too far apart, Washington used these as a fallback strategy to keep the process moving forward. The Israelis desperately wanted the gestures, which would make them feel less despised, or perhaps even grudgingly accepted, by their hostile neighbors. It sounded a lot less positive when Arabs described it: normalizing ties with the enemy. Israel had full diplomatic relations with only two Arab countries, the two countries with whom it had signed peace treaties: Egypt and Jordan. A handful of Arab countries had sporadic trade relations with Israel but from most of the Arab world you couldn't even place a phone call to Israel: the phone would just give you a disconnect signal.

Over dinner at the king's farm, Obama didn't linger on the niceties and got down to business fairly quickly. He presented the eighty-six-year-old monarch with a long list of requests. He wanted the Saudi king to allow Israel's national carrier El Al to overfly the country and asked that Saudi Arabia start receiving Israeli trade delegations. It sounded so simple, but it was like asking an American president to shake hands with Iran's Mahmoud Ahmadinejad to help build confidence before the Iranians had promised to do anything in return. On the campaign trail as a candidate, Obama had said he would be ready to meet with America's foes Iran, North Korea, and Cuba. As president, despite promises to reach out, he had been exceedingly cautious in public. Now he was asking the Saudis to publicly open their arms to Israel and embrace their enemy.

The king paused. "Whoever advised you to ask me this wants to destroy the Saudi-American relationship," he said. He sounded deeply disappointed. Obama had not expected to leave empty-handed.

By definition, a monarchy is traditional, a reminder of days past. In Saudi Arabia, the king is an absolute monarch and Custodian of the Two Holy Mosques, a combination of tradition, conservative mores, and orthodox religion that produces a highly risk averse and opaque foreign policy. Despite bitter rivalries among Arab countries and rulers vying for the position of regional leader, the Saudi king was still regarded by many as a reference, the ultimate protector of Arab and Sunni Muslim interests. He could not be seen to be appeasing the Israelis. But there was also a long history of American presidents asking favors and making promises in their conversation with Saudi royals—and King Abdullah remembered well being asked for CBMs once before by an American president.

In June 2003, at a peace summit in the Egyptian Red Sea resort of Sharm el-Sheikh, American officials had pleaded with Arab foreign ministers to offer similar CBMs and build normal ties with Israel in a communiqué. Conversations went deep into the night. The Israelis wanted it as an incentive; the Arabs saw it as the big final reward for peace. The Saudis just did not do bold gestures. Colin Powell threatened that President Bush would not show up in the morning. The Saudis retorted that their leader wouldn't show up, either. Finally, the Americans relented. In the morning, President George W. Bush told the Arab leaders gathered, addressing mostly Abdullah who was still crown prince, "If I did not think we could do this, I would not be here."[19]

In the end, Bush's peace efforts amounted to naught and the Saudis shrugged—they had been right to be cautious. Who knows whether things would have been different if the Saudis had really reached out to the Israelis? Someone had to make the first step, and the Arabs were rarely if ever willing to do it. Perhaps King Abdullah remembered the disappointment that his own father had felt after his meeting with yet another American president sixty-four years earlier—an encounter that had marked the formal beginning of diplomatic ties between the two countries.

On February 14, 1945, World War II was drawing to an end, the Axis alliance was collapsing, and after meeting with Winston Churchill and Joseph Stalin in Yalta President Franklin D. Roosevelt sailed on the USS *Quincy* from Malta to the Great Bitter Lake of the Suez Canal to meet King Abdul Aziz ibn Saud. Abdul Aziz was the first ruler of Saudi Arabia, which had just discovered oil although no one knew yet the extent of the riches this would bring the desert peninsula. FDR wanted Abdul Aziz's help with Zionism. He explained that the Jews who had suffered indescribable horrors at the hands of the Nazis had a sentimental desire to settle in Palestine. The king suggested that the Allies give the Jews and their descendants "the choicest lands and homes of the Germans who had oppressed them."[20] The king, like so many Arabs, did not understand why they had to pay for the crimes committed by Germany.

FDR complained that the king was not helping, and the king lost patience. There was no resolution, but FDR promised in person and later in a letter that the "U.S. Government would make no change in its basic policy in Palestine without full and prior consultation with both Jews and Arabs."[21]

Eight weeks later, FDR died and Harry Truman became president. Abdul Aziz felt the promise he had received aboard the USS *Quincy* was made by America, not just by the man who was its president. After all, as the absolute ruler of Saudi Arabia, Abdul Aziz's word was law. He was furious to discover that Truman did not feel bound by FDR's letter and did not consult properly with the Arabs before walking down the road toward recognition of Israel. Nevertheless, the U.S.-Saudi relationship continued because the 1945 meeting was also the start of a key agreement between the two countries that has continued, almost uninterrupted, to this day: oil in return for security and arms.

I was stuck in the very back row of an armored car. The hum of the engine as the car sped along on a straight road lulled me to sleep. On the bus, chatting with Saud al-Faisal, Clinton looked out the window as the motorcade whizzed past camel markets and horse farms. An hour into our drive, the vast expanse of light-brown gravel that is the Saudi desert became dotted with more and more brown bushes. We were approaching the oasis of Rawdat Khuraim, the king's desert retreat. Shoots of green appeared, then lone acacia trees, and then a cluster of palm trees and what looked like a small circus: a six-top black tent surrounded by elevated semitrailers and other smaller tents.

The tents were air-conditioned and decorated with tribal rugs; inside one, we sampled dates and cooled off while Hillary freshened up in one of the trailers with gold-plated Grohe faucets. Then, her handbag in her left hand and Nina Behrens, her interpreter, hurrying along one step behind her, she entered the main tent, which was in fact more of a building with a tented top. Clinton walked down the eighty-two-foot-long carpet, past a wall of thirty-two small television sets around one central massive screen, toward the king. Tilting her head to the right, looking slightly demure, she smiled affectionately at the old man with a jet-black goatee, wearing a traditional black flowing robe, known as a *thobe*, and a white and red checkered headdress.

"It's an honor, Your Majesty," said Clinton.

The king held on to Clinton's hand as he inquired about the health of her husband, who had had heart stent surgery in New York the week before. Everybody sat down for the pleasantries that precede any serious meetings. These were unusually long and also, unusually, the journalists were allowed to stay for the duration. The king was showing Clinton extraordinary hospitality by extending his welcome to her entire delegation. Such generosity also meant that serious subjects, teasers for what was to come in the closed meetings, were not even broached. Sitting on an overstuffed, faded turquoise couch, Clinton was in her element, charming the king as she sipped strong arabica coffee. She retold a joke that the Saudi foreign minister had just shared with her on the bus and then started talking about camels.

"I want you to know, Your Majesty, that His Highness thinks camels are ugly," Clinton said with a grin, pointing to Prince Saud who sat next to her.

"I think His Highness was not being fair to camels," the king replied. He mentioned that he had fallen off a camel, and Clinton looked at him with alarm until he clarified that it had happened decades ago.

Clinton had much she wanted to ask the king but, as she often did with her counterparts, she took her time making a connection, before making any requests. She believed that Americans did not always fully appreciate how their get-down-to-business approach to meetings was experienced by others, especially in countries where every conversation started with the same litany of inquiries about the health of family members, from parents to distant relatives. Hillary believed that taking the time to know her counterparts was not only a show of respect but also a smarter way to build relationships. In the twenty-first century America could no longer walk into a room and make demands; it had to build connections first. After twenty minutes, the camel diplomacy petered out, and Clinton and the king rose from their chairs.

"Your Majesty, let me introduce you to my staff," said Clinton. One by one, she introduced Jeff, Jake, and Huma, whose mother had helped found a women's college in Jeddah and still lived there. In the back of the room, the king's aides signaled to everyone to get up and stand in line. When Clinton was done presenting the last person on her team, she was suddenly faced with the traveling press standing sheepishly in line. Clinton thanked the king for extending his hospitality to the media and began to introduce each one of us by our full name and the media outlet we worked for. In her dark navy suit and pearl necklace and perfectly blow-dried hair, the secretary looked amused by the woman reporter who had donned a headscarf to meet the king. Then came the handful of embassy staffers whom she had never met before, so Clinton's much-vaunted memory was of no help, but she offered a general introduction about the great work the staff did at the embassy in Riyadh.

It was time for lunch. Slowly, the king walked out of the reception hall, with Clinton at his side and a slight spring in his step, perhaps thanks to the black sports sneakers that peeked out from below his dark *thobe*. The old monarch, a large, imposing man, suffered from back problems. Across the foyer, a large banquet hall was set up for lunch. Along the side wall, a buffet table was laden with mountains of food—pheasant, lobster, smoked salmon rolls, and three kinds of lamb dishes. On the U-shaped table, more traditional Bedouin dishes awaited us in gold-plated dish warmers. By each of our plates, we found scented Bulgari hand fresheners. The king sat down, Clinton to his right at the head of the table. Suddenly, in the empty space of the U, a huge television screen emerged from a cabinet on a hydraulic lift, hiding Clinton and the king from the view of those sitting farther down the table. Soccer-match commentary started blaring in the room, drowning out all our voices. It was like sitting down for a dinner with your family on football night. Clinton tried each of the lamb dishes while the king spoke to her through his interpreter, the Saudi ambassador to Washington Adel al-Jubeir. More food and desserts emerged from the kitchen. On our way out, servants stood by with bottles of French cologne to spray on our hands.

The king, Clinton, and their close aides retreated to a small side room to talk business. In the large sitting area, the journalists and members of the delegation who were not part of the talks drank cup after cup of tea, courtesy of men with guns wearing white or dark flowing robes.

Inside, the talks were going exceedingly well and stretched beyond the allotted hour and a half. Hillary usually allowed conversations to run their course, and she was certainly not going to wrap up a meeting with a king. The stalled peace efforts, support for the Palestinian president Abbas, sanctions against Iran, the stability of Iraq—there was a lot on the agenda. At some point, the king and his entourage started to fidget.

"Do you mind if I smoke," he asked.

"Your Majesty," Clinton said, "please do as you see fit." But she couldn't help pointing out that smoking was not good for one's health. Out came a cigarette lighter that resembled a blowtorch.

The United States wanted to encourage Saudi Arabia, a Sunni country, to establish a better rapport with the Iraqi prime minister Nouri al-Maliki, a Shiite in a country that was roughly half Sunni. The U.S. troop withdrawal was looming on the horizon, and Iran, a Shiite theocracy, was looking to fill the void. The Sunni-Shiite rivalry dated back centuries and sectarian violence in Iraq had claimed thousands of lives since the American invasion. The whole region was plagued by that tension. Sunni Arabs were eternally in a competition, not only among themselves but also with Iran for regional dominance. They often manipulated the United States into bolstering their position with more arms and support, knowing well that America was scarred by its own history with Iran and would do anything to curb the power of the mullahs in Tehran. The United States wanted the Saudis to reach out to Maliki as a way of fending off Tehran.

The translation was a laborious process that doubled the time required for every conversation. Nina Behrens translated Clinton's words into Arabic for the king. The king, an engaging man with no formal education and a very earthy Arabic, had little time for Iraq's ruler.

"The king regrets to say that he has lost all confidence in Prime Minister Maliki," said his interpreter, the ambassador.

What the king had actually said was "Maliki is a big liar." How often did curt, visceral sentiments like these get lost in translation?

The king suggested the United States itself should be more forceful in reining in Tehran. The Saudi monarch then appealed to Clinton to help with more U.S. student visas for Saudis. It was an issue that mattered to him deeply and that he brought up in almost every meeting with American officials. He deplored the fact that after the attacks of 9/11 the number of Saudis in American universities had dwindled. He insisted that the United States and Saudi Arabia had to maintain a strong relationship, and he believed that the experience of Saudi students in America was essential to that. His own ambassador had spent so much time in the United States, he said, that he was practically an American. Finally, some four hours after their closed meeting had started, Hillary emerged, smiling broadly. If ever a meeting had gone well, this was it.

The caravan made its way through the desert back to the airport, which somehow, unusually, had a small, fully kitted auditorium with interpreter booths and all. Clinton and Saud al-Faisal gave a press conference in which questions about Iran dominated. Washington was pushing for tougher sanctions on Tehran, and journalists asked whether Saudi Arabia supported the move.

"Sanctions are a long-term solution. So we need immediate resolutions rather than gradual resolution to this regard," said Saud al-Faisal. Saudi diplomatic language was so opaque it was almost comic. Had the Saudis just said they would not support America's push for a sanctions resolution at the United Nations? Or was that their subtle way of asking the Americans to take more decisive action, like a military strike? A reporter then asked whether the Saudis would offer more of their own oil supplies to China to encourage them to stop importing crude oil from Iran. The answer sounded like Chinese.

"I am sure the Chinese carry their responsibility as one of the five permanent members of the United Nations very seriously, and they need no suggestion from Saudi Arabia to do what they ought to do according to their responsibility."

Was he saying that Saudi Arabia would not use oil as an incentive to pressure China to back UN sanctions against Iran—the sanctions we weren't sure they actually supported? The statement could also be read as a veiled warning: if Beijing did not back UN sanctions, as was expected from a "responsible world power," it risked upsetting its top oil supplier, Saudi Arabia. Iran was a key crude-oil provider for China, but it ranked third.

When the press conference was over, the line officer grabbed Clinton's personal earphones from the lectern while she was escorted out by the minister. We all scurried behind them, toward the plane. We flew an hour and a half south to the warmer and less conservative Red Sea port city of Jeddah, where Clinton was going to hold a town hall at the Dar Al-Hekma women's college the following day. Huma was excited to see her mother and would be spending the night at the family home.

Saudi Arabia, the birthplace of Islam, is a deeply religious country and has a patriarchal society with a traditional Bedouin past. The culture and customs here are deeply foreign to most Westerners, especially because of the way women are treated. While some Saudi women are just as conservative as their husbands or fathers and don't wish for change, many others resent the segregation that rules everyday life and the restrictions they face at every turn. Everything requires the permission of a male guardian, from traveling to opening a business. Thousands of women work within the gaps in the restrictions and are successful businesswomen, doctors, and lawyers. Women also apparently hold half of the country's bank assets. But they are not allowed to drive, and they have to wear black cloaks at all times—the two most visible signs of the repression women face in Saudi Arabia. Women's rights in the kingdom are often reduced to the single issue of the black cloak, a pet topic for Westerners.

In 2005, Karen Hughes, who was in charge of public diplomacy for the Bush administration, also spoke at Dar Al-Hekma. When she told the audience that driving was an important part of her freedom as an American woman, she was faced with defiance. "I don't want to drive because I have my own driver," said one student.[22] "Americans think that Arab women are not very happy," another said.[23] "We are all pretty happy."

Some of the country's rules were fit for the Middle Ages, but women were not a uniform, black, downtrodden mass. Women did also openly rebel occasionally and took to the wheel in protest, but they bristled at being lectured to by outsiders. Change, they told Hughes, would come, but it would come from them. In the wake of the Iraq War debacle, American lectures about freedom were not welcome in the Arab world.

Hillary had come armed with Egyptian poetry and her deputy chief of staff who had spent almost half her life in Saudi Arabia. Huma's mother, Dr. Saleha Abedin, introduced the secretary on stage, and Hillary paid tribute to her aide to wild applause from the room. She spoke of the vitality and energy of the women lawyers and doctors she had met before the town hall, and she praised the king's effort to advance the education of women.

"I, of course, believe that educating young women is not only morally right, but it is also the most important investment any society can make in order to further and advance the values and the interests of the people. The Egyptian poet Hafez Ibrahim said, 'A mother is a school. Empower her and you empower a great nation.'"

If there were any bitter memories left over from the encounter with Hughes four years earlier, or any pent-up desire to pounce on another American leader who might be telling them that they should drive, Hillary defused them quickly. She praised what had already been achieved—no matter how little she may have thought it was—and combined it with a culturally sensitive but firm appeal for more, and the women felt at ease. Hillary had hoped to engage in a conversation about women's rights, but somehow the students did not pick up on any of her cues, instead sticking to standard subjects like Iran, Israel, and her work as a secretary of state. One question in particular revealed the image many in the region still have of America.

"Everyone knows that everything is almost perfect and strong in the U.S., when it comes to politics and education system, economy. But why there is a big question mark on the health care system in the United States, although President Obama promised to change that. What have the government did so far?" asked one student in English.

A bit later, Hillary laughed when she was asked whether she would immigrate to Canada or Russia if Sarah Palin, the former governor of Alaska, became president of the United States. The rest of the world followed American politics closely, and these women were no exception. The more a country felt its fate was affected by the United States, the more detailed their knowledge was. Tribal leaders in Afghanistan and Palestinian police officers knew the names of American congressmen because they had blocked or approved aid bills that had a direct impact on their towns.

After the town hall wrapped up, Hillary was mobbed by women who wanted to take a picture with her. Huma provided a guiding hand to the protocol. Some of the women had full-face veils. Standing in a corner, away from the eyes of men, they lifted the black cloth to show their faces for a picture with the American secretary of state.

Our five-day trip had come to an end. We arrived at the airport, drove onto the tarmac, and kept going past SAM, stopping only outside the VIP terminal. Clinton may have had a government plane at her disposal at all times, but America was a superpower on a budget. The four aging planes of SAM's fleet rotated between missions and repairs. Congress would not approve the funds needed to upgrade the fleet, and every now and then, the planes broke down. This was one of those times. The fuel valve was kaput. General David Petraeus, the head of the U.S. Central Command leadership, was flying back to Washington from Riyadh that evening. He could swing by Jeddah first to pick up Clinton. Six hours later, the blue secretary of state seal was taken off SAM's door and attached to the new plane. The Velcro wouldn't stick at first, but after a few tries Clinton was on her way home.

The rest of us made our way back home on commercial flights, transiting through various European capitals, wandering aimlessly for hours in airports waiting for connecting flights to the United States until we finally made it home Wednesday in the early afternoon. One of the comments Clinton had made during that trip was still ringing in my ear: "We don't have any magic wands that we can wave."

Of course the United States didn't have a magic wand, but there was something slightly disarming about the candor of that remark by the secretary of state of the world's superpower. American leaders rarely if ever spoke of the limits of American power, even if in fantastical terms. It was of a different nature still from Obama's comment about his peace efforts. This wasn't an admission of failure but an attempt to close the gap between the unrealistic expectations people had, even Americans themselves, especially Americans themselves, of American power and reality. So many countries still expected the United States to do their job for them, tell off their annoying neighbors, or give them pocket money. And then there were countries that thought they could do it all much better than America.

8

WHIRLING DERVISHES
AND BRAZILIAN SAMBA

Ahmet Davutoğlu sat on a stage overlooking the packed conference room at the Washington office of the Council on Foreign Relations, one of the many think tanks that held regular events about international affairs. Turkey's foreign minister was here to promote his country's style of diplomacy in front of an audience eager to hear more about this fast-emerging power on the world stage. With more than three hundred think tanks and research centers operating in the city, I often felt that living in Washington, D.C., was like being on a big university campus with lecture halls where ideas were tested and debated in front of a live audience of experts. I could learn to my heart's content if I wanted to, going from one event to another about subjects as diverse as the future of the American health care system or Islamic Finance in the Central Asia–Caucasus Region and everything in between.

Every world leader, political advisor, opposition figure, or wannabe leader, foreign or American—everyone who had something to say and was in Washington for official or informal meetings—sought to get onto that talking circuit. The more you advertised your vision or theory about a specific issue, the more chances it could gain traction with decision makers inside the administration. In Washington, unlike Paris or London and especially Moscow or Beijing, there was a close connection between public discourse and policy. The revolving door between government and think tanks means that today's China expert at the Brookings Institution could be tomorrow's Asia policy chief at the National Security Council.

Davutoğlu was a popular guest and often gave multiple talks during his visits, at different think tanks around town, all of them oversubscribed. A short man with black hair, rimless glasses, and a permanent smile lurking beneath his salt-and-pepper mustache, Davutoğlu was an eternal optimist, and, like the country he represented, highly energetic, always in motion.

The day before, on April 12, 2010, he had attended a Nuclear Security Summit in Washington. Iran dominated much of the talk. The country upsetting America's best-laid plans everywhere, from Lebanon to Afghanistan, was busy enriching uranium in nuclear plants. Under the Non-Proliferation Treaty, any country had the right to civilian nuclear energy, but Iran's centrifuges were spinning the uranium closer and closer to the level needed to build a nuclear weapon. Tehran insisted that it merely wanted civilian energy for power to light up people's homes. But the West was suspicious: Iran had kept the full extent of its nuclear program hidden for years until an exiled Iranian armed militant group revealed the whereabouts of a major secret facility in 2002. The United Nations had already punished Iran with three layers of sanctions for failing to abide by all the rules, but Iran's centrifuges kept spinning. The United States was now pushing for another round of sanctions.

Turkey, Iran's neighbor, saw an opportunity to play a role bridging the gap between East and West. While Davutoğlu talked to Clinton at the summit, his prime minister Recep Tayyip Erdoğan had conferred with Obama in a trilateral meeting with Brazil's president Luiz Inácio Lula da Silva. Brazil and Turkey were both in a nonpermanent seat at the Security Council, they both wanted to join the club of global powers— and they both had trade ties with Tehran. They didn't want Iran to have an atomic bomb, but they believed that more talking could make a difference. For fifteen minutes, Lula and Erdoğan tried to convince Obama to give their type of diplomacy a chance. Though Obama was not convinced, he didn't categorically say no. His administration was all about multilateral diplomacy, and he wanted to encourage other countries to do their bit to keep peace in their part of the world, especially the rising powers.

Turkey was really the only or, at least, the most sustained success story of the wider Middle East. Just ten years before, Turkey had been stagnating; military coups constantly disrupted its politics, and one aging, uninspiring prime minister seemed to replace the next. But the country had weathered the financial crisis of 2008, and its economy was still growing at around 7 percent a year. Turkey was now the world's seventeenth-largest economy and turning into a vibrant Islamic democracy with a populist, forward-thinking prime minister and an academic-turned-diplomat foreign minister. Both men tapped into the Turkish national sense of pride and grandeur; the Turks, after all, were the heirs of the Ottoman Empire, which had once stretched from the outskirts of Vienna to the Horn of Africa.

Davutoğlu was a ball of energy. He was everywhere and had a plan for everything, his conversation peppered with phrases such as "I've just visited," or "Tomorrow, I'm going to," transiting through Shannon Airport in Ireland to refuel, flying into world capitals just before or just after Clinton. Tehran was often on his schedule. Turkey's government had a small fleet of planes available for its top officials, and Davutoğlu seemed to live on one of them, constantly crisscrossing the world, trying to solve crises from the Balkans to Israel, from Syria to Iran. With one foot in the East and the other in the West, Turkey wanted to be a bridge, especially between the United States and countries that, Davutoğlu liked to insist, America did not understand.

That day in Washington, he spoke at length about his favorite vision—the model partnership between his country and the United States. Unlike previous global powers, he said, America was disconnected not only historically but also geographically from the rest of the world; this isolation gave America security but no strategic depth. Turkey was a regional power, with six very diverse neighbors, a rich history and identity; it was also predominantly Muslim—all of this added up to assets when it came to solving problems, assets that the United States decidedly lacked. Strategic depth—Turkey had so much of it in Davutoğlu's eyes that these two words were the title of his six-hundred-page book on Turkey's uniqueness. He thought it was obvious: the United States needed Turkey.

The two countries had been allies since 1952. During the Cold War, the United States and Turkey shared a fear of Soviet expansionism, and it had made sense then for Turkey to defer to the United States. But though the relationship was strong, in a world of rising regional powers like India and Brazil, Turkey wanted to shine and forge its own path. The

Turks had never been subservient to the United States, but now they were even less willing to let Washington lead. And they were not afraid of irritating the Americans, in ways big and small.

The Obama administration got an early taste of Turkish prickliness at a summit in Strasbourg in April 2009 when Turkey opposed the appointment of the new secretary-general of NATO, Anders Fogh Rasmussen, a former prime minister of Denmark. The Scandinavian country was at the heart of a controversy that started in 2005 when a Danish newspaper published cartoons of the Prophet Muhammad, setting off demonstrations across the Muslim world. The Turks were critical of Rasmussen's handling of the crisis. They also did not appreciate his tolerance for a television station run by the PKK, the Kurdistan Workers Party, a separatist Kurdish party in Turkey that broadcast from Denmark. The Turks could be tough negotiators: to get Erdoğan's backing for Rasmussen, Obama had to promise that the new NATO chief would appoint a Turk as his deputy.

Whenever we traveled with Clinton and a meeting with Erdoğan was on the agenda, his stern bodyguards, as unsmiling as nightclub bouncers, made the secretary's DS agents or the Secret Service look like start-up geeks. The Turks frequently had dustups with other guards who stood in their way, once sending two UN security officials to the hospital. Another time, they came close to a fistfight with an American ambassador over access to a room where Clinton and Erdoğan were meeting. Turkish newspapers would then be full of accounts about how Turkey had safeguarded its honor and stood up to the arrogant Americans. Turkey was pushing back against America again, but this time, American national interest hung in the balance.

For more than six months, Clinton had been working diligently to get the Chinese and the Russians on board for a fourth round of hard-hitting UN sanctions against Iran, which Brazil and Turkey were keen to avoid. Obama had gone from promising to meet with America's foes when he was a candidate to simply calling on those foes to unclench their fists during his inaugural address. But hopes that his persona was enough to transform the dynamics of international diplomacy quickly collided with realpolitik. While pursuing engagement with Tehran, the administration was working to be sure they were ready if diplomacy failed. The Russians didn't necessarily like Iran and especially didn't care for its president, Mahmoud Ahmadinejad, but they shared with Iran a rejectionist attitude toward the West. Moscow enjoyed making Washington's life difficult, so it often banded with Iran to needle the Americans. When Clinton last visited Moscow, she had said there was growing international consensus for more sanctions on Iran. Sitting next to her, Sergei Lavrov, the Russian foreign minister, laconically said he didn't think there was any need for more sanctions. In the end, the Russians always voted in favor of sanctions against Iran, but only after making everyone's life difficult, obstructing the process for months and softening the wording of drafts to the point that the final text barely had any bite. The Russians were also helping Tehran build a civilian nuclear reactor in Bushehr, on the Persian Gulf coast in southeast Iran.

No one had the emotional scars from dealing with Iran that America had, from the hostage crisis of 1979 to the marine bombings in Beirut in 1983. But everybody remembered that the weapons of mass destruction used as an excuse to topple Saddam Hussein were never found. So Washington's warnings about Iran's nuclear advances were often met with skepticism outside of the United States, Europe, and Israel. But in September 2009, the Obama administration, France, and the United Kingdom revealed that Iran had for years hidden yet another nuclear facility deep under a mountain near the holy city of Qom. The Russians were stunned. How could their intelligence services not have known? They were shown the evidence, and it was irrefutable. They were furious; they had been deceived and lied to by their own camp.

Just before the Qom revelations, Iran had agreed to discuss its nuclear program with the P5 + 1 group, which includes the 5 permanent members of the UN Security Council—the United Kingdom, France, Russia, China, the United States, as well as Germany. The P5 + 1 was now planning to use the world's outrage to force Iran into a compromise at the talks in Geneva. But Iran loved to talk; it was an opportunity to buy time and stave off more sanctions.

The five big powers wanted a freeze for freeze: if Iran froze all of its enrichment activities, UN sanctions would be frozen in return. But that freeze was a very elusive end goal. They suggested an intermediary step to help build trust. Tehran had a nuclear medical reactor that needed

new supplies of highly enriched uranium, and Iran wasn't able to produce its own fast enough. So the P5 + 1 made an offer that could both
help ease international concerns about the uranium that Iran was stock-
piling and also help Iran demonstrate that its intentions were peaceful:
give us 1,200 of your 1,500 kilograms of low-enriched uranium (LEU),
they told the Iranians, we'll enrich it further in Russia and France, and
we'll return the nuclear fuel to you to be used in the medical facility.
With only 300 kilograms of LEU left on its soil, Iran's progress toward
a nuclear weapon would be seriously set back. The Iranians said yes, but
then went home to study the proposal further. They never properly
responded. They were too divided themselves, between conservatives and
ultraconservatives, and no one trusted the outside world: they worried
that if they handed over their uranium, they would never see it again. The
Russians were incensed: their credibility was on the line. The sanctions
that Lavrov had dismissed several months ago were edging closer.

The Turks were starting to fret—they didn't have a nuclear program
and didn't want anyone in the region to have a nuclear weapon. But they
were also worried about the prospects of more sanctions on Iran.
Erdoğan and Davutoğlu got to work. They traveled to Iran on several
occasions, working to set themselves up as middlemen between Tehran
and Washington, trying to convince Iran to take the deal. With Brazil,
they started to explore different formulas and variations of the plan.

Perhaps because he was an academic, Davutoğlu was an affable man
with none of the rough edges that came with Turkish pride, but he believed
in his country's destiny. In front of his audience at the Council on Foreign Relations in Washington, he boasted in close-to-perfect English
about his efforts to have excellent relations with countries on Turkey's
borders, which he called a zero-problem-neighborhood policy. Waving
his hands and raising his left index finger, Davutoğlu spoke emphatically
about his country's desire to bring to the region "a new era of stability,
peace, and prosperity." And that included Iran.

"Diplomacy, diplomacy, diplomacy, more efficient diplomacy. Not
military tension, not economic tension, which will affect Turkey, a neighboring country," said Davutoğlu. He was very open about his motivations
to counter the moves toward sanctions at the United Nations. His country had a major stake in this fight: its economy was zipping along and
would be slowed down by sanctions against Iran. Ties between the two

neighbors had blossomed since Erdoğan's moderate Islamist AK Party (Justice and Development) came to power in 2003. From $1 billion in trade with Iran in 2000, it was now $10 billion. Iran was Turkey's second-largest source of energy and its main land route for trade with Asia. Iraq had been Turkey's largest trading partner until it came under sanctions after the Gulf War in 1990, and Turkey's economy had been hard hit.

Turkey was also feeling left out of the discussions about sanctions. At the UN Security Council, China, Russia, the United States, the United Kingdom, and France had permanent seats, with the other ten seats rotating among the 193 member states. Turkey was currently on the UN Security Council, but, sitting in the CFR conference room, an indignant Davutoğlu complained no one had shared with them the details of the sanctions that were being prepared.

"Until now, we didn't get a briefing, we were not consulted, and we don't know what is in the package . . . Maybe the P5, they are consulting among themselves. Of course we are not against this, but we don't know the content."

Perhaps Hillary could answer his questions. He was heading to see her again at the State Department the following day. Clinton had met Davutoğlu on her first trip to Turkey in 2009, when he was still an advisor to Erdoğan, laying the groundwork for his vision of Turkey's foreign policy and its role in the region. She appreciated his intellect and respected his worldview and his energy; she viewed him as one of her more consequential counterparts even if she didn't always agree with him. She liked that he came to every one of their meetings brimming with ideas and a commitment to pursue his country's interests. Developing a relationship with Davutoğlu was also a way of keeping Turkey close, in the orbit of the West. He was one the foreign ministers Clinton spoke to most.

The Turks had wanted to become part of the European Union, but Europe—France, especially—was hesitant to open its arms. The Turks were deeply insulted. Parts of Europe had once fallen under the Ottoman Empire; now Old Europe was going to keep Turkey out of the EU? The Turks looked East and tried to re-create part of their old Ottoman space with a visa-free zone with Jordan, Lebanon, and Syria. They embraced their Muslim identity and bluntly criticized their old friend and military ally Israel for oppressing the Palestinians. Their new ambition to be a regional power, a bridge between West and East, meant they were cultivating ties with countries and groups that were hostile to the West—countries like Iran but also groups like Hamas, the Palestinian radical militant group. The Turks appeared to be slowly drifting away from the United States' orbit. Turkey was a NATO ally in a key strategic area, and Washington could not afford to let go of Ankara's hand.

Clinton and Davutoğlu called each other by their first names and always started their conversations by talking about their families. She gave him a high five in public when he became a grandfather; he praised her in front of the cameras, saying her leadership went well beyond the institution of the State Department. They had developed a good rapport, and there was never enough time to talk about all the subjects on the agenda. Both were voluble, and the conversations could sometimes get intense, like on this occasion. Iran diplomacy was intricate and emotional for everyone.

Clinton and Davutoğlu first spent a few minutes chatting in her office and then walked across the hall with their teams to the conference room to get down to business. Surrounded by four peach-colored walls, senior American officials sat on one side of the long table and Turkish officials on the other. P. J. Crowley, the State Department's spokesperson, took notes so he could update journalists with any details about the conversation that could be made public. Most of the time, Clinton gave a small press conference with ministers after their meeting in the round, blue Treaty Room, around the corner from her offices. But neither minister had the time or desire to be quizzed by the media, so on this occasion P. J. would answer our questions at the Daily Press Briefing.

"Two minutes till the briefing, two minutes." The announcement over the public address system into the bull pen alerted the State Department press corps that P. J. was on his way down. The briefings usually took place around noon. The meeting with Davutoğlu was expected to last forty-five minutes; it ended just before three in the afternoon, clocking in at almost two hours. Half a dozen journalists exited their cubicles in the bull pen and walked thirty steps around the corner and into the briefing room on the Building's second floor.

Several dozen journalists were already there, mostly foreigners who worked for their country's national media. Any journalist with a press card was allowed to attend the briefing and ask a question. Sometimes the briefing started with an announcement, but this was no press conference—it didn't matter whether anyone in the Building really had anything new to say, whether there was a breakthrough in Mideast peace talks or China had jailed another dissident. Journalists representing countries around the world wanted to know what the United States had to say or what it planned to do about the smallest incremental development in the politics of their own countries. Unless he or she had a meeting scheduled afterward, the spokesperson would call on every journalist who raised a hand. The briefing was filmed in full and broadcast to news agencies worldwide. Officials would comb through it for reaction to international events or a mention of their country's name. On the evening news, in Japan, Tripoli, or Islamabad, the anchor would say, "The State Department spokesperson today congratulated Japan on the election of its new prime minister," or "The U.S. today offered its condolences to Pakistan after a bomb killed fifty people." No matter how many episodes of *The West Wing* TV series with White House briefings my friends and I had watched in Beirut, lifting the veil over the real thing was still startling. When we heard on television that the United States was talking about us, we could not fathom that if a State Department spokesperson mentioned our country it wasn't necessarily because American officials had held a meeting, discussed the situation at length, and consciously decided to make a statement about Lebanon, but rather because someone in the briefing room had raised a hand. I experimented a couple of times, asking a question about Lebanon and watching the answer appear on the news in Beirut when there had been no real movement in the United States on the issue. The look of disappointment on people's faces in Beirut, as well as other countries, when I told them how the briefing worked was revealing of the extent to which people thought they were America's sole concern.

Standing behind the light-brown wood lectern with a State Department seal, a glass of water at hand, P. J. rifled through his white ring binder with a Red Sox sticker on the cover. The binder was divided by region, country, and issue and contained detailed talking points; it was a visual aid that helped him spell out American policy on an ongoing issue or update us if something had moved. But depending on who showed up, the range of questions was like a political knowledge pop quiz, totally disconnected from the news. Sometimes, there was nothing in the binder, and P. J. would have to recall from memory the exact position of the United States on countries he hadn't thought of for a while.

On that day, Turkey only came up briefly toward the end, and reporters were mostly eager to know whether there was any sign that Ankara was going to support Washington's drive for another round of sanctions against Iran. P. J. said Turkey was being helpful. Really? Yes, really, he insisted. He referred to Turkey's efforts to continue engaging with Iran and said the United States and Turkey shared a common objective, which was to make sure Iran did not become a nuclear state.

"Did the secretary show the Turkish foreign minister a draft of the resolution, which they hadn't seen up until now?" asked a Turkish journalist.

"[The meeting] was about a strategic approach to Iran. This was not about the nuts and bolts of a resolution."

"But only yesterday, he complained that you didn't show him the draft. He made a speech yesterday. He complained that the Americans refused to give us a plan."

"And we pledged during the meeting that we would have further discussions and consult closely with Turkey as a resolution draft emerges," P. J. answered.

Forty minutes later, we had run out of questions and left the room, unaware of what had been a crucial item on the agenda for Clinton and Davutoğlu. They had continued the discussion started at the Nuclear Summit by Obama, Erdoğan, and Lula. None of it had been reported yet, but Erdoğan and Lula weren't simply making a vague proposal for more diplomacy; they were suggesting hands-on deal making.

The meeting between Clinton and Davutoğlu had not been about the nuts and bolts of a Security Resolution as P. J. had accurately told us. I would learn later it had been about the nuts and bolts of a deal with Iran that would help avoid further sanctions.

Davutoğlu began by explaining to Clinton again, as he had so often, why Turkey understood Iran better than the United States did. We've known Iran for hundreds of years, he would say. As a friend of the Iranians, we can speak bluntly to them, something the West could not do. Mostly, he insisted that Turkey's foreign policy was about giving a sense of justice and vision to the region; they would not admonish or threaten the Iranians in public, American-style.

The Turks were still looking for ways to revive the deal put on the table in October in Geneva—1,200 kilograms of low-enriched uranium shipped out of Iran, highly enriched uranium (HEU) sent back. Iran had told the Turks it would consider shipping out the uranium but only after it had received the nuclear fuel for the research reactor. This was not acceptable to the P5 + 1. It would take a year to produce the fuel, during which time Iran's own centrifuges would continue spinning, augmenting its uranium stockpile. But Davutoğlu insisted this was still a good first step to build trust.

It's a good deal, this will work, he said. You can't just expect the Iranians to give up their uranium; you have to understand them, he argued. And he insisted that Turkey was a tough negotiator; it would be strict with the Iranians.

Clinton had no trouble understanding Davutoğlu's motives: he was trying to protect his country from the impact of sanctions and conflict. She disagreed with his approach. This was becoming the bazaar. Bob Einhorn, the State Department's nuclear expert, was brought in to explain in detail what was wrong with the deal the Turks were proposing: this was no longer about when the uranium left Iran and when it was sent back in. Almost six months had passed since the deal was put on the table, and Iran's centrifuges had continued spinning. Iran now had much more than the 1,500 kilograms of uranium it had in October. The 1,200 kilograms were no longer 80 percent of Iran's stockpile, but barely 50 percent. Iran would be left with enough uranium to continue working toward a nuclear weapon. Back in October in Geneva, the Russians had refused to make the offer based on an ongoing percentage. Even they were keen to just pin down a number and get the uranium out quickly. More importantly, the P5 + 1 wanted Iran to stop enriching uranium to the level of 20 percent. The more such uranium Iran produced, the closer it would get to what it needed for an atomic bomb.

If the Turks wanted to go ahead, Clinton and Einhorn said, they had to ask for much more than 1,200 kilograms. If you can pull a rabbit out of a hat, more power to you, Clinton told Davutoğlu, but we are really skeptical. With his sunny, positive disposition, Davutoğlu didn't hear no.

As rough and assertive as Americans could be in negotiations, there were times when they were also too polite. Again, Obama attempted to encourage responsible leadership among the rising powers, as he had in person during his meeting with Lula and Erdoğan a few weeks earlier. On April 20, Lula received a letter from the White House that explained again why their proposal was not acceptable—this would not work as a confidence-building measure, certainly not for the United States and the P5 + 1. But in an attempt to be encouraging, Obama's letter ended by describing possible compromises with Iran, including the possibility that 1,200 kilograms of uranium would be put in escrow immediately in Turkey, a country Iran trusted. Twelve hundred—that number just wouldn't go away. When the State Department officials read the letter, they were alarmed by how vague it was about red lines for the escrow proposal to be acceptable. Mostly, they were distressed to see the mention of the 1,200 kilograms.

Deep down, American officials perhaps did not believe that the new powers could make any progress in their talks with the Iranians. Washington continued to negotiate the text of a sanctions resolution with Moscow and Beijing. But by May 13, alarm bells were ringing wildly in Washington. Clinton got on the phone to Davutoğlu. The 1,200 kilograms were not enough, she explained, the United States and its allies would never accept a deal with that amount in it. Crucially, Iran still had to stop enriching its uranium to 20 percent. She was going against the letter that the White House had sent to Lula, in essence contradicting the president, something she had never done before, but the situation required urgent damage control. This was not going to delay the sanctions, she said. Finally, Clinton told Davutoğlu that it was time for the Turks to put an end to their enterprise with the Brazilians.

But the Turks had stopped listening to Clinton. In front of them was a letter, in black and white, by the president of the United States mentioning the magic number 1,200. They were certain that their escrow proposal would work, and they were going to prove to Washington that Turkey could be a trusted broker, an indispensable problem solver, a new world power. Obama's letter was all they needed to go to Iran. And they were now locked into their approach with Lula.

It was less clear what Brazil wanted out of the deal. Trade relations between the Latin American giant and Iran were also growing, and sanctions would affect Brazil's economy. But from Washington's perspective, it looked like a freelance mission, good old contrarian politics to spite Uncle Sam. Brazil was part of the Non-Aligned Movement formed in the 1960s to counter American imperialism. Celso Amorim, the Brazilian foreign minister, and Lula, a former union leader, were driven by reflexive third-world ideology; they believed deeply in Brazil's rise and saw America as an obstacle to their emergence on the global stage. The Brazilians were the B in BRICS—with Russia, India, China, and South Africa, newly developed, emerging economic powers. Apart from Russia, the other BRICS were also testing their newfound political power. The author and foreign policy columnist Fareed Zakaria called it the "rise of the rest." The BICS, sans Russia, protested that the international institutions set up after World War II, from the United Nations to the International Monetary Fund, were anachronistic, relics of an antiquated status quo. France and Britain had long lost their empires, the Soviet Union had disintegrated, and America was no longer the superpower it once was. China and Russia had permanent seats on the UN Security Council, and Brazil, India, and South Africa argued that they should get one too. Along with Turkey, the emerging powers felt they should be given the power they deserved. This was their chance to grab it.

On May 15, Lula arrived in Tehran to attend a summit of developed and developing countries. Iran was not part of the movement but was an honorary member as a country that stood against U.S. hegemony. After a phone call between Davutoğlu and his Iranian counterpart, Manouchehr Mottaki, the Turkish ball of energy got on a plane to Tehran. Mottaki, Amorim, and Davutoğlu spent eighteen hours hammering out the details of an agreement. On Sunday evening, when they felt a deal was in sight, Davutoğlu called his boss and told him to fly to Tehran.

On Monday morning, a deal was finalized. Iran had agreed to put 1,200 kilograms of low-enriched uranium in escrow in Turkey, in return for nuclear fuel. The uranium would remain the property of Iran, and Tehran could ask that it be sent back at any time. It looked like refreshing, creative diplomacy on an issue of international magnitude by someone other than America.

"My expectation is that after this declaration there will not be a need for sanctions," Erdoğan said in Tehran. He posed for a picture with the Brazilian and Iranian presidents. Mahmoud Ahmadinejad was a small man from a modest background, a hard-line conservative animated by religious fervor. Standing between the portly Lula and the tall Erdoğan, he grabbed their hands and lifted them in the air like trophies. He had pulled Turkey and Brazil into his orbit, splitting the international community.

The Turks often boasted that their president was the only leader who could go to Iran and meet the supreme leader, Ayatollah Ali Khamenei, and then fly across the Atlantic and sit in the Oval Office with Obama. They were needed; they played a key role that no one else could fill. But Erdoğan looked slightly uncomfortable in the picture. He never showed many teeth when he smiled, but the corners of his lips were barely turned upward as he stood next to Ahmadinejad.

A few hours later that Monday, Washington awoke to the picture of a victorious Ahmadinejad and news of the pact. At the White House and the State Department and on Capitol Hill, people looked at Erdoğan standing next to the Iranian leader and they saw the image of betrayal—America's ally and its archenemy were brothers? Someone had hit the accelerator button on the rise of the rest, and the result was a chaotic mess. The Turks had not consulted with Washington before signing; in fact no one had called Washington since Clinton and Davutoğlu had spoken on the thirteenth. For the United States, this was like a sixteen-year-old with a learner's permit taking his new car for a spin and forgetting he still needed an adult sitting in the car.

The Obama administration had also worked for eight months to get Beijing and Moscow on board with the sanctions, and Washington was stuck on that path as well. One official told me that it was hard to predict what Washington would have done if the Turks had actually managed to secure an ironclad deal involving the removal of 80 percent of Iran's uranium. Perhaps the United States would have been willing to take a diplomatic gamble and test the Turkish deal with Iran, on the condition that Russia and China would commit to going ahead with the agreed sanctions if Iran did not ship out its uranium. No one had a sure answer to that hypothetical question.

Hillary Clinton's official portrait on the State Department website, taken in early 2009. She conceded the race for the Democratic nomination on June 7, 2008, and soon after endorsed and started campaigning for Barack Obama. (STATE DEPARTMENT)

President-elect Obama leaves a Chicago press conference on December 1, 2008, with Clinton after formally announcing his picks for national security positions in his administration. Many were surprised by Obama's choice, including Clinton herself. There were predictions of drama between the two former rivals. (AP)

Clinton is sworn in by Vice President Joseph Biden during a ceremonial event in the Benjamin Franklin room on the eighth floor of the State Department. Standing next to her are husband and former president, Bill; daughter, Chelsea; and her mother, Dorothy Rodham. (STATE DEPARTMENT)

The crowds cheered wildly when Clinton arrived at the State Department on the morning of January 22, 2009, for her first day at work. There was a campaign feel to the event as she shook hands while people screamed, "We love you, Hillary." Behind her on the left, diplomatic security special agent Fred Ketchem, chief of her security, is standing guard. (AP)

A polarizing politician in the United States, Clinton had built a worldwide following as a First Lady and was welcomed like a rock star on her maiden voyage as secretary of state, which included this stop in Jakarta in February 2009. (STATE DEPARTMENT)

Clinton and her staff believed that public diplomacy was key to improving America's image. They planned to beam her into living rooms around the world, starting with this town hall–format interview on the *Dahsyat* television show in Indonesia on February 18, 2009 (*left*). "Townterviews" were held on every stop of every trip for four years, including Jeddah in Saudi Arabia in January 2010 (*below*). (GETTY IMAGES/AFP)

Clinton spent a lot of time with varying success repairing America's frayed ties around the world and strengthening others, from the gimmicky "reset button" with Russia's foreign minister Sergei Lavrov to the more comprehensive approach to ties with China. She built a close rapport with State Councilor Dai Bingguo; here she greets him at the State Department in July 2009. (AP)

During her first months in office, Clinton welcomed almost every foreign leader who requested a meeting, from close allies to less savory characters, such as Mutassim Gaddafi (*right*), son of Libya's dictator Muammar Gaddafi. Meetings were usually followed with a statement in the State Department's seventh-floor Treaty Room. (STATE DEPARTMENT)

Clinton's deputy chief of staff Jake Sullivan (*left*) first started working for her during the presidential campaign and took on an increasingly important role in advising, policy making, and messaging during four years at the State Department. Deputy chief of staff and longtime aide Huma Abedin (*right*) was always by Clinton's side, doing everything from advising her on cultural issues in countries such as Pakistan to holding her handbag. (AP)

By the end of 2009, Clinton and Obama were settling into their new roles as team players and Clinton was making her voice heard more forcefully within the administration. She had always had a good rapport with Biden. (WHITE HOUSE)

Clinton congratulates Obama in the Situation Room on March 23, 2010, after the health care reform bill was passed. During the Clinton administration, Hillary took on a leading and controversial role in the health care reform project. It was an unprecedented move for a First Lady and her role in the failed effort continued to haunt her into her presidential campaign. (WHITE HOUSE)

In July 2010 Clinton traveled to the Demilitarized Zone, which straddles the 38th parallel and divides the Korean peninsula into North and South Korea. A North Korean soldier peers through a window as Clinton and Defense Secretary Robert Gates get a tour of a UN building. The visit was meant as a display of soft and hard power. Clinton forged strong ties with Gates and his successor, Leon Panetta. (AP)

Clinton believed in building close ties with world leaders and in being accessible, in order to gain added leverage during diplomatic crises. At the Elysée Palace in January 2010, she had a "Cinderella moment" with French president Nicolas Sarkozy (*left*). She also had good ties with Afghanistan's president Hamid Karzai but had little to show for it—here the two take a stroll in Dumbarton Oaks gardens in Washington (*below*). (AP)

Clinton worked to engage leaders in emerging powers, including Brazil, though exchanges with President Luiz Inácio Lula da Silva and foreign minister Celso Amorim (*above*) were often testy. Clinton also made women's and children's rights a central part of her work as secretary of state and met with nongovernmental organizations everywhere she went. Here she visits an orphanage in Cambodia (*below*). (AP)

Clinton's efforts, along with President Obama, to bring peace to the Middle East got off to a terrible start and ended with possibly the shortest round of talks ever between the Israelis and the Palestinians, in Sharm el-Sheikh in September 2010. Egyptian President Hosni Mubarak, second from the right (flanked by Benjamin Netanyahu and Mahmoud Abbas), would be ousted from office in a popular revolution in February 2011. (AP)

On March 16, 2011, Clinton took a stroll in Cairo's Tahrir Square. The square had been taken over by hundreds of thousands of protestors during the revolution. The Arab uprisings were spreading, two dictators had already been deposed, and one thousand miles to the west, Libya was next. (AP)

Life on the road with Clinton was gruelling, often with up to ten events and four countries in day. Philippe Reines, Clinton's media gatekeeper, and Victoria Nuland, the department spokesperson (*left*), keep up with the world while on the road. The traveling journalists filed their stories wherever they could—here in a palace in Bahrain—often while waiting for Clinton to finish her meetings (*above*). The delegation traveled by motorcade, often in heavily armored vehicles, right up to Clinton's plane on the tarmac. (Kim Ghattas/Nicole Gaouette)

Clinton took her diplomacy to remote places, such as this women's cooperative farm in Tanzania, and made top government officials, including the country's prime minister, Mizengo Pinda, travel with her. (AP)

The traveling press took occasional breaks from the drudgery to pose for pictures in front of the secretary's plane. On almost every trip, Clinton gave interviews to the television reporters traveling with her—including the author. She often came to the back of her plane to brief journalists en route to the next stop. (Kim Ghattas/ Nicole Gaouette/ John Sullivan)

The secretary's plane was part of the bubble in which the delegation traveled for days. Here Clinton gets off her plane in Dar es Salaam with security officers standing guard. The Ravens watch over the plane twenty-four hours a day. (Kim Ghattas)

Clinton and Turkey's foreign minister Ahmet Davutoğlu built a close relationship, part of the Obama administration's approach to managing the rise of other powers. This picture was taken during a diplomatic summit in Abu Dhabi in July 2011 to discuss the NATO military campaign in Libya and the country's future. Some Arab papers said the two officials were celebrating the death of Libyans but the high five was actually in honor of Davutoğlu's newly born grandchild. (AP)

Diplomatic action on Libya consumed much of the summer of 2011 and continued after the fall of Tripoli in August. On September 1, Clinton walks to a meeting at the Elysée Palace in Paris with Libya's interim leaders Mustafa Abdul Jalil and Mahmoud Jibril to her right and Assistant Secretary of State for Near Eastern Affairs Jeffrey Feltman (at far left). (AP)

Clinton travels to Tripoli in October 2011 on board a military plane; Jeffrey Feltman is sitting directly behind her. The shot was turned into an Internet meme that went viral. Clinton submitted her own meme, met the authors, and signed a picture for them "Hilz." (KIM GHATTAS)

Clinton is welcomed on the tarmac of Tripoli International Airport by a motley crew of Libyan militiamen who had been part of the effort to topple Gaddafi and were all eager to have their picture taken with her. A rare moment of thanks to America in the Middle East and a moment of celebration before tragedy less than a year later. (KIM GHATTAS)

Clinton walks hand in hand with Khin Khin Win, wife of Burma's president Thein Sein (ahead of Clinton wearing glasses), in the cavernous gilded palace in Nay Pyi Taw. Clinton was the first U.S. secretary of state to visit the isolated, repressive state since the 1950s. Obama said he had seen "flickers of progress" in Burma and sent Clinton to test the intentions of the country's leaders in December 2011. (AP)

Clinton and Nobel Prize laureate Aung San Suu Kyi met for the first time in Rangoon and had dinner tête-à-tête on the patio of the U.S. mission there before a work meeting the following day with their aides, after which they embraced like long-lost sisters. (AP)

From Timor-Leste, Hillary watches her husband, former president Bill Clinton, give the keynote speech at the Democratic National Convention on September 5, 2012. Bill delivered an enthusiastic, unstinting endorsement of Obama and was the other star on the campaign trail. With Hillary's own sky-high approval ratings, the restoration of the Clinton brand was complete. (NICHOLAS MERRILL)

President Obama signs the condolence book at the State Department on September 12, 2012, after radical militants in Benghazi attacked the U.S. consulate, killing Ambassador Chris Stevens and three other Americans. The tragedy cast a shadow over Clinton's last months as secretary of state and became a highly politicized issue in the run-up to the election. (WHITE HOUSE)

Clinton traveled a million miles to more than one hundred countries in four years. Like Obama, Clinton aged considerably during her tenure and the difference is noticeable when comparing this photo with her portrait from her first day in office. Clinton seemed to come into her own during her years at the State Department, though her aides argued it was the public's perception of her that had changed. (AP)

Either way, the Turks and the Americans had both failed at the exercise: the Turks hadn't listened when Hillary had warned them the devil was in the detail of the 1,200 kilograms. The White House was guilty of a vague letter, perhaps unable to accept that the Turks could get the Iranians to sign off on a deal, any deal. The Brazilians had gotten what they wanted—making life difficult for the United States. And Iran had hoodwinked everybody. An editorial in the state-run *Kayhan* newspaper the next day boasted about Iran's cunning gamble, insisting that Tehran had not signed an agreement, just a nonbinding declaration. Another "written agreement and proper arrangement" was needed before any fuel exchange would take place. Ahmadinejad had seen the Brazilian and Turkish effort as a gift from heaven: he could buy time, delay sanctions, and cause havoc in the established channels of international diplomacy.

Despite their fury, the Americans were still delicate in their reaction to the Turks. Standing behind his lectern, P. J. acknowledged the Turkish and Brazilian effort but said Washington was still studying the details of the deal—a diplomatic way of saying, "The deal is awful, but we can't get ourselves to say it." He faced an onslaught of questions. Matt Lee of the AP went first.

"Why is this [deal] even remotely acceptable?"

Others chimed in.

"Why don't you just reject this?"

"Were you informed of the Turkish and Brazilian effort while they were under way?"

P. J. tried his best to defend American diplomacy without alienating proud Turkey. But the Turks were not into nuances: they weren't picking up on the coolness of the American reaction. The Russians were more forthcoming—President Dmitry Medvedev said the deal would not satisfy the international community and indicated that work at the UN would continue.

The following morning, on Tuesday the eighteenth, fresh off the plane from Tehran and more ebullient than ever, Davutoğlu gave a press conference in Istanbul.

"With the agreement yesterday, an important psychological threshold has been crossed towards establishing mutual trust," Davutoğlu told reporters.

"Sanctions, the discussions on sanctions, will spoil the atmosphere, and the escalation of statements may provoke the Iranian public opinion," he added. Turkish diplomacy had won the day in his view: there would be no sanctions against Iran.

But a few hours later, just after ten in the morning in Washington, Clinton was appearing in the Senate for a hearing and she announced her own diplomatic coup. After victory had been announced in Tehran, she had helped seal the deal the administration had been working on for months—consensus with Russia and China on the text of a resolution, the broadest, most comprehensive set of sanctions against Iran to date.

"With all due respect to my Turkish and Brazilian friends, the fact that we have Russia on board, China on board and that we're moving early this week, namely today . . . put[s] pressure on Iran which they were trying to somehow dissipate," Clinton told the senators.

Across time zones and oceans, word was starting to reach Turkey that America was displeased. Journalists were calling up officials at the foreign ministry to ask for their reaction to Clinton's announcements.

"Are you kidding?" one of them asked when a journalist shared the news about the sanctions. "This can't be good." The Turks were in disbelief—maybe they were misreading something. A few hours later, when Clinton was back from Capitol Hill, Davutoğlu called her. He was still on a high and spent forty-five minutes trying to explain to her why this was a great achievement, a great day.

I don't think so, replied Clinton tersely. The Turks felt like they had been stabbed in the back. They bristled at the way Russia, China, and the United States had looked past their own differences and banded together to elbow out the rising powers. The powers of yesterday behaved like they still ran the planet, the Turks thought, it was so Cold War.

A few weeks later, the sanctions were put to a vote at the UN Security Council, and everybody relived the trauma of old and new powers pulling in different directions. Despite much lobbying, Turkey and Brazil voted against the resolution. The United States was outraged and this time stated clearly and publicly how disappointed it was in its NATO ally. The vote was excruciatingly painful for Ankara, but the Turks felt stuck. They had worked hard to gain Tehran's trust and couldn't suddenly vote to punish them at the UN; it would have been their undoing as a broker in the region. And they were in lockstep with their new partner Lula, whose presidency was coming to an end in six months. The Turks were bitter about the Brazilians and dismissive about their role. Months later, a Turkish official would tell me: "Lula said no at the Security Council and then left. Who remembers Lula today? But for us it was very difficult to say no to the U.S."

Washington's relationship with countries in its backyard, like Brazil, had always been fraught, but Turkey was a NATO member, a stalwart ally of the United States in the region, and home to American military bases. Turkey undermining the United States on an issue of such strategic import as Iran was not part of the agreement. Something was broken. With so many countries clamoring for a share of the global power pie, power was becoming more and more diffuse, and it clearly wasn't just because China was becoming stronger. The Obama administration was trying to harness the energy of these new powers and encourage them to take on world responsibilities. But the United States also wanted and needed to remain at the center of all the action; the superpower wasn't about to let go of the reins. It was a learning process, and this first real-life exercise on a key issue had gone terribly wrong. Even dealing with the Chinese seemed easier—at least their rivalry was predictable. The United States still had the world's biggest military, bigger than those of the next three countries combined, and this was unlikely to change for some time. But military might alone was no longer enough to project power, especially when budgets were being cut. America had to reinvent its diplomacy.

Although the United States had regularly acted outside the multilateral institutions it had helped set up after World War II, especially in cases of national security imperatives, America mostly behaved like a convening power. But there were more and more countries to convene and more coordination was needed outside the big traditional institutions. From day one, Hillary's State Department began formalizing connections with countries big and small, starting with Asia, ASEAN, and the TAC. Over the course of Hillary's tenure, the department would set up twenty-five formal initiatives that would place the United States at the heart of a web of diplomacy and encourage others to feel involved in managing the planet. There were bilateral strategic dialogues with India and South Africa, in addition to the already existing one with China; smaller countries like Indonesia and Nigeria got bilateral commissions.

There were global programs of all sorts: entrepreneurship, civil society, maternal health, climate change, counterterrorism efforts. Many initiatives relied on a key partner, from Turkey to Norway, from nongovernmental organizations to businesses—stakeholders in a new system. Every day, the State Department worked to connect with countries, players, and people everywhere. Even in the midst of the Iran debacle with Turkey and Brazil, the State Department was announcing a "conference for the U.S.-Brazil joint action plan to eliminate racial and ethnic discrimination and promote equality" in Atlanta a few days later. Diplomacy was no longer just about formal talks with leaders. Smart power was exhausting but, in Clinton's view, essential.

She was working hard to project an image of continued American dominance by engaging the world relentlessly, feeding the perception that America still mattered on every level and hoping to turn it into a reality. But though technology had shrunk the world to the size of a village, Hillary quickly learned that her counterparts still wanted to look her in the eyes to make sure they still mattered to Washington or to seal a deal. It was still essential to show up—everywhere.

9

MEET ME AT
THE FAIR

S hanghai was drenched by a steady spring drizzle that beat down on the metropolis of futuristic skyscrapers, sending ripples into the gray waters of the Huangpu River. When Hillary last visited China's financial capital, in November 2009, it had rained too, and she had had to hold on to her dark-blue umbrella with two hands, in the wind, before a shell of a building. She had sounded like a coach, rallying her team around a flagging project: America's pavilion at the world expo to be attended by 189 countries. Now, in May 2010, she had come to see the result of her work and make sure with her own eyes that it had really been built. She stepped out of her car and under a red, white, and blue umbrella printed with the words "Shanghai Expo." Two mammoth gray ovaloid steel structures stood in front of her, connected in the middle by a low-slung glass structure. The architect had intended the design to suggest an eagle stretching its wings in welcome. Instead it looked like a bunker, drab, foreboding, and cold, more like the fortresses that housed American embassies in hostile parts of the world. At least it was there.

World fairs began in the nineteenth century to showcase industrial and technological innovations and to introduce faraway countries to one another. Over the years, fairs had become more and more about nation branding, a way to improve a country's image. For China, the Shanghai World Expo was another opportunity, almost as important as the Beijing Olympics of 2008, to prove that the Middle Kingdom was opening up and rising onto the world stage as a peaceful power. The Chinese Communist party also wanted to show off its economic prowess when the rest of the world was mired in recession. Beijing was spending $45 billion just sprucing up Shanghai ahead of the fair, and more than $200 million on the Chinese pavilion alone. Each exhibitor hoped that the millions of Chinese expected at the fair would be inspired to visit their country on holiday, buy some of their goods, strike a business deal in the pavilions' VIP rooms—anything to get those Chinese yuans flowing into flagging economies. It was a costly sales pitch, but countries hoped for good returns on their investment. America had almost missed the party.

In the early 1990s, American lawmakers decided that taxpayer money could no longer be spent on international fairs. They just didn't see the point; they were willing to make some exceptions but not many. It became mostly up to private investors to fund America's participation in world expos. When Clinton had arrived at the State Department in early 2009, the plans to take part in the 2010 Shanghai Expo were in disarray. America felt like it was in economic meltdown during the financial crisis of 2008. There was no point asking Congress for an exception to use government funds, and no company could be convinced to spend money on what looked like a nonessential junket in a distant country.

But America's absence would only reinforce all the talk about decline, like a once well-off family refusing to spring for a daughter's wedding. The family's limited funds might be better spent elsewhere, but nothing signals a drop in status as dramatically as slashing back the pomp. People would gossip. Every day the empty plot allocated for the USA pavilion would scream at millions of expo visitors: the United States is missing in action. Even Beijing didn't really want such a message proclaimed so loudly: though the Chinese viewed the United States as weakened by the financial crisis, they still wanted their party to be complete, and the United States' absence would reflect poorly on Beijing.

When Clinton traveled to China on her maiden voyage as secretary of state in February 2009, Dai Bingguo, the state councilor, and the foreign minister Yang Jiechi had asked her to ensure that the United States would attend the fair. Something had to be done. In 149 years of world expos, the United States had absented itself only once before, in Hannover in 2000, for very different reasons. The 1990s had been a golden decade for the United States: America was rich and felt like it ruled the world.

The Clinton administration didn't need to advertise the United States around the world; Bill, the president, had even turned down an invitation to visit the fair while he was in Germany that year.

Times had clearly changed. Though Hillary herself didn't believe in the so-called American decline, she was intent on fighting that perception. She gave her Rolodex to two longtime Clinton fund-raisers, and they started working the phones to collect the $60 million needed to build the pavilion. Finally, there it stood, with big red letters on its side spelling out "USA" and thousands of Chinese queuing up to get inside. We filed past everybody and into the sixty-thousand-square-foot bunker.

We felt as though we had been transported into a typical American convention center. In a hangar-sized room, bright advertising displays from the corporate sponsors of the pavilion covered a white wall— FedEx, American Airlines, General Electric, Pepsi. A crowd of several hundred people stood on a maroon carpet, giggling and snapping pictures. The State Department had requested that the pavilion stay open to the public; Hillary wanted to remain accessible to visitors and to project a physical sense of informality and openness, reflecting the values that were key to her country. It was a powerful message in China, where repression and corruption meant that aloof politicians were always ringed by security. The crowd was almost all Chinese, their eyes trained on the two young Americans in jeans speaking to them from bullhorns.

These were the "student ambassadors," two from a group of 160 college-age Americans, perfectly bilingual, not just linguistically but also culturally. The visitors were delighted to be greeted in their own language by smiling young Americans after they had waited in line in the heat, sometimes for three hours. It was public diplomacy par excellence, Hillary's favorite kind.

"Ni hen lihai," the students said and then translated, "You are awesome!"

The audience was transfixed. Some of the Chinese visitors, who were coming from all corners of the vast country, had never met a foreigner before, let alone heard one speak their language. As best as they could, they screamed back, "You are awesome!"

"Nong lau jie guen eh," said the young girl, offering another translation of "You are awesome." Giggles erupted. A foreigner speaking Shanghai dialect! Then, led by the American students, in English, everybody screamed, "China. Is. Awesome!" The student ambassadors were constantly surrounded by a swarm of people. Everybody wanted a picture with them as though they were celebrities.

Suddenly, basketball legend Kobe Bryant from the Los Angeles Lakers appeared on the screens on the red wall on our left. "Ni hao," he greeted the viewers in Chinese. Stunned silence. The video continued as ordinary Americans filmed on the streets of the United States were taught how to say "Welcome" in Mandarin. The Chinese giggled with laughter as the men and women tried, failed, and ultimately succeeded at uttering a few words in Mandarin. Famous skateboarder Tony Hawk did a stunt and then spoke into the camera in apparently fluent Chinese, possibly picked up during his trip to the country a few days earlier to inaugurate a Woodward skateboard camp in Beijing. Olympic medalist Michelle Kwan slid up to the camera on her skates, speaking Cantonese. A group of white, Latino, and Asian firefighters standing in front of their red truck; two dozen schoolchildren of mixed backgrounds in a park; a black shopkeeper; stockbrokers on the trading floor—all of these Americans offered their greetings to China. Wild applause.

In the next room, courtesy of Citicorp, a giant Hillary was projected on the wall.

"Ni hao," she said, "I'm Hillary Clinton." Warm applause from the crowd and excited "woo-hoos."

"As you explore the pavilion, you will discover American values in action: diversity, innovation, and optimism," Hillary said in the video. A film meant to be about the creative power of children followed, though the speakers were representatives from Chevron, GE, PepsiCo, and Johnson & Johnson. At the end of the video, Barack Obama appeared with his own message welcoming visitors to the pavilion. Some of the Chinese in the audience stood up from the benches, turned their backs to the screen, and handed their camera to someone to snap a picture of them with the American president in the background.

The pièce de résistance was a film screened in the "Pfizer Room." A silent movie told the story of a young girl who wants to transform a junkyard into a garden. With a lot of cajoling, she convinces everybody in her neighborhood to help. The project is a communal success. To the delight of the audience, at some point during the film, the seats started shaking and a light mist was sprayed all over the room.

The traveling press kept rolling their eyes. The feel-good films with soaring tunes, sappy story lines, and big American flags fluttering on poles were just too much for seasoned reporters with a critical eye. The corporate stamp gave everything an unrefined, inelegant feel. There was no subtlety, no history, no talk of democracy, of the constitution, or of American traditions, nothing about American technology and innovation, nothing about tourist destinations. There was no mention of George Washington, no pictures of Mount Rushmore. There was nothing to see beyond the ubiquitous corporate logos and superficial entertainment.

Coverage in the United States was scathing. Writing in the *Washington Post*, Ezra Klein complained that "the inattention to aesthetics might work as a signal of power and wealth, like Bill Gates being rich enough to wear denim when he goes to meet the Queen. But then you get to the three videos that make up America's message to the word. Message? We're bad at languages, in hock to corporations, and only able to set up gardens when children shame us into doing so." American officials on the delegation were also taken aback by the corporate-branding onslaught. This was a whole new way of contracting out U.S. diplomacy.

Yet the queue outside the American pavilion was the longest at the expo except for China's own pavilion. Was it just the pull of the three big red letters on the facade? Were the Chinese leaving disappointed? Or did they experience something inside that Americans just weren't getting? I was appalled too by what I saw as a crass sales pitch, but I wondered whether I'd been in America too long and had lost my outsider's perspective.

The Chinese mostly smiled politely though some were no doubt disappointed by the lack of frills (the Saudi pavilion, for example, had an IMAX 3D movie theater that was a sensation). But the audience reaction to the American pavilion seemed mostly positive. A young couple said they were touched by "American humanity"; one man said he was impressed by how children had such heart. China was a country where the individual was subordinate to the Communist Party and children served their parents and society, and where despite the booming economy millions of citizens were poor and left behind. A film focused on children was a novelty; a little girl getting older people to gather around a project was unheard of in a country where civic activism had long been suppressed.

But I could see how the videos were also a small window into a normalcy that was out of reach for millions of Chinese and billions of others around the world. The roads looked safe, the streets were neat and lined with trees and grass; people looked friendly, and most importantly they seemed carefree. It was a film, of course: people in the United States weren't all carefree; they toiled long hours, lacked health care, lost their jobs. But there was something in those films to envy. Trying to tap into whatever it was the Chinese might have been feeling, I thought back to my first visit to the United States in 1996. My sister Ingrid lived in San Francisco then, and we had gone for a walk around the campus of the University of California, Berkeley, a half hour drive across the San Francisco–Oakland Bay Bridge. A group of students was playing a ball game on the green grass on campus. Others lay around chatting, studying in the sun, their books scattered around them. Everything about these young students—their expressions, the way they reclined so easily in the sun, their postures—radiated a graceful ease. It was so peaceful it looked like a movie; but it was real, I could feel it. "So that's what it feels like to be carefree," I thought. For a fleeting moment I was painfully envious. I had never had that. Even affluent people in Lebanon with penthouse apartments overlooking the Mediterranean didn't look carefree. Fear was a constant in our lives. Just as it was in the lives of people from Pakistan to China, places where the rule of law was a joke, baby milk was tainted, policemen dragged you out of your house in the middle of the night, and the greed of corrupt politicians left little behind for people to feed on. The Chinese government may have made economic success available to a vast number of its citizens, but life for the middle class was still precarious, too dependent on the whims of the powerful. The gap between rich and poor in China was also bigger than in most of the other big economies, and much of the country's wealth was concentrated in the hands of families all connected to the ruling elite.

The image of America that the Chinese received inside the pavilion was not that of the country distrusted by proud nationalist Chinese, of the superpower that made unreasonable demands, encircled them in the Pacific, and lectured them from on high. This was the America where many Chinese dreamed of immigrating even as their own country boomed; it was the America that people thought of if they sought refuge in the U.S. embassy from persecution in their own country.

In the USA pavilion souvenir shop, everything seemed to be made in China. The Chinese manager asked Hillary to autograph her book *Living History* and then asked for a picture, handing her digital camera to a colleague behind the till. The two women smiled. The camera switched itself off. The manager grabbed it and fiddled with it. Hillary smiled. The camera was working again. The cashier tried to snap a picture. The screen went dark. The manager fiddled some more, determined to get her picture. "Why don't I sign the book while you do that," Hillary said, smiling. Finally, the digital screen captured a shot of the two women. There were cameras all around; a swarm of journalists always covered Hillary's every move. It was hard to tell where her warmth and patience ended and where her acute self-awareness as a politician started.

By the main entrance, at the other end of the fairground, the Chinese pavilion, the size of one thousand soccer pitches, straddled both sides of the Huangpu River. The government had built the expo in a poor area of the city. Authorities had evicted more than eighteen thousand families and some two hundred factories by force, clearing the area with wrecking balls. Government-led development in China was relentless and brutal, but you would never know it inside the expo.

Our motorcade snaked its way past the endless lines of visitors who were sweating in the humid rain. Fleets of electric cars ferried around rich or important Chinese. When we got out of the vans, we felt like dwarfs at the feet of China's towering, flamboyant red "Crown of the East." No pavilion was allowed to exceed China's in height, and to ensure that no pavilion came even close, the Chinese produced a structure three times higher than anything around it. The traditional interlocking wooden brackets formed what looked like an inverted pyramid with its tip buried in the ground or a monumental emperor's crown. The fair's motto, "Better City, Better Life," motivated many of the foreign exhibitors to showcase energy-efficient and sustainable designs. China's pavilion was a display of power and might that seemed designed to appeal to patriotic pride.

While Clinton sped to the top of the emperor's crown in a VIP elevator, the rest of us made our way up with Chinese citizens. VIP visits to such a pavilion in China or even in some other countries usually prompted security officials to shut off the whole building or sections of it from the general public. But Hillary's team had insisted there need not be any closures on her account.

Shanghai's mayor Han Zheng guided Clinton through the main attraction of the pavilion, the jewel in the crown: a mesmerizing, animated recreation of a twelfth-century panoramic scroll depicting life during the culturally vibrant Song dynasty. All the tiny details in the twenty-foot-high display of "Riverside Scene at Qingming Festival" came to life in the darkened room—men poled river junks, caravans passed through the forest, women carried goods back from the market, and lanterns lit up as day turned to night in a continuous loop. A bed of water ran all along the four-hundred-foot-long tableau, mirroring the ancient Bian River in the painting.

Fred and his agents struggled to keep the crowd from trampling all over their diamond, the formation of four agents they constantly maintained around the secretary. This was a highly policed country and she was surrounded by officials from the Communist Party, but even a friendly crowd could get out of hand and crush Evergreen, especially in the semi-darkness of the seemingly never-ending hall. After a buffet lunch of assorted indistinguishable Chinese fare, it was time to leave, with a detour through the regional Chinese pavilions, where women in traditional dress smiled, mostly silently, at visitors. Occasionally, groups of visitors shrieked, "We love you, Hillary!" to which she responded with her signature big smile and a wave. Just before exiting, Hillary posed with Haibao, the expo's cuddly blue mascot. According to the expo's website, the sky-blue color, which matched Hillary's coat, symbolized "latitude and imagination," representing "the rising and potential of China."

Other than the cheap-looking Haibao, who resembled the clay Gumby character, the Chinese pavilion was as grand as a museum; the contrast with the USA pavilion could not have been greater. They were emblematic of their respective country's history, values, and attitude toward the world, but mostly they reflected their current states of mind. China had smaller provincial pavilions across the fairground and other structures showcasing the "State Shipbuilding Corporation" and China's "glorious railways"—never mind that design flaws in the country's high-speed rails were causing accidents.

We asked the secretary what she thought of the house she had helped build.

"It's fine. Can you imagine if we had not been here?"

Showing up was what it was all about, and America had been part of the show.

O ver the next six months, ten million visitors would walk through the Chinese pavilion. Seven million visited the American one, the second most popular exhibit. It was an astounding number considering that China had the home turf advantage. Washington and Beijing had shared the stage at the expo, and they were doing so increasingly around the world. They received an almost equal amount of the world's love, hate, and attention—but for very different reasons.

The two world powers were sparring over Iran, one of China's top suppliers of oil, and North Korea, China's poorer and unruly ally, both of which were at the fair. In fact, China had paid for North Korea's first-ever pavilion at a world expo. It stood wall-to-wall with Iran, and together in a forlorn corner, they formed two-thirds of the axis of evil. There were no lines outside either pavilion; whatever they had to offer was apparently of no interest to visitors. The Democratic People's Republic of Korea, or DPRK, as it was officially known, proudly advertised that it was a "Paradise for People." A fountain stood in the middle, though with its green and red lighting and cherubs, it looked more like Las Vegas than paradise. The tiny fake meadow with a small bridge over a tiny stream, symbolizing the country's Taedong River, and the video of children intercut with footage of a missile launch didn't help North Korea's image. Photographs of its dictator since 1994, Kim Jong Il, hung on the walls, as well as pictures of an eerily empty Pyongyang—more reminders, as if any were needed, that North Korea was not a happy country. The pavilion was small and felt bare; you could see the exit the instant you entered. The handful of people who walked into the neon-lit structure every now and then seemed to head straight for the way out.

Next door, China's second-largest supplier of oil attracted many more visitors than North Korea. Built to showcase traditional Islamic architecture, Iran's pavilion boasted its own fountain, Iranian musicians performed six times a day, and Iranian rugs were on sale on the upper level. A huge picture of Iran's political and religious leadership at prayer covered one of the walls, including President Mahmoud Ahmadinejad and Supreme Leader Ayatollah Ali Khamenei. The pavilion also displayed Iran's achievements, from medical equipment to a harp with lasers rather than strings and a stuffed goat. A proud placard declared that, apart from Iran, "Only a few countries such as the U.S., the UK, Canada and China have a cloned goat in their list of achievement." Despite belonging to that exclusive club of goat cloners, Iran somehow felt it still needed a nuclear program to feel powerful.

Hillary could be a mischievous diplomat, often prodding people out of established patterns to elicit different outcomes or more candid answers, but at the world expo she did not attempt any creative diplomacy by visiting the two pavilions. The stakes were too high. Iran was facing more sanctions, and there was no room for a free gesture of engagement. And North Korea stood accused of sinking a South Korean military ship, the *Cheonan*, that past March, killing forty-six seamen. Pyongyang denied it had done anything wrong; China claimed the ship had touched an American sea mine. The Russians were vague. Cold War reflexes died hard. Everybody had been waiting for the results of the international investigation that was attempting to determine exactly what had happened.

The results had been released just as we had arrived in Asia for the expo. "Based on all such relevant facts and classified analysis, we have reached the clear conclusion that the [Republic of Korea's] 'Cheonan' was sunk as the result of an external underwater explosion caused by a torpedo made in North Korea. The evidence points overwhelmingly to the conclusion that the torpedo was fired by a North Korean submarine. There is no other plausible explanation."

The North Koreans spouted angrily. On their state-run television stations, melodramatic newscasters who generally praised their leader Kim Jong Il in wavering lofty tones switched on the hatred and delivered warnings to the outside world at the top of their voices. Newspapers ran long diatribes.

"We had already warned the South Korean group of traitors not to make reckless remarks concerning the sinking of warship 'Cheonan' of the puppet navy. We sternly warn the U.S. and Japanese authorities and riff-raffs, their poor lackeys, to act with discretion. The world will clearly see what dear price the group of traitors will have to pay for the clumsy 'conspiratorial farce' and 'charade' concocted to stifle compatriots."

The expo had been a welcome interlude of cultural diplomacy, but tomorrow, in Beijing, Hillary would have to wade into this quagmire with the Chinese.

n the Chinese capital, Paul Narain was holding his last countdown meeting before our Sunday arrival. He had been assigned as the advance line officer for this trip and had been here a week already, his longest advance in two years on the job. He had already been on a four-day pre-advance trip a month earlier. He had clocked 130 hours and thousands of e-mails to Washington this week and was more sleep deprived than he had been on any other trip, worse even than the previous fall's Pakistan-to-Morocco-to-Egypt extravaganza. Every advance required two or three countdown meetings with about twenty embassy officials to make sure everything was running on schedule and every detail had been taken into account. This advance required four meetings and a gymnasium. Paul ran through all the details one more time. "This must be a mistake," he thought when he first caught a glimpse of the schedule and list of more than three hundred attendees. "We can't possibly take this many people on a trip."

There was no mistake. The U.S. government always arrived in a big way, but this group was monstrous. The United States and China were holding the Strategic and Economic Dialogue, a yearly, somewhat unwieldy, diplomatic exercise between two world powers. The S&ED was a two-day talkfest where anything and everything on which the two countries collaborated was on the table, from climate change to logging, education exchange programs, and China's currency exchange rate. It was a way for China and the United States to learn how to stay focused on everything they could agree on while working out their differences. A version of the dialogue had taken place during the Bush administration, but with Obama it became even more comprehensive.

Several hundred U.S. officials would be coming to town: every government agency, every department, every senior official wanted in on the dialogue with America's banker and was eager to be in the room with the world's next superpower. Even more than that, they wanted airtime to prove their relevance in the most important bilateral relationship their country had. Without it, the rest of the U.S. bureaucracy might think they were dispensable, and furthermore, if the Chinese didn't hear your voice in a room with three hundred people and dozens of U.S. government agencies, you were irrelevant. If the Chinese didn't know you existed, then you were out of the game. The S&ED was not just about tangible agreements but also about perception.

The United States had become obsessed with staying ahead of China. Nothing else seemed to matter. Just under half of Americans[24] believed that China had already surpassed the United States as the world's superpower, or was at least well under way to do so. They looked at the numbers and saw an economy still growing at a rate of 10 percent per year while theirs was sputtering along at 2 or 3 percent. Everything they bought at home seemed to be made in China. America was being drained by war while China was buying up Africa. China was booming, and the United States was going bust. It was the same middle-of-the-night anxiety that had suburban parents in America scheming for ways to afford Mandarin lessons. But the United States seemed fixated rather than motivated, a worry fueled by neurosis. The figures were certainly a reality, but America seemed to be thinking itself into further decline. Even Obama kept referring to China's faster trains and newer airports. The comparison was meant to entice Americans to buckle down and get to work, but it often had the opposite, depressing effect. The United States had fretted about being overtaken by Japan in the 1980s, and the Asian economic giant had eventually gone bust. But this time, Americans were sure it was real—China was going to swallow them.

Although 63 percent of Chinese believed their country had already overtaken, or was going to overtake, the United States as the world's superpower,[25] they were ambivalent about having the spotlight on their country. The *Global Times*, a government-backed newspaper, published an editorial in reaction to one of Obama's speeches, accusing the United States of China bashing, a "strategy that intensifies and exploits public fear of the unknown."

The importance of the relationship between the two countries was perhaps best symbolized by the size of the American embassy in Beijing—it was the largest in the world. Paul's first countdown meeting had taken place in a small auditorium with several dozen embassy employees. But every minute of the day, another employee approached him to say they should be included because they were a guide on one of the motorcade buses or in charge of food for the teams that would await the delegations' arrivals at the airport. So he held his final countdown meeting in the embassy gymnasium, and two hundred people attended. He ordered pizza for everybody. It lasted three hours. An entire team was assigned to organizing the motorcade. Usually, details of who sat in which car or which bus were included in the daily mini-schedules that each member of the delegation received. But in this case, there were buses and buses and buses, and the list of passengers was thirty-two pages long. Staple guns were brought in to handle the three hundred schedules. Paul and his colleagues from the State Department and the Treasury had planned everything down to the last detail. Their eager and meticulous Chinese counterparts went even further: at two in the morning, they knocked on Paul's door to review the planning one more time, just in case.

Paul just kept plugging along on the details. Part of the job of advance officers was to make sure that the form didn't destroy the content. The two days of talks would consist of one hundred hours of dialogue (a dream for the Chinese, who loved to dilute substance in the fluff of meetings and make grand statements that revealed little). But if Paul and his team rubbed their hosts the wrong way, demanding that four thousand credentials be printed in a day or trampling all over the flower beds on their way out, it would undo all the diplomatic efforts. In China, the form was almost more important than the substance. The obsession with preserving face drove everyone's actions. It was a concept that combined reputation, honor, and pride, and the threshold for losing face in China seemed higher than even in Arab societies. Paul also wanted everything to be perfect and wanted to make sure the secretary and all the other U.S. officials who were coming would look good, but for Americans small hiccups were not experienced as collective national embarrassment.

And now weeks, no, months of preparations were being overshadowed by the *Cheonan* crisis. Hours of talks on every single issue of interest to China and the United States had been planned, but the only topic anyone was interested in asking about was tension on the Korean peninsula. Washington wanted Beijing to acknowledge what had happened and scold Kim Jong Il, the "Dear Leader" in Pyongyang. All eyes were on China. How would it perform in this international crisis? Was it indeed turning into a responsible world power, telling off friends after bad behavior? Or would the cult of face prevail?

The *Cheonan* sinking was an unprecedented event for this generation
of Chinese leaders. They were treading very carefully. Bellicose
North Korea, a Soviet ally since 1948, became China's protégé during the
Korean War in the early 1950s. The relationship was a legacy of the Cold
War: it perpetuated a proxy war between China and the United States
and created a balance of power. The United States military was still seven
times larger than China's, but with its nuclear program and missile testing, Pyongyang was helping Beijing to keep Washington on its toes.

Kim Il Sung, North Korea's first ruler, had been installed in the
North after the end of World War II by Soviet leader Joseph Stalin. Below
the 38th parallel that divided the country, the South was in the American
camp. But in 1950, Kim decided he wanted to unify the country under his
command. He convinced China's Mao Zedong that North Korean troops
would be able to march south of the 38th parallel that divided the country and conquer it—so quickly, in fact, that the United States would have
no time to send troops to help its ally, Syngman Rhee, in Seoul even if it
wanted to.

Mao started planning China's entry into the Korean War before U.S.
troops even got close to the 38th parallel, just in case, although he entered
the war only when the Americans overreached.[26] Mao wanted to make
sure North Korea wouldn't fall; he wanted to prevent American imperialism from becoming victorious, dizzy with success and in a position to
threaten China.[27] Mao also did it to mobilize public opinion in China and
consolidate his own power in a country emerging from civil war. Although
tens of thousand of Chinese troops died in the war, they fought the United
States to a stalemate on the 38th parallel and held on to North Korea. The
Communist country emerged with its sense of national pride and unity
restored. Crucially, the Chinese were led to believe that the war started
because of America's expansionist designs rather than an invasion
launched by their North Korean friends. Decades later, the narrative per-
sisted: North Korea was the underdog, America the imperialist hegemon.

Unlike the United States, which had some fifty formal military alliances and countless programs of cooperation binding it to dozens of
countries around the world, China's friends were strategic liabilities.
Many of China's friends were weak, like Nepal and Cambodia; its closest
allies were really client states, and rogue ones at that: North Korea and

Burma. Pyongyang was proving to be increasingly unpredictable and capricious. The North Koreans saw China as their ATM, and though Beijing kept them afloat with food and aid, North Korea was always trying to attract America's attention, pushing for direct talks with Washington while the United States insisted that any negotiations with Pyongyang had to include the Chinese, the Japanese, and other world players. The North Koreans just wanted a deal with America. The Chinese were relieved that at least Burma seemed reliable, staying in their camp. China also had many business partners, but its checkbook was meant for resources to feed its own growing economy—not love.

Sitting on the tarmac in Shanghai, with dozens of planes ahead of us lined up for takeoff, we settled into our seats for a long wait. SAM rarely, if ever, requested special treatment. But the Chinese were not about to let the American secretary of state bake in the midday sun in an aluminum tube, so we taxied to the head of the line and took off for Beijing, where we landed two hours later to a hiccup that no amount of planning by Paul and his team could have foreseen.

The DS agents and the traveling press corps were always first off the plane, through the back door and down the stairs, giving Fred's team time to take up their positions on the ground and allowing the camera crew traveling with us, recording the secretary's every move, to be ready to film her waving hello as she came out of the front door of the plane. During those few minutes, with Huma's help, Hillary would freshen up in her cabin, putting on the finishing touches to her attire.

But in Beijing, airport workers had trouble lining up the stairs with the front door of the plane. The hydraulic lift didn't seem to work. There was frantic yammering in the walkie-talkies and running around. Chinese officials, impassive at first, stood in line waiting to greet their VIP guest. Airport workers drove a second set of stairs to the plane, but America's plane and China's steps just did not want to line up. The Chinese officials were starting to fidget. This was an embarrassment to their country. Third time lucky—the American ambassador to China, Jon Huntsman, walked up the steps and escorted the secretary down. As always, Fred emerged a few moments later, followed by Huma, to make sure photographers could first get a clear shot of the secretary as she walked down.

State Councilor Dai Bingguo hosted Clinton at dinner, as always a stunningly delicate display of hospitality with elaborate meals and entertainment. The Chinese always devoted the first meeting or meal to small talk and entertainment. They asked her about her trip so far and how she had enjoyed Shanghai.

Since her first trip to Asia, in February 2009, Clinton had grown more comfortable at managing the conversation with the Chinese and was able to draw her interlocutors out of the established script. In a very affable way, she told Dai that while there would be many opportunities over the coming two days to discuss heavy subjects, she needed to touch base on a few things right away. Lee Myung-bak, the president of South Korea, was giving an address to the nation the following day, and Clinton wanted to hear from Dai about how China viewed the situation, what it was prepared to do to make sure the *Cheonan* situation did not escalate. She was also keen to hear more about the state of mind and health of Kim Jong Il, who had just visited Beijing. As usual, Dai didn't say much. The Chinese were reticent about their North Korean friends, as they knew American officials would brief the press, and it would be in the newspapers in no time.

The following day, the S&ED was logistically flawless, but not free of worry and tension. Discussions between the Chinese and the Americans were a very polite tug-of-war on many issues. China kept its currency artificially low so that its goods stayed cheap and appealing to buyers around the world. Washington said this was unfair competition and regularly pushed Beijing to appreciate its currency. But now Europe was in a financial crisis, Greece couldn't pay its debts anymore, and the euro was looking shaky. The Chinese worried about the impact the crisis would have on their exports. This was not the time to make their products more expensive. The United States insisted the European crisis would not affect global growth, but the Treasury secretary Timothy Geithner was worried enough that he was planning to travel to the Old Continent to tell the Europeans to get their act together before they jeopardized America's own, very slow, economic recovery.

And there was, of course, the *Cheonan*. All day long, the Chinese had said almost nothing in public about the incident. At the end of the day, Clinton held a press conference, alone, to commend the wise and prudent leadership of President Lee, who had just given his address. When journalists prodded her about what the Chinese were ready to do about their rogue ally, Clinton appealed to China's sense of responsibility.

"The Chinese understand the reaction by the South Koreans; and they also understand our unique responsibility for the peace and stability on the Korean Peninsula," Clinton replied. She praised the cooperation with China in the past in response to North Korean "provocations" and said they were discussing how to cooperate again now. The *Cheonan* had become a category of its own in the S&ED.

Clinton also said a few words about an important announcement that had been made farther east, in Tokyo.

"I want to commend Prime Minister Hatoyama for making the difficult, but nevertheless correct, decision to relocate the Futenma facility inside Okinawa," she said.

The announcement by Yukio Hatoyama to stick to the agreement with the United States and relocate the American base on Okinawa itself was the fruit of a year and a half of negotiation with the Japanese. It had started on Clinton's first trip to Asia, in February 2009, when she had met with the Democratic Party of Japan—at the time, the opposition party. The *Cheonan* incident and growing Chinese bluster reminded Japan of the dangers lurking in the region. Earlier in the spring, Chinese helicopters had buzzed a Japanese destroyer, a few hundred miles away from Okinawa, and ten Chinese warships had sailed worryingly close to the southern tip of the Japanese archipelago. China was flexing its muscles, and Japan was suddenly feeling rather exposed. These were all good reasons to keep the Americans happy and close.

"As a former politician," Hillary continued, "I know how hard Prime Minister Hatoyama's decision was, and I thank him for his courage and determination to fulfill his commitments." Hillary saw her past as a politician who had had to make difficult compromises as one of her key assets: she empathized with her interlocutors, and they felt valued and understood. It didn't mean they were ready to sign away their country if she asked, her efforts to reason with Afghanistan's president Hamid Karzai would have little impact. But such empathy did sometimes help leaders travel that last mile to make a decision, such as now.

"This is truly the foundation for our future work as allies in the Asia Pacific region," Hillary added. The Obama administration was laying that foundation very quietly, block by block.

* * *

After two full days in Beijing, it was time for the grand finale inside the Great Hall of the People, just off Tiananmen Square. The two sides were keen to show that the two days of dialogue had produced something tangible. So with some pomp, a signing ceremony took place for a handful of memorandums of understanding on random topics from nuclear safety to eco-partnership and infectious diseases. American officials and their Chinese counterparts sat down at a long table, one after the other, to sign the documents, with a floor-to-ceiling dark-blue backdrop behind them, with the words "US-China Strategic and Economic Dialogue" at the top. Standing behind them, Clinton looked on with a slightly amused face, Geithner to her right and Vice Premier Wang Qishan and Councilor Dai on her left. The signing done, the four top officials sat down at the table with microphones in front of them, their faces peering from behind big colorful bouquets atop a green tablecloth, rows of journalists facing them. It looked just like a press conference, but this was China. There would be no questions to China's top officials, only statements from them. Clinton and Geithner would hold a press conference later at their hotel.

Dai Bingguo praised the "successful conclusion" of the dialogue. What did that mean in Chinese terms? Everybody agreed on everything? No big fights erupted? Difficult topics were avoided? It was hard to tell from listening to Dai. He sounded like a self-help business guru, talking about advancing cooperation to achieve results, the spirit and principles of communication, and the need to handle sensitive issues properly. It was all peppered with profuse use of the words "respect," "mutual trust," and "core interests."

"Only by helping each other out as passengers in this gigantic ship of the China-U.S. relationship will we be able to move forward, braving winds and waves," he added.

Meanwhile, China's own, real ships had been causing waves in the high seas of the region. There was the Japanese destroyer incident earlier in the spring; the warships close to the southern tip; and in the South China Sea, the Chinese were making ripples that were upsetting neighbors from Vietnam to Malaysia and the Philippines.

We woke up on Wednesday, one week into our trip, eager to go home, but we still had to swing by Seoul. America's best friend in the region needed some loving reassurance after the *Cheonan* attack. Clinton went to lunch with President Lee at the Blue House, but there would be no statements for the media, so we camped out at the Foreign Ministry waiting for the press conference to start. An e-mail arrived about Hillary's next trip, to Latin America, in two weeks' time. Philippe and his team were always busy planning trips, during trips, after trips—it was never-ending.

After the press conference, we ran to the vans and drove off to the airport to be reunited with SAM. The stories had already been e-mailed, broadcast, and telephoned to the world; we had a sixteen-hour-long plane ride home ahead of us. Sixteen hours to recover from sleep deprivation. Some officials were still high on adrenaline, and they wanted to share their views of what they thought had been a good trip. In general, we were constantly asking officials for briefings, but sometimes we just wanted to be left alone.

Two officials crossed the Line of Death to share with us what they had gleaned from Chinese officials. With one of them standing in the aisle, the other sitting on an armrest, those of us in the back rows leaned over the chairs to hear.

These types of briefings were done "on background," meaning we could not name the people who were speaking to us, only identify them as senior officials. The anonymity allowed them to speak more freely by giving them a degree of plausible deniability, if things didn't develop as they had anticipated. There was, of course, spin: officials wanted to shape the story to their advantage and put their version of events forward with the facts that suited them. But they could also be very open about the content of their talks, the goals they were aiming for, and the obstacles in the way. There are always exceptions, but as a rule, there were no lies: if officials couldn't share information, they would ignore the question or work around it. Nevertheless, even on background, the candor of comments by American officials could infuriate the countries that were the subject of the conversation, countries like Russia, Pakistan, and China, where information is opaque, access to officials severely controlled, and the version of events put forward by the state often wildly divergent from the reality.

Somewhere above the Pacific Ocean, we were told that China was likely to abandon its caution and join international condemnation of North Korea's role in the sinking of the *Cheonan*. The prime minister of

China, Wen Jiabao, was traveling to South Korea for a summit over the weekend, and he was expected to express regret for the loss of South Korean lives and accept the findings of the international investigation about the *Cheonan* sinking. The officials told us the Chinese were frustrated by the erratic and irresponsible behavior of the North Koreans. The current leadership did not have the same strong, historical ties to Pyongyang as their predecessors did. They felt stuck with their ally and its sick, aging leader, Kim Jong Il.

We also learned that China's military, the People's Liberation Army, was finally going to extend an invitation to visit Beijing to Robert Gates, the U.S. secretary of defense. Gates had been trying to visit for a while, but the PLA, a powerhouse of its own, weighed in heavily on the country's domestic and foreign policy decisions. For a while, it had expressed its discontent with Washington by refusing to welcome Gates and minimizing military-to-military contact.

Hillary always promoted both government-to-government and people-to-people contact around the world in her visits, but she also understood the need for displays of strength. She looked after diplomacy and development; Gates, her ally in Obama's cabinet, was the implementer of defense. Together, the two secretaries formed a close team in Washington, usually taking the same side on issues. Clinton had purposely included top officers in her delegation to force the door open on military-to-military conversation. With a wide grin, the officials on the plane told us that the PLA might soon have an opening on its schedule for a Gates visit.

There was a collective eye roll from all the journalists. This background briefing was clearly all positive spin, and we were not buying it. It was clear to us that while the Chinese had nodded with a smile to Hillary and her team, the delegation had really come up empty-handed on the issues that were of core interest to Washington.

But if the United States was often a reluctant world power, the Chinese barely wanted to dip their toes, let alone dive, into the sea of world responsibilities. They weren't sure their big new shiny boat would actually float, and they certainly didn't want to lose face if it sank; they tried to stay as neutral as possible, sitting under a formal, elaborately constructed beach umbrella on the shore. On Sunday in South Korea, Wen offered his condolences for the families of the South Korean sailors; he also called for restraint and warned in general about the consequences of war. But there was no expression of regret for the incident and certainly no public condemnation of China's protégé. Gates would not be invited to visit Beijing for another six months.

Watching from Washington in the days after our return, I thought back to the conversation on the plane. My colleagues and I had been right; it was all wishful thinking. But before the end of the year, I would come to understand why the American officials had sounded so positive.

10

MEET ME IN
THE SEA

The *Cheonan* crisis carried on into the summer. At the United Nations, members of the Security Council listened to the South and North Koreans present their version of events and the results of their investigation. South Korea and its allies wanted to send a clear, unequivocal message to North Korea that its behavior would not be tolerated. But no one was sure how to do that. China would veto any UN resolution condemning the DPRK. The U.S. ambassador to the UN, Susan Rice, explored different options, while Kurt Campbell, the top man in charge of Asia at the State Department, traveled to Seoul to discuss these options with the South Koreans. The Security Council finally compromised and, in a presidential statement, condemned the *Cheonan* attack without naming North Korea as the perpetrator. Such statements were not resolutions; they were not binding and carried little weight.

Hillary had been keeping tabs on the discussion while juggling other crises and traveling twenty-one thousand miles to Latin America and Europe. Now it was time for her to show more support for South Korea. But because the earth was round and everywhere was always on the way to everywhere else, when we left at the end of July for South Korea, we first made stops in Pakistan and Afghanistan.

Clinton's schedule in Islamabad was once again full of public diplomacy events. She was plowing ahead, trying to maintain good relationships with the civilian leadership, the military, and the people. It was important to show that the United States didn't reduce its relationship with Pakistan to one person, as had happened in the past with military rulers. But it was exhausting to be Pakistan's friend. Washington still promised a long-term relationship, but the Pakistanis didn't fully trust the offer. Every now and then, Hillary would ask Vali, the Iranian American expert on Pakistan, "We gave them all this money, why are they still screaming at us?" Or she would ask how Pakistan would respond if the United States made a certain move or launched an initiative. Vali never had a clear, black-and-white answer for Hillary; there were none in countries like Pakistan, where political behavior was not always dictated by reason—or at least not the same rationale as the West.

In Kabul, Clinton was attending an international conference to show support for Hamid Karzai's government. Our stops here were short and felt claustrophobic. The Bubble shrank all the way down to the embassy compound and one outside location—the presidential palace or the foreign ministry, both barely a five-minute drive away, in heavily armored cars. Clinton met "real" Afghans during events held at the embassy, people the U.S. embassy trusted enough to bring into the compound. We slept in "hooches," a Vietnam War–era slang word for a thatched hut, except that in Kabul they were drab trailers, and it was always cold.

This was a country that the United States was trying to get out of; our stops seemed to reflect that. In and out, quickly, in one piece. Afghanistan was not America's future; it was the past, a painful, bloodied, scarred past and a bottomless money pit like Iraq. The military adventure in those two countries had been dragging America down for years, morally and financially. Like so often in the past, the minute U.S. troops set foot in a country, they started looking for the exit, perhaps understandably. The reluctant superpower never planned to stay long, but that was exactly why it was so hard to get out: missions were ill-prepared and ill-defined. Success, too, was ill-defined.

"You'll know it when you see it," Richard Holbrooke, the envoy for Afghanistan Pakistan, had said. But most Americans didn't have the patience for that. They were upfront, efficient, result-driven people who expected quick turnarounds and believed every problem had a solution.

In Iraq, Afghanistan, Pakistan, the Middle East, and so many other places, time was elastic. Tomorrow meant sometime in the future. Yes could mean no, no was sometimes yes.

Eventually, before anything was really fixed in Afghanistan or elsewhere, and sometimes before the real problems had even started, Americans had moved on, they had other problems to tend to. People on the ground could feel invaded, abandoned, and betrayed all at once. They saw America as an impatient, fickle friend. It didn't matter how much money the United States had invested, wasted, spent; it didn't matter how many U.S. troops had died.

They wanted more, just like we had in Beirut during the war.

O n the flight to Seoul, we ate a light dinner: blackened chicken salad with cut melon and watermelon for dessert. We chatted to some of the officials in the nook near the lavatory. Hillary's daughter, Chelsea, was getting married that summer, as well as Hillary's deputy chief of staff, Huma. Huma told stories about dresses and guest lists for both weddings.

We landed ten hours later, just past seven in the morning, groggy and crumpled. Even the gray morning light of Seoul was too glaring. We had an eleven-hour day ahead of us. Clinton's suitcases, black garment bags and a large red cabin carryall, came down the steps and were carried down the red carpet to the waiting limousine. Two rows of South Korean men in wide yellow silk pants, black coats, and red flowing sleeves stood guard on either side.

Clinton emerged at the top of the stairs a few minutes later. She had changed into a red jacket and blue trousers just before landing. Beaming behind her sunglasses, she walked down the steps to be greeted on the tarmac by the South Korean ambassador to the United States. She was excited about this stop. It was one more building block in the administration's policy toward Asia that had been carefully choreographed.

We would have a bit of time at the hotel to freshen up before the one-hour drive to the Demilitarized Zone, or DMZ, the border between South and North Korea. We would be long gone by the time Lew and his team brought our luggage to the hotel, so the trick on trips like this was to pack toiletries and a change of clothes before handing over your luggage for pickup—in this case, pickup had been twenty hours ago.

Outside the hotel our motorcade grew bigger. The U.S. defense secretary Robert Gates was joining Clinton on her excursion for a display of soft and hard U.S. power. It was rare for American secretaries of defense and state to travel together, and it was the first joint visit to the DMZ. America was making its presence felt in Asia in an unprecedented fashion. The South Korean officials traveled to the border by helicopter, a much faster ride. But Hillary didn't like noisy, windy helicopter rides and avoided them whenever possible. Our press buses, rented by the embassy for the delegation, had green "Foreign tourists on board" signs on the windshields. An odd warning, but South Korea was working hard to be friendlier to foreigners, who often felt discriminated against in one of the most racially homogeneous countries in the world. Seoul was going to host the G20 summit later in the year, and the Ministries of Education and Culture had just announced a new initiative to educate students in global etiquette. The guidebook used in classes instructed students on their "role as global citizens and on how to interact with foreigners."[28]

If the green signs were meant to encourage motorists to let the clueless foreigners through, they failed. As soon as we departed from the hotel, the back of the long motorcade was separated from officials at the front by a swarm of cars that jutted in between our buses. Our bus drivers were not embassy employees, and despite the police escort, they did not feel empowered to drive through red lights.

The State Department media handlers on our buses were frantically e-mailing their colleagues in the cars up ahead to inform them that the press was trailing behind. Without the journalists, there would be no photos of the event. News eventually reached Fred, in the secretary's car, and the front of the motorcade slowed down to a snail's pace on the highway while the rest of us caught up.

Bernadette Meehan was the line officer with us on her first advance trip. She had moved back to Washington recently from Dubai. During the long car ride, her mind raced with the same thoughts that troubled all her colleagues. Did she have the number of the site officer at the next stop saved in her phone? Did she have a set of earpieces with her for the secretary for the translation at the press conference later? Did she remember to tell the secretary that Gates was getting into her car when they reached the DMZ? Did she check that the toilet was clean and the door unlocked at the Freedom House building? Did she tell the site officer at the observation post to make sure they took off the lens caps before handing the binoculars to the two secretaries? Did she have her briefing paper for the next event? She thought of everything, again and again, nine hundred times. All night, she had tossed and turned going through every minute of the day. Every mundane detail mattered. It could be tomorrow's headline or front-page picture. The power was in the details, and she was in charge of them

The visit to the border with North Korea had been conceived as a message, a photo opportunity to project American power in Asia but also to poke North Korea in the eye. Behind the strutting was some frustration. For more than a year now, the Obama administration had tried to get Pyongyang to sit down again for talks about giving up its nuclear program. There had been many rounds of negotiations before 2009, but the "Dear Leader," Kim Jong Il, was recalcitrant and wary of giving up leverage. Without nukes, he was nothing, just another dictator with a famished people on a territory of no consequence. If he was to give them up, he wanted something big in return, like eternal American friendship. He demanded attention with erratic behavior like firing missiles or sinking South Korean ships.

The DMZ is a two-mile-wide buffer zone through which runs the Military Demarcation Line (MDL), one of the last two remaining Cold War–era dividing lines splitting a country into north and south. The other is the Green Line that divides the island of Cyprus. There are many other tense borders between countries around the world, between Lebanon and Israel, or Pakistan and India. At the Wagah crossing, Pakistani and Indian officers mount an elaborate daily drama, standing eyeball to eyeball, in colorful costumes, as they shut the border crossing between the two countries at dusk, to the sound of horns, while villagers and tourists on both sides cheer and clap wildly.

But the MDL had separated one people into two countries for so long that they had become two people—the north was poor, ravaged by famine. Scientists found that North Koreans had become a few inches shorter than their cousins to the south. South Korea, meanwhile, had prospered into the world's fourteenth-largest economy, its well-fed people growing taller by a few inches. Seen from the sky at night, North Korea was a dark spot with one speck of light, Pyongyang. On Google maps, the North was one large, unknown patch of white while the South was bright and covered in a yellowish-orange grid of highways and roads.

Like at Wagah, North and South Korean soldiers came face-to-face, in one location along the 160-mile line splitting their country—the Joint Security Area (JSA) in the abandoned village of Panmunjom. Also known as the Truce Village, it was a circular enclave that straddled the demarcation line, and we were heading there with Clinton and Gates. Despite the lush greenery on both sides, the area felt barren and desolate, bristling with hostility. Signs warned about land mines. The drizzle added a feeling of despair.

While we waited below in the "village," the limousine carrying Clinton and Gates drove up the hill to Observation Post Ouellette, a small outpost with a watchtower, overlooking the northern side of the DMZ. In the front seat, Fred's eyes scanned his surroundings carefully. The American and South Korean soldiers from the UN mission were on full alert, but he had ultimate responsibility for his package. North Korean soldiers from the Korean People's Army were easily provoked, and the Joint Security Area had been the scene of several violent incidents over the years, including the gruesome "axe murder" incident in 1976, when North Korean soldiers seized axes being used by a UN team to prune a tree and killed two American soldiers. Since then, the demarcation line was enforced within the JSA, which had been a neutral zone until then; South and North Koreans now had to stick to their side of the area. There had been no violence since the 1980s, but the North was unpredictable and on edge following the condemnation it had faced after the *Cheonan* sinking.

Holding a large black umbrella, Clinton walked up the steps to the observation post, ringed by low walls covered in camouflage netting. Gates followed, and the two of them shook hands with the soldiers manning the post. Fred stopped halfway up the stairs, staying out of the range of the camera lenses. The drizzle stopped briefly, the umbrellas were put away, the two secretaries were handed binoculars, and perfect pictures were produced: America's war and peace envoys, wearing a matching red tie and a red coral necklace, respectively, standing at the frontier of liberty, peering into the distance, with the American, UN, and Republic of Korea (ROK) flags fluttering on tall poles behind them.

In the Truce Village below, a cluster of rectangular blue one-story huts with windows straddled the demarcation line. ROK soldiers from the Joint Security Area stood guard, positioned at the southern corners of the buildings, half their bodies hidden by the stark structures. The stance was meant to give the North a smaller area to target and allow the soldiers to signal to the South if needed. A modified tae kwon do stance, known as ROK-ready position, it signaled readiness to fight or to take cover if needed. The soldiers maintained it as long as there were visitors in the JSA, including inside the buildings.

Gates, Clinton, and their South Korean counterparts were escorted into one of the blue huts: the Military Armistice Commission building, where talks take place between North and South around a green-felt-covered conference table. One door opened onto the South, the other onto the North.

Inside, a soldier also stood in an ROK-ready position, with his back against the blue door that opened onto the other side—the "Paradise for People." Why would any North Korean want to leave paradise for the South? But if they did, they'd have to walk over his dead body. The soldier kept his fists clenched and his reflective sunglasses on, even indoors, no winks or smiles, no humanity. To the North Koreans, he looked cold and ruthless; he was the enemy incarnate. It was almost comical, except that people were dying on both sides of the demarcation line, which, in this building, ran through a table.

Peering through the window, an unusually tall North Korean soldier stood outside, likely wondering what the commotion was all about. This was a popular tourist destination, like Checkpoint Charlie at the Berlin Wall. But tourists did not come with bulletproof cars or a retinue of bodyguards as this group did. North Koreans posted here were elite soldiers, and this soldier would have been briefed by his superiors when they picked up indications that a high-profile visit was being prepared. I couldn't help wondering whether he recognized Hillary. Had he seen pictures of her? What did he know about the outside world? What did he wish for?

Fed a steady diet of propaganda about America's evil designs on his country, the soldier may have simply wanted to make sure no one crossed into his territory. For a few minutes, he was unsuccessful. Clinton and Gates had stepped to the North's side of the blue room. They were in North Korea. They did not look back at the soldier, though Gates, a slightly mischievous smile on his face, seemed to have trouble resisting doing just that.

We drove back into Seoul, for a visit to the twenty-thousand-square-foot War Memorial of Korea, part war museum, part history lesson, about the many wars that have shaped Korea over the centuries until the Korean War of the 1950s. The conflict killed hundreds of thousands: almost 40,000 American soldiers were killed in action or missing, the South Koreans lost at least 45,000 soldiers, and several thousand from allied countries died, too. Over 700,000 Chinese and North Koreans died.

The soldiers who had died fighting for South Korea, against the advance of Communism, were remembered in a way reminiscent of the sober Vietnam Veterans Memorial Wall in Washington. In a long outdoor gallery, tall black panels set against stone walls were engraved with the names of all the soldiers who had died, with a mention of the country or the American state.

As soon as we arrived, Clinton, Gates, and their entourage took a pause in a room inside the museum. They were going to pay a choreographically complex homage around the large memorial, and though they'd received a printed briefing from their teams—in Hillary's case, her usual truncated briefing checklist—Bernadette was going to walk them through it one final time.

Clinton outranked Gates in the cabinet, but the secretary of defense was very easygoing and followed Clinton's schedule and preferences without complaint. Hillary could power through the day and munch on an apple or a sandwich in the car until there was a break in the schedule for a meal or until she was done for the day: she didn't need to eat at a set time. But Gates had one demand: he needed to stop for twenty minutes for lunch. Two packed lunches had been arranged: a burger and fries for him, a chicken sandwich for Clinton. Bernadette had gobbled down a packet of trail mix, and now the two secretaries ate while listening to her instructions about stages, bells ringing, and rope lines.

Outside, the traveling press corps was also being briefed about the event, the photographer and cameraman so they knew how the subject of their pictures was going to move and the rest of us so that we could make sure to stay out of the shot.

Perfect pictures of Clinton and Gates at the DMZ and at the memorial ran on the front pages of South Korea's morning papers. The United States had just slapped more sanctions on North Korea. The nuclear-powered aircraft carrier USS *George Washington* was docked in the southern port of Busan. In just a few days, 8,000 American and South Korean troops would come together for a large military training exercise, Invincible Spirit, with a U.S. Navy carrier as well as the South Korean air force and submarines. That was on top of the 28,500 American troops already stationed in South Korea.

The South Koreans would sleep better tonight. Their big, powerful friend was there, its reassuring presence and soothing words giving them strength in the face of their belligerent northern cousins and their Chinese protector. It looked like it was all just a show, but there was an imperceptible yet definite shift under way in the region.

From Afghanistan and Pakistan to South Korea, we were now moving on to Vietnam. Our trip was a tour of America's wars, past and present. The Obama administration saw America's future very much tied to the Pacific area. For Clinton, there were also lessons to be drawn from the past.

"We saw South Korea struggle to become a functioning democracy—huge amounts of instability, coups, corruption, scandal, you name it," Clinton said.

"I think it's good to remind ourselves that the United States has stood with countries that went through a lot of ups and downs for a lot longer than eight years, and it is important to recognize what's at stake . . . in Afghanistan. This is a country that we left before, much to our dismay, and we can't do it again."

Hillary had a keen eye and memory for detail, but she always tried to look at the bigger picture. Success can be elusive for decades, but eventually, with careful work, she believed things would fall into place. A country once as hostile to the United States as it could have been, Vietnam now welcomed Clinton to celebrate fifteen years of friendship with the United States. The past seemed to weigh much less on Southeast Asia than it did on Pakistan or the Middle East.

Clinton was also in Vietnam for another serving of alphabet soup. ASEAN and TAC were back. As promised in February 2009, she had signed the Treaty of Amity and Cooperation and attended several Asian summits already; goodwill toward the United States was on the rise in a region where symbolic gestures meant a lot. Almost simultaneously, countries were also coming closer to the United States because a giant was awakening in their region.

For decades, China has sparred with neighbors around the South China Sea over the Spratly and Paracel island chains. Chinese forces seized the western Paracels from Vietnam in 1974 and sank three Vietnamese naval vessels in a sea battle in 1988. China had recently announced plans to develop the islands for tourism. Vietnam was furious because it had never recognized China's control over the Paracels. The South China Sea provided rich fishing grounds and was believed to have large oil and natural gas reserves. Busy sea-lanes were also a crucial conduit for resources feeding China's economy. In March, the Chinese government had told American officials at the White House to stay out of the South China Sea. They would solve any dispute with individual countries. At the S&ED in May, Hillary had heard the same message. The Chinese were elevating the South China Sea to a key national interest, at the same level as Taiwan and Tibet, and they were starting to serve notice to other countries to back off.

Vietnam, the Philippines, Malaysia, and others were looking for help and for strength in numbers, and the United States saw an opportunity to push back against China. Hillary, Kurt, and Jake worked with all the Asian representatives to choreograph carefully their approach to the Chinese during one of the meetings. The Asian countries would speak first. Clinton would go last. One after the other, the Asian ministers voiced their anger and concern about China's aggressive behavior on the high seas. The Chinese foreign minister Yang Jiechi was taken aback. As the session progressed, he got angrier. By the time Clinton spoke, he was furious. When it was his turn to speak, Yang Jiechi was still fuming at the temerity of the small countries that had brought up the South China Sea, twelve in all. "China is a big country and other countries are small countries and that is just a fact," said Yang, staring at his counterparts.

Chinese maps dating to before the Communist revolution appeared to place most of the South China Sea under Chinese sovereignty, and China was ready to reclaim its territory. Over the last couple of years, China's swagger had grown. Beijing may not have wanted to be a superpower, but it was becoming more assertive. After initially fawning over the new American president and working to make the transition of ties successful, the Chinese government had sized up the Obama administration, its conciliatory tone, its attempts to reach out to foes, Hillary's apparent soft-pedaling on human rights, and, most of all, the financial crisis of 2008. Weighing all of this, it concluded it could push America around. There had been much debate among ruling officials in Beijing about American decline and many of them believed it was indeed happening. The coordinated move during a diplomatic meeting behind closed doors took the Chinese by surprise.

"The United States, like every nation, has a national interest in freedom of navigation, open access to Asia's maritime commons, and respect for international law in the South China Sea," Clinton said a bit later during a press conference at the end of the summit. She was only getting started.

"The United States supports a collaborative diplomatic process for all claimants to resolve the various territorial disputes without coercion," she went on. "We encourage the parties to reach agreement on a full code of conduct. The U.S. is prepared to facilitate initiatives and confidence building measures consistent with the [2002 joint China-ASEAN] declaration."

The United States? Facilitate initiatives? The Chinese were livid. Not only was the United States carrying out naval exercises with South Korea in China's own backyard, but now America was wading into an Asian family dispute. Washington was supposed to be retreating from the world, not sailing into the Pacific. Something had gone terribly wrong.

Suddenly, China the rising Asian giant looked very lonely. Though it shared borders with fourteen countries, when it looked around, China saw no real allies, no one it really shared values with, no one it could count on. China was standing in a crowded room and was utterly lonely. Over the last century, China had been at war with India, Russia, and Japan. None of these countries really liked or trusted each other. Sure, Pakistan was a friend, but it was a heap of problems. And North Korea and Burma were in a whole different category.

China's ruling Communist Party was obsessed first and foremost with its own survival. Its leaders needed to keep 1.3 billion people fed, housed, and happy enough so that they wouldn't threaten the stability of the regime. Nationalism was frequently used to dismiss criticism of the current system as part of a historic conspiracy by foreigners to denigrate

China. The bellicose behavior on the South China Sea fed into that narrative, helping the party's quest to look powerful and to stay in power. Chinese officials seemed unwilling or unable to make conciliatory gestures toward their neighbors to calm their fears. Suddenly, America seemed a much more appealing superpower to China's neighbors, and China lost an opportunity to take the lead in the region. Instead of becoming an Asian giant that could challenge Western hegemony, China remained a scary ogre.

America's careful diplomacy combined with China's missteps meant that Asia was a bright spot in the Obama administration's foreign policy, but the good news made few headlines. There never seemed to be much room for optimism on front pages covered with stories about the dismal state of the world. Even administration officials who worked on other regions and hot spots were unable to recognize the nascent success in Asia, a policy that would become known as the "Asia pivot."

The news back at home wasn't great, either.

11

MAKING THE CUT

Yellow leaves were starting to fall, and the mood in Washington was grim as the end of 2010 approached. The newspapers were full of stories about people losing their homes, towns trying to balance their budgets, and industries struggling to stay alive while Wall Street executives got paid million-dollar bonuses.

A government town, Washington suffered much less than the rest of the country; restaurants were full and new ones continued to open, new residential buildings were under construction, and international institutions brought a steady stream of visitors into the city. But the District was not immune to the pervasive nationwide malaise about where America was heading. My American friends worried not just about their jobs but about the future of their country. What was America really about these days? It didn't feel like the land of opportunity to them, so what did it represent? The contrarian, radical-right Tea Party movement looked like it was sweeping the country. America's first black president was not uniting or transforming the country. In fact, the United States felt more divided than before, politics as partisan as ever. Unemployment stagnated around 9 percent—a nagging reminder that Obama's efforts to revive the economy were still failing. The extent of the financial crisis that had hit the United States—and much of the world—in 2008 was more extensive than anyone had first realized. It would take patient, diligent work to unravel years of damage, but unemployed and frustrated people could not wait any longer.

In November, Americans voted in the midterm elections for Congress and showed their lack of patience on the home front. Americans often seemed to dole out time like accountants: the minute something didn't work, they gave up and tried something else. Two years after electing change, they voted for change again. The Democrats lost sixty-two seats and their majority in Congress. They still had a tiny majority in the Senate. Obama had only barely managed to get his health care reform plan through Congress in March, even with a Democratic majority in both houses. The next two years were looking exceedingly difficult.

Around the globe, it appeared that chaos had broken out too. World news was never an orderly event, and wars, economic meltdowns, and earthquakes didn't politely wait their turn, but somehow, during this time, the globe felt rudderless.

I headed out after work one day in mid-November to meet a high-level official for an informal conversation about American diplomacy; such conversations were a staple of life for journalists in Washington. A lot of the conversations were had on the phone or by e-mail when you needed a quick comment or one quote for a story, but whenever possible breakfasts, coffees, lunches, drinks, and dinners were arranged. Quality face time was important to develop a level of trust that enabled officials to part with some of their more interesting information, beyond the talking points issued in statements. If you were a reporter for a top national American media outlet, your access was almost guaranteed. Others, especially foreigners, had to work a bit harder. It was naturally in the interest of officials to talk to the press, so they could put their mark on the stories that were published. Sometimes they called you because they wanted something out there—all sources have an agenda. As a journalist, your responsibility was to read between the lines and corroborate the facts. In a country like Lebanon or Pakistan, the task was even harder as it involved determining whether officials were giving you facts or outright lying and rumormongering. There was often a remarkable openness to what American officials said in private, a tangible connection to the heart of the decision-making machine. On the plane, Hillary spoke to us often, off the record, which meant we could not use the information, but it added context to the knowledge we had about a developing story. Robert Gates did the same with reporters on his plane.

The briefings we got regularly by lower-ranking administration officials allowed us to understand what they were thinking, what they were trying to do, and, sometimes, what they were trying to hide. Even when European or Arab diplomats took on a confidential tone and said, "Let's talk off the record," what followed was often just a repetition of what they had said in public. Occasionally, briefings by U.S. officials were utterly useless: when negotiations were in a delicate phase or they had nothing to show for their efforts or, as in any government, if they simply didn't want to share sensitive information. President Obama gave regular interviews and answered questions often, either alone or in press conferences with visiting foreign leaders. Reporters did not get to speak to the president as often as they did with Clinton or Gates, but White House reporters would be able to question someone very senior who was in the room with him when a key decision was taken, for example. American officials—from cabinet secretaries to the CIA chief and the top military brass—were regularly grilled in Congress, in lengthy testimonies that were televised for all to see.

In relatively closed countries like China, journalists' access to officials with real power is close to nonexistent; barely anyone knows what is going on at the top of the leadership. Journalists may be able to speak to lower-level bureaucrats or foreign officials who have met senior leaders like we did after every trip to China, but sitting down with Councilor Dai Bingguo or President Hu Jintao or Zhou Yongkang, China's security chief, was impossible. Of the nine members of the Politburo Standing Committee, the body that governs China, only the prime minister Wen Jiabao occasionally spoke to the foreign press and held a regular press conference—once a year.

A cold wind was blowing when I sat down over a cup of coffee in a Starbucks with the high-level official. The gloom from the midterm elections had permeated deep into the foreign policy–making machine at the State Department and the White House.

"We're holding things together with chewing gum and rubber bands," said the official. "It's bad, really bad."

He went through the list. More desperate efforts to get peace talks going in the Middle East had resulted in nothing, despite high-profile summitry at the White House and in the region over the summer. The Israelis were being a pain, demanding rewards for doing what they were meant to do anyway, and mostly, the official complained, the Israelis didn't care that their obstructionism was further eroding America's cred-ibility in the Arab world. The Palestinians refused to yield to any pres-sure or make any gesture whatsoever. They were stuck in their own version of a Greek tragedy. Afghanistan's president Hamid Karzai was being his unreliable, moody self. The Pakistanis were as impossible as always, gobbling up American money but dragging their feet on any-thing that could be helpful to the United States. And Iran? Let's not even go there. Nothing was going America's way. It felt as though everybody was testing the limits of American power, pushing Washington around to see how much ground they could gain themselves.

"Success begets success," the official went on, obviously implying that the opposite was true as well. If a sense of failure settled in, things could unravel, and America's prestige would be eroded even further, its power reduced even more. The foundations that the Obama administration had been carefully laying for two years to position America for the twenty-first century were still extraordinarily fragile. Nothing had really taken root yet, except in Asia. But even that progress could be jeopardized if the trajectory took a downward turn.

I went home feeling deeply unsettled. Gum and rubber bands? I was stunned by the candor. I knew America couldn't get things done just by pushing a button. I'd heard Hillary say there was no magic wand, and for two years I had watched American officials do the heavy lifting required to get anything done around the world. But this was too vulnerable, too raw. Was this what decline looked like? I thought back to those days in Beirut, when America had taken a beating. The headlines had been all about decline then too. Were we wrong then but right now? Were things really worse? It was one thing to believe that mighty America was wilting because you were looking at the ruins of its embassy in Beirut and you believed history started and ended in your country. It was quite another to be sitting in Washington with American officials who had all the pieces of the puzzle in their hands but felt they were losing control.

I read former secretary of state Madeleine Albright's memoir and found she had shown some of the same despair when writing about 1998. "It seemed that wherever I looked, I saw either gridlock or peril. For all the power of the United States, we were not able to dictate events. The North Koreans, Serbs, Israelis and Palestinians, Indians and Pakistanis, Iraqis, Russians, African leaders, even our allies seemed indifferent or hostile to our requests. My personal confidence level was down." I was surprised. The Clinton presidency was thought of nostalgically by some as the heyday of American hegemony and unchallenged power in a unipolar world in the years after the Soviet Union collapsed.

I dug further. In early 1975, American diplomacy, with Henry Kissinger at the helm, seemed to lie in tatters around the world as well, especially in Asia: the Vietnam War had been a disaster; the Khmer Rouge was about to take over Cambodia; a key ally of the United States, King Faisal of Saudi Arabia, had been assassinated by a member of his own family; and the Israelis were making Washington's life so difficult in the aftermath of the October 1973 Arab-Israeli War that President Nixon was ready to go toe-to-toe with Israel no matter what the domestic political consequences.[29] During the war, the "oil-for-arms" agreement between the U.S. and Saudi Arabia, which had started back in 1945 with Truman, had broken down for the first (and so far last) time. Saudi Arabia and other Arab oil producing countries had decided to use oil as a weapon to punish the United States for its military support for Israel. They imposed an oil embargo, which caused oil prices to quadruple and provoked lines at gas stations in the United States.

All the way back in 1950, there had been dire warnings, including a key National Security Council document about America not having the military or financial means to meet all its global strategic commitments, and fears there could be a serious relative decline of America and the free world in the face of a rising Soviet Union. Chairman Mao was convinced that the United States was in decline, that it could not take on any more commitments around the world and would be incapable of maintaining its hegemony in its part of the world.[30] This all sounded rather familiar.

The talk of decline seemed cyclical; feelings of confidence ebbed and flowed. It was not a clear curve going up or down. But there were some inevitable facts showing that America was no longer the giant it had been, especially economically. America's share of the world's GDP was 50 percent after World War II; it had fallen to 25 percent in the 1970s as Europe rebuilt itself, and has lingered there ever since. The rise of other economic powers was often a benefit to America itself. They traded with the United States, and American companies found new markets. But there was no doubt that as other countries prospered and lifted their populations out of poverty or found political stability, they started vying for a bigger share of the pie.

If America had less and less of a say in the world, where did that leave me? Would I be better off if America was less powerful? Would Lebanon? The Middle East? Pakistan? Like so many around the world, growing up in Lebanon I had often thought America should mind its own business, go home, and leave us to sort out our own affairs. But I had never seriously thought about what or who would replace America as a superpower. I'm not sure anyone who ranted against America around me had gone to the end of that thought process. And Americans who wanted their government to retreat from the world didn't seem to have fully thought through the consequences on their daily life. What would happen if China monopolized shipping lanes in the South China Sea unchallenged and the price of rice or iPads shot up? Or if Turkey and Brazil enabled Iran's nuclear ambitions and Tehran developed an atomic bomb, using its newfound power to further assert its control over Lebanon? In part it was perhaps because American power seemed to be a given and no one could actually imagine a world without it or picture the far-reaching consequences on the world system if America suddenly "went home."

And yet the United States hadn't been a superpower long enough to have perfected the art of governing the world. On a historical scale, six decades were nothing. America was still maturing and finding its footing, but was American power benign or nefarious? America's faults were many: from fomenting coups in Latin America to backing dictators in the Arab world. So why did so many countries and people appeal for American help?

I had come to appreciate many of the officials I dealt with on a daily basis. There was something rather earnest about American diplomats. But did their actions amount to making America a force for good around the world? Surely, their primary concern was protecting their country's national interests. Were national interests and moral choices mutually exclusive?

Life in the United States was free of the kind of fear I had experienced in Lebanon—fear that was a staple in so many countries. Rule of law prevailed here. There were no thugs grabbing you out of your house in the dead of night, no extrajudicial killings, no gangs chopping off people's heads or militants setting off bombs in markets. I felt safe. But if you lived on the receiving end of American foreign policy, as I had in Lebanon, it could be painful. Was it worse to suffer at the hands of your own government or as a consequence of American actions? Was an Iranian tortured in Tehran's notorious Evin prison worse or better off than an inmate in Guantánamo Bay detained for years with no trial? Was it worse to live under Syrian occupation in Lebanon or to live in fear of night raids by U.S. soldiers in Afghanistan? Was it worse to be humiliated in Abu Ghraib prison at the hands of American soldiers or tortured in an Uzbek or Chinese prison?

The thoughts racing through my mind were constantly pushing me into a reductive discussion about the essence of American power, about values that were hard to define, but I knew the world was not good or evil, black or white; it was shades of gray. There was no simple answer, but the difference seemed to be recourse to the law. I was astounded by the fervor with which American officers were serving as lawyers for defendants on trial in Gitmo. When I asked Lieutenant Brian Mizer how he could be defending a man who was accused of having aided Osama bin Laden, America's enemy number one, he told me everybody deserved a fair trial. In theory, yes, except that in Lebanon, for example, few if any would dare defend someone accused of aiding Israel, officially Lebanon's enemy. Both defendant and lawyer could be accused of treason. In countries like Syria, China, or Russia, the law meant nothing if you were poor or had no connections to the powerful. Laws didn't protect you against the whims of your own government, and the feeling of utter powerlessness this could engender was mind-numbing. I thought of Brazil's refusal to condemn the stoning of women in Iran, China's crushing of dissent, Russia's hunting down of journalists. Would they help save a dissident from brutal repression in another country? Perhaps world governing wasn't anyone's responsibility, not America's either, but I still wondered about a globe where present-day China called all the shots.

Perhaps a real multipolar world was better, with power distributed more evenly among the different players around the world. Checks and balances were a healthy way to make sure might was not concentrated in the hands of one. In 1998, when U.S. dominance was unchallenged, France's foreign minister had compared America to a steamroller, calling it a hyperpower. The hubris had led to the excesses of the Bush administration. The war in Iraq had been the exception to the rule of American reluctance to intervene abroad, and the United States had enthusiastically plunged headfirst into a war of choice. But the end of empires and eras usually involves an outbreak of violence as the balance of power shifts, and someone inevitably tries to take the upper hand. For now, and probably for decades to come, no single country would have more power than America. So the competition for world leadership wasn't between America and China, or America and the BRICs. It was America or no one. New rising powers pushing against American influence, asserting themselves on the world stage, were also pushing against each other. They may have resented America, but they disliked each other even more. So unless America maintained the edge, a multipolar world sounded like a recipe for global gridlock.

Suddenly, the idea of American decline seemed utterly unappealing to me. But it seemed to be under way already or, at least, everyone was saying it was inevitable.

And just when things couldn't get worse, a virtual hurricane engulfed the Building and blew its classified documents to the four corners of the world.

In the summer of 2010, an organization called WikiLeaks had started to release videos and cables from the Pentagon about Iraq and Afghanistan that showed the war effort in its raw, unvarnished form. The logs revealed the extent of the failures in Afghanistan and a higher number of civilian casualties than had been officially disclosed. The group wanted to shine a light on the dark workings of governments and warned that the information they were revealing was cause for war crimes prosecution. In the end, there wasn't much in the cables that hadn't already been in the public reel, but it was now all in one location, conveniently accessible on the WikiLeaks website. WikiLeaks promised that the State Department was the next target. The rumblings started in late October: the group had gotten hold of 250,000 diplomatic cables.

Bradley Manning, the young army private in Iraq suspected of having been the source of the leak, had been arrested in the spring. Officials at the State Department were furious that their confidential cables had been disclosed, especially by someone who had no business reading them. The

United States had tried to encourage more openness within the government after the attacks of September 11, 2001. Lack of communication between different agencies was one of the reasons why no one had been able to connect the different warning signs. A new system called SIPRNet meant that State Department and Pentagon officials could read some of their respective classified correspondence. The cables were missives written by American diplomats posted around the world and sent back to the Building. They contained accounts of their conversations with local officials or dissidents and analysis of the political situation in a country or the stability of a regime. The content helped provide other officials involved in foreign policy decision making with a more nuanced perspective about various issues. But Foreign Service officers wondered why a lowly soldier in Iraq should be given access to accounts of the conversation between General David Petraeus and Yemen's president in Sana'a, or cables from the American embassy in London giving Hillary a background briefing about British politics before her visit?

In the Building, no one knew exactly which cables had been leaked. Moods swung wildly from dismay to disbelief—surely it couldn't be that bad. The CIA had set up an investigation into the leak called "Wikileaks Task Force" and its unfortunate acronym—WTF—aptly summarized how people felt. Top officials like Jeff and Kurt worked with their sections and with American embassies in their region to identify which cables might become public and what damage their content might cause, not only to America's relationships with other countries but also to the secretary herself. As the days went on, the magnitude of the problem became clear. This was going to be a long-term crisis, and it wasn't something that ambassadors or assistant secretaries of state could fix alone. The top tier of the Obama administration would have to help with the damage control. Ambassadors in capitals around the world called foreign ministers to warn them of the crisis that was about to unfold.

The call came around mid-November. Top editors from the *New York Times* informed the White House that they had been given access to the cables. WikiLeaks was working with international news organizations to spread its treasure trove over front pages everywhere. State Department officials pleaded and pushed for the cables not to be revealed. But WikiLeaks and the newspapers did not budge. The Building decided to cooperate with the media organizations publishing the documents to make sure that while a light was shone on the inner workings of the American foreign policy machine, no one got killed in the process. American diplomats everywhere spoke to dissidents, human rights activists, opposition politicians; it was critical that their names be redacted from the documents or their lives could be at risk. Julian Assange, the bleached-blond Australian behind WikiLeaks, was initially opposed to the redactions. He told Declan Walsh from the *New York Times* that he saw those who spoke to American diplomats as "informants" who'd had it coming to them if they got killed.[31] The leaks were going to be made public sometime during the Thanksgiving weekend.

Hillary was spending the Thanksgiving holiday with her family at their New York State home in Chappaqua. She had left D.C. on Tuesday evening, on a commercial flight as always, with two DS agents assigned to protect her. In the Building, on the road, aboard SAM, Hillary was always on the phone to leaders around the world. She sometimes walked around the seventh floor with her earpiece in her right ear, catching up, finalizing details of an agreement, or touching base before an upcoming visit. I'd seen firsthand how Clinton schmoozed. I'd watched her position herself at the heart of the world's community of foreign policy deciders and experts and become the connector. Just as Washington sat at the heart of a web of connections tying it to the world, Hillary was a center of gravity to herself. From the day she took office, she had worked hard to be available to her counterparts, both because she believed in being accessible but also because availability was political capital. Her personal contacts with ministers, presidents, and princes, either recent or decades-old, meant there was a huge amount of bandwidth that allowed for communications not to clog up or break down when a major crisis erupted.

Kissinger believed that "it's very important to establish relationships before you need anything, so that there is a measure of respect in negotiations once they occur or when a crisis develops. When you travel as secretary, one problem you have is that the press comes with you and wants an immediate result because it justifies their trip. And sometimes the best result is that you don't try to get a result but try to get an understanding for the next time you go to them."

Now Hillary was coming to her counterparts to ask for understanding. She took her task very seriously. It was unclear how other countries would react to the content of the cables, and she believed that the best way to soften the blow was to use her own charm and appeal. Presidents and foreign ministers expect to hear from me personally, she said, and she got to work. It was important to make sure the apologies were not mishandled or it could compound the problem. She knew she wasn't going to do this alone. Others were making calls too, from the president to the vice president, to the secretary of defense. Everybody called their counterparts or the people they knew best.

At 6:31 in the evening of November 24, the Wednesday before Thanksgiving, Hillary sat down in her study on the second floor of her Chappaqua home for the first call of the holiday weekend. The study was fitted with a secure line and the State Department's Operations Center (OPS) connected her to the Japanese foreign minister Seiji Maehara. It was 8:31 in the morning on Thursday in Tokyo. They spoke for about fifteen minutes. At 6:48, another call—this time to the Korean foreign minister Kim Sung-Hwan. Then Kevin Rudd, the Australian foreign minister. The cables were not public yet, and it wasn't clear how much the media organizations would print, so Hillary was doing some candid but cautious preemptive diplomacy. There was no point divulging too many details over the phone. In later conversations with lower-ranking officials, Rudd would erupt furiously. He had been described as abrasive, impulsive, and a control freak in the cables that were splashed on the front pages of Australian newspapers. He blamed the American government for the leaks, not WikiLeak's founder, Julian Assange, and said there were real questions about America's security system.

Thursday was sacred turkey and family day. There would be no calls. The flurry started again in earnest on Friday at 7:00 in the morning with a call to China. The OPS center sent e-mail alerts to officials at the various echelons of the Building. The content ranged from breaking news to must-read newspaper articles. Notifications about the secretary's phone calls were sent to a handful of her closest aides. All day, the e-mails dropped, one after the other.

07:33: The Secretary is speaking with Emirati FM al Nahyan.

07:37: The Secretary is speaking with Abu Dhabi Crown Prince al Nahyan.

08:17: The Secretary is speaking with German FM Westerwelle. (He had been described in the cables as anti-American, a burden on U.S.-German relations, an exuberant wild card who had none of his own ideas to solve international problems.)

09:01: The Secretary is speaking with French FM Alliot-Marie. (Her president, Nicolas Sarkozy, was an "emperor with no clothes.")

On and on it went. There was other business to be dealt with as well, but WikiLeaks dominated the day. Saturday brought some light relief. Just after 9:00 in the morning, Clinton spoke to the Canadian foreign minister Lawrence Cannon. Don't worry, Hillary, he told her. You should see what we say about you guys.

On Sunday, everybody was poised for the release; it was being called a "dump" of cables, and it was expected to start at 3:00 in the afternoon. But just before lunch, an e-mail flashed on Hillary's BlackBerry.

From: Ops Alert
Sent: Sunday, November 28, 2010 1:10PM
Subject: First Wikileaks articles appear in Jerusalem Post and Der Spiegel
At approximately 1305, the Jerusalem Post and Der Spiegel published articles with multiple sensitive quotes from the State Department cables referencing world leaders. The Jerusalem Post says it is quoting from the Der Spiegel article.

Hillary started working the phones again. She had to have the same conversation over and over. It was one thing to deal with a problem in one conversation and then move on to another set of issues in the next meeting. But when she was done with one conversation, there was a long line of people still waiting to have the exact same conversation. Regardless of how she handled it and whether her interlocutor was appeased, she had to tango all over again with every leader she spoke to, in the same way or a bit differently, repeatedly. There was no blanket apology, no conference call, and no meeting to be held at the UN for a mea culpa speech. The next best thing, as it conveniently happened, was Hillary's upcoming trip: a conference of the Organization for Security and Co-operation of Europe.

*   *   *

We were leaving that Monday afternoon for another whirlwind tour, starting with the OSCE summit in Astana, Kazakhstan. Dozens of leaders would be in attendance, all of whom had been mentioned in at least one cable, from Germany's "Teflon" Angela Merkel, to the "feckless" Silvio Berlusconi, Italy's prime minister. It would be a long day of contrition, without the buffer of a phone line and hundreds of miles of distance. Before boarding SAM, Hillary would have the opportunity to hone her approach for the face-to-face WikiLeaks conversations with the representative of a prickly, proud country, the subject of some seven thousand cables.

Turkey's foreign minister, Davutoğlu, had long been scheduled for a visit to Washington. There was, as always, much to discuss, but now WikiLeaks caused serious upset for the proud Turks. The number of missives relating to Ankara seemed disproportionate, a sign of both how important Turkey was to the United States and how worried Washington had been about some of its ally's actions.

Davutoğlu, whose efforts to transform Turkey into an indispensable broker had gone awry that spring, had been described in a 2004 cable as an "exceptionally dangerous Islamist" with "delusions of empire." Davutoğlu had been an advisor to the prime minister at the time. Erdoğan himself was being lacerated in the cables as a man with unbridled ambition who believed God had anointed him to lead Turkey. Luckily, these cables had been written under a previous administration, so there was comfortable distance with their author. But Clinton still spent forty-five minutes alone with the man she had worked so hard to befriend in an effort to reassure him that the Obama administration valued its friendship with Turkey. They sat in her office at the State Department, just the two of them, while their staff waited outside. The Turks, who had been considering bringing their paper-based diplomatic communication system fully into the twenty-first century, quipped that perhaps it was best to stick to methods of communications that were less vulnerable to problems like WikiLeaks. Davutoğlu liked Clinton and prized his relationship with her. He was quick to state very publicly that the cables would not affect Turkey's relationship with the United States.

Beyond the hurt feelings of world leaders, the Building worried about dissidents, activists, or even confidential sources whose names might not be redacted or who could be identified from the context of the cables. A matrix was created to identify vulnerable subjects around the world. Most people told U.S. officials who contacted them that their government already knew about them so there was no reason to worry. In some cases, though they were known to the authorities, the content of the cables provided details of sensitive conversations and tipped the balance against them so they asked to be spirited out of the country and elaborate planning was required to construct a valid, innocuous reason for them to leave. In some cases, officials concluded that contacting certain people to ask if they needed help would only endanger them further. In China, where information was so scarce and access to insiders so difficult to attain, the revelations were damaging to diplomats' sources. Even journalists or professors with a modicum of knowledge about the inner workings of the Communist Party risked their jobs by sharing that information with outsiders.

For everyone involved, this was a breach of trust, albeit one that the United States had not intended. Would anyone ever speak to an American diplomat candidly again? The cables were being read as bibles of U.S. foreign policy when they were not. They were observations at one point in time about the situation in a specific country, which informed decision making in Washington. In fact, ambassadors complained that their missives to headquarters often ended up in the recycling bin. The State Department did not confirm that the WikiLeaks documents were indeed its classified diplomatic cables—a necessary diplomatic charade. Everyone knew the cables were real, but there was no need to confirm it publicly. Clinton and other officials referred to "alleged" stolen cables.

Anyone who fought against government secrecy or resented American influence hailed the leak as a great event. Enemies hoped it was a fatal blow to the imperial hegemonic power, another marker on the downhill trajectory of a country in decline. Rivals and even some friends greeted the event with a degree of glee—invincible America was not so invincible after all. There was also widespread disbelief: mighty America can't keep its secrets safe? Mostly, it was seen as a blow to U.S. prestige and power. Clinton, who had given a tough and widely applauded speech about Internet freedom earlier in the year, rejected the notion that the leak was about freedom of expression or access to information. After her morning meeting with the Turks, she called a small press conference in the Treaty Room.

"I am aware that some may mistakenly applaud those responsible, so I want to set the record straight. There is nothing laudable about endangering innocent people, and there is nothing brave about sabotaging the peaceful relations between nations on which our common security depends," she said. "There have been examples in history in which official conduct has been made public in the name of exposing wrongdoings or misdeeds. This is not one of those cases."

Instead of heading to Andrews Air Force Base ahead of the secretary as usual, we first filed our stories about her statement from our offices in the bull pen on the second floor. Then we piled into the vans and drove with her motorcade to be reunited with SAM, just after two in the afternoon, under a sunny blue December sky. The classified books had already been laid out for the delegation, and Lew had overseen the loading of our luggage. We did our seating lottery rapidly on the tarmac and embarked.

We were flying east, into the future, across eleven time zones. After sixteen hours, we arrived in snowy Astana late in the afternoon on Tuesday. As we rode to our hotel in overheated vans, our eyes widened at the sights produced by Kazakhstan's recent oil wealth: this really was the future. World-renowned architects had been commissioned to design buildings to populate the capital's sparse skyline. The result of their unbridled creativity included a purple yurt-shaped structure by British architect Norman Foster, which was actually a mall, featuring a fake sandy beach with palm trees. There was a building in the shape of a rocket and another that was described in our hotel city guide as the "most arrogant" building of the capital. No one could figure out where the translation had gone wrong. The city also had a replica of the White House, but with a blue dome and golden spire on top, sitting on Astana's own, tiled version of the National Mall.

On Wednesday morning in Astana, the Apology Tour, as we had dubbed the trip, was about to enter full swing. The day started with a family photo of all the leaders attending the summit. Hillary looked relaxed and chatted comfortably with those around her. Almost none of them had escaped unscathed from the acerbic or humorous descriptions by America's diplomats. In the massive hall, the tall, lanky advance line officer took one step forward to stand out of the crowd of photographers and cameramen. He stood next to the exit and made eye contact with Clinton. She started walking toward him. Her aides and Fred followed. Line officers always made sure something about them stood out—a tie, a colorful handbag, something Clinton could spot so she could find her way to her next appointment with no awkward wild hand waves and without ever looking lost.

Every day, Huma briefed Clinton about the schedule. Hillary's cordovan leather-bound daily briefing book also contained the "truncated briefing checklists" with the detailed scenarios of every event she was to attend, but the secretary didn't devote much energy trying to retain or worry about the details of the logistics, as long as she got the big picture. Over the years, since her days as First Lady in Arkansas, she had learned to turn off the part of her brain that asked, "Where do I go now?" or "Have we sorted out lunch?" and "Where will I sit?" This was the only way she could devote her full attention to the content and substance of an eighteen-hour day like this conference in Astana, with eleven different events and a handful of one-on-ones.

Hillary trusted those around her and relied on them to help her glide through her heavy schedule, and her easygoing social nature allowed her to manage herself on the rare occasions when the system failed her for a few minutes. She rearranged people's positions for pictures, laughed at her own missteps, and filled in awkward silences with shy activists or, in this case, world leaders with bruised egos.

International summits were an intense intellectual effort, juggling all the different issues at the heart of the gathering and then the multitude of bilateral meetings that counterparts always requested. At the yearly General Assembly at the UN, Clinton participated on average in sixty meetings and events, multilateral or bilateral, alone or with the president, over the course of about five days. It required an exceptional level of mental multitasking to keep all the countries and their issues straight. The OSCE was much smaller, but the list of bilateral meetings was growing, and no matter what other pressing issues had to be resolved, every meeting would start with the WikiLeaks talk. There was some guesswork involved as well: WikiLeaks was releasing cables by dribs and drabs, and the State Department was not entirely certain of every missive in Assange's possession. Clinton kept some of her conversations very general, careful not to draw attention to content that may never become public.

The secretary didn't try to ignore the issue, pretend it didn't matter, or reject responsibility because the cable had been written by someone else during another administration. This was a failure of America, and she was angry too. She tried as best she could to explain the context of each cable, why it had been written, what was the background. But mostly she tried to empathize with her interlocutors as a politician. I get it, she would say. I know how you feel. I too have suffered slings and arrows. Russia's Sergei Lavrov waved WikiLeaks away; he just wanted to get down to business. In Moscow, even ultranationalist Russians who loved to badmouth the United States were surprisingly dismissive of the leak. The foreign minister of Kazakhstan was delighted to find out he was important enough to be the subject of an American cable detailing his nightlife and restaurant habits; he said it was great publicity. From Georgia's Mikheil Saakashvili to Britain's deputy prime minister Nick Clegg, Clinton diligently calmed upset egos and gave reassurance about steady alliances.

After their private talks with Clinton, the ministers went away, somewhat appeased. But one man wanted a public apology. Italy's flamboyant prime minister Silvio Berlusconi gave Hillary an impassioned presentation about how much he loved America and why it was so painful for him to read the cables. He had brought her a gift: silk scarves from Naples's famous E. Marinella artisans. He told her about his father, who used to take him to the cemetery to see the graves of American soldiers who had fought and died to liberate Italy in World War II and how it had cemented his love for America. Clinton was not exactly an admirer of the Italian leader as a person, with his reputation for raunchy parties and allegations of sex with underage girls. But she felt bad for Berlusconi the politician, who had been such an ally for the United States. I will stand here with you, she told him. We will bring the cameras, and I will convey our gratitude to Italy and to you personally for what you have done for our relationship. An e-mail was sent around to the traveling press corps alerting us that Clinton was about to make a statement. The camera crew, photographers, and a couple of reporters hurried into the room.

"The United States highly values the relationship that we have with the prime minister and with Italy," said Clinton. "We have no better friend, we have no one who supports the American policies as consistently as Prime Minister Berlusconi has, starting in the Clinton administration, through the Bush administration, and now the Obama administration."

We have no better friend—how many times did American officials say that about a country? Canada, the Netherlands, the United Kingdom, France, Italy, India, the Philippines, South Korea. A montage of statements by Obama and Clinton, and by all their predecessors, praising different countries as America's best friend, would be an entertaining comedy sketch. And yet it was a sought-after mention that revealed each country's neuroses and insecurities. The publication of the cables seemed to have sent the world into a tizzy, as people everywhere pored over them, eager to find out whether they had made the cut and what America really thought of them in private. Were they in fact America's best friend?

Washingtonians are often mocked for what is called the "index read," a quick scan through the index to find one's name. Find the relevant paragraphs, read them to determine how you're portrayed, maybe check the index for names of friends and see how they come across, derive pleasure if you come out looking better. Don't bother buying the book if you're not in the index.

WikiLeaks was the State Department's "Unabridged Guide to the World: Our Relationship with Every Country and Quirks of World Leaders." The globe did a quick "index scan." Which country got the most mentions? Which came out most favorably? Which close ally was actually being disparaged in diplomatic cables? What did American diplomats think of this world leader? Countries kept a score board: they complained that their information was being revealed and took comfort from the fact that their country was cited most often.

Zauresh Batalova, the head of a local NGO in Astana, was waiting excitedly for a meeting with Clinton when I asked her what she thought about the leak.

"The cables are a confirmation that America is still a global leader in geopolitical affairs," she told me. A simple but astute observation that made me wonder whether any other country had diplomats sending cables from every single world capital. China? Possibly. But America, whether in decline or not, clearly still had a finger in every imaginable pie.

The reaction to the "dump" in different countries was also very telling of their national personality. China blocked Internet access to anything WikiLeaks. The cables could not be read by average Chinese citizens in a country where the media were tightly controlled. The content would reveal too much about their government's workings and corrupt the minds of the people. In Pakistan, members of the cabinet angrily dismissed the leaks as a conspiracy against the country and an attempt to undermine the political and military leadership. A few days later, someone in Pakistan planted fake cables in which American diplomats heaped praise over Pakistan's military while attacking India, describing its military as vain, egotistical, and genocidal. When the hoax was revealed, some newspapers apologized quickly to their readers but others, like the *Nation*, which had so shocked me during our visit to Pakistan with its rabid coverage, continued for days to print articles about "India's True Face."

On Thursday, we left our hotel in Astana at seven in the morning, driving through deserted streets, white with snow. SAM was having trouble getting deiced, and our departure was slightly delayed. We flew south to Kyrgyzstan. Clinton met the president, gave a press conference, spent an hour with students in a town hall, greeted the U.S. embassy staff, and then we went to Manas Air Base, where she shook hands with American troops. We got back on the plane and flew another hour west to the warmer temperatures and repression of Uzbekistan. We spent a few hours being stared at by menacing government goons in black leather jackets who looked more Soviet than the Russians. Clinton sat down with the local dictator Islam Karimov for one of those meetings where values had lost out to national interest. The United States worried about relying too much on Pakistan as a route in and out of Afghanistan. Uzbekistan bordered Afghanistan too and provided an alternative—Hillary would have to pinch her nose. She would make up for it by meeting with civil society representatives in the embassy. Four hours after landing in Tashkent, SAM took us on a five-hour ride southwest to Bahrain. We landed in Manama just before midnight local time. In Astana, where we had started that morning under the snow in twenty degrees Fahrenheit, it was already three in the morning. We shed our coats, gloves, and hats and walked down the steps onto the tarmac and into Bahrain's balmy sixty-degree weather.

The flight had given me some more time to delve into the WikiLeaks cables, which were turning into the foreign policy equivalent of a gossip column. As I skimmed through the batch that had been published so far, a theme emerged: everybody still relied on the United States to sort out their problems. Countries and world leaders didn't just want America's attention or another photo opportunity; they somehow expected action. While the United States was struggling to advance its own agenda, other countries were waiting for it to help them with theirs. The cables showed the extent to which the Arabs feared Iran's rise as a nuclear power but refused to say so in public—because what scared them even more than Iran was the reaction of their own people if they were exposed trying to bring America's wrath onto another Muslim country. Instead, they privately called on the United States to "cut off the head of the snake," in the words of the Saudi official ambassador to the United States Adel el-Jubeir, who was quoting the king himself. If America did attack Iran, the same Arab leaders would publicly curse the imperialistic American warmongers. Pakistan's leaders called for more American drone strikes in private and then protested against it in the National Assembly. Yemen's president Ali Abdullah Saleh did the opposite: he wanted more American drone strikes against militants from al-Qaeda who were challenging his grip on power. In public, he pretended the Yemeni army was carrying out the attacks so he could look like a strong leader and avoid anti-American protests that would strengthen the militants. In Bahrain, Hillary had also for the first time said she would not serve a second term as secretary of state. She wanted to step out of the limelight and said she was done with the high wire of politics. Her statement dominated the headlines at home, even if no one believed her.

On the endless journey back to Washington, at the end of a weeklong trip, I battled jetlag by reading more cables. They were a treasure trove for historians. I couldn't believe it when I read that even China seemed to want the United States to do its bidding. The Chinese appeared increasingly worried about North Korea's reckless behavior but refused to criticize it openly, hoping instead that the United States would continue to flex its muscle with military exercises in the region, enough to scare Pyongyang into submission and cool tempers on the Korean peninsula. I suddenly realized that on that flight out of Seoul in the summer, while my colleagues and I had been dismissive of the administration's official line that China was being helpful on a few issues, there was actually some truth in what American diplomats were telling us. China wasn't about to ditch North Korea, but it appreciated a bit of American help keeping the crazy Dear Leader in check.

There were a lot of juicy details about the habits of foreign leaders but no real surprises—there was no sign of coups being fomented or secret supplies of weapons no one had ever heard of before. The gap between what America said it did these days and what its diplomats were actually doing seemed rather narrow. The cables showed a superpower at work, cajoling, pleading, reassuring, and bullying. American diplomats came across as sharp-eyed and earnest, detailing the corruption of the Tunisian regime, the frustrating pace of almost nonexistent reforms in Egypt, or the lavish lifestyles of various dictators around the world. They were also hard at work advancing their country's interests, detailing China's growing influence in Africa and access to resources there or reporting on the ties between Beijing and Islamabad. The biggest gap was between what foreign leaders said in public to their own people and what they said in private to American diplomats.

Obviously, the American cables were of the lowest classification category. They were not top secret, they were not CIA missives; even senior officials in the Building admitted they didn't know everything their government was involved in. People suspected there were covert operations to sow unrest in Iran. American officials would soon openly acknowledge the use of drones, but it was already an open secret. American newspapers had long uncovered CIA rendition flights and black holes where suspects were being interrogated. This was not the age of the Pentagon Papers of the 1960s, which, once revealed, showed that the U.S. government had consistently and systematically lied to Congress and to the public about decision making during the Vietnam War.

Italy's foreign minister Franco Frattini had emphatically declared that the leak was the 9/11 of diplomacy. There was indeed less openness in conversations with American diplomats perhaps for a while, and dissidents in repressive countries shied away from contacting American officials, but overall, Secretary Gates laconically summed up why diplomacy wouldn't change all that much: the United States was too big to ignore.

"The fact is governments deal with the United States because it's in their interest, not because they like us, not because they trust us, and not because they believe we can keep secrets." The cables showed the web of connections, ties, alliances, and partnerships that the United States had had around the world for decades. Over the last two years, almost imperceptibly but very methodically, the Obama administration and Clinton in particular had been working to strengthen and build on that foundation to make sure the United States remained the indispensable partner of the twenty-first century.

For the months to come, every time the administration made a statement or staked a position, everybody would rush to compare that to what American officials had said about the issue in their classified documents, to see how big or small the gap was between public and private statements. The WikiLeaks cables became part of the furniture. New cables kept being published, and Hillary continued to make calls well into the following spring, a spring that brought its own share of momentous events.

PART III

The genius of you Americans is that you never make clear-cut stupid moves, only complicated stupid moves which make the rest of us wonder at the possibility that we might be missing something.

—Gamal Abdel Nasser, 1957

12

I WANT TO
BREAK THROUGH

wanted to ignore the tweet, but something about it grabbed my attention. I had spent Christmas of 2010 with my family in Beirut, and life by
the Mediterranean was a slow, languorous affair of lunches, dinners, and
socializing over coffee in between. I was having a hard time stepping
back into the fast-paced, BlackBerry-driven world of Washington politics.
Just four days into the new year, the news was already speeding ahead:
the Ivory Coast was slowly imploding, the Chinese foreign minister Yang
Jiechi was in town, and Clinton had just issued a statement condemning
the assassination of Punjab governor Salman Taseer, shot dead by his
bodyguard in Lahore. Hillary also called his wife, Aamna, to extend
condolences to her and her children. They talked about the time they'd
all met in Lahore in October 2009, and Hillary relayed how much she'd
admired Taseer's work to promote tolerance. Taseer was a staunch liberal
and had spoken out forcefully against a law that punished blasphemy
with death. His positions had cost him his life; the bodyguard would
later say he had shot the governor because he was an "apostate." Pakistan's
unending problems remained a headache for Washington. As usual, my
editors in London wanted to know Washington's reaction to everything.

I wanted to ignore it, but the tweeter was persistent: Why was the
White House not saying anything about Tunisia? I was puzzled. Tunisia?
The small North African country hadn't been on my radar recently, and
I was intrigued by this tweeter reaching out to America the only way he

knew how. I did a quick search on the news from Tunisia. Protests had been spreading slowly since December 19, when a twenty-six-year-old man, Mohamed Bouazizi, set himself on fire in the southern town of Sidi Bouzid. Bouazizi had been the provider for his mother and six younger siblings and he struggled to make enough money as a fruit and vegetable vendor. Humiliated repeatedly by the police, who pushed him around and confiscated his cart, he had preferred self-immolation to a life with no hope. It was an iconic, powerful gesture for anyone, but especially for a Muslim whose religion forbade suicide. Few people were paying attention. Bouazizi's gesture had barely received any mention in the media. I had been 1,500 miles away on the same seashore just a few days ago, and no one had mentioned Tunisia. Protests in the Arab world erupted occasionally, then fizzled out with no further impact but never before in Tunisia, a tightly policed country that had had only two presidents since gaining its independence from France in 1956. The current ruler Zin el-Abidine Ben Ali had been in power for twenty years, oblivious to his people's misery.

Bouazizi had just died in the hospital from his wounds, and I asked @ferjani9arwi why he wanted the White House to say anything. "US must stand up for people's rights" came the reply "US silence = more people killed and imprisoned." But would it really matter if Washington spoke? Another tweeter from Tunisia, @samieleuch, said, "For religious people, nothing happens without the will of God. For secular people, nothing happens without the will of the US."

At the State Department briefing on that January 4, I raised my hand to ask a question.

"On Tunisia, there's continued, sort of, civil unrest there, and I was just wondering . . ."

"What country?"

"Tunisia. Tunisia. And I was wondering what you made of the situation there."

P. J. rifled through his binder. Nothing.

"Actually, I didn't get updated on Tunisia today. So we'll save that question."

Matt from AP chimed in, laughing.

"When was the last time you did get updated on Tunisia?"

The following day, we asked again. P. J. had an update. He told us the United States was concerned about economic inequality in the country, and the embassy warden had issued a message to American citizens in the country warning them about the unrest. By January 6, the State Department had summoned the Tunisian ambassador, and Jeff Feltman protested the use of force against the demonstrators. The Tunisian authorities were also hacking into their citizens' Facebook and Twitter accounts, for which they were harshly criticized by the State Department. In Europe, there was a very different reaction. The French foreign minister Michèle Alliot-Marie offered to send French riot police to help quell the unrest in France's old colonial backyard. Tunisia continued to simmer, but no one quite knew what to make of the protestors—and they were competing for headlines in the news. On January 8 in Tucson, Arizona, Congresswoman Gabrielle Giffords was shot in the head by a lone gunman whose bullets killed six others. The world was also watching the birth of a new country as South Sudan got ready to secede from Sudan. SAM was waiting for us again.

We landed in Abu Dhabi, in the United Arab Emirates, at eleven at night on Sunday, January 9. This time the hotels had been booked in advance, and Bernadette was with us on the plane as part of the line officer plane team, rather than scrambling to assemble a motorcade.

Our hotel, the Emirates Palace, appeared like a glittering mirage at the end of a long monotonous road. A gigantic brown building with dozens of domes, it was a cross between an Indian palace and a mosque with a two-mile-long private beach. My room key looked like a gold coin. Ten pounds of gold were used every year to sprinkle flakes into glasses of champagne and on caviar and other delicacies. Gold, it was thought, was a powerful aphrodisiac. The hotel offered $1 million custom-made holidays. This was the Arab-world version of the "1 percent." The other 99 percent were like Bouazizi, desperate and ready to kill themselves for a job and some dignity.

By Monday morning, the fire had started slowly spreading across the region. There were three dead in food riots in Algeria, and 250 university graduates had staged a protest in Riyadh—and it was all in the United Arab Emirates' English-language newspaper the *National* with the front-page headline "The Frustrated Generation." The United Arab Emirates was small and rich, and though under its modern facade there were human-rights abuses and censorship, it didn't have to worry about frustrated youth. Emirate newspapers could afford to write in English about unrest elsewhere with an editorial reminding rich Gulf countries of their duty to help poor North Africa by boosting trade ties. Other Arab newspapers, most of them controlled by the state, ignored the protestors, fearful of stoking the anger and inciting their own population. They were seemingly unaware of the futility of their efforts. Privately owned satellite television stations like al Jazeera and al Arabiyya were already showing extensive footage of the protests.

On page 2, the *National* ran a picture of Clinton meeting the minister of foreign affairs Sheikh Abdullah bin Zayed in Washington in April 2009. She was the same woman who had traveled from Washington with us on the plane, and yet in that old photo she looked different. Her hair had grown from her sharp presidential campaign cut into a softer style, blond locks framing her face a shade lighter than in years past. Chelsea had asked her mother to grow her hair for the wedding, and Hillary had liked the result. The one-tone pantsuits still made guest appearances, but her wardrobe now included more fashionable, sleeker styles.

The politician burned so often by the media in the past had relaxed; released from the acrimony and gutter fighting of American domestic politics, she was coming into her own, allowing the world to see the real Hillary more often than at any time in the past. Democrats and Republicans praised her performance on the world stage, and world leaders, even those who resented U.S. influence, always seemed eager to welcome her. People did ask what it was that she had actually achieved so far as secretary of state. After all, there was still no peace in the Middle East, Iran was still enriching uranium, and Pakistan was still a mess. Few of her predecessors had managed tangible successes either and Hillary believed her success would be more intangible but longer lasting. Her public diplomacy efforts were often scorned by foreign policy wonks, but she believed it was an essential part of maintaining American leadership.

Before leaving, officials had told us that the whole trip had been organized around the idea of engaging with civil society. If in the past it was an element that was tacked onto every stop, Clinton had wanted this trip designed around it. Even in the United Arab Emirates, where dry diplomatic talk with the foreign minister always centered on Iran and Iraq, Hillary was to sit down for a town hall with women and would meet with students at a green-energy research center. Civil society was a buzz word on every part of the trip, including on our surprise stop.

As usual, it wasn't on our printed schedule to keep it under wraps, but everybody was excited about going to Sana'a, Yemen. It was one country on a shrinking list of places that Clinton had not been to yet, and over dinner in Dubai the day before our visit, the secretary asked who had visited and what their impressions had been of the country. She was always keen to get the opinions of people outside her circle of advisors and listened intently to the stories of photographer Stephanie Sinclair, who had spent some time in the country photographing child brides to draw attention to their plight.

Walking down the steps onto the tarmac in Sana'a, we were greeted by the sight of a plane with a red tail adorned with a white crescent. The Turks were here as well! It wasn't Davutoğlu, but his president, Abdullah Gul. Our motorcade of armored vehicles sped through wide, empty roads into the center of the city, banners welcoming President Gul fluttering above our heads. There were none for Clinton since no one was supposed to know she was coming. But Gul had just spent two days here and was leaving the palace of President Ali Abdullah Saleh just as we were arriving. The Turkish president had signed dozens of agreements, encouraging trade between the two countries and abolishing the need for visas between them, and he had fought back a few tears as Yemeni students sang a eulogy to Ottoman soldiers who fell in Yemen during World War I. Turkey's policy for a neighborhood with zero problems was clearly expanding beyond its immediate borders.

In the front passenger seat of Clinton's SUV, Fred was tense but satisfied with the security measures he saw in place. He had worked in Yemen in the aftermath of the bombing of the USS *Cole* in 2000, but having a mental image of the country did little in this case to abate his concerns about security. Yemen was worse than Pakistan. No matter how upset the Pakistanis were with America, the last thing the government wanted was an attack against the American secretary of state, and they had enough control and power to ensure it didn't happen. In Yemen, however, it didn't matter how happy Saleh was that Clinton was gracing his country with a visit—he was not fully in control of his own territory. Tribes kidnapped Western tourists, al-Qaeda targeted the American embassy, and political opponents used guns to express their anger. This was where the Christmas Day underwear bomber, Umar Farouk Abdulmutallab, had been trained and sent on his mission aboard a plane to Chicago in 2009.

On quick day visits with no hotel rooms to set up a mobile office on a secure floor, the plane team of line officers often went for a tour of the city they were in, with some help from the U.S. embassy, while the secretary went about her official business. But here, Fred forbade anyone from leaving the airport. Securing Evergreen's package was enough of a challenge and required all the resources at hand. Bernadette stayed on the plane with a handful of others, including Lew and his metal case full of passports. The Ravens stood guard at the bottom of the steps, in the sun, awaiting our return several hours later.

Yemen was one of the poorest countries in the world, so despite the corruption that goes with power in the region, Saleh's palace was modest compared to the opulence that his oil-rich neighbors displayed. But it had as much, or as little, style. Beyond the tall, elaborately carved wooden doors was a dark, carpeted, windowless foyer. The walls were lined with aging wood-and-glass display cases for the various gifts he'd received from visiting foreign dignitaries, mostly guns, including some from American generals. There was also a gold-plated MP5 9mm submachine gun: a gift from Iran in 1986. Clinton had brought him a silver tray, perhaps a symbol of what the United States had to offer him if only he listened to them more.

As First Lady, senator, and secretary of state, Hillary had stood next to countless political leaders and smiled for the cameras. Most of the time, it was genuine. She had a knack for becoming friends with everyone, from the boorish Boris Yeltsin to the quiet president of South Korea, Lee Myung-bak. She often ended up liking people she never expected to like because she had come to understand and empathize with their history and background. Sometimes with less savory characters, the smile was forced, but still she tried to always focus on why she was there and what she was trying to achieve.

With her delegation, Clinton was ushered into a room that hadn't been updated since the eighties, taking a seat on a faded pink and earthen green upholstered chair. The local Yemeni press corps overran the American reporters and almost pushed Fred and his agents out of the way as they competed to snap pictures of the historical event. Above the pink and green curtains, the sun shone through stained-glass windows. An old TV in a wooden frame with legs stood in a corner, silent, unlike the Saudi king's television from a year ago. A silver sculpture of two rearing horses stood on a low wooden table between Clinton and Saleh.

Hillary had never met the Yemeni president before. He had been at the White House in 2000 to meet President Clinton, but their paths had not crossed at the time. She looked at the man sitting in front of her and saw a stereotype of a man who had ruled too long. Wily and ruthless, he told her that governing Yemen was like dancing on the heads of snakes—that was how you governed Yemen for thirty years and survived.

He had come to power in 1978, after two decades of civil war in the country, as the president of North Yemen. He presided over the union with South Yemen in 1990 and navigated its tribal politics with shrewd cunning, crushing political opponents and using a system of patronage to keep people loyal and dependent. He had opened the doors of his country to Islamic jihad fighters returning from Afghanistan after the fall of the Soviet Union and then sent them to fight against secular tribes in the south when the war broke out again in 1994. Counterterrorism was all that American officials talked about when they came to the poorest country of the Arab world. The United States saw Yemen as a necessary partner in the fight against al-Qaeda and gave the country $300 million a year in counterterror aid. Saleh always argued for more, warning, or more likely threatening, that without aid his country would turn into a failed state like Somalia. American officials sitting down with him felt a sense of foreboding around him; despite the smiles, his history, arrogant demeanor, and dismissive talk of his people's rights gave the impression that he was a violent ruler.

On the wall of the dark lobby, a fading portrait of Saleh in earth tones showed him as a larger-than-life figure sailing a boat full of people, leaving choppy seas behind him. "Through the waves of rebellion and the storms of treason, you have sailed us to safe shores," said the Arabic lettering in one corner. But the people of Yemen were unhappy, and after quickly going through the counterterrorism aspect of the agenda, Clinton spent her meeting explaining to Saleh why he had to engage with the opposition, embrace reform, and be smart about his budget. She didn't try to pretend she understood the complex tribal politics of the country, but with her politician's cap on she attempted to explain to him why even he would benefit from reform. Saleh insisted he was not like other Arab leaders; he did listen to his people. Well, I am going to sit down with members of civil society, she told him, our diplomats from the embassy see them all the time, and I will listen to what they have to say.

Like so many leaders around the world who crave attention from the United States, Saleh, with his bottle-black mustache, was basking in the glory of the visit, probably barely listening. He had been to the White House five times since 2000, but now Hillary Clinton, the representative of the world's superpower, was sitting on his dark-pink couch, in his palace. He repeatedly thanked her for visiting his country, telling her many times that it was historic. American counterterrorism officials visited often, and he relished the leverage it gave him over the United States. But no American secretary had come to visit him since James Baker in November 1990. Yemen held a rotating seat on the Security Council then, and Baker had come to ask Saleh to vote in favor of a resolution authorizing force to get Saddam Hussein's troops out of Kuwait. He had warned Saleh that he would risk losing the $70 million of yearly aid he was getting from the United States if he voted against it. Saleh, a long-time ally of Saddam, decided he could live without American aid. The Iraqi leader had been doing his own wooing and was hoping to build an anti-American axis in the region, starting with Baghdad and Sana'a.

But when the U.S. aid was cut down further to a pittance, Yemen descended deeper into poverty and crucial ties between the two countries withered. Pakistan had experienced something of the same in the 1990s after aid had been cut. America lost touch with a troubled country that then veered off course. It was a vicious cycle: the United States could not keep pouring aid into countries to keep them steady, but the aid it was giving fed an addiction to external support that often encouraged corruption. Projects that the United States believed were necessary were not a priority in these countries, and America didn't always listen, often believing it knew best: democracy and prosperity had to fit the American template. Countries started feeling entitled to the money and resented the United States when aid was cut because they hadn't abided by the guidelines. There was little understanding outside America of how Congress operated and the hold it could have on the government's purse.

Standing on the steps of the palace after an elaborate lunch, Clinton was not her usual effusive self. She had replaced her own pearl necklace with the elaborate traditional silver necklace that Saleh had given her, but it was the only warm gesture she was willing to make in public toward a man whose arrogance had been revolting. She gave only perfunctory thanks for his warm hospitality and moved on to give a quick overview of what had been discussed. Standing to her left, his sunglasses on, Saleh looked her up and down. There were no questions.

In 1990, Saleh had taken Secretary Baker on a walking tour of the heart of the city, the merchant souk. This was well before al-Qaeda, the attack against the USS *Cole*, 9/11, and the underwear bomber. We would still get a tour, though in armored vehicles. The day before our arrival, DS agents had tested the route through the souk full of people and vendor carts. It had taken over an hour to get through; long enough to give someone time to launch an attack. DS cleared the path as much as possible. Thankfully, Gul's own visit and drive through the souk meant all the diplomatic activity was not necessarily a giveaway about Clinton's impending arrival. Just as on all such visits, Fred's "assets" were invisible to my eyes, but I knew they were everywhere, on rooftops, on corners, in civilian clothes.

Children waved and screamed, "Ahlan, ahlan," Arabic for welcome, as we drove through the souk. Men with their traditional large daggers on their belts looked ever so slightly threatening but smiled broadly. It was an unusually warm welcome in a country that was so vilified in the American press and that arguably could have the same reasons to resent America as Pakistan did. Perhaps they were too amused by the novelty of seeing American vehicles making their way uphill through the narrow alleys, barely an inch to spare between the heavy armored vehicles and the sandstone walls of the buildings along our path.

The contrast between Saleh and his people could not have been greater. The questions at the town hall were some of the most thoughtful and politically cogent we'd heard in two years of endless Hillary-style public diplomacy. Young and old, students and members of parliament, they knew exactly what ailed their country and what the solution was; they were asking for very specific assistance from the United States. There was no ranting, no hatred, no lecturing, just facts. Saleh was perhaps right to say he was not like other Arab leaders: his people had not lost their spark, despite his dictatorship. He had in fact failed to ever fully control this tribal society and what we were witnessing was a fringe benefit of chaos. The women were feisty, everyone's criticism of their leader was remarkably vocal, and their respect for America astonishingly intact. They thanked Hillary for American aid because it had high impact, and they asked for more. They said there had to be an end to the one-party rule because it bred terrorism—and wasn't the United States trying to fight terrorism, after all? They also pushed her on American foreign policy decisions. One man asked her about Obama's failure to close Guantánamo Bay but said he wanted a "real answer, not a politician's answer." The moderator got the signal from the line officer that it was time to wrap up, but Hillary was enjoying this breath of fresh Arab air too much. She did her own moderating.

"Oh, no, no. We will take two more, two more questions. Just two more."

One man told her that Yemenis like him who had lived and studied abroad were sometimes regarded with suspicion back home, like "intruders." He wanted to know how we could make his fellow countrymen accept him as someone who wanted to help build up the country. The final question came from a woman who said that the key to fighting terrorism was improving human rights, so she suggested that the best way to fight terror was for America to declare a war on human rights violations.

We were clearly in the presence of a very thin slice of the population in a poor rural country with high rates of illiteracy and 40 percent unemployment. Rabid, radical militants were unlikely to have made it through a security screening for a town hall with the American secretary of state, and many of those attending were known to the U.S. embassy through exchange programs and NGO work. But that still left a pool of random people whose opinions were never vetted in advance of these events. Even compared to Iraq, where we had attended a town hall organized under similar conditions, the contrast was great. Hillary was delighted by what she heard.

"Wow. I was quite hopeful about Yemen before I came today. And having listened to all of you, I am more so. But these last two young people really give me a lot of confidence in Yemen's future."

Dusk was falling and it was time to move on. After a night and half a day in the Sultanate of Oman, we landed in Doha, just as a crisis erupted in Beirut, a three-hour flight away. Hezbollah and its allies had been threatening to walk out of the coalition cabinet, and they carried out their threat at the exact minute that Lebanon's prime minister Saad Hariri walked into his first-ever meeting with President Obama at the White House. He walked out a former prime minister. Hezbollah, Syria, and Iran were closing in on the country. Clinton's first meeting in Doha, with Gulf ministers, turned into a crisis meeting about Lebanon. The Sunni monarchies, as usual, were fretting about Shiite Iran, and now they were in a panic about losing Lebanon to Hezbollah, which they viewed as a cloak hiding Ahmadinejad and Khamenei. The battle between East and West, between the United States and Iran, between pro-America and pro-Iran, Sunnis and Shiites, was fought on a daily, sometimes hourly, basis in Beirut. The battle lines had ebbed and flowed since that bloody day in Beirut in 1983 when a bomb truck had driven into the marine barracks.

At a press conference with the Qatari foreign minister, Clinton answered four questions, all about Lebanon, Hezbollah, and Iran's influence. Tunisia wasn't on anyone's mind. I called my mother in Beirut. Watching Lebanon from afar, its crises seemed more alarming to me.

"So, the cabinet fell," I ventured.

"Well, my child, we have been without a government for decades," my mother said, speaking to me in Dutch as she often did. "Another one goes, another comes, it's their problem. We just keep going." Forty years in Lebanon had taught my Dutch mother a thing or two about resilience. Though we were a country at peace, there was barely ever any city water or power. Potholes were everywhere. Landfills of garbage destroyed our coast. Red tape and bribes were normal. But we had adapted. We bought power generators, ordered trucks of cistern water to fill up our tanks, and averted our eyes from piles of rubbish. Like others around the region, we got used to the sad state of affairs; defeated, we endured in silence. My family was luckier than most, but I recognized this attitude in many countries, from Syria to China. It was hard to protest against your government when your day was consumed with trying to feed your children and stay alive, and when dissent was punishable with humiliation, torture, or death, even if you were powerful.

In Lebanon during the Syrian occupation, I was frustrated by politicians who in private complained about the humiliation of being at the mercy of their masters in Damascus. I asked why they didn't rebel, push back, and wondered whether they were cowards, worried they would lose the privileges that working with an occupying power did provide—until the former prime minister Rafic Hariri was assassinated. Then a spate of car bombs targeted politicians and journalists who vocally opposed Syria's stranglehold on the country. The country's upcoming leadership was wiped out. The investigation continues, and no one's been convicted yet, but there are few doubts about who did it. One politician's wife told me about the calls she received at work every day from Syrian intelligence officers, recognizable by their accents, warning her that her husband would come back to her in a coffin if he continued to openly criticize Syria.

The politicians who were assassinated did not have pristine records; they had not been perfect democrats or incorruptible, but it didn't matter who owned the truth, who was right or wrong, good or bad—one party was willing to kill to advance its agenda.

At two in the morning on the secure floor of our Doha hotel, it was time for Hillary and her team to forget about the day's crisis in Beirut and take a step back. In makeshift offices in hotels around the world, on the seventh floor of the Building, in the West Wing, at the Pentagon, or aboard SAM, officials went from one crisis to the next, from one urgent matter to the following. The adrenaline never receded. The news cycle was relentless, and long gone were the days when top officials in Washington stopped working at six thirty to watch the evening news and then awaited their morning paper to find out if there were any agenda setters. Every tweet, every blog, every morning, midday, and evening show was a news maker and a crisis alert, and every pundit declared the administration a failure if it hadn't found a solution within five minutes of a problem erupting. There was hardly any time to think about the long term, but like others in the administration, Hillary, Jake, and the rest of the team tried as best they could.

Clinton was often criticized for not having adopted a signature issue to which she had devoted her heart and soul. By the end of her tenure, Condoleezza Rice was in the weeds of the Palestinian-Israeli conflict, negotiating the removal of a checkpoint here and restriction on movement there. She was criticized for losing sight of the bigger picture, shuttling to the region every month and ending up empty-handed. Clinton had steered clear of that approach, partly because none of the problems in her in-box had an easy solution: there was no point tying your reputation to a sure failure. She also believed it was more important to establish long-lasting trends that could deliver more for more people—like empowering civil society and women. This empowerment could, in turn, bring about lasting solutions to conflicts. But she also wanted to manage the bigger picture: America's position in the world. American power was bigger than just the sum of its successes and failures.

Sitting in a staff office with Dan Schwerin, one of Clinton's speechwriters, Jake was reviewing the speech that his boss would be giving at the conference she was here to attend. The Forum for the Future was a yearly gathering of government officials, business leaders, and civil society organizations from G8 countries and the Middle East, and Clinton wanted to deliver a warning about the negative trends in the region. On January 3, Jake and Dan had gathered with Huma and Jeff, the Middle East man, in the secretary's office to prepare for this trip. Clinton wanted civil society to be the focus at every stop, every speech.

In the summer, President Obama gave a directive to review American policy toward the Middle East, a region not only plagued by conflicts but also ruled by dictators, many of them reliable friends of Washington. They provided stability, and America gave them military aid and economic assistance. Those who were not friends with America were somehow part of the system too.

But Washington knew that any perceived stability of the region was false. Condoleezza Rice had spoken in the past about the need to push for reform and not choose stability over democracy, but neither Arab leaders nor Arab civilians were in the mood to listen to America's talk about democracy after the debacle of the Iraq War. Yet there was a growing realization that the price of being friends with rulers like Mubarak of Egypt or Saleh of Yemen was about to rise exponentially. The presidential study ordered by Obama had come to tentative conclusions: be more assertive on pushing reform, find points of leverage, work more with civil society, and ally with people inside the government who understand the urgency for reform. No formal decisions were made, no plans drafted; after all, there was no rush—the Arab world moved at a glacial pace.

Hillary was personally frustrated. She had been traveling to the Arab world for two years as secretary of state by now, and she had seen the region amble aimlessly forward for years. She had read all the UN reports about the lack of development, the booming demographics. She had pleaded with leaders to embrace reforms and had tried to explain how a more open system would benefit everyone. She was fed up with Arab officials not listening to her. Her admonitions were becoming background noise. During that meeting to prepare the trip, Hillary had got more and more agitated as they delved deeper into the challenges of the region.

"I want to break through," she said. "We have to come up with a way to wake these people up. They are sitting on a time bomb."

Not even Hillary knew how prescient her words were. Now in Doha, Jake and Dan were trying to find the one sentence that would help her break through. Was it too harsh? Was the metaphor clichéd or too scathing? Bernadette walked in to pick up a stack of files. They read it to her.

"So what do you think?" asked Jake.

Bernadette paused for a few seconds. She had barely slept since leaving Washington. All she could think of was whether she had prepared enough mini-schedules for the morning. But in the tedium of the grind, Clinton's deputy chief of staff was asking her what she thought about a key policy speech. Suddenly she was reminded of why she was doing this job and what it was all about.

"I like it. It is tough, but it's a good line," she said.

On the morning of January 13, with colleagues from the traveling press, we met Amr Moussa for a quick cup of coffee in the hotel café. The secretary-general of the Arab League didn't have his cigar this time, but he offered more pricelessly useless assessments.

"Ben Ali has called for parliamentary elections. He is serious about finding a solution," he said. He hadn't spoken to any Tunisian officials yet, but as we all walked out of the restaurant, he said he planned to call the foreign minister in the coming days.

Clinton's intervention at the Forum for the Future conference was about to start. In going over the speech in the morning with her team, she had decided she liked the line that had given Jake and the others some anguish. She kept it. She didn't think chaos was around the corner, but the region's young population was only growing and unemployment only rising, with militants keen to fill the void—a combustible combination. It was time to grab the region's leaders by their lapels, others by the golden trimming on their *bishts*, the loose dark coat that men in the Gulf wore over their *thobes*.

"In too many places, in too many ways, the region's foundations are sinking into the sand," she said to the conference attendees. Silence.

"Those who cling to the status quo may be able to hold back the full impact of their countries' problems for a little while, but not forever." More silence.

Clinton was just getting started. The region's leaders needed to listen to their people, she continued. They had to view civil society as a partner, not a threat; they had to create opportunities for their people and rein in corruption.

"Trying to get a permit, you have to pass money through so many different hands. Trying to open up, you have to pay people off. Trying to stay open, you have to pay people off. Trying to export your goods, you have to pay people off. So by the time you finish paying everybody off, it's not a very profitable venture."

When she was asked why the United States couldn't stop Israel from expanding settlements in the West Bank, she gazed pointedly across the room full of officials from countries that were U.S. allies—Bahrain, Jordan, Morocco, Saudi Arabia.

"We can't stop a lot of countries from doing things we disagree with and that we speak out against. We see it all over the world," she said.

"The United States bears a disproportionate amount of the burden for trying to maintain peace and security and prosperity across the globe. I wish there were a way we could tell a lot of countries what they should do," she said.

Clinton was frustrated because the United States, along with Europe, was one of the biggest donors to the Palestinians and constantly had to beg countries like Saudi Arabia to pay up too. The Saudis had pledged close to $2 billion in the preceding few years but so far had transferred only a third of it to the Palestinian government. Arab money was often pledged yet rarely made it to the recipients. The United States often tried to shame Arab countries into disbursing the money they had promised, making very public, elaborate announcements whenever the United States released a portion of money to the Palestinian Authority.

Clinton's role in the forum had come to an end. Our vans were waiting outside the hotel, ready for the race to the airport with the usual detour to the U.S. embassy to rally the troops. No matter how far behind we might have been, embassy stops remained an essential part of our schedule on every trip, in every country. Hillary gave those stops her full attention and her customary warm, energetic thank-you. She felt strongly that embassy employees were the implementers of U.S. foreign policy on the ground. They needed to believe in what they did and feed off her energy to carry forward at a time when doubts about America's role plagued people's vision.

After we left, Egypt's foreign minister Ahmed Aboul Gheit offered his own vision of the urgency for reform.

"History and contemporary practice have both proven that any reform process is by its nature evolutionary, cumulative, and gradual, which are all essential prerequisites in order to guarantee its success and continuity along with the preservation of stability and social cohesion."

The opaque statement reflected the inability of Egyptian leaders to understand the needs of their people, the urgency of reforms. Their obfuscation blinded them to what was awaiting them and their country.

We had a twelve-hour journey back home, stopping through Shannon, and would be landing midevening on U.S. soil. In the front section of the plane, staffers were working on Hillary's speech for the next morning on American-Chinese relations. Jake took a break and came to the back of the plane to chat about the content of her address and all the other preparations that were under way for the visit to Washington the following week by China's president Hu Jintao. We talked about Richard Holbrooke, who had died suddenly a few weeks earlier. Without the special representative for Afghanistan and Pakistan, U.S. policy toward the two countries would soon be adrift. Not everybody had agreed with Holbrooke, and there was much infighting within the administration about him, but he kept people's minds focused on the issue. Soon,

Vali and other people on the team would move on to other jobs inside or outside the State Department. The focus would change, decrease. The Pakistanis would feel abandoned again because Holbrooke's replacement wasn't as high caliber.

After her China speech on Friday morning, Clinton had a ten thirty meeting with the Malaysian deputy prime minister, an eleven o'clock meeting at the White House with President Obama and President Zardari of Pakistan, and a one o'clock meeting with all the special representatives for Afghanistan and Pakistan—Holbrooke's counterparts from all the other countries in the coalition fighting in Afghanistan. They were all in town to attend Holbrooke's memorial service later that afternoon at the Kennedy Center. Hillary and her husband would each give a speech, alongside all the others paying their respects. It was rare for the two Clintons to share time in the same location. Hillary and Bill spoke almost every day on the phone, but coordinating their schedules was an exercise in improbability.

There was also an unscheduled event for that Friday, January 14, all the way in Tunisia. Zine el-Abidine Ben Ali got on a plane and flew into the night, looking for a country that would take him. As with every significant world event, the American president and the secretary of state sent out statements, e-mailed to journalists around town and farther afield.

"The United States continues to closely monitor the rapidly evolving events in Tunisia, where earlier today President Ben Ali left his country following several weeks of demonstrations and popular unrest. We condemn the violence and urge restraint on all sides."

No one said anything about history in the making; no one knew for sure what it meant. But at the White House and the State Department, they rushed to the phones and dialed country code (+20): Cairo? We have a problem.

13

THIS IS NOT
ABOUT US

The Egyptian prime minister Ahmed Nazif and Omar Suleiman, the country's spy chief, had no patience for any more lectures by America. A few months earlier, U.S. officials had called them and even spoken to President Hosni Mubarak himself to press on them the need for urgent reform after the country held fraudulent parliamentary elections in October. A bomb explosion on New Year's Day in Alexandria had also killed twenty Coptic Christians, and in the daily briefing, Egyptian journalists were imploring P. J. and the United States to do something, anything to help protect Egypt's minority. As usual, Mubarak was not receptive to outside advice. But now, the Americans seized on the popular rebellion in Tunisia to make their case again. This could happen in Egypt, the officials warned. Don't you think you're going to have to open things up? No, came the answer. The Egyptians insisted their country was different. It can't happen here, they said. Well, why not? asked Washington. Egypt was just different, replied Cairo.

Ten days after Ben Ali left Tunisia, Clinton traveled to Mexico for a one-day trip full of meetings and public events. SAM flew her back and dropped her off at Andrews Air Force Base at two in the morning on January 25. Later that day, she would be attending President Obama's State of the Union Address in Congress, and she was sending her input to the White House. Obama's advisors were debating whether to mention the events in Tunisia and decided to make an oblique reference to the rest of the region as well. "The United States of America stands with the people of Tunisia and supports the democratic aspirations of all people," Obama would say that evening. But first Clinton had a meeting at ten thirty with the Spanish foreign minister Trinidad Jimenez after which they took questions in the Treaty Room. Those little press conferences, called press avails, were an occasion for journalists to ask Clinton about any world event, not just the content of her meeting.

Earlier that day, protests had erupted across Egypt. A wave of small-scale demonstrations against Mubarak's stranglehold on power had taken place in 2004 and 2005 under the slogan "Enough." Mubarak had been president since 1981, reelected regularly with a surreal 98 percent of the vote. He was grooming his son to take over. The "Enough" movement petered out while another protest group started up: the April 6 movement was launched on Facebook in 2008 and called for a national strike in support of textile workers. Inspired by the nonviolent Otpor! group in Serbia, which helped bring down Slobodan Milošević, one of the movement's members also attended a youth conference organized by the State Department in December 2008. He told U.S. officials about a plan to replace the Mubarak government with a parliamentary democracy by 2011. In a diplomatic cable, revealed by WikiLeaks, U.S. officials said this was a highly unrealistic goal. The April 6 movement did little between December 2008 and January 2011. But now the simmering anger and frustration in a country of eighty million people had been inflamed by Bouazizi next door, and the youth movement in Egypt seized its chance.

One of its members, a young, veiled activist named Asmaa Mahfouz, made a home video exhorting her fellow citizens to take to the streets on January 25 if they really cared about their country. She posted it on You-Tube and the video went viral. Thousands of Egyptians discovered they had a voice and took to the streets. In some of the largest demonstrations Egypt had seen in decades, protestors outnumbered police for the first time. But it would take all day for the world's media to notice something was different about these demonstrations. As the day ended in Cairo, in Washington a reporter sitting in the front row of journalists at the morning press conference asked Clinton about the violence in Egypt. Three people had been killed so far in clashes with the police and forty-nine wounded.

"Is there concern in Washington about the stability of the Egyptian government, of course, a very valuable ally of the United States?"

Hillary was being asked whether a steadfast ally of the United States for the last thirty years, a country of eighty million people, with a powerful army that received more than a billion dollars in American aid every year, was stable. She didn't seem to think twice.

"We support the fundamental right of expression and assembly for all people, and we urge that all parties exercise restraint and refrain from violence. But our assessment is that the Egyptian government is stable and is looking for ways to respond to the legitimate needs and interests of the Egyptian people."

Since Egypt was a behemoth state with a massive army and police force with total control over its territory, it would have been difficult to say that the Egyptian government was *not* stable, because that wouldn't have been entirely accurate either. There was unrest, and the United States was certainly concerned, but Egypt was not Yemen. Mubarak's forces were in charge of every village on the Nile, every slum of sprawling Cairo. Egypt had been stable, it had been a valuable ally, and, through its accord with Israel, it had been (indeed, still was) the cornerstone of the region's cold peace with the Jewish state. Clinton had known Mubarak and his wife since her days at the White House and described them as friends. But if there was often method to Clinton's off-script comments, there was nothing to be gained from using the word "stable." It was superfluous and damaging. A few days later, in a television interview, Vice President Joe Biden said Mubarak was not a dictator and should not step down. Washington just couldn't fathom letting go of Mubarak instantly: the stirrings on the streets of Egypt did not signal a sea change in the country just yet. Despite the corruption, human rights abuses, and repression by a police state, Mubarak was not a ruthless dictator like Saddam Hussein had been, for example; he was an eighty-two-year-old stubborn, greedy pharaoh. But mostly, the United States was keen not to alienate Mubarak. He barely listened to their calls for reform when the country *wasn't* protesting; they couldn't risk shutting down all lines of communications with him now. But when Clinton next spoke in public, she said nothing about stability. She urged the Egyptian government to implement real reforms and said that the United States supported the democratic aspirations of all people.

Many Egyptian protestors had already drawn an instant conclusion—

that America did not support them. They had wanted the United States to ditch Mubarak and take sides with the people unconditionally, immediately, to fulfill everything they believed America stood for, to be on the right side of history, human rights, and freedom. On Tahrir Square, Abdullah al-Murhoni, a middle-aged engineering professor, said he had hoped that the United States, a country that always spoke about freedom and democracy, would have supported the protestors rather than stood by the dictator oppressing them. Past American administrations had happily and quickly voiced their support for popular revolutions attempting to topple dictators that the United States disliked, like in Ukraine, but these Egyptian waters were uncharted, and while Obama recognized that the way the United States approached the Middle East was outdated, there was no instant new script. At this early stage of the protests, Washington was also unsure how far the Egyptian people themselves wanted to go. Did they want Mubarak out, or did they just want radical reforms? Did they want him out now, or would they wait till the next presidential election? Did the hundreds of thousands on the street represent the millions of Egyptians? There was no way of telling, and Obama, who had so carefully avoided the "freedom agenda" of the Bush administration, did not want to get out in front of the Egyptian people. The protests continued to swell through the week as officials in Washington watched closely, trying to take their cue from the streets of Cairo.

In the West Wing, at the Pentagon, in Foggy Bottom, everywhere, there were human beings without all the facts agonizing over difficult decisions. They were euphoric to discover "people power" in the Arab world but torn about how to handle it. Excited and disbelieving diplomats told me they couldn't peel themselves away from their television screen but that they were also at a loss about what to actually do. When crowds chanted "death to America" around the world, as they had been doing for several decades, American officials took it in their stride; they were used to such sentiment by now, a bizarrely comforting background hum, maybe like the sound of shelling was to me when I was child, scary but familiar. But there was no America in the slogans now; instead the streets echoed with "The people want the fall of the regime." "This is not about us," American officials kept telling me. "This is about what Egyptians want." And yet everyone still wanted to know what Washington had decided about Egypt's future: Would America drop Mubarak or prop him up? The reality wasn't that simple.

There were endless interagency meetings as a debate erupted within the administration. The debate wasn't about whether Mubarak should stay or go but about how and how quickly; it was a battle between the idealists and the pragmatists inside the administration. Some officials were trying to avoid a protracted face-off between the people and their rulers or the total collapse of institutions that would send Egypt into a black hole if Mubarak departed too quickly. Mubarak had often warned that the alternative to his rule was a takeover by Islamists. The Muslim Brotherhood, once banned for its espousal of violence, was still repressed by Mubarak and shunned by the United States, even as a peaceful political party. In 2005, Condoleezza Rice had said that the United States had not and would not engage the Islamist group. Egypt's neighbor Israel was also fretting about the prospect that Mubarak could be replaced by an Islamist government. Their peace with Egypt was cold. Mubarak had only ever visited Israel once in thirty years, but he kept the peace treaty alive. For decades, both the United States and Israel seemed unable to understand that Arab dictators who wore ties or spoke English and warned that the alternative to their rule was chaos were only feeding radicalism with their repression. Israel was at peace with one man, Mubarak, not with eighty million Egyptians. Mubarak himself fed anti-American and anti-Israel sentiment and then used it to justify his control over the country.

Younger, more idealistic advisors around Obama, like Samantha Power, were more carried away by the winds of history: we can't stop it; we can't look like we're trying to hold it back because it could backfire and destroy our credibility. Obama took something from each school of thought. His administration would listen to the people and let them set the tone while trying to coax Egypt's leaders in the right direction. Clinton and Gates represented the more traditional thinking inside the administration. They were averse to uncertainty and cautioned against pushing Mubarak out too quickly. America was constantly accused of abandoning its allies; this would be the ultimate and terrible proof that America was a fickle friend. The Saudis were already furious that Washington had refused to show unconditional support for Mubarak. King Abdullah called the Egyptian leader to offer his backing. "Some infiltrators, in the name of freedom of expression, have infiltrated into the brotherly people of Egypt, to destabilize its security and stability," the king said, according to the Saudi Press Agency.

Arab rulers often blamed outsiders—more specifically, the West—for anything that went wrong in their countries. The Egyptian foreign minister Aboul Gheit was convinced that because one member of the April 6 movement had attended a conference in the United States, the whole revolution had been plotted by Washington. On Tahrir Square, some protestors were also wary of too much public support by America, worried that it would only feed the government's attempts to dismiss them as agents of the West.

The leaders still believed in this lie of foreign interference, which was their own falsehood, but the people had woken up to the truth. Now, someone had to wake Mubarak up. Clinton suggested sending someone to Egypt to explain to him, privately, that he must start heading toward the exit before the situation got out of hand. Presidential elections were due to take place later that year, and the message from Washington was that they had to be real—not fixed: neither he nor his sons should stand, and there had to be open competition. There was enough time to prepare for a proper exercise in democracy.

Clinton chose Frank Wisner, a former ambassador to Egypt, to deliver the message, and he prepared to fly out to Cairo on a secret mission. Meanwhile, Mubarak sacked his cabinet on Friday evening, January 28. He also appointed his intelligence chief Omar Suleiman as vice president, but these were futile gestures. Mubarak was still the boss. At the end of that day in Washington, President Obama made a speech.

"When President Mubarak addressed the Egyptian people tonight, he pledged a better democracy and greater economic opportunity. I just spoke to him after his speech and I told him he has a responsibility to give meaning to those words, to take concrete steps and actions that deliver on that promise."

On Sunday, Clinton sat through interviews with all five of the Sunday shows on American network television and delivered the next installment of Washington's policy. On air, she made clear that Mubarak had to listen to his people, that there had to be a national dialogue, and she called for an "orderly transition to democracy." It was a new term in the diplomatic panoply, though what it meant exactly was open to interpretation, to be defined by the Egyptians themselves. On Monday, the thirty-first, during the briefing, a journalist asked P. J. whether the United States would prefer that President Mubarak not seek reelection. "These are decisions to be made inside Egypt." In public, the administration was exceedingly careful not to sound like it was driving the process or imposing its will—this was not about what the United States wanted.

Behind the scenes, gentle advice to the Egyptian leader continued. Wisner landed in Cairo and met with Mubarak, delivering his instructions from Washington: the president had to make way, for the good of the country. But the crusty old man had no ears for that. He had no new tricks in his bag. He was ancient and knew how to do things only one way.

At the White House and the State Department, officials worried about the fixation on the streets of Cairo with specific individuals: Mubarak in, Mubarak out, Suleiman in, Suleiman out; the protestors didn't seem to take into account that there was a massive institution and apparatus that stood behind Mubarak and could remain fundamentally intact and manage the process even without him. On the Sunday shows, Clinton had warned that there was no point removing Mubarak just to have him replaced by a military dictatorship. The United States knew how powerful the military was: just as in Pakistan, the army was a corporation with entrenched interests, underwritten by American money to the tune of more than $1 billion a year—in many ways, a good investment since the army was promising today not to shoot at the people. But who knew what they would do tomorrow? There were limits to how much influence the United States had over a sovereign army.

Democratic and Republican senators were starting to call on Mubarak to step down, pressing the administration to publicly call for his resignation. Some of my American friends were furious it was taking Obama so long to say Mubarak had to step down. If I were still living in Lebanon, I may have thought the same, infuriated by America's typical reluctance, its pursuit of narrow interests. But after several years with a front-row seat in Washington, I was starting to understand the complex decision-making process and I could see how the United States tried to weigh its actions. I found myself debating with a friend the deliberate approach taken by the administration. Was it the responsible choice? Empower the people but make sure it's not an American-driven process; don't say things you can't deliver on; don't push people out front only to leave them hanging because you can't protect them when the police arrest them or beat them to death (or both). In 1991, after the Gulf War, the United States had encouraged Shiites in Iraq to rise up against Saddam Hussein. But Washington was unable or unwilling to provide cover or help to the rebellion. Tens of thousands of people died as Saddam crushed the uprising.

America was perhaps finally learning the impact of its words. Expressions of support were often misinterpreted. When American leaders winked, strange things happened, like Georgian presidents going to war with Russia thinking America would back them up. The Obama administration believed that a somewhat more neutral expression was best. If the United States had rushed to say Mubarak should step down, but he had stayed and trampled on the protestors further and with greater loss of life, the United States would have been lambasted for not stopping Mubarak when all America could really have done was call for the violence to end. The United States wasn't going to send in the cavalry, and cutting military aid for the Egyptian army wouldn't have had an immediate impact and was only a last resort.

In May 2008, when Lebanon had descended into another bout of violence with pro-Western and anti-Western forces clashing on the street, the liberals in Beirut had been buoyed by expressions of moral support from the United States. And when their paltry forces were defeated by Hezbollah, armed to the teeth and backed by Syria and Iran, they accused the United States of abandoning them. But what did they expect the United States to do? I asked around, and responses ran the gamut. In all seriousness, some politicians replied that they had requested the White House to buzz Bashar al-Assad's palace in Damascus with U.S. fighter jets or, even better, send American marines to Beirut. Lebanon was definitely not the only country with crazy ideas about how American power worked.

While people around the world feverishly speculated about America's plans for Egypt, officials in the United States were in the dark. "We are entering the unknown. This could be 1989 or it could be 1979," one of them told me. The fall of the Berlin Wall or the Iranian Revolution: two world events in which the United States had been a player but the consequences and outcome of which it couldn't and didn't dictate. The aftermath had been widely different: one event had ushered in an era of openness in Europe, the other had brought a theocracy to Iran. No one knew what the revolution in Egypt would produce, but there were warnings in

Washington that America's influence in the region would be undermined by events. After all, this was an American ally being ousted by his own people, and many read it as a rejection of the American order. Countries that opposed U.S. influence in the region, like Syria and Iran, were gleeful.

In Beirut, some of my liberal friends worried that Hezbollah would emerge more powerful in what appeared to be a battle for the soul of the Middle East, Iran's influence over Lebanon only growing as America retreated from the region. Ayatollah Khamenei, the supreme leader in Iran, was thinking precisely that and shared as much in a tweet to the world. @khamenei_ir : "Ayatollah Khamenei: the time has come for an end to the dominance of the superpowers & a gradual decline in their power."

I was particularly struck by how, despite all the talk about the end of the American empire, no one seemed to be curious about what the Chinese were saying to Mubarak. The Chinese of course had even less leverage over him than the United States did, but the protestors craving outside recognition were neither asking nor getting it from China—or from Russia for that matter. Beijing was quiet, too busy blocking the Internet at home to make sure the Chinese didn't see what people power could do to autocrats in the age of Twitter and twenty-four-hour news. Reacting to a major international crisis by looking inward with paranoia was not exactly the stuff of a superpower. Even the European countries barely uttered a word. Somehow what America said, what it did or didn't do, still mattered, even if people's grasp of what made up American power was out of touch with reality.

"This is the irony here," an American official complained to me. "On the one hand, we're being accused of dominating everything and dictating everything. On the other hand, we're being accused of not dictating everything and dominating everything. These are choices to be made by the Egyptian people." No matter what Washington did, the world expected something different.

The truth was somewhere in the middle between dominating and not dominating. And so every day, America waited and listened to the people on the streets of Egypt. When the crowds roared, the tone in the United States toughened. When the anger ebbed, Washington spoke more softly. Every day, everyone in Washington called everyone in Cairo, and they waited for the next speech. But Mubarak was always one step behind.

*   *   *

On February 1, Mubarak announced that he would not seek reelection. But he said nothing about whether his son would stand. He gave some hints about reform and dialogue. On the streets of Cairo, opinions were divided. The president had made a gesture. He had listened. Some didn't trust him. Others did. In Washington, there was a sense that perhaps things were calming down. The pharaoh had announced he was going to retire, and perhaps Mubarak should be given a bit of time to make those changes. There was no point making him grovel.

Obama, however, wanted to hold Mubarak to his word. He wanted to clarify exactly what Mubarak needed to do to make sure the political transition was real, started right away, and didn't last forever. No one wanted months of protests on the streets of Egypt. Mubarak and Obama spoke on the phone in English for thirty minutes. Obama was respectful of his elder but firm. You are a leader who has served his people for a long time, Obama told Mubarak, someone who is committed to serving his people. But this isn't going to work this way, you are going to have to accelerate the transition and hold talks with a full range of opposition leaders. Obama appealed to Mubarak's sense of pride and love of his country. After committing his whole life to Egypt, surely the last thing Mubarak wanted was instability.

"You don't know my people. They know only I can create stability."

"What if you're wrong?"

"But you don't know my people."

"Let's talk in twenty-four hours."

"No, no, we'll talk in a few days. You will see, everything will be fine."

"You could be right, but what if you're not. The stakes are high for you too."

Obama tried to be respectful and empathic as he tried to explain to a man who was old enough to be his father that it wasn't because things had been a certain way for a long time that they would stay like that. Mubarak was too old to listen.

"I know my people. You don't know them."

They would never speak again. Obama gave a speech soon after the call. He was frustrated. He wanted to lock Mubarak into the promises he had made about reform. In a stern address, Obama put Mubarak on notice.

"I spoke directly to President Mubarak. He recognizes that the status quo is not sustainable and that a change must take place. What is clear—

and what I indicated tonight to President Mubarak—is my belief that an orderly transition must be meaningful, it must be peaceful, and it must begin now."

The next day, regime thugs forged into the crowds on horseback, beating demonstrators. Three people were killed, another 1,500 injured. The ferocious attack was a turning point in the protests and gave the lie to Mubarak's assurances that only he could bring stability to the country. Tahrir Square erupted again, united once more in fury, demanding Mubarak's departure. Any illusion that there was still time for the president to be part of the transition was gone.

Clinton called the intelligence chief Omar Suleiman, who had just been appointed as vice president a few days earlier. She was firm: this would not be tolerated. Suleiman reassured her it wouldn't happen again and that the violence would indeed be kept under control. You can't put the salt back in the shaker, she told him. You have to preside over a real transition. You can't just do some window-dressing reforms and stick around for another ten years. Real change had to come. Fast.

Every day, Clinton went to the White House. She met with Obama alone. She met with Bob Gates and the national security advisor Tom Donilon. They met all together. Clinton had always said that what had surprised her most about her job was how often she was at the White House. Now she was spending half her days there. Obama was surrounded by his own trusted circle of advisors who saw the world as he did, but over the course of the last two years, he had been listening more closely to Clinton. And she, in turn, voiced her views and gave advice with more and more confidence. Clinton had spent her first year in Obama's cabinet trying to be, for the most part, the good soldier. Now she added to that role her own pragmatic views and a voice more forcefully heard. During national security meetings, the national security advisor would kick off with the agenda, and if the focus was foreign policy, Obama would turn to Clinton to ask for her input before the advisor had even finished. If she wasn't present, Obama would say, I want to know where Hillary is on this. They didn't always agree, of course, and he was still the ultimate decider, but Clinton was a steady hand and, perhaps most importantly, she was the implementer. If Obama wanted something done, he needed to know Clinton felt confident she could deliver the outcome that was required.

Hillary took the long view on Egypt, keeping one eye on the bigger picture. She had warned about moving too fast and making it look like the United States was abandoning its allies. She believed deeply in empowering people and in the need to support reform, but she was also the one who had given a speech in Doha just a few weeks earlier warning that the choice was not between reform and stability but between reform and chaos. Now, chaos was knocking at the door, and it was important to manage this properly. The United States had a reputation to think of. It wasn't just a question of values but also one of credibility. And it was about money. Washington was already underwriting the Egyptian army, but the aftermath of any upheaval would require an influx of aid to fuel the economy. The United States had its own economic woes to worry about and could soon find itself knocking on Riyadh's door to ask for their riyals to flow toward Egypt. It was unwise to alienate the rich uncle in the Gulf just before asking for his wallet. Israel's fears about an Egypt without Mubarak also weighed on Clinton's mind.

On February 5, a few days after Obama's call for the transition to "begin now," Wisner, by now a former envoy, gave a talk at a conference in Munich. He volunteered his opinion that it would actually still be best if Mubarak stayed in power to oversee the whole process of the transition toward democracy. This is what Wisner had been sent to tell Mubarak, but since then everything had changed. Conspiracy theories erupted across the globe. What did he mean by that? Hadn't Obama said the transition started now? Didn't that mean that Mubarak himself had to go now? Was Mubarak suddenly part of that transition? What was America's plan? Once again, here was proof of America's changeability: saying one thing, doing another. U.S. leaders claimed that they were with the people, but really they were protecting their ally, hedging their bets, waiting to see which way the wind would blow. The foreign minister Ahmed Aboul Gheit complained during a television interview with PBS that America was sending mixed messages that were utterly confusing even to the Egyptian leadership.

The Obama administration was trying so hard to find the right words, to weigh every message, yet its response looked messy and uncoordinated. But what people often forgot was that American officials didn't have it all figured out, every statement was not part of a methodical plan, and not everybody agreed on the best course of action. And this was not China, where decision making was hypercentralized and officials did not deviate from the party line, whether in public or private. The United States was a country where people loved to express their opinions, and it wasn't always easy to stick to one message. If you had been hired as a freelancer and your mission was over, as in the case of Wisner, surely you could express your own opinions again. Hillary, who was at the same conference in Munich, was frustrated when she heard the news. She canceled her dinner plans and tried to fix the damage. Obama was annoyed by the uncertainty the different statements were creating about Washington's policy. The White House issued clear instructions: not a word would be uttered anymore that hadn't been approved; no one was to stray from the talking points.

After days of defiantly poking his finger in America's eye, Mubarak finally promised the military he would announce his resignation in a speech on the evening of February 10. The army had been watching with alarm as the protests swelled. Their own power was at risk. Egypt's generals told officials in Washington that everything was set for Mubarak's departure. Speaking to Congress that morning, CIA chief Leon Panetta said there was "a strong likelihood that Mubarak may step down this evening."

Clinton was convinced Mubarak was going to hedge. His first speech had been so ambiguous that she expected this one would be equally so. Chatting with her aides, she said she just couldn't see how this old man could stand up and say, "I'm leaving." It just wasn't in his DNA.

Hillary watched the speech in her office on the seventh floor. Her television set, usually sitting silently behind a panel in the wooden wall unit to the right of her desk, had been turned on for the occasion. Mubarak's speech was so convoluted that for seventeen long minutes, no one knew what he was trying to say. At some point, he did utter the sentence "Transfer all powers under the constitution to the vice president." On Tahrir Square, barely anyone was listening anymore: there were howls of rage, tears, and protestors who had been chanting, "The people want the downfall of the regime," started singing, "The people want to understand the speech." When Mubarak was finished, I asked American officials whether the speech was satisfactory.

"We're trying to decipher his words," one of them said.

Panetta would later issue a correction about his statement to Congress, explaining that he had been relying on what he'd heard in the media. He made himself look like a fool: if the CIA director relied on the media for his information, the world was in trouble. But it was Mubarak who was really in trouble. Panetta knew Mubarak had promised to resign, but the pharaoh had reneged on his promise.

Obama watched the speech on board Air Force One, returning from a trip to Michigan. Mubarak had included a special message for him. "It is shameful and I will not, nor will I ever, accept to hear foreign dictations, whatever the source might be or whatever the context it came in."

What on earth was going on? That evening, the White House sent out a written statement by President Obama.

"The Egyptian people have been told that there was a transition of authority, but it is not yet clear that this transition is immediate, meaningful, or sufficient . . . We therefore urge the Egyptian government to move swiftly to explain the changes that have been made."

The focus—at least publicly—was on the Egyptian people.

"The Egyptian people have made it clear that there is no going back to the way things were: Egypt has changed, and its future is in the hands of the people . . . In these difficult times, I know that the Egyptian people will persevere, and they must know that they will continue to have a friend in the United States of America."

Later that evening, Defense Secretary Gates called Field Marshal Mohamed Tantawi, Egypt's defense minister, and told him this was a dangerous crossroads: Mubarak had to go. The army now needed to clean this up and help manage the transition. The United States stood ready to mentor them and help the Egyptian army do something they'd never done before—give birth to a democratic process.

Many in the administration worried that the army would do everything possible to preserve its own power and privileges, but Washington couldn't tell how big of a problem it might become; the country would descend into chaos unless the crowds were calmed and the protestors got what they wanted. The army was Washington's only recourse. The generals were tired and tense, worried about bloodshed. They had so far avoided shooting. The people kissed soldiers on the streets and praised the army, but it could all be lost in an instant. The generals weighed their options all night and all of the next day. Mubarak was a military man, and he had ruled for three decades. The generals may not have liked being bossed around by the United States, but it was that or risk destroying the whole edifice.

But it truly was not in Mubarak's DNA to announce his departure, so he sent someone else to utter the fateful words. On February 11, at eleven in the morning in Washington, six in the evening in Cairo, Clinton arrived at the White House for a meeting. In Cairo, Omar Suleiman faced the cameras in a wood-paneled hallway of the presidential palace. Standing under neon lights, in a blue suit and tie, the seventy-five-year-old man looked like death, all color drained from his face. He spoke for thirty-five seconds. The president had resigned. The Supreme Council of the Armed Forces was in charge.

"God help everybody," he said. The people had won.

On Tahrir Square, they celebrated and cried with relief that the decades of frustration, humiliation, corruption, repression, and poverty had come to an end. All their dreams had come true, said one woman. Few paused to wonder whether being ruled by the army was cause for celebration. They thought the revolution was the answer to all their problems, unaware that revolutions simply lift the veil that concealed the extent of problems plaguing a country, problems hidden for years by the state's propaganda.

The State Department briefing for that day was canceled. On big momentous occasions such as this, the White House spoke first. No matter how big a star Hillary was on the world stage, the president was the president. Four hours later, Obama stood in the marble grand foyer of the White House. It had been a roller-coaster few days and weeks as the battle between American national interests and American principles was fought in offices in Washington, in people's minds, in Obama's heart, and on the streets of Cairo.

"There are very few moments in our lives where we have the privilege to witness history taking place," the president started by saying. "This is one of those moments. This is one of those times. The people of Egypt have spoken, their voices have been heard, and Egypt will never be the same."

Nothing would be the same again. Not Egypt, not the Middle East, and not America.

"The word 'Tahrir' means liberation," Obama said at the end of his speech. "It is a word that speaks to that something in our souls that cries out for freedom. And forevermore it will remind us of the Egyptian people, of what they did, of the things that they stood for, and how they changed their country, and in doing so changed the world."

In Tahrir Square, Obama's speech was carried live on big screens, his words texted around by jubilant protestors. Though they had been disappointed by what they saw as America's initial reluctance to support them, they were now proud to be recognized by a president they still admired. But this was their victory. They had done it.

Throughout the process, Hillary didn't call Hosni or Suzanne Mubarak, and they didn't call her either. This was politics. Clinton wasn't cold-blooded, just realistic. Democratic forces were at work, and leaders lost power. She was a veteran politician who had faced loss herself. She would shed no tears for a guy because he didn't get to rule the way he'd ruled for the last thirty years.

That evening, some 1,080 miles west of the jubilant scenes in Cairo, Yael Lempert was glued to the television with her husband and some friends. She had recently served as an American diplomat in Egypt and was transfixed by the scope and pace of events. She thought of her Egyptian friends who had expressed such frustration about life under Mubarak. How elated they must be. She was now the acting deputy chief of mission at the brand-new U.S. embassy in Tripoli.

"It's such a shame that this will not happen here," she said. They turned off the television and went out for dinner at a Chinese restaurant.

An hour later, Libyan state television's news ticker carried a short sentence about Mubarak's resignation. The country's own much more colorful demagogue, Colonel Muammar Gaddafi, had been in power even longer—forty-two years—wearing purple or blue silk suits and epaulets, carrying a gold scepter, and surrounding himself with female bodyguards. But he was certain of his people's love. They would not let themselves be used by foreign plotters. He was convinced that he was different from his neighbors on his eastern and western borders.

Three days later, on February 14, protests erupted in Bahrain, a small island state where Sunni monarchs ruled over a Shiite majority. For years, Shiites had faced discrimination in jobs and society, and now they were taking to the streets. The crackdown was shocking in its brutality. But Clinton chose her words very carefully when she spoke out about the violence.

"Bahrain is a friend and an ally and has been for many years, and while all governments have a responsibility to provide citizens with security and stability, we call [for] restraint."

When the United States looked at Bahrain, it didn't just see protestors demanding respect for their rights; it saw Iran lurking behind and the picture blurred. Shiite Iran had long had claims over the small island. But Bahrain was home to the U.S. Fifth Fleet and a key pillar for the U.S. regional military infrastructure. Sunni kingdoms like Bahrain and its bigger neighbor Saudi Arabia were a crucial counterweight to Tehran's growing influence in the region. The undertone of sectarian tension, real or imagined, meant the United States was taking no chances. In Egypt, they had gambled on an army underwritten by Washington, but Bahrain could very well be the first domino to fall into the Iranian camp. Blinded by its fear of Iran, the United States would do nothing that risked bringing down Bahrain's rulers.

With each revolution in each country came a new set of issues, a new set of headaches for the Obama administration, and challenges to the exercise of American power in the region and in the twenty-first century. Each one was a lesson about the challenges and possibilities for the United States as a world leader.

14

SARKO'S WAR

On the night of February 18 when Yael Lempert went to bed in her home in Suqal Jumaa, Tripoli's sprawling eastern suburb, she could hear shooting in the distance for the second night in a row. Earlier in the day, the American diplomat had asked Libyan officials about it, but they had brushed the gunfire away.

"Just a few excited *shabab*," they had said.

Shabab means "young men" in Arabic, and it's often used to describe a group of them, hanging out on street corners, rowdy, restless, bored, and underemployed. They harass girls, smoke cigarettes, and occasionally fire guns for fun or to mark their territory. There were *shabab* in Lebanon, in Jordan, in the Palestinian territories, places where young men often had little to do and where the state afforded them some latitude. But the tightly controlled Jamahiriya of Gaddafi? Not so much.

At three in the morning, Yael's home phone rang. The cell phone network was out of commission. It was one of the embassy drivers.

"I'm in Green Square," he said. "Fifteen people just died in front of me. The revolution has started." Click.

All night the shooting continued. In the morning, Yael drove to work in her SUV. Suddenly, halfway into the fifteen-minute ride, she saw the Arabic writing scrawled on the walls. Anti-Gaddafi graffiti, pictures of the leader defaced. It was true: the revolution had started. Her mind raced through the different scenarios. How would this unfold? Would Gaddafi use violence? Would millions take to the street? The only thing Yael was certain of was that it wouldn't be quick like in Egypt. There were no checks and balances here, no institutions, just a dictator with a Green Book of rules and slogans. She had to start planning with the embassy staff. And she had to think of her baby; her first child was due in just a month.

The embassy was a start-up mission. The United States had closed down the mission in 1979 after mobs attacked the building, the same week that the U.S. embassy had been torched in Pakistan, all in the aftermath of the siege of Mecca. Libya had started turning into an international pariah soon after Gaddafi came to power in 1969, as he waged war against Egypt, supported anti-Western militant groups around the world, and developed a stockpile of weapons of mass destruction. Gaddafi, or Brother Leader, as he called himself, was most infamous for ordering the 1988 bombing of Pan Am flight 103 over Lockerbie in Scotland, in which 270 people died. In the late 1990s, Gaddafi had slowly begun his rehabilitation. In 2005, he announced he would give up his WMDs and then agreed to pay compensation for the Lockerbie victims. In 2008, the United States reopened its embassy in Tripoli after removing Libya from the list of state sponsors of terrorism. But unlike every other American embassy around the world, there were no marines standing guard. Gaddafi had refused to allow U.S. Marines into the country, and it was difficult to argue with an unpredictable leader prone to tantrums. Under the Bush administration, the State Department had conceded the point to Gaddafi, not an unreasonable decision in a police state where no one breathed without permission from the leader and where crime was nonexistent. The first sign that perhaps the concession was not so wise came after the WikiLeaks debacle. Gaddafi had been incensed after the leaks revealed that the newly arrived American ambassador, Gene Cretz, had speculated about Gaddafi's health and mentioned his voluptuous nurse. Gaddafi's security men started tailing Cretz around town, and out of concern for his safety the State Department ordered him to leave the country.

Now, at the start of a revolution, with embassy buildings and staff spread out across the city and no reliable radio communications network, the mission was vulnerable and exposed—every diplomat's worst nightmare. Cell phone coverage in Tripoli was already patchy, and the authorities were trying to cut off the country's Internet connection. In a matter of days, Yael and her colleagues would have no e-mail, no working cell phones, and just one landline at the embassy that could still reach both the sixth floor of the Building in Washington and the operations center.

In my tiny cubicle in Washington, I waited for e-mails to appear in my in-box. Throughout the Egypt crisis, I had been in constant e-mail contact with American officials in the Building. Stuck in endless interagency meetings, they weren't always free to talk on the phone, but no matter how busy they were, they always found the time to fire off a quick reply to my e-mail queries. E-mail was the communication method of choice in Washington, BlackBerries an extension of people's hands. In short missives, officials engaged in a lively back and forth electronic conversation. They had shared fears about the unknown that was engulfing the region and their hopes about a better future for Egypt. And they often shared information beyond what was being said in front of the cameras by P. J. Crowley or White House spokesperson Robert Gibbs. They told me what they were telling Mubarak, what the generals saying were saying, how frustrated they were that Mubarak was always one step behind, how they were adjusting their statements to the clamor on Egypt's streets.

Now every morning, I sent e-mails asking about Libya: When were they going to tell Gaddafi he had to step down? What leverage did they have over him? When were they going to evacuate all embassy staff? I waited and waited. I called their offices, but they weren't there or were too busy to take the call. Hours, days passed. Nothing. The daily press briefings too were frustrating. Even P. J., prone to making jokes and often getting out ahead of the policy talking points in his binder, much to the annoyance of the White House, was exceedingly careful during the briefing, and even in private, when we cornered him for a few minutes away from the cameras.

On February 21, the State Department ordered families of diplomats out of the country. The situation was deteriorating quickly. The protests were spreading around the country and becoming more violent. More than one hundred Libyans had already been killed as Gaddafi unleashed his police forces and army on civilians. Washington still did not call for Gaddafi to step down nor order all Americans to leave the country. The praise for the demonstrators was lukewarm and general. I was baffled. In the briefing, Matt, from the AP, was poking P. J. with a hot stick.

"Is there a reason why no one, none of the officials who have spoken to this yet, have actually used Gaddaffi's name?"

"Well, this—as I just said, we hold the Libyan government, including its leader, responsible for what is occurring in Libya."

"And that leader's name is?

"Colonel Gaddafi."

"Everybody looks at Washington, and they see a very tepid, if at all, enthusiasm for toppling Gaddafi, while they have shown more enthusiasm towards what happens elsewhere. Could you explain that to us?"

"Well, as I suggested yesterday, who leads Libya is a matter between the government and the Libyan people. As we have said throughout this historic period, it is not for the United States or any outside power to dictate who should rule or not rule a particular country."

Outside of the United States, as usual, people paid close attention to every statement made by American officials. A few days earlier on Twitter, P. J. had criticized Congress for banning U.S. funding for a UN panel on climate change and cutting funding for the State Department's special envoy for climate change. A Libyan Twitter user replied instantly: "Mr Crowley, we appreciate your environmental consciousness, but here in Tripoli we are getting killed."

When a reporter asked P. J. during the daily press briefing if the United States had heard from the Libyan foreign minister Musa Kusa, P. J. said the minister hadn't picked up his phone for a few days. The next morning, Kusa called Jeff Feltman, the Building's Middle East policy man: "Mr. Crowley says you're having trouble reaching me?"

Unbeknownst to many of us haranguing American officials in Washington, the regime in Tripoli had made clear that the American diplomatic staff was not to leave the country. Americans had been evacuated from Egypt and look what had resulted—a revolution had toppled Mubarak. Gaddafi wanted to keep the diplomats as leverage, an insurance policy to guarantee his continuing power: a hostage situation was developing. Gaddafi had been linked to bomb attacks in Europe in the past, and Washington as well as European countries worried that he still had operatives in the West he could activate. Yael and her colleagues pleaded with the administration not to publicly call on Gaddafi to step down until they were able to negotiate a way out of the country for everyone and had a secure exit route. In the Building and at the White House, the mood wavered between anguish and fury. The Americans were at the mercy of an erratic dictator who brought down planes, planted his tent in public parks in Europe, and demanded public apologies from American officials even if they sounded sarcastic when speaking about him.

On February 23, Clinton gave a short press conference in the Treaty Room with the Brazilian foreign minister after their talks. A reporter asked the secretary of state what the United States was doing about the violence in Libya. She gave a long, circuitous answer involving pressure at the UN and the Human Rights Council in Geneva. Suddenly, toward the end, she slipped in a statement calling on all Americans to leave Libya immediately.

"And we are encouraging Americans to leave Libya," Clinton said. "We have taken the step of providing a chartered ferryboat today to take off not only all the Americans who could get to the ferryboat pier, but also other nationals from other countries who we have offered to similarly take out of Libya. We urge Americans to depart immediately." Within hours, the State Department would issue its standard notice in such cases, widely e-mailed and posted on the website of the embassy in Tripoli.

After days of pleading, Yael and her colleagues had finally secured permission for safe passage out of the country. A top Libyan official had somehow agreed to an evacuation. A ferryboat had arrived in Tripoli, but it would still take a few more days for everyone to get out. Storms and choppy seas had delayed the ferry's departure, and the four hundred Americans whose passports had been stamped for departure out of the country would have to spend two nights on a boat, with almost no supplies, docked in the port of a country slipping into chaos.

They were close enough to freedom that later in the evening, President Obama made his first public statement about Libya. The suffering and bloodshed were outrageous, he said. The United States was looking at all the options. He was sending Clinton to Geneva to a special session at the UN Human Rights Council.

During his seven-minute statement, Obama did not once mention Gaddafi by name.

On Sunday morning, February 27, SAM sat on the tarmac waiting for us. In the VIP lounge, we drank weak coffee, nibbled on some air force chocolate chip cookies, and had our little lottery. I got a window seat. Clinton's black armored Cadillac came to a halt by the nose of the plane. Seven DS agents spilled out of two vans and sprinted up the steps and into the aircraft, while two others stayed on the tarmac to help unload luggage from the car, whose trunk was unusually empty: just a couple of bags for a thirty-six-hour-long mission to Geneva to stop a madman who was on a rampage against his own people. More than one thousand people had been killed by now. Gaddafi called the protestors "rats." He threatened to hunt them down and execute them all. His problems were America's fault, he said. He was already starting to lose territory: the eastern city of Benghazi had fallen to the opposition, soldiers were fast defecting, and rebels were organizing themselves in the east of the country.

Hillary emerged from the car, sunglasses on. She always wore sunglasses outside, even on gray, melancholy days like this. She made her way into her cabin on the plane. On the table, by the secure phone with which she could call president Obama or other foreign leaders while above the clouds, was the usual sheet of paper with the weather forecast for our destination, mostly cloudy with a chance of rain or snow—high: 45° F, low: 35° F. Clinton had traveled to seventy-nine countries by now and covered almost five hundred thousand miles. But no trip, no crisis, had tested her and her country's role as a superpower like the eruption of anger that brought millions of Arabs onto the streets demanding to be rid of the leaders who had deprived them of hope and freedom.

She never wore makeup on our morning flights out of Andrews Air Force Base. Her freckles showed, and she looked fresh and much younger without the layers of foundation and powder that television required. She always smiled when she came to the back of the plane to chat with us before takeoff. By then, she would be wearing her rectangular Giorgio Armani glasses, and in her booming voice, a twinkle in her eye, she would exclaim, "Hi, guys!"

But that day, she looked tired and tense, worn out by two months of an Arab upheaval that was only gathering momentum. Jake, in his trademark blue fleece, clutching his notebook, stood behind her, looking more gaunt than ever, the black circles around his blue eyes even bigger than usual. Only now were people in Washington starting to grasp the full extent of what was happening. The revolt was engulfing the whole region, American allies and foes alike. Arabs were rising up against their leaders, brutal and delusional old men who still dyed their hair jet-black, who gave three-hour-long speeches because no one had ever dared tell them to shut up, who thought the Botox injected into their faces served as a facelift for their country. They presided over a people bored into submission, swindled into poverty, beaten into obedience, tortured to death. No one knew yet who or what would replace them, but America's global leadership and even its economic recovery hung in the balance.

Some also saw an opportunity within the crisis, a chance for America to bring its stated values and principles into line with its policies, a better way to protect its national interests in the long term. Oil prices were rising steadily. Oil companies in Libya had shut down production and evacuated staff, taking Libya's daily production of 1.6 million barrels a day off the market. What better way to maintain access to oil resources and trade routes than to have all the Arab people on your side, not just their autocratic leaders? Equally, it could turn into another episode of world history over which the United States had no control but that could deal another blow to the slow recovery of America's power and standing in the world.

Doug, the flight attendant, handed out mimosas in plastic cups. We'd never had those on SAM before, but perhaps a Sunday morning departure in the midst of a huge crisis warranted a nod to brunch. We were all tired enough to be immensely grateful. I sipped my drink and took one last look at my Twitter feed before takeoff. I had been staying in touch with Libyans in Tripoli and Benghazi thanks to this twenty-first-century personal telegram, with minute-by-minute updates about the latest outburst of shooting, which room of the house someone was sheltering in, what the noise around them told them about the weapons unleashed against them.

I could read the fear in their tweets just as I could hear it in the voice of the woman who two days earlier had called in to CNN imploring from Tripoli, in very basic English and a halting voice, "Please help us, Mr. Obama, please help us." Gaddafi was threatening to hunt down his opponents alley by alley. His army was shelling neighborhoods indiscriminately, dragging people out of their houses and shooting them on the street. A UN resolution had imposed sanctions on the country; an arms embargo was in place. Now pundits and politicians were talking about the need for more. Maybe a no-fly zone to protect civilians? This was like a demilitarized zone but in the sky, a swath of territory over which Gaddafi's military aircraft would not be able to fly and bomb civilians on the ground. But someone had to enforce the zone by patrolling it with fighter jets. No one liked Gaddafi, but military action was a whole different ball game. And Gaddafi wasn't really deploying his airpower anyway. He was mostly sending in mercenaries and tanks to shoot and crush people to death.

In Geneva, foreign ministers from around the world were attending the session at the UN Human Rights Council, the perfect occasion for Clinton to gauge which way the international winds blew. On Monday morning, on the ground floor of the Intercontinental Hotel, a ballet of trays with glasses of juice and cookies mirrored the comings and goings of foreign ministers who had all come to the hotel to meet her. In one conference room, she sat down with the Russian foreign minister Sergei Lavrov. He was adamant: no no-fly zone, absolutely not. Clinton was still unconvinced herself about the way forward. A no-fly zone was fraught with dangers and didn't protect civilians from ground fire. But she wanted to keep all options on the table. She pressed Lavrov, saying that they all had to think about it seriously.

She stepped out into the foyer and into the conference room next door, where she sat down with the Germans, Italians, and French. More trays, more juice. The Europeans made their way out. Clinton crossed the hall and walked into a third conference room. A large table had been set up with little name tags with mini American flags on one side of the table and a red flag with a white crescent and star on the other. Davutoğlu stood waiting for Clinton, and the two friends shook hands, greeting each other warmly. Hillary knew this would be another tough conversation. The Turks were still talking about their zero-problem policy in the region, especially ironic now that the Arab world's problems were multiplying by the day. Erdoğan had emphatically accused the international community of acting on Libya out of self-interest, motivated more by the country's oil riches than concern for its people. Turkey in fact already had a blossoming relationship with the North African country: $2.4 billion in yearly trade and $15 billion invested in construction projects. A war now would slaughter the cash cow.

After listening to all her counterparts, Clinton returned to Washington to brief Obama. She had a sound sense of where each country stood, but she was the clearest on where they diverged—there was no consensus about military action, let alone consensus about a no-fly zone, unlikely to protect civilians from artillery shelling anyway. The French and British were the most gung ho about reining in Gaddafi. More importantly, the Arabs were still far behind the rest of the world. They had suspended Libya from the Arab League but had done little else.

This American administration was not about to embark on a war with a paltry and hastily assembled coalition to remove a dictator who for now posed no or little strategic threat to the United States, only to be left with the broken pottery. For two years, the Obama administration had worked to embed the United States in multilateral organizations around the world, to make the United States a partner in decision making everywhere. Obama had invested far too much in not being a bully—at least not on issues that were of no immediate strategic value to the United States—to undo that work by stampeding into a war without a UN resolution. The United States also didn't have the money or the appetite for another war, but mostly, it didn't want to do everyone else's expensive, dirty work. People were dying, and the United States would do all it could to bring pressure on Gaddafi, but the calculations that propelled American power were changing; the world itself was changing. It was time for other countries, other regions, to take ownership of their problems. For decades, the first reaction of people around the world had been to ask what America was planning. Now America wanted first to know what the rest of the world had in mind, and second, what they were willing to contribute to that plan.

The French and the British had made their own gaffes on Tunisia and Egypt, and had been even further behind the United States in catching up with the popular mood on the Arab street. Nicolas Sarkozy's government had shipped tear gas to Tunisian police just two days before Ben Ali had boarded a plane into exile. The French foreign minister Michèle Alliot-Marie had vacationed in Tunisia during the crackdown, flying on the private plane of a regime crony. Sarkozy sacked her within weeks. While people demanded freedom and respect on Tahrir Square, the British foreign minister William Hague had warned that the unrest was detrimental to Middle East peace efforts—no matter that the peace process was dead. In an attempt to undo some of that damage, the British prime minister David Cameron rushed to Cairo to be the first world leader to visit postrevolution Egypt, just ten days after Mubarak resigned. Now France and Britain seemed to be trying to make up further for the damage to their images by calling on Gaddafi to step down. They started to talk about the need to intervene in Libya and protect civilians. A flood of Libyan refugees was sailing across the Mediterranean and landing on European soil. Europe didn't want more immigrants. It had enough problems.

On March 3, Obama gave a press conference; this time, he named Gaddafi and called on him to leave power. A few days later, the Gulf Cooperation Council called on the United Nations to impose a no-fly zone over Libya. The Arab League, long a hollow and impotent body, was plagued with the same ills as the region: it didn't represent the people and was beset by rivalry and disagreements between its twenty-two member states. The league never took decisions of any consequence, and its secretary-general Amr Moussa was a former foreign minister of Egypt who had served under Mubarak. But on March 12, Arab foreign ministers attending a special meeting at the league's headquarters in Cairo voted unanimously in support of a no-fly zone. Syria and Iraq abstained.

I was flabbergasted: Arabs calling for military action against one of their own? Not even in 1990, when George H. W. Bush put together an international coalition to liberate Kuwait from Saddam Hussein's army, did Arab countries unanimously participate: those who did were in it ostensibly to help Kuwait, not to rein in one of their own as they would be doing in Libya. The old myth of Arab solidarity had been truly punctured. Of course, Gaddafi's antics, his bizarre wardrobe, his rambling, interminable speeches at the UN General Assembly every year, and his delusions about being the king of Africa drove the Arabs crazy. At an Arab League summit, he had once called the Saudi ruler a liar. No one would be sorry to see him go. The Turks still insisted that military action was a ridiculous idea. But the clamor for action was growing, as was criticism of Obama for standing idly by while civilians were being killed.

Sarkozy had come out ahead of everyone and recognized the Libyan opposition group, the Transitional National Council, as the legitimate representative of the Libyan people. The Libyan opposition was pushing the United States to follow suit. But Washington was still only saying "a" legitimate representative. I sometimes rolled my eyes at how much time U.S. officials spent on nuances and semantics. It was lost on people who were being shot. But I could see that in this case the definite article made all the difference because it had legal and financial implications. And I knew the weight that America's words carried. Cameron and Sarkozy, even Erdoğan, were scrutinized mostly at home, their words or missteps the subject of some opinion pieces here or there. There would be a ruckus in the House of Commons in London if the British prime minister met with the wrong political representative. But once Washington embraced the new Libyan opposition, it would be hard to undo. The United States first wanted to know more about the rebels.

With the world debating what to do about Libya, Clinton planned to check in on the state of postrevolution Egypt and Tunisia, Libya's neighbors. Huma, Philippe, and Jake were putting the final touches on the planning, weighing every event, every location, and every meeting on the schedule for Cairo and Tunis. Here again, if Hillary met with the wrong activist or visited a specific location, it could send an inadvertent signal of a change in U.S. policy. But the secretary would first stop in Paris, deal with a nuclear crisis, and get an American out of the claws of Pakistan's intelligence agencies.

The Book was in chaos, a reflection of the state of the world. The Building was struggling to keep up. Every day brought new changes in Egypt and Tunisia, and the briefing notes that the Near Eastern Affairs section was contributing to the Book were already outdated by the time they were printed. While Libya's revolution had been gaining momentum, a devastating earthquake and tsunami had hit Japan on March 11, and the country's nuclear energy reactors were failing. Washington worried the Japanese were not moving fast enough to contain the crisis and was concerned about the health and safety of thousands of American troops in Japan, who were also being drafted into the relief efforts. The U.S. Navy was also on its way to help. The crackdown in Bahrain was continuing. Egypt was navigating its transition. Tunisia was learning to live without Ben Ali. Protests had erupted in Syria. In Pakistan, Raymond Davis, an American contractor suspected of being a CIA agent, had been arrested after allegedly shooting two men on the streets of Lahore in January. And then, of course, there was Libya.

* * *

On Sunday evening, March 15, Molly Montgomery and Andrew Johnson, the line plane team, settled down to work through the nighttime flight to Paris. They needed a definitive version of the secretary's daily briefing book in seven hours. When SAM landed at nine the next morning, Clinton would head into a long day of meetings. Molly snacked on beef jerky that her husband had made for her. They asked Washington for extra briefing materials, for more information. Every official Clinton would be speaking with in Paris wanted to discuss the Japanese nuclear crisis, what the United States would do to help. Molly and Andrew also had to think about Tunisia and Egypt. The American embassy in Egypt was overwhelmed and barely finding its footing—it didn't know all the new players on the scene. Huma wanted to know whether the secretary could meet with this activist or that minister. No one had any firm answers. All the usual talking points that Molly and Andrew were getting from the relevant country desks in the Building were now irrelevant and out-dated; with Jake, they rewrote and refined policy on the plane from scratch and then rewrote it again. Hillary was reading the Book as usual and somehow stapling papers. She kept walking out of her cabin and borrowing Molly and Andrew's stapler.

Jake had fleetingly thought about how exciting it was to be going to Egypt, but now all he could think of was Libya, that the clock was tick-ing, how Gaddafi was threatening to flatten the rebel city of Benghazi. He checked in regularly with the White House, relaying the latest to his boss.

The back of the plane was packed with a record twenty-one journal-ists. SAM hadn't seen such a large press contingent since Madeleine Albright had traveled to Pyongyang in November 2000. DS agents and officials had been sent ahead to the different stops on commercial flights to make room for the journalists who would record the historic visit of the American secretary of state to post-Mubarak Egypt.

When we landed in Paris, our in-boxes contained an updated list of events. There was now a meeting with the representative of the Libyan Transitional National Council sometime on Monday, to be determined (TBD). A note said it could end up being Tuesday. There was a meeting with the Japanese foreign minister. Though she would see Takeaki Matsu-moto at the G8 meeting, they would meet à deux to discuss the response to the earthquake in Japan in detail. Clinton wasn't just meeting with the new French foreign minister Alain Juppé. Now she would also be received by President Sarkozy himself.

Sarko was a fan of the United States and was often referred to as Sarko l'américain. He loved Hillary, and she enjoyed his charming French je ne sais quoi. Sarko saw her not just as the American chief diplomat but as Hillary the woman. A year ago, she'd come to the Elysée Palace to meet him. As she walked up the steps on her way in, her black kitten heel shoe had slipped off her right foot, and Sarko caught her hand in time and supported her while she found her footing. The moment was immortalized in a picture, a copy of which Hillary sent to Sarkozy with a note: "I may not be Cinderella but you'll always be my Prince Charming." After the hour-long meeting, he didn't just wave good-bye to her from the steps of the Elysée, he walked her to the door of her car. The warm ties and trust would come in handy to keep the impetuous Sarkozy from dragging America into an uncontrolled spiral in Libya. He was becoming increasingly vocal about military action, but the contours of what he was proposing were very vague. Exasperated American officials at the UN were accusing the French of grandstanding and dragging America into "their shitty little war."[32]

Hillary had arrived in Paris with a reasonably clear vision about what needed to be done in Libya but uncertain about whether all the factors were aligned. So she came with her legendary checklist. Her critics mocked her for being a good Methodist girl who simply checked things off a to-do list, to which she would retort that at the end of the day what mattered was that she got the job done.

She got to work. She sat down with Sarkozy and explained to him what a no-fly zone entailed and what it did not deliver. It wouldn't be enough to protect civilians. The rebels would need more. But before implementing a no-fly zone, it was necessary to take out Gaddafi's air defenses. Was France ready and able to do that?

Next she sat down with the Emirati foreign minister Abdullah bin Zayed to talk about Libya but also Bahrain. Bob Gates had been in Bahrain over the weekend, urging America's ally to implement quick reforms to respond to the demands of the protestors. Baby steps were simply not enough with Iran looking to exploit the unrest.

"Time is not our friend," he had said. The Sunni Gulf monarchies were always ready to crush their Shiite minorities out of religious hatred for their sect and historic discrimination. The United States sympathized with the Bahraini protestors, though it worried more about Iran. Blinded by its own history with Tehran, the United States feared Shiite radicalism more than Sunni orthodoxy.

The Bahrainis agreed that time was key and watched Iran's extending hand with horror. But they had a better idea about how to push back against Tehran, and democracy had nothing to do with it. Just as we were landing in Paris, two thousand Saudi and Emirati troops were driving across the causeway and onto the island of Bahrain to restore their vision of order. They gave no notice to the United States of their plans. Officials who got wind that something was under way were told to stay out of it. Saudi Arabia had its own restless, alienated Shiite population in the Eastern Province, and the military move was a message to them as well.

Clinton admonished bin Zayed for the deployment of troops. This looked nothing like reform. But almost in the same breath she also asked exactly what the Gulf countries and the Arab League had in mind when they called for a no-fly zone over Libya. Hillary wanted to get a sense of people's real intentions, not just their public statements. She was ready to go as far as the Arabs were ready to go, and now that they had made those statements, she wanted to assess their sincerity—theirs and that of everyone else so desperate to dispatch fighter jets over Libyan skies.

In Libya, Gaddafi's troops were advancing quickly east, beating back the opposition. Soon they could be in Benghazi, the rebel stronghold. The pressure for action was mounting by the hour. In Washington, no decision had been taken yet about the course of action. Hillary continued working on her checklist.

Over dinner with all the G8 ministers, she spoke to William Hague. The British were pushing for a no-fly zone as well. She spoke with Lavrov, who opposed it less vehemently than when she'd seen him in Geneva in February. It was no longer "no, no, no" but simply "no." The Germans were not keen at all.

Clinton still needed to get a feel for what the Libyan opposition was made of, or at least its American-educated leader, Mahmoud Jibril. The advance line officer for this trip, Antoinette Hurtado, was doing everything possible to make that happen. While Clinton went from meeting to meeting, Antoinette had been on the phone all afternoon with the representative of the Libyan Transitional National Council, trying to get a sense of when she might be able to get him into the same room with Clinton and change that TBD event on our schedule into a confirmed meeting. Antoinette had arrived in Paris herself only a couple of days ago, for one of the shortest advances she had been on. Before leaving, she had been given an Emirates cell phone number with instructions to get the man on the other end of the line to Paris safely.

Being on European soil was not protection enough against Gaddafi's wrath and long arm, so Jibril's arrival and the location of his meeting with the secretary were kept secret. He was flying into Paris from the Gulf on a private jet lent by a benefactor, his exact arrival time uncertain. The meeting was first slated for the early afternoon, but then he called to say the plane wouldn't be able to take off in time. Antoinette found it nerve-racking but inspirational to speak to the man who was risking his life by standing up to a dictator. She conferred with Huma. Clinton was going into a series of meetings. Perhaps they could slot him in before the G8 dinner. Too tight. It would have to be after the G8 dinner, at Clinton's hotel. All evening, as she guided Clinton from meeting to meeting to the dinner, Antoinette nervously checked her BlackBerry to make sure Jibril had arrived and was in place. As an additional security precaution, Jibril had asked to avoid the front entrance of the hotel, so Antoinette arranged for him to be taken in through a back entrance. He was waiting in a hold room on the secure floor, just down the hall from Clinton's suite, chatting to Gene Cretz, the spiky-haired ambassador to Libya who had feared for his own life after WikiLeaks released his diplomatic cables about Gaddafi. Chris Stevens, a tall, lanky career diplomat with hunched shoulders who had also recently served in Libya and knew Jibril, was in the room as well. Chris, who spoke good Arabic, had just been appointed Washington's liaison with the rebels and would soon be making his way to Benghazi. Just after ten in the evening, they got word that Clinton was on her way up.

The Libyan rebel leader looked nothing like a revolutionary. No beard, no camouflage, no bandana on his forehead. Short with glasses and wearing a suit, the fifty-nine-year-old business management consultant had come to Paris to find out what America had to offer. The gulf between perception and expectations—he knew all about that. It was at the heart of his PhD thesis on the U.S.-Libyan relationship at the University of Pittsburgh years ago. He had written about the influence of images and perception in the very rocky U.S.-Libyan relationship from 1969, the year Gaddafi took power, when Libya was still an American friend, until 1982, when Libya had moved from being an agitator against the United States to being firmly in the camp of the enemy.

"We tend to see that countries we like do things we like, and to see our enemies pursuing policies that would harm our interests," Jibril had written in 1985.

Now again, America's perception of Libya changed depending on what its own objectives and interests were in the region. Jibril needed to get Clinton to like him and convince her that a no-fly zone was in America's interest, but in real life, perceptions and expectations could not be neatly charted the way they had been in his thesis.

On the top floor of the Westin Hotel, Clinton welcomed Jibril into the living room of her presidential suite. The Eiffel Tower was lit up, shining through the corner window. The tasteful purple and gray couches and settees and the checkered armchairs had been rearranged into a more formal meeting setting. Clinton asked a few questions, but she mostly listened. In his perfect but heavily accented English, Jibril eloquently explained that without a no-fly zone, without U.S. intervention, there would be a massacre in Benghazi. His plea was passionate but delivered calmly, his bushy eyebrows only barely moving up and down under his dark rimmed eyeglasses. Clinton said America's vital interests were not at stake. America, he replied, had to be coherent in its foreign policy; it could not speak of the defense of democracy and abandon the Libyan people. Clinton asked very detailed questions about the Transitional National Council, its composition, how representative it was of all of Libya, his vision for the future of the country. She also asked him for an update about the military situation on the ground as well as the humanitarian aid needed.

After forty-five minutes, the meeting came to an end. Clinton walked Jibril into the hallway. They shook hands, and he thanked her for the meeting. She smiled, he bowed slightly, looking relieved it was over. Clinton conferred very quickly with Cretz and Stevens. She added what she had heard to the information she'd gathered all day. She had checked all her boxes, and she could make her case to President Obama about what she believed should be America's next move.

Jibril left the hotel through the back door again. He had been pleasantly surprised by how attentive Clinton had been and how much time she had given him to make his case. But she had made no commitment to him either way. He had given it his best shot, but he didn't know whether he had convinced the American secretary of state to help his country. Was the cavalry coming? Perhaps the Arabs and the French, but he wasn't sure about the United States. Libya could be on its own, but he was hopeful.

The day wasn't over. At half past midnight, we were called to a background briefing with three senior officials from the delegation. There was no filing center, where we usually held those briefings, so we agreed to meet up in the hotel bar. It was a Monday night, but the Tuileries Bar was crowded. The hotel was in the heart of Paris, in the first arrondissement, between the place de la Concorde and the place Vendôme, lined with the world's finest jewelry shops.

We tried to huddle away from indiscreet ears in a nook in the back of the bar. The large, plush black chairs kept us well apart from each other, two tables separating us from the officials sitting together on the red velvet banquette. Why weren't they ready to take more definitive steps? Were they simply in the dark about what was going on in Libya? Were the divisions about what to do next simply too big? The first official tried to answer our question, walking a fine line as he described the discussions at the G8 dinner.

"I wouldn't claim that all eight who were at the table tonight are exactly in the same place. As you know, the French have already recognized the opposition, some were more forward-leaning about a no-fly zone or the use of force than others, there's no doubt. But at the same time they all shared a sense of urgency. The ministers spoke very passionately about what is happening and the need for us to move as quickly as possible to accomplish these goals."

"But this has been going on for weeks!" Matt from the AP interjected.

"But there's another set of principles that's also very important to have on the table," the official replied, "which is not to act without regional support."

"But you have regional support!" Matt said. "You have the Arab League, you have the GCC. It may not be spelled out exactly the way you would like it but . . ." A loud, nasal American female voice from a table nearby drowned out the rest.

"That's precisely why the secretary asked for clarifications," the official butted in. "So that when the Security Council takes this up, we understands exactly what it is we're talking about."

A chorus of voices interrupted him, all talking over each other but all saying the same thing.

"It sounds like nobody wants to do this."

The first official paused, a frustrated look on his face. The second one pursed his lips. The third stared at his two colleagues.

"People don't want to take action based on a misunderstanding," volunteered the first official. He explained it was important to have more than just vague regional support. But what did that support actually mean? What were they not telling us? These briefings were key to helping us understand the context of what was happening behind the scenes but also to get a sense of where things were going. For the officials, it often seemed like agony, worse than the daily grilling at the lectern in Washington. They wanted to make sure they gave us their version of history in the making, but there was only so much they could tell us. Diplomacy didn't flourish in the limelight. Their guarded statements left big blanks that we filled with our own conclusions. In this case, it made the Americans look reluctant to do anything for the Libyans beyond issue statements and wait for someone else to deal with Gaddafi.

"Well, this sense of urgency you talk about doesn't seem to exist," said Matt. "No one is going to do anything about this, except talk more about it and stay in nine-hundred-euro hotel rooms in various world capitals."

It was almost one thirty in the morning—dinnertime in Washington. We ordered more drinks, got more salted almonds, and prodded further.

"Why are you still trying to figure out what a no-fly zone entails. Isn't that obvious?" asked Elise Labott from CNN.

"What would constitute clear support from the Arab League?" I asked. "They have never called for any sort of military action against another Arab country. What more do you want? Do you want Arab military involvement?"

There was a long silence filled by the bar chatter, which suddenly sounded deafening. Twenty seconds passed.

"Whatever action is taken we are asking them to take the lead in carrying it out," replied the second official. "For the United States or NATO or France to carry out any military action without clear regional support poses significant risks that everyone in this room fully understands," he went on. "Past no-fly zones have required significant military action."

A no-fly zone, they explained, had to be enforced. If anyone sent planes over Libya, Gaddafi would try to bring them down, so you first had to take out his air defenses. Nonanswer answers were a classic play by American officials. He hadn't confirmed they were seeking Arab military participation, but he hadn't denied it either. So we were onto something. But why did the United States want Arab military involvement? To do what?

Just as we were sitting down with the officials in the bar around midnight, high up on the secure floor, past the marines standing sentry in the hallway, Molly and Andrew were putting the final touches on the daily briefing book for the secretary's meetings for the following day in Paris and then Cairo. Thirty mini-schedules had been printed out, cut, and stapled. The two hungry young officers had had enough of eating beef jerky; it was time for real French food. They headed out to Montmartre, betting they could find late dining in the lively, artistic neighborhood. A couple of steak frites and a few glasses of wine later, back at the Westin Hotel, Molly collapsed in her bed at two in the morning and closed her eyes for the first time in thirty-eight hours. Ten minutes later, she half opened them, brought her BlackBerry closer to her face, and glanced at her e-mails. She closed her eyes again, her BlackBerry still in her hand. No one ever slept deeply on these trips. Half an hour later, with her thumb she clicked the scroll button, lighting up the screen of her mobile device. All was quiet.

At four in the morning, the dim light shone again on Molly's face. Her eyes opened wide. A cascade of OPS alerts, with bad news from Japan. There had been a third blast at a reactor of the Fukushima plant, the U.S. Navy was repositioning ships after detecting airborne radioactivity, the United States was considering evacuating thousands of American citizens, and a fire had broken out in a cooling pond at one of the reactors. Molly called Andrew. Five minutes later, they were back in the office. Clinton was meeting the Japanese foreign minister at eight thirty in the morning at the Hotel Le Meurice, a short walk around the corner from the Westin. The daily Book had to be redone.

The United States had been very sensitive about the guidance it was giving to citizens and military personnel so as not to offend Japan, which was downplaying all the risks. Now it was clear how overwhelmed Japan was. No one was really in charge. The United States wasn't going to wait to be asked for help, it was time to step in. The dangers of a nuclear catastrophe were too big, the consequences dire for hundreds of thousands of people in Japan and beyond. In the morning, Clinton went to the Meurice and had her meeting with the Japanese foreign minister. In public, all the statements were about total support for Japan and its people. In private the message was tougher: get your act together.

Off we went to Cairo.

At the Egyptian foreign ministry, Clinton was meeting the new man in charge, Nabil Elaraby. The last time we had been in Cairo, Clinton had stood next to Aboul Gheit. She had just met Mubarak, and they had talked about peace and settlements in front of a small crowd of journalists. This time, around a hundred journalists were crushed into a room, and cameramen were pushing and shoving trying to set up their tripods. The wait was long and the room overheated. I headed out for some fresh air.

Outside, inveterate smokers were lighting up cigarette after cigarette.

"How come so many people are attending this press conference?" I asked one of the Egyptian reporters. "Do you still care what America has to say?"

The man stared at me, incredulous. "It's America!"

Inside, on an improvised desk, the advance line officer for the Cairo stop had set up a laptop and printer to print out the latest version of the remarks Clinton would be giving shortly. He was waiting for final clearance from Washington—everyone with a say on Egypt had to sign off on the document. The Wi-Fi Internet was acting up, and the e-mail just wasn't landing. The remarks had to be waiting for her on the lectern as she walked out of her meeting. She was going to praise the Egyptians for what they had achieved in Tahrir Square and tell them repeatedly that this moment in history belonged to them, that they had broken barriers and overcome obstacles to pursue the dream of democracy—and the United States stood by them.

There was still some convincing to do. A number of democracy activists who had been part of the uprising had been invited to meet Clinton at her hotel and a handful had refused, still resentful over her January 25 comment about Egypt being stable. The revolution had started long before that date in their hearts, and they couldn't forgive America for weighing interests and values before speaking out. Clinton asked those in the meeting, including Asmaa Mahfouz, the woman who had spurred mass demonstrations with her YouTube video, how they were preparing for the upcoming parliamentary elections. She was stunned when they told her they were revolutionaries; they "didn't do politics." They believed that the momentum and emotions of the revolution would win the day at the ballot box. On this occasion, Hillary's instincts as a politician were the right ones, and the naive activists would soon find themselves out-maneuvered by the well-organized Muslim Brotherhood and even the remnants of Mubarak's ruling party.

In the morning she had more meetings, with the army generals, the defense minister, and civil society representatives, and she took a walk around revolution central—Tahrir Square. The crowds were gone and traffic was back, but Hillary still found it emotional to see the square with her own eyes. She then had to deal with Pakistan. An agreement had been reached with Islamabad, and CIA contractor Raymond Davis was being released from jail. Then interviews. On every trip, Clinton gave interviews to the television reporters with her on the plane. Sitting in a hotel room that had been transformed into a makeshift television set, Clinton would subject herself to the interviews back-to-back, with barely a few minutes to spare between them.

I sat down and started grilling her. Was the United States going to support action at the UN? Did the United States want a no-fly zone? Were the Arabs going to participate? Even the French and the British were getting frustrated. Why was the United States dillydallying?

Clinton said there were many ways to help the Libyan people; they had to make sure that a resolution was carefully crafted so it didn't get vetoed. She insisted the United States was on the same page as its allies. Her answers felt like they amounted to nothing. I pushed further.

"Gaddafi's forces are advancing on Benghazi. The rebels seem to be losing ground day by day, perhaps hour by hour. If Benghazi falls to Colonel Gaddafi because the United States was seen to take its time deliberating, history won't judge the Obama administration very kindly, will it?"

Clinton sat still, her face impassive.

"The United States under President Obama is engaged in numerous efforts around the world to ensure peace and stability. It is important that no one sees the United States acting unilaterally. This is what we were criticized for in the not-so-distant past . . . But I believe that we are moving in the right direction and that hopefully there will be a consensus and the United States will be part of that consensus."

I wondered whether the United States was shirking its responsibilities. I understood the reluctance to go to war, but I was still perplexed by this apparent lack of urgency.

Sitting down with Clinton for the cameras, I didn't know that the day before, around ten in the evening while my colleagues and I were having dinner in the restaurant hotel overlooking the Nile, the secretary had been on the phone to the White House with her checklist. From her hotel suite, on a secure line, she had joined a National Security Council meeting in the Situation Room: President Obama, Robert Gates, Vice President Joe Biden, Mike Mullen, the Joint Chiefs of Staff, Susan Rice on videoconference line from the UN, and others.

Obama was trying to get American troops out of Afghanistan and out of Iraq—two Muslim countries where the presence of infidels in camouflage continually stoked anti-American sentiment. A war in a third Muslim country, with American jets in the sky, was the last thing he wanted. Libyan rebels were clamoring for America to save them, but around the world, saviors turned into occupiers or oppressors very quickly. For weeks now, different options had been weighed, all the military and diplomatic scenarios carefully scrutinized. Gates was a quiet, reticent man; he was fed up with what he described as "loose talk" about a no-fly zone. People just didn't think through what this meant and what was needed to make it happen: the U.S. military would first have to take out Gaddafi's air defenses. America would be going to war again. Together with the vice president and Mullen, he argued against action.

In Paris, Hillary had checked all her boxes; she knew how she would proceed. In general, whenever she wanted to make her case, she didn't necessarily state her objective explicitly. Instead, she would lay out the facts with a slant toward the conclusion she wanted to reach. By the time she was done with her presentation, her interlocutor could see things from her perspective. This was how she handled her foreign counterparts; it was how she went into the meeting with the president. As usual, he wanted to know from her what and who she could deliver.

She laid out what she had heard in Paris. Sarkozy was intent on having his war. He wanted a no-fly zone. The British also wanted action. They were going to push a resolution at the UN for a no-fly zone. But she had told them such a move wasn't going to make a real difference, and she had spent time assessing their intentions. Did they just want to take their fighter jets out for a spin so they could feel good about themselves, or were they ready to stick it out and do things right? She had spoken to the Arabs and gotten their commitment that they would contribute military assets and would not get squeamish after the first shots were fired. She had sat down with the Libyan opposition chief and assessed what kind of leadership he offered for the Libya of tomorrow.

Obama was also convinced that a no-fly zone would not cut it. America could feel good about being on the right side of history, but people would still get killed. Not acting was not an option; it could affect America's long-term interests in the region and set a terrible example for Arab leaders who might take U.S. inaction as an inability to act. They might deduce that they could kill their people with no consequences whatsoever. Clinton made clear that a vote was going to take place in New York—the United States could either lead or be led.

"Let's drive this," she said. Susan Rice chimed in. She already had a draft for a tougher resolution that went beyond a no-fly zone and included a call for "all necessary measures" to protect civilians. All necessary measures meant that the United States and its allies would be able to actively impede the advance of Gaddafi's force and strike them from the air. This was well beyond just a sky patrol. Clinton had set the stage about a discussion for broad action. After the call ended, others, like Samantha Power, chimed in, telling Obama to go for the "all necessary measures" option.

Obama asked the military to present him with more detailed plans. When they all reconvened a few hours later, Clinton was fast asleep in Cairo, where it was four in the morning. She was represented at the table by one of her deputies, Jim Steinberg, with orders to say yes to "all necessary measures." The president was given the details of the three options available: no action, no-fly zone, or all necessary measures. He went for the last one.

Later, I also came to understand the extent to which the United States was worried that it could enter this battle, believing the Arabs and Europeans were securing its flanks, only to find itself alone on the front line with everyone hanging back. What guarantees did it have that, once the strikes started, the region's rulers wouldn't publicly wash their hands of the operation and condemn the deaths of Muslims at the hands of the American bully?

Washington had in the past openly, publicly, and very loudly driven the process of building a coalition to drive out an invader or stop a massacre, but this was a new style of American leadership—a more modest one, one that made it possible for unlikely partners, such as the Arab League, to cooperate with Washington. The shadow of the Iraq War was ever present. To a world unaccustomed to a silent superpower, this nuanced diplomacy gave the impression that the United States was reluctant. The United States *was* reluctant: to get burned alone. It was time for Europe to grow up and assume its share of responsibilities, and it was time for Arab leaders to develop a spine.

So Washington kept its cards close to its chest. American officials didn't want to make any statements that would allow others to suddenly sit back and push America to the front. If the United States was suddenly seen leading a war effort, it would undermine the careful work being done at the UN and, more crucially, it could scare the Arabs away. But the silence meant that Clinton and Obama were being harshly criticized for not helping to stop an impending massacre.

We flew into the might from Cairo to Tunis, over the Mediterranean, steering clear of Libyan airspace and a country at war. The flight path on our screen showed Benghazi, just south of the plane. Hillary had been given her own stapler, which sat on her desk in her cabin with the words *The Secretary* taped on it. There hadn't been much time to think of Tunisia yet. The line officers had asked the Building for talking points ahead of the town hall in Tunis. They wanted to know what young people in Tunisia wanted to hear from the secretary. Instead, they got vague, outdated generalities. Molly, Andrew, and Jake got to work on the plane rewording all the documents. Molly felt like the world was ending. If America's bureaucracy had reached its limit, there was no hope for others.

Our stop in Tunis was the usual Hillary template: official meetings and public diplomacy. But the real action was taking place on the phone, away from our prying ears. Earlier in the day, the operations center had sent an update about the secretary's communications to her close aides.

From: OPS Alert
Sent: Thursday, March 17, 2011 5:41 AM
To:
Subject: The Secretary has requested to speak with Russian Foreign Minister Lavrov

Then seven hours later, as she stepped off the stage at the end of a town hall, Jake handed her a cell phone.

From: OPS
Sent: Thursday, March 17, 2011 1:09 PM
To:
Subject: The Secretary is speaking with Russian FM Lavrov

Clinton needed to make sure Russia wasn't going to veto the resolution. She had told Lavrov that if Gaddafi was crazy before, he was only going to get worse if international pressure was suddenly lifted. The clampdown had to continue, and this resolution was the next step.

"C'mon, Sergei, this is important. And the Arab League and the Arab countries are behind us," Hillary told him.[33] He told her it was a mistake but that Russia would not use its veto.

We got on the plane and headed home; everyone was exhausted. Clinton got on the phone to Obama, Gates, and Donilon. Jake seemed to be melting as the trip proceeded, despite Molly's and Andrew's efforts to keep him fed with beef jerky. The first meal of the flight had been served while he was in the secretary's cabin talking about the vote coming up at the UN, and he had missed it. In New York, the Security Council chambers were filling up with delegates. Susan Rice was making sure all the delegates needed for the vote were there for the crucial moment. Jake came to the Line of Death to chat with the traveling press. Engrossed in our travel bubble, we were not fully informed of the precise details of events at the UN and the exact wording of the resolution being voted on. We pounced on Jake.

"So is America really going to just stand by while Gaddafi marches on Benghazi?"

Somewhere above the Atlantic, an OPS e-mail dropped. This one was for wider distribution. The line officer printed it out and passed it around to the senior officials in the front area. The UN resolution had passed in New York. Russia and China abstained, as expected. More shocking was Germany's abstention. Washington would not forgive that very soon. Also disappointing were the abstentions of Brazil and India, The rising powers were on the Security Council, and they were showing worrying signs of staying on the sidelines, unable to get over their own historic wariness about Western-led interventions, even to stop a dictator from killing his people.

Clinton came out of her cabin in her red fleece jacket and black kitten heels. Rarely did a trip end with such a visible result. Diplomacy was all about chipping away slowly. But for once there was a piece of paper being passed around the plane, with the words "all necessary measures" underlined. There was a definite buzz among the officials in the front cabin, the sense of a job achieved. Clinton had helped seal the deal. The United States had carefully orchestrated its approach, in a deliberate manner that got the international community in lockstep. Obama may never have gone to war at all if Sarkozy hadn't been so intent on bombing Tripoli, but once the march toward war had become inevitable, the U.S. administration had stepped in to drive the effort in a way that would actually deliver results, not just knock a few buildings down.

Standing by the lavatory, the journalists who just moments ago had criticized Jake for the administration's inaction on Libya turned on him again.

"So you're taking America into a third war?" asked one of the journalists. "As if Iraq and Afghanistan are not enough! Are you insane?"

Jake rolled his eyes and walked back to his seat.

15

SUMMER OF
DISPARATE DISCONTENTS

The stifling heat of D.C. summer had arrived, and I left for a short holiday by the Mediterranean. Lebanon was by no means cooler, but the sea breeze and open horizon made up for the humid chaos of Beirut. Amid all the upheaval in the region, Lebanon was, for once, unusually calm.

The war in Libya was still raging and made the front page of the local newspapers every day. The bombing campaign had started just a few days after the March 17 vote at the UN authorizing the use of all necessary measures to protect civilians. From an informal alliance of countries, it had become a NATO-led operation, and the Russians were fuming: the campaign meant to protect civilians was turning into a de facto full-blown operation designed to help the rebels advance on Tripoli and forcibly bring down Gaddafi. Toppling Gaddafi was not what the resolution had stated, although early on in the campaign, whispers of these unstated motives had abounded. I wondered if the shrewd Russians had really not seen beyond the subtle wording of the resolution when they agreed not to use their veto. Either way, Russia would in the future conveniently hold up this episode as proof that the West could not be trusted.

As the war dragged on, Hillary spent much of her time keeping the coalition together, refereeing spats between the French, Italians, and others who threw fits and threatened to quit. Through Amr Moussa, the Arab League's cigar-smoking secretary-general, the league predictably criticized the military strikes the minute they started. Moussa stated that the attacks went beyond what had been called for. Qatar and the UAE got cold feet: four days after the war had started, the fighter planes they had promised to contribute were nowhere to be seen. Clinton picked up the phone and spoke to the Qatari and Emirati foreign ministers and other Arab leaders.

"This is important to the United States, it's important to the president, and it's important to me personally," Clinton told them.[34] The following day the Qatari Mirage jets and Emirati F16s appeared over Libya's skies. She had attended four meetings of the Friends of Libya group, with dozens of other foreign ministers and the Libyan opposition, focused on putting together a vision for a post-Gaddafi Libya. Hillary was struggling with buyer's remorse. She had weighed heavily in favor of intervention, and the Obama administration had publicly and repeatedly said the campaign would last weeks and not months. But more than four months later, there was no end in sight.

In the region, opinions and editorials were divided as usual: some deplored the fact that America wasn't deploying all its firepower to finish the job; others were furious about American military intervention. Despite the very public Libyan plea for intervention—as well as a wider Arab call—many Arab citizens and pundits believed the United States had engineered the conflict to get its hands on Libya's oil, that it was yet another ploy by the neocolonial imperial power to take over the region's riches, using U.S. regional allies like Qatar and Saudi Arabia to give the campaign legitimacy. Much had changed in the region, but much remained the same.

Back in Beirut, I found myself on my friend Rania's[35] couch in an affluent Christian neighborhood, chatting about her daughter, common friends, new restaurants in the city. The conversation inevitably turned to politics.

"I think there's something weird about all these revolutions, don't you?" she asked. "It's just strange how all of a sudden people in Tunisia, Egypt, Yemen, Syria, they all woke up and started a revolution. I mean— what got into them?"

"Well, you know, this was boiling under the surface for a long time," I ventured, uncertain about where she was going with the conversation. "No one predicted it would explode like this, all at once, but there had been warnings for a long time that the situation in the region was unsustainable. You know, dictators, poverty, demographic explosion, unemployment, it's a very combustible combination. Then one guy killed himself, and it started a revolution that spread across the region. I think the region was ripe."

"I don't know," she replied. "I think it's strange. I guess the Americans decided all these dictators had outlived their usefulness or something. But I don't know what their plan is exactly."

Plan? I thought of Jeffrey Feltman, the former ambassador to Beirut now sitting in Washington, shuttling endlessly to the Arab world, trying to keep track of which leader was about to fall, had fallen, or was ruthlessly trying to hold on to power. He was exhausted and selfishly hoping that amid their awakening, the Arabs would take a nap so he could catch his breath. American officials and their Arab counterparts barely bothered to pretend that the peace process was still alive. Some American officials were asking me what I thought was going to happen in Syria. Others expressed their frustration with Yemen's Ali Abdullah Saleh, who couldn't sign an agreement and stick with it, or with the Bahrainis, who refused to rein in their security forces, or with the Saudis, who were still upset because the United States had let down Mubarak. Everybody was making America's life difficult, and unless chaos was actually the plan, I failed to see how the United States was pulling any of the strings here. There were no doubt many layers of the American foreign policy machine that were hidden to me, but it was hard to believe that everyone in the State Department and the White House was in on the ploy to look unprepared and scrambling to cope.

A bit later that afternoon, I went shopping in downtown Beirut. A close friend of mine, Randa,[36] was a fashion designer, and I loved picking a few items from her collection to show off everywhere I traveled, my own tiny effort to advertise Lebanon. I always arrived too late in the season to buy anything, as rich women from the Gulf had usually bought up all the good stuff. I walked into the shop; the racks were full. The rich women had stayed at home that summer since there was so much uncertainty in the region. No one was buying.

"So what do you think is going to happen to Lebanon? What are you hearing in Washington?" Randa asked. I wasn't hearing anything; for once, Lebanon was not high up on Washington's agenda. American officials kept an eye on it mostly because it was Syria's neighbor and home to

Hezbollah. Instead, I offered my own prognosis about how this time Lebanon would probably muddle through the turbulent times, and stay out of trouble.

"But what do you think they have planned, you know, for Lebanon, for Syria?" Randa asked. I looked at her, eyebrows raised. "Plan? Randa, there is no plan. You know, Americans are trying to figure this out day by day and manage it as best they can."

A look of horror descended on her face. She raised her hands in the air.

"Kim, Kim! What are you saying? What do you mean there is no plan? If the Americans don't have a plan, then who the hell is in charge of everything?"

The idea that the United States wasn't masterminding anything was too alien a concept to my friends. It didn't seem to matter that popular revolutions were sweeping the region, that people were bringing down dictators and taking charge of their countries, that all the headlines were about America being on the decline—again. The United States somehow must have been behind everything. In one breath, people both praised their own newfound power and accused the United States of bringing down their leaders. The image of a plot being cooked up in an office in the United States, so popular for all those decades, was so ingrained in people's brains it was hard to dismiss.

In 2005, when Lebanon had gone through its own popular uprising after the assassination of Rafic Hariri, the Bush administration gave it unequivocal support. Jeffrey Feltman, who was still in Beirut at the time, was at a dinner with politicians from the pro-Western camp when he casually mentioned that he was going on holiday for two weeks. The table fell silent.

"But what will we do?" one of the politicians suddenly wailed. The anti-Western camp often accused Jeff of being the real ruler of Lebanon and pulling all the strings. This politician's reaction seemed to reflect that belief—except that Jeff was frustrated that none of these politicians actually ever seemed to listen to his advice.

So who was in charge? This was the paradox in much of the Arab world and beyond—the U.S.-as-puppet-master provided a tidy explanation for the problems in the region, though America also seemed to be expected to swoop in and fix everything. Despite the fear and loathing of America, people still pinned their hopes on the United States for answers or even support. Even as they excoriated Obama for not coming out early enough to support their revolution, Egyptians had called on him to do more and faster to precipitate the fall of Mubarak.

M any countries seemed to have a hard time letting go of their reli-
ance on the United States, which was, for now, the top super-
power. America had long fed that dependence. But now the Obama administration, trying to empower other countries to do some of the heavy lifting, was finding that the world wasn't catching on that quickly to the idea. The phones were still ringing off the hook at the Near Eastern Affairs bureau at the State Department. The Yemeni opposition was desperate for the United States to come and remove Ali Abdullah Saleh. The Bahraini opposition wanted Washington to force the authorities to accept their demands for better representation, but they didn't want to enter into a dialogue with the authorities themselves. The Libyan National Transitional Council wanted all the African countries to turn their backs on Gaddafi, but they didn't want to do the asking themselves; could Wash-
ington please lobby on their behalf? And although the United States had walked slowly and reluctantly down the road to action in Libya, Ameri-
can military airpower had been crucial to delivering crippling blows to Gaddafi's forces in the first few days of the military campaign. When the United States stepped back to allow others in the coalition to drive the operation, the Obama administration was criticized for entering the war halfheartedly, for failing the rebels who wanted more drone strikes and more intelligence. President Obama was criticized for "leading from behind," even though the United States had played a key, albeit little-
advertised, role in framing the debate about intervention and ultimately shaping the platform that allowed it to happen.

The Libya war had been a new experiment for Europe. Though the United States and Europe had waged war together through NATO before, America had always been the leader. Europe would never have imagined leading a military campaign: in the past, they simply followed. Libya was a more cooperative process. The Europeans were much more willing to work with America when Washington wasn't being a bully. But it was a steep learning curve, and even the Americans seemed shocked to find out how much their own hardware was still needed. Europe wanted to pedal on its own, but the United States still had to supply the wheels and, in fact, the pedals themselves. The United States worried that Europe would fall off the bike. It was a confidence- and trust-building exercise for everybody.

Washington hoped that this approach would allow European countries to achieve a new and much-needed maturity on the world stage. No one knew whether future wars would be waged in the same way, but each party had learned how to pull off international action in situations when America did not want to act unilaterally or could not foot the entire bill.

The Arab Spring both inspired Obama and distracted him all at once. The slow economic recovery and unemployment rate that still hovered around 9 percent were his real concerns. The United States' debt ceiling was about to be broken, and the United States could default on its debt if it couldn't borrow more money. The Treasury regularly adjusted the limit but this required permission from Congress. For decades, it had been a routine affair but with a Republican majority in Congress and the Tea Party movement angling for a showdown, the process became opaque. Raising the ceiling automatically meant more spending, but Congress wanted the ceiling to be raised only as part of a bigger deal to cut government spending over the coming years. No one was willing to cave in first.

The Lebanese media did a fair amount of coverage on the acrimonious bickering between Democrats and Republicans, politicians and pundits, a sorry spectacle somewhat bizarrely reminiscent of the partisan spats among Lebanese politicians with differing worldviews. But we seemed to bicker on forever, in circular arguments, whereas others would eventually find a resolution, however imperfect, to their dispute.

The debt crisis was unfolding right as Clinton was embarking on one of her craziest trips yet—ten days, Greece, Turkey, India, Indonesia, Hong Kong, and China. Greece was crumbling under its own debt crisis and being bailed out by France and Germany. At each stop, Clinton was asked whether America would come to its senses and raise its debt ceiling, or take the world down with it.

"Let me assure you we understand the stakes. We know how important this is for us and how important it is for you," she told an audience of business leaders—and through these leaders the world—in Hong Kong on July 25. Acknowledging the other side's concern was a classic Hillary Clinton first step in calming fraying nerves. She had faith in her country because she had seen it all before. America went through slumps, economic and psychological, in cycles. She remembered the late 1970s, when oil prices had skyrocketed, cars lined up at gas pumps, and unemployment was above 10 percent. She believed in American innovation, ingenuity, and resilience, and she believed in the American political system because she had seen it close to collapse before as well when she was at the White House.

"These kinds of debates have been a constant in our political life throughout the history of our republic. And sometimes, they are messy," she told the audience of anxious businessmen. "I well remember the government shutdown of the 1990s; I had a front-row seat for that one. But this is how an open and democratic society ultimately comes together to reach the right solutions."

On July 31, the showdown in Washington was over. Congress and the White House came to an agreement that raised the debt but also cut spending over ten years by an almost equal amount.

From the island of Hong Kong, Clinton's motorcade drove two hours across a bridge toward the Special Economic Zone of Shenzhen in southern China. State Councilor Dai Bingguo was waiting with a lavish lunch and army of staffers to make the American delegation comfortable.

Over a four-hour meal in a government guesthouse, the two officials and their delegation talked in detail about all the issues that mattered to both countries, in a smaller, informal version of the Strategic and Economic Dialogue. Clinton's ability to manage a diplomatic conversation had matured, and she had learned to draw Dai out of the formulaic conversations Chinese officials preferred. The discussion flowed more freely, even though Hillary was the woman who had dared challenge the Chinese in their own backyard about their behavior on the high seas. Worse, she had stated in an interview with the *Atlantic* magazine a few months earlier that China's system of rule and its attempts to stop democracy from taking hold in the country were a fool's errand. And yet here she was talking about how to tackle global problems together.

The relationship itself was maturing, and the two rivals were learning to keep ties steady even as crisis erupted. Although they now understood that Hillary and America could not be pushed around, Chinese leaders still seized on every detail that appeared to show their system was working and America's wasn't. The meltdown in Washington was an appalling display of American decay in the eyes of a Communist Party that never allowed the outside world to see its divisions.

"It seems that the American system is not producing fast results," Dai said.

Clinton laughed gently.

"We can devote the next lunch to talk about the Chinese system if you want," she said, gently suggesting that he probably wouldn't want to open that door. Clinton had no way of knowing that in less than a year the Communist Party would be rocked by the biggest political scandal in decades when one of its rising stars, Bo Xilai, would be purged from the party and his wife detained and later convicted of murdering a British businessman. The Chinese would get a glimpse of how their rulers and their relatives, known as princelings, had amassed enormous fortunes in a country where there is no separation of powers and no independent judiciary.

But in July 2011, while others in Asia had sought assurances from Clinton that the United States would eventually get its act together and pull through, Dai acted as though Clinton needed his reassurance. Everything would be okay, he seemed to be telling her. He always used a pleasant, diplomatic tone, but there was a condescending tinge to it. Clinton gently pushed back, signaling that neither she nor president Obama needed China's pat on the back. Perhaps Dai was trying to reassure himself.

After the 2008 financial crisis, China had boasted about its own prospering economic model, lording over others that China hadn't taken a hit. But the possibility of American default was a very different situation, and Chinese officials got cold sweats just thinking about it. Over the years, China had bought $1 trillion worth of U.S. Treasury bills, which meant that the United States owed China $1 trillion. If you owe the bank $1 million, the bank has you by the neck. If you owe the bank $1 trillion, then you basically own the bank, and if you default on your debt, you take the bank down with you. China was trying to diversify the foreign currencies it owned, but the euro was in crisis and Japan's economy had taken a hard hit after the March earthquake. America and China were stuck together. And the lure of the dollar and of America remained strong.

In public, the Chinese still sounded cocky, condescending of the wasteful Americans whose government was unable to get its lawmakers to behave.

"China, the largest creditor of the world's sole superpower, has every right now to demand the United States address its structural debt problems and ensure the safety of China's dollar assets," China's official news agency, Xinhua, said in a commentary. China also urged the United States to apply "common sense" to "cure its addiction to debts" by cutting military and social welfare expenditure.

"The U.S. government has to come to terms with the painful fact that the good old days when it could just borrow its way out of messes of its own making are finally gone."

A week later, a large advertisement for Xinhua went up on the large facade of the building located at 2 Times Square: China had made it to the world's crossroads, as Times Square was known. No Chinese company had ever had a permanent foothold on the iconic square. It was just a forty-by-sixty-foot neon sign, but even the news agency that poured such scorn over America was proud to have a presence in the Big Apple. China seemed to have confidence in its future but not in its own present. If you wanted to guarantee China's continued growth, you had to make it in America, in its private high schools and Ivy League universities, and on Times Square.

While I watched Libya on the evening news in Beirut every day, I was also keeping an eye on events to the east, across the border in Syria. The popular uprising there had erupted in mid-March, after a group of teenage boys scribbled some graffiti on the walls of their town of Daraa, south of Damascus: the people want to overthrow the regime, the graffiti said. These words had been the rallying cry in Tahrir Square as well as on the streets of Benghazi and in Yemen. In Syria, the boys were detained, beaten, bloodied, their fingernails pulled out. Business as usual for Syria's secret police.

Just as Mubarak and Gaddafi had insisted before him, President Bashar al-Assad had declared in January 2011 that his people loved him, that his country was different, and that there would be no uprising in Syria. In some ways, Assad was different. Those who saw the world through the prism of anti-imperialism and resistance against Israel believed Assad was one of the only remaining leaders in the region, along with Iran's president, standing up to the West and pushing back against its hegemonic designs. But resentment against the totalitarian regime, its ruthless intelligence services and economic monopoly, had been simmering for several years already. Hundreds of thousands of Syrians were fed up with oppression for the sake of an abstract concept of someone else's freedom, like that of the Palestinians.

Thousands of Syrians started to take to the streets in peaceful demonstrations. "Selmiyya, selmiyya," chanted the Syrians, as Egyptians had done a few weeks before them. Syria was mostly closed off to the international media, so coverage relied on amateur footage taken with cell phones of protestors in various towns. The grainy shots were fascinating not only to watch but also to listen to because of the unguarded comments of those filming. "Look, oh my God, look, they're coming out. They're coming, dozens of them. God bless them. Maybe we should join them?" was the commentary on one of the videos I came across on the Internet. Just then shooting erupted, and the man holding the cell phone retreated inside and most likely didn't join the protestors, at least not this time.

There was a raw quality to the emotion of people who were discovering their collective identity as Syrians for the first time. In a country where neighbors didn't trust each other and family members spied on one another, reporting any dissent to the local offices of the ruling Baath Party, people were suddenly finding strength in numbers.

At the start of the Obama administration, Washington had reached out to Assad, as it had done with other American foes. Obama appointed an ambassador to Damascus, the first one since the Bush administration had withdrawn its representative in 2005, in the aftermath of the assassination of Rafic Hariri. Engagement wasn't yielding many results yet, but overall the United States could live with Assad as an irritant. He had shared just enough intelligence about al-Qaeda after the attacks of 9/11 that the United States considered him mildly useful. Mostly, officials in Washington, as well as their counterparts in European capitals, hoped that by engaging Assad it could peel him away from his best friends in Tehran and convince him to make peace with Israel. Under President George H. W. Bush, Washington had engaged with Hafez al-Assad, with some success for American interests in the region. The younger Assad was in many ways more radical and more of an ideologue.

Two weeks after the Syrian uprising had started, Clinton told CBS, "What's been happening there [in Syria] the last few weeks is deeply concerning, but there's a difference between calling out aircraft and indiscriminately strafing and bombing your own cities and then police actions, which, frankly, have exceeded the use of force that any of us would want to see." Syrian forces were still behaving with restraint in comparison to Libya.

"There's a different leader in Syria now," she added, trying to highlight the difference between Bashar al-Assad and his father, who had razed whole neighborhoods to the ground in 1982 to crush a rebellion in Hama, in the north of the country.

"Many of the members of Congress of both parties who have gone to Syria in recent months have said they believe he's a reformer," Hillary said.

One of those members of Congress was Democratic senator John Kerry, who had traveled to Damascus several times to meet with Assad. Kerry had said that the Syrian leader was a man of his word who had been "very generous with me." He insisted that under Assad, "Syria will move; Syria will change as it embraces a legitimate relationship with the United States."

Such was the conventional thinking in Washington, and it was hard to shake. Assad was making promises to lift the emergency laws and hold free elections and offering to hold talks with the opposition, keeping the hope for reform alive. Inside Syria itself, not everybody was taking to the streets: large swaths of the population also believed the younger Assad was different. With his gorgeous, British-educated wife, Asma, by his side, Assad projected the image of a modern leader and had brought a modicum of change since his accession, mostly by opening up the country's economy cautiously and reforming the banking sector. I had reported extensively in Syria from 2000 to 2007 and heard Syrians from all walks of life express their admiration for the president and their hope that he would continue to reform. They blamed the corruption, widespread arrests of dissidents, and continued climate of fear on the old guard still surrounding the young Assad. He just needed more time, they insisted.

After the demonstrations started, the Obama administration released a crescendo of statements, at first only slowly increasing pressure, as though unable to accept that yet another dictator was falling. Assad was fast losing his legitimacy, officials said. The window was closing. The window was almost closed. He was not indispensable. His legitimacy was gone. They imposed sanctions on his coterie. Then on his generals. Then on him. Not even President Mahmoud Ahmadinejad of Iran was personally under sanctions. As the violence deployed against the protestors escalated and the death toll grew by several hundred every month, calls increased for the administration to say the magic words: "Assad must go."

The Obama administration resisted making that statement. Obama was still eager to ensure that the United States did not look like it was encouraging the uprisings. He and his advisors wanted the people on the ground to own their revolution. Public American support was often the kiss of death. Assad, predictably, blamed a foreign plot for the unrest in his country. In Washington but also in the region, some people argued that since Arab leaders used the plot excuse anyway, whether America spoke out or not, Washington might just as well throw its weight behind the protestors. But with a war still ongoing in Libya, Obama didn't want to say anything that could lead to demands for another intervention: you said he has to go, now take him out. The U.S. presidential election was also already a consideration.

For outsiders, it seemed simple to call for a leader to step down; once those words are uttered, however, the United States is essentially declaring it will never deal with that government again. The United States' careful deliberations behind closed doors were seen in the region as intentional inaction, driven by a desire to see Assad prevail. Yet more proof of America's nefarious designs and hypocrisy when it came to supporting human rights and freedom. The cost of saying nothing was rising. Finally, on August 18, Obama issued a statement.

"We have consistently said that President Assad must lead a democratic transition or get out of the way. He has not led. For the sake of the Syrian people, the time has come for President Assad to step aside."

When Obama made his statement, anti-Assad protestors cried victory.

But statements by the United States did not necessarily have an impact on the ground. Obama had said Gaddafi should go in March, but five months later he was still holding on to power in Libya, despite a NATO bombing campaign. Now, Obama had said Assad had to leave, and the Syrian leader did not appear to be shaking in his boots. When nothing happened after an American president spoke, it made the United States look powerless.

The uprising in Syria was unlike the other revolutions in the Middle East. Tunisia had happened so fast, no one had had time to think. In Egypt, the United States had leverage because it gave money to the army and the army hadn't shot at the protestors. The revolutionaries had been well organized, bringing millions onto the street. Libya was a fringe country in North Africa with a fringe leader no one liked. There were strategic interests involved, but mostly for the Europeans because it was their backyard. Washington was not developing a comprehensive strategic approach to the Arab Spring. It dealt with each country separately.

Assad had his hands on many destructive levers, more so perhaps than most dictators in the region. Syria was a supporter of Hezbollah in Lebanon on its eastern border, was a friend of Hamas, which had its headquarters in Damascus, and had links to the networks of insurgents in Iraq. Assad himself, as well as his relatives, who were all in positions of power, often made veiled threats. Syria, they said, had influence over groups like Hezbollah and Hamas, so they could rein them in and counsel them to stay quiet. But the obvious implication was that thanks to these groups, Syria could unleash chaos across the region. In keeping with that attitude, Assad's cousin Rami Makhlouf, the country's most powerful businessman and a lightning rod for dissent, had warned in an interview with the *New York Times* in May that if anyone dared touch the Syrian regime, no one could guarantee the stability of Israel or the region. Ironically, Assad kept his own border with Israel quiet. Not a shot had been fired since the last conflagration in 1973, and Israel was keen to keep it that way, often pressing Washington not to push Assad too hard. It was a classic case of the "the devil we know."

The biggest problem was Syria's alliance with Iran. Tehran wasn't going to let Assad fall without putting up a fight for him. The United States constantly worried about Tehran gaining influence and political clout in the region, and when the protests had erupted in Bahrain, American fear of Iran had come at great cost to the protestors. Now the problem was reversed. The end of Assad in Syria could deal a strategic blow to Tehran but American officials worried that, if they pushed to make it happen, the United States could suddenly find itself at war with Iran.

Back in Washington, Jake was keeping an eye on events in Libya. His BlackBerry rang.

"Hi, Jake! What's going on in the world?" asked the voice on the other line. It was the secretary. He was always ready for that question. In his pocket he kept a scribbled list of the top issues and developments of the day, just for these phone calls. Hillary checked in every evening during the week, no matter how often they spoke during the day or in the office. Jake kept a low profile, he was a behind-the-scenes operator, but Hillary's longtime aides remarked that she had rarely relied on someone as much as she relied on Jake. His debate skills helped her refine tactical points, his knowledge of policy nuances allowed her to hone her arguments, and his pocket list of hot spots assisted her in visualizing the big picture, the trends that were shaping the world—her specialty. Hillary excelled with details, but she was even better at long-term plotting, strategic patience.

Hillary had been criticized by U.S. pundits for spreading herself too thin at the start of her tenure. Why was she talking about women and not getting down in the weeds on the Middle East peace process? Why was she touring Africa and not shuttling between Pakistan and Afghanistan herself to close the deal? Why was she revamping the way the Building operated when nuclear talks with North Korea were stalled? Hillary believed that it was no longer possible to devote all your attention to one hot spot or one issue, ignoring the others. All the issues and all the countries were increasingly connected, and if she wanted to help solve any of the problems, she had to connect all the dots. She also didn't want to invest all her energy in a losing venture, like Middle East peace. Besides, Hillary just didn't know how to focus on one task. It was a quality and a flaw. She always wanted to do it all, and then she wanted to do some more. But her overarching concern was that America had to change the way it did business around the world if it wanted to remain a relevant leader in the twenty-first century, not only tackling traditional diplomatic concerns but empowering people to solve their own problems. Hillary deployed an army of special envoys, from human rights to women's rights to climate change to youth issues, to help the United States reach out to civil society around the world, harness the power of new technology, and modernize the way the United States handled diplomacy. The State Department had become the world's leading foreign ministry in using social media, with 150 full-time social media employees working across twenty-five different offices and nine hundred diplomats at U.S. missions around the world using it in their day-to-day diplomacy, from Twitter to YouTube and Facebook. Victoria Nuland, the department's new spokesperson, didn't just brief from the podium but also on Twitter, taking questions from around the world. Jake didn't just discuss the administration's foreign policy priorities at think tanks in Washington but also on live Internet broadcasts where journalists from the four corners of the world could send in their questions. The State Department also set up programs for mobile banking in Africa, tip lines in Mexico to fight drug cartels, text message donation programs to raise money for Haiti. America was expanding its reach and redefining its role, though no one could guarantee that this new approach would deliver in the longer term. Smart power on the part of America seemed too avant-garde for a world that still judged power in a very traditional way, and still expected the United States to be a bully.

The economic crisis continued to grow in Europe: Greece had cheated in its national accounting books and was now heavily in debt. Italy, Spain, and Portugal were all on the verge of a crisis as well. Europe was facing its own decline. I traveled around the continent asking various officials what they thought of the theory of American decline.

"American decline?" asked one senior French official with a laugh. "There is no such thing. It's a joke." Italians were adamant that America wasn't in decline. Italy was, but America? No.

Decline, apparently, was highly relative. The Old Continent had often looked at America with condescension, a legacy of anti-Americanism that predated George W. Bush, the Iraq War, and freedom fries. In 1947, just two years after the end of World War II, the French writer Simone de Beauvoir traveled across the United States and recorded her impressions of the world's new superpower. Her writings contained much disdain. A very proud, patriotic French friend of mine had often scoffed at Uncle Sam's arrogance and dismissed Americans as incompetent bullies who had no understanding of how the rest of the world worked. Now he was telling me how worried he was about American decline. It would be a terrible thing for Europe, the world, the Middle East, where he now lived. I reminded him of his previous statements about America, and he confessed that his words were partly driven by envy—America was bigger, better. It was the world power that France had once been, and he was loathe to admit that France now played only a cameo role on the world stage.

I had a hard time accepting my friend's change of heart. I prodded deeper with others, journalists and diplomats, architects and hotel owners, in Italy, in the United Kingdom, in the Netherlands. They all expressed concern about the possibility of American decline. If America is in decline, what about us? The rivalry was gone, the scorn had vanished. Europe now looked to America and saw that the country it had mocked for its lack of sophistication, history, or refined culture was the first line of defense against its own decline into total irrelevance. Together, they could face the new powers on the global stage, new powers that didn't have the same values or interests as the West.

On August 21, Tripoli fell to rebels. Although the fighting around the capital had intensified and the assault had been carefully and secretly planned, it was still very sudden. Months later, an American official would tell me that luck had also played a role, so the Obama administration did not see the military operation as a guarantee of success anywhere else. Gaddafi was still on the run, but Sarkozy, Cameron, and Erdoğan made a very public triumphant appearance in the city, with chants of "Thank you, France, thank you, Turkey" ringing around them. On October 17, 2011, we were on our way to Libya.

Clinton was greeted on the tarmac of Tripoli airport by a chant no American official has ever associated with gratitude to America.

"Allahu Akbar, Allahu Akbar." God is great, in Arabic. A phalanx of uniformed, bearded fighters, who were part of a militia that now controlled the airport, stood on the tarmac as she emerged from the plane. SAM had remained in Malta, and we had flown over in a military C-17, better equipped to fly into what was, in effect, still a war zone. In the West, "Allahu Akbar" is now so closely associated with the cry of radical militants before their worst acts of violence that few are able to accept that in Arabic it is often simply a cry of joy or exasperation or a reaction to fear, as common as "Oh my God" or "Dear Jesus."

The fighters raised their hands in signs of victory and asked to pose for pictures with Hillary. She also raised her fingers in a V. The militiamen then escorted Hillary's heavily armored motorcade into Tripoli, zigzagging on the road ahead of us in their own SUVs, driving alongside us, grinning widely, some of them leaning out of their windows with their guns.

"I am proud to stand here on the soil of a free Libya," Clinton said after one of her meetings with the country's new interim leaders, including Mahmoud Jibril, who had played a key role in convincing the West that the Libya opposition was worth betting on.

After Tripoli, we went on to Kabul and Islamabad. The policy on Pakistan had been drifting for a while. After Richard Holbrooke died, his team had disbanded. Vali Nasr was gone too. The United States and Pakistan still didn't trust each other; even worse, they confused the hell out of each other. The relationship between them seemed to be only getting worse, partly because of American actions and partly because Pakistani honor—*ghairat*—was applied selectively. When Pakistani soldiers died in friendly fire by the Americans, the news was plastered all over television and Pakistan demanded an apology and more aid. When Pakistani soldiers died at the hands of the Taliban or in a snow avalanche, the deaths, divergent from Pakistan's narrative that it was being bullied by America, barely received a mention in the news.

A lot of bruised egos followed the Navy SEAL special operation that killed Osama bin Laden in May 2011. The Pakistanis didn't just feel betrayed by the United States. They were worried about having been caught unaware and what that said to the world about their intelligence and army. If we didn't know the United States was flying into our country, they thought, who knows what else, who else, might be flying in.

In Islamabad, Clinton soldiered on with her efforts to engage the people, the members of parliament, though the types of questions and the reception she received had barely changed in the two years since she first visited.

From Lahore, Shehrbano Taseer, the daughter of Aamna and the assassinated Punjab governor Salman Taseer, was watching the coverage of the visit to Islamabad. She had missed Clinton's last visit while studying in the United States, but now she was back in Pakistan, fatherless and helping her mother with the family business. Shehrbano's brother Shahbaz, the eagle, whose name had so pleased Hillary, had been kidnapped that summer. There had been no claim, no ransom demanded. His family believed he was being held somewhere along the border with Afghanistan. Shehrbano had come to Washington in the fall to ask if there was any intelligence about his whereabouts, as the whole area was under heavy surveillance by the Americans, who hunted down militants and then struck them down in drone attacks. The family kept any information they gleaned to themselves for fear it would compromise Shahbaz's safety. The harsh winter would set in soon, and Shehrbano worried about her brother, in the cold. Drone strikes were ridding her country of militants, but her brother was now in their hands. As she lay awake at night, she wondered, "What if my brother dies in a drone strike meant to kill his captors?"

Our stop in Kabul, as always, was about getting out of the country as fast as possible. Fred was now based there, in charge of the embassy security. Another tall but blond and heavily built Diplomatic Security agent, Kurt Olson, looked after Clinton. Antoinette Hurtado had also joined the embassy for a yearlong stint and thought back fondly of the Paris escapade. On October 20, news reached us that Gaddafi had been caught alive and then shot dead in Sirte.

"We came, we saw, he died," Clinton said in an unguarded moment caught on camera.

Dictators were being brought down, walls of fear falling, but some things never changed. The minute Obama had announced a surge of troops to stabilize Afghanistan and defeat al-Qaeda in November 2009, he had been looking for the exit out of the war. The motto had been "Clear, hold, build, transfer," which had proved too ambitious. In Kabul,

Clinton announced a new, more modest strategy. Any hint of nation building was gone. As so often before, grand plans had been shelved, more millions of dollars had been wasted by short-sighted ambitions and petty turf wars within the U.S. government and military. Naive good intentions dried up on the arid plains of a country known as the "graveyard of empires."

16

HELP US HELP YOU

The e-mail arrived in our in-boxes in late November. We would soon be flying twenty-two hours across the Pacific until we reached our destination, a country almost untouched by the outside world, a land of white elephants and bejeweled temples. There were detailed clothing instructions. Don't bring white, pink, or black clothes; these are considered mourning colors. Tone down your rusts and saffrons; these are the colors of protest. For the men among us, whose closets were full of black suits and white shirts, these strange instructions presented an unwelcome hassle the day before the Thanksgiving weekend. We women had more options; there were enough colors left for us to assemble our attire.

The second memo, titled "Facts before you come," was more problematic: no BlackBerry service, no high-speed Internet, no credit cards, no cash machines. Foreign journalists were a rarity, and sensitive areas were off limits to foreigners. Though this would make our work as journalists a particular challenge, the reward of reporting from inside this isolated nation would only be that much greater. On the Monday after Thanksgiving, we settled into our seats in the back of good old SAM.

The package pulled up on the tarmac just after two in the afternoon. Hillary had already been to four events that day, including a summit at the White House with European leaders. The Euro-zone crisis was still in full swing and threatened to land on America's shores every day.

Clinton stepped out of her limousine in a chic black pantsuit, her sunglasses on as usual, her blond windswept hair now past her shoulders. Hillary had many reasons to be excited about this trip, both professionally and personally. The trip added a new country to her list of places she had visited and represented the result of three years of work. Clinton would be the first American secretary of state to set foot in the country since the 1950s. She was also going to meet a personal heroine.

Burma beckoned. The Land of the Golden Pagodas, once known as the Jewel of Asia, a fertile country traversed by the Irrawaddy River.

"This is Burma, and it will be quite unlike any land you know about," Rudyard Kipling had written in 1898, in his *Letters from the East.*

Today's Burma was a pariah state called Myanmar by the military junta that had ruled the country since a coup in 1962. The ruling junta stood accused of the worst abuses—forced labor, including of children, forcible relocations of ethnic populations, and using rape as a war weapon. The country was mired in poverty, civil war, and corruption. Uprisings by monks demanding more freedom for the country were violently put down, whole monasteries emptied of their populations as the monks were sent to prison. Tough sanctions imposed by the West were meant to choke the regime, but the strategy wasn't working and the people were only getting poorer.

In his inaugural address, Obama had called on America's foes to unclench their fists. Iran and North Korea weren't sure they wanted to unclench anything and didn't seem to know how. But that year, surprising everyone, Burma's junta made contact. During her travels to Asia, Clinton had heard from her Indonesian counterpart that the sanctions alone weren't working and that the Burmese were trying to figure out how to move forward. Indonesia could help bring Burma back into the fold of the international community. She listened closely, registering the importance of what she was hearing. A regional approach to solving a vexing problem appealed to the Obama administration. And unlike Brazil and Turkey with Iran, Asian countries didn't want to make friends with Burma just for the sake of making friends, just for the sake of a deal. They were willing to listen to Washington's advice about how to navigate the process and Washington was open to their approach. This could work.

Burma and the United States waltzed with each other all year, but the dance didn't really go anywhere. There were no diplomatic breakthroughs beyond one high-level meeting at the UN between Burmese and U.S. officials. The country had its own groundwork to do first, including parliamentary elections and the election of its first civilian president in decades, a former general, Thein Sein. The strongest signal for change came when the generals released from house arrest a woman as famous as Hillary—Aung San Suu Kyi. In 1990, her party had won the elections, but the military ignored the results and instead imprisoned her, sometimes in her own home, sometimes in a jail. The way Burma's generals treated Suu Kyi, a Nobel laureate, would become the barometer of how close or fast the West was ready to engage with Burma. Obama had consulted with Aung San Suu Kyi before sending Clinton to the country, and soon the two iconic women would be face-to-face. First, however, Hillary would deploy her people-reading skills to gauge whether Thein Sein and his colleagues were serious about change or simply trying to con the world into lifting sanctions. Obama said he saw "flickers of progress," and Clinton was going to find out if they could be fanned into a real flame.

Soon after takeoff, Clinton came to the back of the plane for a chat. It was such a shame there wasn't more time to travel around Burma, Clinton told us. She would have wanted to visit Mandalay, the country's former capital. Clinton had repeatedly insisted she was stepping off the high-wire of politics at the end of her tenure at the State Department. She said she felt cheated traveling the world for work with no real time to experience the places she was visiting. She was still energized by her trips, but this one was especially momentous. Copious briefing material produced by the State Department had not been enough for her. She had asked for books and films, poring over the history and politics of the country for a week before the trip.

After our taco salad lunch, Kurt Campbell, the assistant secretary of state for East Asia and the Pacific, crossed the Line of Death to brief us about the visit and what to expect. Kurt also spent his life on planes crisscrossing the region, building on the work done by the secretary or preparing for her upcoming visits. America's relationships with its allies, in Asia or elsewhere, required constant tending. On the plane, everyone was preoccupied with one central question—after years of maintaining a close, repressive grip over the nation, why were the generals now finally unclenching their fist? No one knew for sure.

Burma's leaders were able to travel around Asia, unlike their North

Korean friends, whose travel was confined to China because of extensive travel bans. The Burmese attended ASEAN summits, spoke with other leaders, and could see their country falling behind, choked by sanctions, while the rest of Asia prospered. Burma had a large expatriate population that fed news back into the country. Burma was cut off, but it was no North Korea. So, unlike Arab leaders who had utterly rejected reforms, the Burmese leaders appeared to have understood that if they could open up the country slowly, on their terms, perhaps they could stay in power and reap the rewards, as well as avoid international justice.

Despite all the hard work that had gone into diplomacy with Burma, no one on the plane was claiming credit for the stirrings of change. It was too soon to claim success anyway, but American officials were also aware of the many converging elements that had made this moment possible. The hard work of other Asian countries and Burma's own will and intention had been key, but the real game changer for the Burmese had been China. The Burmese were feeling used by their bigger neighbor. Chinese companies were building hydroelectric projects in Burma and bringing in workers from China rather than creating jobs for the Burmese. The Chinese were planning a huge dam on the Irrawaddy River, a holy flow of water for the Burmese. The dam would greatly damage the river, and the Chinese were planning to send 90 percent of the power generated back to China. *What kind of a friend was that?* the Burmese wondered. The generals wanted the United States to be a buffer, a balancer.

After a quick stop in South Korea for a conference about international aid, we flew to Nay Pyi Taw, Burma's new capital. The landing strip was narrow and unlit; we had to be wheels down before nightfall. SAM could not be kept secure in Burma, so the Ravens would spend the night guarding the plane in neighboring Thailand. Clinton walked down the steps wearing an intense fuchsia jacket and black trousers. Men in white shirts and dark *longyi*, the traditional Burmese wrapped skirt, greeted her on the tarmac. Clearly, Hillary and her Burmese hosts had not read the memo.

A red billboard stood at one end of the tarmac, barely thirty feet away from the nose of the plane. The country welcomed the prime minister of Belarus, who had just visited, in big white letters. There were no banners welcoming Clinton—the generals didn't seem to want to get ahead of themselves or appear too eager in public—but this country was clearly aspiring to keep better company than other dictatorships.

We had been promised white elephants and stunning, pastoral landscapes, but we got water buffalos, startled farmers, and a road paved with concrete. For probably the only time in our travels with the secretary, we all actually watched the country go by our windows: no BlackBerries. We entered the town, which looked deserted, and pulled up to our hotel, the Thingaha, a small resort of teak villas where we were the only customers. Waitresses bearing trays of watermelon juice welcomed us, some overcome by emotion when Hillary greeted them like long-lost friends.

Dusk fell as the waitresses set a long table on the terrace for drinks and snacks with the secretary. Over the last three years, Hillary had grown to like and trust the traveling press corps. Every now and then on the road, she joined us for drinks or dinner and talked frankly about everything from the policy issues she was facing to what films she had watched the evening before in her hotel room or gossip about celebrities. The agreement was always that those conversations were private and their content not to be shared. It allowed her to be herself, or as close to that as was possible while still in the company of journalists. She often had a couple of drinks. This evening it would be tea for the secretary—she was coming down with a cold and needed to be fit for the next day. Her hair was up, her makeup removed for the evening, her contact lenses replaced by her glasses. She was relaxed, comfortable, and funny, holding court for over an hour.

The next morning we readied for our visit to the presidential palace in Nay Pyi Taw, Abode of Kings, the country's new capital, a brand-new city with twenty-lane-wide streets. There was a street for hotels, one for restaurants, a section for government buildings, another for housing of government employees. The modern ultra-planned city was unlike anything else in the country. In the past, royals had moved the capital around the country according to their whim; the British had set up in Mandalay, and the capital then moved to Rangoon in 1948 after independence.

The generals who took over in 1962 grew increasingly isolated over the years and became paranoid about an attack by the country they perceived as their enemy—the United States. Rangoon was also becoming congested, so the generals started clearing hundreds of square feet of tropical scrubland to make way for Asian-style buildings with a Soviet bulkiness. They chose an area so remote that no one was even aware a new city was being built, except for residents in a logging town two miles away, who were tipped off when Chinese engineers suddenly began frequenting local cafés. The outside world, watching on satellite imagery, wasn't sure what the construction was all about.

With the help of an astrologer, the generals chose an auspicious date and time to move to Nay Pyi Taw, and on a Friday in November 2005, they announced that Myanmar had a new capital. Two days later, whole government ministries started moving up to Nay Pyi Taw, a ten-hour drive from Rangoon. Burma's rulers and its bureaucracy were retreating inland. Six years later, they let the "enemy" into their bosom.

Our motorcade, usually an overwhelming sight in any city, could do nothing to fill the twenty-lane highway in the government zone of the city. The annoyance of having a foreign dignitary closing off streets meant nothing in this oversized ghost town that appeared completely depopulated. After we drove past a few cars and motorcycles near our hotel, there was not a vehicle or a person in sight anymore as we approached the presidential palace. We entered the compound through the golden gates, across a bridge over what looked like a moat, and pulled up outside the palace—a massive marble building that could have been the work of Donald Trump.

The man awaiting Clinton had been a general and a prime minister for the junta when the country was still ruled by the fearsome General Than Shwe, who had kept Aung San Suu Kyi and thousands of others in prison. As part of Burma's efforts to present a softer face to the outside world, Thein Sein had resigned from the army in 2010 to run in the elections as a civilian. He was now president. The country was nominally governed by civilians, but the generals were still the bosses.

Thein Sein was a blushing, somewhat shy host. It was unexpected behavior from a former junta leader. Admittedly, he'd mostly been a bureaucrat and not a field commander, but the diminutive, bespectacled man in a traditional blue silk *longyi* seemed overwhelmed by the size of his own palace. He was waiting for his guest, the first American official to ever visit the city, in a room the size of a football field with a crystal chandelier so large it was menacing. Clinton, in a turquoise pantsuit and matching necklace, walked in with barely a smile on her face. There was no coddling to be done here.

"Your Excellency's visit will be a historic milestone," said Thein Sein.

"I am here today because President Obama and myself are encouraged by the steps that you have taken to provide for your people," said Clinton.

The two leaders shook hands for the cameras and then sat on large gold thrones against a red and gold backdrop framed by a gold curtain. The press was ushered out. The chairs were too far apart for a quiet conversation, and four microphones were set on the table between the two thrones for the officials and their translators. Their staff, sitting on chairs along the walls, separated from each other by a sea of a carpet, could barely participate in the discussion. For forty-five minutes, Thein Sein explained why he was serious about reform and all the steps his government was planning to take to make it happen. His list matched each of America's concerns—Clinton was not here to start a dialogue in the dark, and the Burmese knew what she expected to hear. American officials had prepared the visit with numerous trips to Burma. The recitation of America's own demands could have been a clever ploy, but Thein Sein was also open about the difficulties he was facing from within his government—not everybody believed in reform, and he had some convincing to do around him. His unexpected candor made his promises of reform sound more sincere.

Clinton went through her presentation, outlining the requirements to keep the dialogue going and for the relationship between the two countries to be normalized. There was a long way to go but the United States was willing to match every gesture the Burmese undertook with a reward. From releasing prisoners to allowing Aung San Suu Kyi to run for parliament, the list was extensive. In return, the Burmese could host an American ambassador and sanctions could be eased. One day, American companies would be allowed to invest in Burma. Trade could flourish.

The talks ended, it was time for lunch. The president's wife, Khin Khin Win, had appeared, and the two delegations walked over the marble floors, below more chandeliers, toward the dining hall. Hillary and Khin Khin Win, who were the same age, quickly connected. The Burmese woman told Hillary she was relieved the visit had finally come to pass because her husband had been nervous and lost much sleep in the preceding weeks, so anxious had he been for everything to work out perfectly. He wanted to make a good impression on the American secretary of state. His country's future depended on it. His future depended on it.

Khin Khin Win and Hillary walked with clutched hands, their elbows bent, fingers interlocking as the Burmese woman told her about her desire to see a better future for her country and an end to the suffering in the ethnic areas that had endured so much fighting.

While officials ate their way through twelve courses, from deep-fried crab to fried rice with egg and green peas, the hungry traveling press corps lingered on large, gaudy chairs, gazed at the small Buddhas, squinted at the chandeliers and all the gold. The style was an odd combination of Asian culture, bland Chinese design, and Gulf-style nouveau riche ostentation. The money poured into building the capital—the cost of the palace alone was estimated at $4 billion—had further drained Burma's economy. The opulent city belied the fact that this was a country where malaria was still endemic, and people lived on less than a dollar a day.

The visit was over. Clinton and her delegation said their good-byes, and we all settled into our seats for the ride. Burmese journalists snapped pictures of her black limousine. The president, his wife, and their entourage stood on the steps watching the departing motorcade drive away over the bridge. The tiny president waved back to occupants in one of the vans, looking slightly forlorn on the steps of his giant marble palace.

In the distance, we could see the Uppatasanti Pagoda, an exact replica of the Shwedagon Pagoda in Rangoon. Uppatasanti also stood 325 feet tall, but its jade Buddha apparently bore a striking resemblance to Than Shwe. Now we were off to see the real thing in the old capital.

We landed in Rangoon as the sun was setting and raced up the Singutarra Hill to see the golden pagoda in daylight. The oldest Buddhist pagoda in the world looked more like a spire than the usual multitiered pagoda. Scintillating in the twilight, with its gold plating and hundreds of rubies and diamonds, it could be seen from almost anywhere in the city.

Everybody had to take off shoes and socks to enter the site. Clinton revealed dark-red toenail polish. DS agents, in their suits and ties, were not amused. Padding around barefoot, whispering into their earpieces, they looked cartoonish. The site had been kept open to tourists and locals, and we heard a couple of screams of "We love you, Hillary" and clapping. Burmese police pushed the crowds away roughly while Clinton's staff and DS tried to allow people to come closer to the secretary.

The site was quiet and contemplative, colorful and raucous—a place of meditation where the only noise, apart from the shrieking fans, was made by Clinton when she sounded one of the forty-ton bells, a sanctuary of beauty and precious stones punctuated by odd neon Buddha halos. The visit to the holy site was a rare occasion for the secretary to do some sightseeing, a moment of peace before the most anticipated meeting of the trip.

At seven in the evening, a tattered white sedan drove up to the residence of the U.S. chargé d'affaires in Rangoon, a colonial-style house of understated, hushed elegance with a portico, teak floors, and a patio. A frail-looking ethereal woman sprang out of her seat as soon as the car door was opened for her and darted up one step to the house's threshold for a meeting she had been looking forward to for weeks.

They could not have had more different lives or been more different in personality and outlook. But when Hillary and Aung San Suu Kyi came face-to-face for the first time after years of reading about each other's struggles and dreams, there appeared to be a moment of instant recognition. By coincidence, they wore matching outfits for the occasion—white Asian-style jackets, their hair tied at the back, Suu Kyi's low ponytail pinned with flowers.

Hillary had, perhaps for the first time ever, met her match in the equally world-famous, prodemocracy activist with a quiet demeanor hiding a steely determination. Likewise, the Nobel Peace laureate, revered in her country and an inspiration to millions around the world, a political royal treated with deference by her entourage, found herself in the presence of a woman who was truly her equal.

Hillary's usual booming "Hello" was replaced with a more subdued tone as she welcomed Suu Kyi for dinner at the mission. Suu Kyi appeared slightly nervous shaking hands with her host in the doorway. Though they had never met in person and had spoken on the phone only once before, Hillary felt like she was meeting a friend after a long time apart.

The tone was familiar but emotional. The two women stood in the doorway smiling for the cameras, talking softly.

Suu Kyi told Clinton she still had the poster from the 1995 UN conference on women in Beijing, when Hillary had given her groundbreaking speech on women's rights. Hillary, Madeleine Albright (the then U.S. ambassador to the UN), and others had signed a copy of the poster, and Albright had delivered it to Suu Kyi on a quick visit to Burma.

In Clinton's packed travel schedule, there was rarely the time—or perhaps even the desire—for a lengthy one-on-one dinner and this one had initially not been on the schedule at all. There were only plans for a formal meeting at Suu Kyi's house on our second day in Rangoon. But Clinton couldn't travel all the way from Washington to Rangoon and meet this iconic woman just to have a diplomatic business discussion. A table with a white cloth and white china awaited the two women in the front room of the mission; in the kitchen, the Burmese chef had been laboring all day over a dinner of Burmese food, including some of Suu Kyi's favorites.

First they had drinks on the patio with Hillary's team—Kurt, who had met Suu Kyi before, and others who hadn't, like Cheryl Mills, Hillary's chief of staff. The anticipation subsided, and the two women slipped into an easy conversation, as if they had known each other for years and had spoken regularly. On the plane on the way over, Clinton had also watched a new film about Suu Kyi's life, *The Lady*. Suu Kyi had read Hillary's and Bill's autobiographies. The entourage departed, and the two women sat down for dinner. The weather was cool, so the dinner china had been moved out of the dark dining room and onto the patio's glass table.

Clinton presented her dinner guest with rare editions of books authored and signed by Eleanor Roosevelt. There would also be a chew toy and bowl for Suu Kyi's dog the following day. Suu Kyi gave Clinton a traditional silver necklace she had made herself. Over three hours, they talked about their lives and their hopes for Burma.

When they met again the next morning, they were ready to get down to business. Clinton's black limousine pulled up at Suu Kyi's home just after nine in the morning. The aging home, by one of the city's many lakes, had been Suu Kyi's prison for years. I had seen it on television, so I instantly recognized the large front portico, the red-tiled roof, the lawn, and the water in the background. The Lady stood waiting in the doorway. Hillary's hair was pulled back in a chignon, and she wore her new silver necklace with a light-blue pantsuit.

The two women greeted each other with a kiss on the cheek. Suu Kyi introduced the secretary to her relatives and staff and showed her the house, laughing about how much cleaning had gone into the preparations for Hillary's visit. They sat down at a round table with both their aides and talked about how to connect the country's leaders with the opposition and the outside world as a way to keep the reforms moving forward. Suu Kyi had been developing a rapport with Thein Sein and indicated she trusted his intention to reform. She told Hillary she'd been reading books about military men who had become politicians, including U.S. president Dwight Eisenhower.

But while Thein Sein seemed determined to pursue reforms, it was unclear to Clinton whether he had the temperament needed to push beyond the initial stages of a process that would be long and messy. Suu Kyi had faith, and she appealed to Clinton to make clear to those in the United States who opposed engagement with Burma to listen to the Burmese people, who wanted contact with the United States. There were some members of Congress who refused to make any gesture toward the Burmese regime until officials addressed every single concern of the outside world and righted every wrong. Clinton disagreed. She had come to believe it was important to seize on every indication that a regime was willing to reform and try to encourage it, which is why she had come here. She had listened to the Burmese people, to their leaders, and to the country's neighbors. Her presence was the result of a desire for change by the people, steps taken by the leaders, legwork by other regional leaders, all in coordination and with the quiet leadership of America. It was the diplomatic version of the Libya war, a successful version of the failed Turkey-Brazil mediation. Every situation was different, but they all required the same ingredients— active efforts for change by the people, willingness of the leaders, regional ownership, and patient, hands-on American coordination.

After their meeting, Clinton and Suu Kyi strolled through the garden, the dog bouncing around them. The cameras snapped away. The two walked back to the house and up to the back porch to speak to the media.

The prodemocracy activist had already said she would run in the upcoming parliamentary elections. There were hints of an electoral campaign in her statement to the press as she called for equal rights for all ethnic communities in this "union of many people."

Suu Kyi clasped hands with Clinton as she thanked the United States for its help and its "calibrated" approach to reengagement with Burma's government. Hillary leaned forward tentatively to hug the activist. She was embraced warmly. The two women then exploded in laughter before walking away together, like two long-lost sisters. In the midday sun, on the back porch of a colonial home, the power of America and the power of Hillary had blended into one. It was time to go home.

17

CHAIRMAN OF
THE BOARD

The uprising in Syria was almost a year old, the death toll stood at nine thousand, the revolution was no longer peaceful, the rebels were taking up arms. But Bashar al-Assad was still there. The international community was deeply divided about how to end the violence. Even those who agreed that Assad had to go could not agree on how. There was no talk about any Libya-style military intervention. But something had to be done. So a conference was organized in support of the Syrian people to pledge humanitarian aid and discuss a post-Assad Syria. The conference would be held on February 24, 2012, in Tunisia, the country where the Arab Spring had started in December 2010. Keeping the Libya war effort on track had been hard work, but Hillary found that bridging the gaps between her counterparts on Syria was near impossible. The conference hadn't even taken place yet, and the UAE, Turkey, and France were already jostling to host the next meeting. The Turks and the French were also at each other's throats over plans to introduce a bill in the French parliament that would punish those who denied that the 1915–16 mass killings of Armenians by Ottoman Turks was genocide. Getting them into the same room was going to be a challenge. The British barely wanted anything to do with the Syria quandary. Clinton tried to reason with everyone, keeping them focused on the task at hand.

Russia and China were both blocking action at the UN, so the conference in Tunis, blandly dubbed Friends of the Syrian People, was the only way to get any forward diplomatic momentum. Twice already, in November and earlier in February, Beijing and Moscow had vetoed a resolution condemning the mounting violence in Syria. The text of the resolutions was weak and did not even call for sanctions, yet Moscow was adamant that it would not sign on to any more resolutions that could pave the way to military intervention and regime change. Russia felt burned by the Libya episode; the anti-Assad protestors were paying the price.

Russia had motivations beyond Libya too: Syria had been a client state of the Soviet Union and remained an ally of the Russian Federation. Russia supplied the Syrians with arms and maintained a naval base in the city of Tartous, on the Mediterranean, one of its few military bases abroad. Moscow wasn't going to give up on its ally, no matter how many people had already died.

Both Russia and China looked at the Arab uprisings, especially in Syria, through their respective prisms. In Syria, Russia saw echoes of Chechnya, a rebellious Muslim region that tried to break away from Russia after the dissolution of the Soviet Union and lived through two ferocious Russian military campaigns to crush the rebellion, devastating cities like Grozny and killing tens of thousands of civilians. The rebels carried out a number of horrific attacks inside Russia proper, which killed scores of civilians. Beijing had its own history of crushing dissent both at home and in Tibet, a territory over which Beijing had forcibly declared Chinese sovereignty. Assad was doing what China and Russia had done in the past when faced with a rebellion. They understood and approved of his tactics, and were ready to stick by him. They were not going to Tunis.

Russia also appeared eager to make a stand on the world stage in a way that it hadn't been able to do since the end of the Cold War. Today's Russia was not the same world player that the Soviet Union had been. Its areas of influence were limited, and there were not many big strategic games in which it could participate. China had once supported people who rose up against colonial powers but now worried about setting any precedents of outside interference that could be used to challenge the tight grip of the Communist Party on China.

After each veto at the UN, U.S. ambassador Susan Rice expressed her outrage and disgust, saying it was clear "who on this council supports [Syrians'] yearning for liberty and human rights." The Americans could be seen as hypocrites—unwilling to take any forceful action, they were grandstanding while hiding behind Russia's veto. But the United States and the European Union had already gone beyond condemning the violence, imposing sanctions on a growing number of Syrian officials. The United States was adamant that Russian action at the UN would have sent a clear signal to Assad that he had to stop shooting and start a real political transition to a Syria where he was not president.

On our way to Tunis, we stopped in London for another conference, on Somalia. Many of the ministers who would be attending the Syria conference were there too, and after spending hours with them on the phone from Washington, Clinton was going to make sure, in person, that everybody was on the same page.

Behind the scenes, American officials were busy helping the divided Syrian opposition coalesce into a group that represented all of Syria's religious and ethnic communities and could engage in a serious dialogue with the Syrian leadership to start a real political transition to a post-Assad Syria. If no one wanted to remove Assad and he wasn't going to fall any time soon, a negotiated transition was the next best thing. The opposition was represented by the Syrian National Council, led by Burhan Ghalioun, a white-haired, uninspiring sociology professor who had lived in exile in Paris for more than three decades. Since its creation in August 2011, the SNC had been mired in internal divisions and was accused of being corrupt. The SNC was criticized for being too close to the Muslim Brotherhood, which had been banned in Syria for almost fifty years. SNC members resigned regularly and new rival opposition groups kept springing up. There was no Mahmoud Jibril here. The SNC also seemed unable to put together a document laying out its vision for the post-Assad period, one that was inclusive of all the nation's communities, including Christians and Assad's own Alawite sect, which each made up roughly 10 percent of the Syrian population. The SNC failed to include any Kurdish representatives, Syria's largest ethnic community. American officials were dropping as many hints as they could about what the opposition needed to do to galvanize support, but they didn't want to write the program for them: screams about American interference would erupt, overshadowing the tragedy unfolding in Syria. Washington also worried about the fact that the SNC did not properly represent the thousands of activists, trapped under fire inside Syria, risking their lives each day to coordinate protests and send out news of their rebellion. The last time the

United States had relied on advice solely from an opposition in exile, in Iraq, it had been a disaster. The State Department hoped that the opposition would manage to smuggle some representatives out of Syria or have them join the conference by Skype. Clinton wanted the Syrian opposition and the outcome of the conference to represent the will of people on the inside who were angry with opposition leaders in exile for failing to galvanize international support fast enough, if at all.

The Tunisians were nervous about their first foray into international crisis solving since removing their own dictator. The conference in London provided an opportunity for some hand-holding before the big day. There, they received help on how to run the gathering and formulating the final communiqué of the conference and advice about how to run the conference. Some sixty countries and organizations would be attending the gathering. There had to be broad consensus on a text that would be powerful enough to send a clear message to Assad. The Emirati sheikhs gave the Tunisian minister a ride back to Tunis and provided even further guidance and advice, practically dictating the text of the statement in an effort to speed things along.

We arrived in Tunis at two in the afternoon and headed to the seaside Gammarth Palace hotel, where the conference was taking place. We were still on our way to town when the motorcade came to a standstill on a deserted highway, in the middle of a small forest. Diplomatic Security agents got out of the car and for a moment I wondered whether we were in the middle of an ambush of some sort. But DS agents posted at the hotel had informed agents in the motorcade that a pro-Assad demonstration under way in front of the hotel had gotten out of hand, and we were hanging back waiting for the crowds to calm down.

After a brief pause, we were back on our way to the Gammarth and to the mayhem. The hotel lobby was heaving with delegates and journalists. Tunisian security guards seemed in a panic, the restaurants out of food. Behind closed doors, key participants in the conference were giving their speeches. The Tunisians upset the SNC when they abruptly suggested that Ghalioun shouldn't take the podium but finally agreed to let him speak. They had also been unable to find a table large enough to accommodate all the ministers around it, so they seated delegates in rows and the French, sitting in the third row, were fuming. No panic, the

American delegation thought, the first Friends of Libya meeting had also been a challenge. Clinton was going to give her own speech at the conference and then hold a series of talks with several of her counterparts.

The Saudis were there, no longer sulking about America, the fickle friend that threw its allies under the bus. Iran, their nemesis in the region, seemed to create antibodies that pushed countries closer to the United States. Fear of Iran and rivalry with Shiites drove everything in the Sunni kingdoms. Now the Saudis were sulking about something else. Before his meeting with Clinton started, Saud al-Faisal answered questions from reporters, instead of sticking to pleasantries in front of the cameras. Was it a good idea to arm the rebels?

"I think it's an excellent idea," he said. "Because they have to protect themselves."

Sitting next to him on a red upholstered chair, Clinton was taken aback. Arm the rebels? The focus of the conference was humanitarian aid and the political transition. The UN and the Arab League were about to name an envoy to Syria, Kofi Annan, a former UN secretary-general, to implement the transition plan suggested by the Arab League, bringing monitors to oversee an end to the violence. Arming the rebels would only feed the conflict. This was not part of the agenda. Washington was wary of any move that would further feed the violence and militarize the uprising. For months, American officials had repeatedly and publicly exhorted the protestors in Syria to remain peaceful, "selmiyya," until the repression by Assad's forces became so violent that Washington's position was no longer tenable. But openly arming the rebels was yet another story. In Libya, the Transitional National Council, led by Jibril, represented the political and the military wing of the rebellion. The United States had also sought and received assurances that the fighters were not affiliated with al-Qaeda. But even then, the United States had supplied the Libyan rebels only with non-lethal equipment, no weapons. The Free Syria army, on the other hand, was not the armed wing of the SNC and the two bodies were in fact often at odds. The SNC had initially rejected the use of violence in the Syrian uprising. The fighters in Syria were not all under the FSA command and there were signs that radical Islamists were increasingly taking up arms.

With reporters out of the room, Clinton and her delegation probed some more, asking who those rebels were exactly that Saudi Arabia wanted to arm. Saud al-Faisal gave a vague answer.

"We know who they are, we know."

He suggested putting money in a bank account and letting the rebels use it as they saw fit.

On the hotel doorstep I bumped into a senior Saudi official I knew from my days reporting in the Middle East.

"What do you think the conference will achieve?" I asked.

"It's a waste of time, all this talk about humanitarian aid, fine, but it's time to get rid of Assad, and all this talk isn't going to help," he said.

"So are you going to arm them? Do you think that's going to help get rid of Assad?" I asked.

"We think something needs to be done," he responded. "All this talk is useless. Assad is an occupier now. It's time to take Syria back."

Those were very strong words. In the Arab world, "occupation" and "occupier" had become synonymous for Israel's occupation of Palestinian territories. Whenever an Arab talked about "the occupation," it was understood he meant the Israeli occupation. The rulers of Saudi Arabia, the Custodian of the Two Holy Mosques, had now put Assad in the same category as Israeli leaders.

But no matter how nefarious or violent Assad was, arming the rebels was a risky business. The last time Saudi Arabia had helped armed rebels, it was in Afghanistan in the 1980s with Washington's cooperation, to fight the Russian occupation. That effort gave birth to a generation of jihadi fighters, the Taliban and al-Qaeda, all of them still wreaking havoc in Afghanistan and beyond. But my Saudi friend was adamant that concrete action had to be taken and that actively arming the rebels was a first step. He seemed to indicate that what was really needed was a military intervention.

"So is Saudi Arabia going to intervene and take him out?" I asked.

The Saudi official looked at me as though I had just lost my mind.

"We're not a superpower. America is the superpower," he said.

Superpower or not, Saudi Arabia and the United States had just sealed a $30 billion deal for eighty-four new F-15 fighter jets. Another seventy fighter jets were being refurbished. A year earlier, hundreds of Saudi troops and army vehicles had been sent across the border into Bahrain to help quell Shiite demonstrators rising up against the country's Sunni rulers. In 2009, Saudi jets had bombed Yemeni rebels challenging the rule of Ali Abdullah Saleh, their neighbor. Though the Saudis had the means to intervene and had done it before, they did so only when it was in their immediate backyard and when the solution was straightforward. Syria was a bigger challenge, a viper's nest: better leave that to America.

During the Libya crisis, the Obama administration had said it was willing to go as far as the Arabs; the United States had then led the way to intervention. But on Syria, the Arabs were divided. The Tunisians opposed arming the rebels. The Bahrainis said armament was premature. The rebels were not just an unknown quantity, they also held no territory. Unlike in Libya, there was no safe haven where they could organize themselves and mount an organized attack against Assad. But the key player here was Turkey, Syria's neighbor to the north. Ankara made vague reference to the need for a safe haven but stopped short of calling for one to be forcibly established.

Erdoğan and Davutoğlu had initially been keen to demonstrate the benefits of their zero-problem-neighborhood policy and their close relationship with Assad. They asked Washington to give them the time to bring Assad around. They had met and spoken to the Syrian leader repeatedly at the start of the uprising, counseling dialogue and reform, but Assad had said one thing and done another. By the end of 2011 Erdoğan felt personally let down. The Turks started calling for action, in vague terms. When American officials had asked exactly what they envisaged, it appeared that Erdoğan and Davutoğlu had not exactly consulted their generals. Once they actually looked down the barrel of military action, their public ardor for action became more measured, and Turkey's discussion with Washington focused on what Ankara's red lines were: floods of refugees and a spillover of the conflict. With Washington, they set up a defensive military planning contingency cell.

The Syrians themselves were divided about calling for military intervention. After weeks of working with opposition leader Burhan Ghalioun to help him put his best foot forward, his performance at the conference had been uninspiring. Even worse, he told journalists that the gathering "doesn't meet his people's aspirations." Hillary's team was furious—the secretary had come all the way from Washington to show support, Ghalioun had said nothing during the meeting that indicated he was disappointed, and now he was declaring that all of this just wasn't enough for Syria. At least the opposition activists had been able to join the conference, speaking from Syria by Skype.

Night had fallen and the rowdy gathering came to an end. The Tunisian chair gave a press conference, and at nine in the evening it was Clinton's turn. Faced with questions about what had really been achieved and how the talking in Tunisia could end the killing in Syria, the secretary sounded both combative and reassuring, like a chairman of the board praising participants for what had been achieved, including pledges of humanitarian aid, and detailing the path that still lay ahead.[37]

"Let's stay focused on what we accomplish today. I've been to a lot of meetings over many, many years—rarely one that was put together with such intense effort on such a short timetable that produced so much consensus. So let's stay on the path we have begun on."

She appealed to soldiers and officers and others around Assad to defect so the fighting would end. She reserved her toughest words for the Russians and the Chinese.

"They are basically saying to Tunisians, to Libyans, to others throughout the region, well, we don't agree that you have a right to have elections, to choose your leaders. I think that is absolutely contrary to history. And it is not a position that is sustainable," Clinton said.

"It is just despicable. And I ask, whose side are they on? They are clearly not on the side of the Syrian people, and they need to ask themselves some very hard questions about what that means for them as well as the rest of us."

After another half a day in Tunisia and a few hours in Algeria, Hillary awoke on a Sunday morning, in her suite on the eighth floor overlooking the white Moroccan city of Rabat, frustrated and angry. The pace had been frenetic since Washington. London had been a long, busy day. The Tunis conference had been a zoo. The day-stop in Algeria was exhausting. She had barely had time to reflect on where things stood on Syria. But that morning, the full extent of the deadlock in Tunisia dawned on her. Hillary just couldn't see how this played out, how it ended. When I sat down with her for an interview in the hotel restaurant converted for the occasion into a television stage, I asked her the same question I had asked her almost a year earlier: how did she think the Obama administration would be judged by history if it allowed Assad to level a town like Homs while Washington dillydallied, wondering what to do.

"I wish that people inside Syria were responding as people inside Libya responded," she said. "They are not, at this point, perhaps because of the firepower and the absolute intent that we've seen by the Assad regime to kill whomever."

But what about her criticism of Russia and China; surely their obstructionism made it easy to avoid action that no one wanted anyway?

"No. If they had joined us in the Security Council, I think it would have sent a really strong message to Assad that he needed to start planning his exit, and the people around him, who are already hedging their bets, would have been doing the same. [But] they know they've got Iran actively supporting them, Russia selling them arms and diplomatically protecting them, and China not wanting anybody to interfere with anybody's internal affairs. So that gives them a lot of comfort."

The extent of her disappointment at the conference became more and more apparent as the interview went on.

"I would not be doing my job if I were not looking at the complexity. I mean, I could come on and I could do an interview with you and I could say, 'Oh, we're all for them. Let's go get them.' But what would that mean? Because clearly I know how complex this is, and anybody who is thinking about it and having to actually consider what could happen next understands it."

As a reporter, my job was to grill her with tough questions and never be satisfied with the answers. As a woman who had grown up during a war, this was the kind of frank and human response I wished American leaders gave more often. The truth was painful but I felt it was better than empty promises of help.

But on a policy level, Clinton's candor was often a double-edged sword. This was not the message that the administration wanted to put out, but this is where she was in her head that morning. Her words were seen as a blow to the opposition—was the United States abandoning them? Pundits warned that Clinton's statement would be comforting to Assad.

Calibrating a message in this day of instant news was a struggle. Should American officials be up front about the limits of their power and make clear to those waiting for help that they should help themselves? Part of the responsibility to protect people in danger was perhaps to admit to them that the cavalry wasn't coming and that they had to do a better job organizing and helping themselves. A hard message to send to people under fire, but then they also deserved better than the poor excuse of a leadership in exile that they had ended up with.

Clinton also had little by way of facts to deliver to Obama. When she had gone to Paris just over a year prior, not fully decided about military action in Libya, she had methodically crossed off every item on her political shopping list. She spoke to the French and the British, who assured her that they were on board and understood that more than a no-fly zone was needed. The Arabs had promised her face-to-face that they would put their money where their mouth was. The Libyan opposition chief looked like someone you could do business with. A year later, Libya was not exactly a shining example of democracy, but at least the dictator was gone and people had tasted the freedom of their own power. The rest was up to them, this was their country, and they had to drive it. Soon, parliamentary elections would be held that would be touted as historic with Mahmoud Jibril's centrist coalition in the lead.

But at the Tunis conference on Syria, Hillary hadn't been able to cross off anything. The French didn't want to do anything too close to the presidential elections. The British didn't want to mount any sort of coalition. Some of the Arabs wanted to arm the opposition, and others didn't. The Arab League hadn't called for action, neither had the Gulf Cooperation Council. Turkey talked a lot but didn't actually want to do anything. The Syrian opposition was useless. The bar was not high—no one was trying to organize a coalition for a military intervention—but Hillary had nothing to work with: no international unity, no unity within the Syrian opposition. She didn't even have something in her hands that she could sell to Lavrov. There were no clear answers; the diplomatic stars weren't lining up, not yet. But the longer the fighting continued in Syria, the messier it was going to become. I began to see echoes of Lebanon.

Back in Washington, I continued to watch the footage coming out of Syria. More reporters were finding their way into the country, but most of the pictures were from activists and citizen journalists. Their unverified footage made it hard to confirm what was happening exactly on the ground, and there was no doubt that a propaganda war was under way as well, with the anti-Assad rebels keen to show the extent of the regime's crime and none of their own abuses.

In one of the videos, a Syrian soldier stood in a field with two gun-toting colleagues on either side, dozens of others behind him. Some of them held up Syrian revolution flags—the black, white, and green flag with three red stars that fluttered in Syria between its independence from France in 1946 and 1963, when the Baath Party seized power in a coup. Under a gray March sky, villagers and children looked on. The soldier gave his name and announced his defection from the Syrian national army. On camera, he read his new oath of allegiance as a member of the Free Syrian Army.

"I promise to defend villagers from the assault of the government forces," he said. "Long live Assad's Syria." He paused a moment, then burst out laughing, his hands to his head, his body tilting backward in the laugh. Everybody laughed. "Long Live Assad's Syria" was seared on every Syrian's brain, branded like cattle from infancy. Every Syrian belonged to the Assad family; the country belonged to the Assads. The motto was tagged on walls, printed in schoolbooks, repeated like a mantra for generations. It was hard to get rid of. Just like Assad himself.

For years, Lebanon had suffered from the Machiavellian politics of the Assad family. Several dozen prominent politicians had been assassinated over the course of three decades. Syrian soldiers had invaded, occupied, looted, and raped in Lebanon with the outside world often paying scant attention. In 1972, Hafez al-Assad declared that Lebanon and Syria were one country, and he pursued that goal of unity assiduously and ruthlessly from the first time he sent troops into Lebanon in 1975, until he completed his control with the invasion of 1990 that had marked me so much. In the process, across Lebanon, people were humiliated, detained, or beaten up by Syrian troops or intelligence officers, many languished in Syrian jails for years, and some had never resurfaced. Damascus did also have staunch allies in Lebanon who either benefited from that alliance or espoused the same worldview—resistance to Israel and the imperial West. Syria was now being torn apart, and while many Lebanese had often wished the worst for their occupiers, this was heartbreaking. I looked at the images coming out of Syria and I thought of Lebanon. There were many differences between us. Syria was poorer and more rural than Lebanon, and its cities still bore the mark of the Soviet influence, but in many ways we were similar, not one country, but cousins, people of the Levant. The fact that Syria was stuck somewhere in the 1980s because of dictatorship only reinforced the feeling that, when I looked at the conflict unfolding in Syria, I was seeing Lebanon from the 1980s.

The idea that Bashar al-Assad was a reformer was buried in the rubble of cities like Homs and Daraa, which had so far borne the brunt of the military assault. Assad after all had never rebelled against his father, Hafez, never broken ranks; he was truly his father's son, along with his brother Maher. Just like Saif Gaddafi, who had deceived so many with his talk about change, appearing to lead the way toward reform, or Gamal Mubarak, who ended up being partly responsible for the downfall of his father in his desperate desire to keep power in the hands of the family. Syrians who had hoped that Bashar was their country's savior were disappointed and angry. Smart, educated, Westernized liberals started to break ranks, bitter about how they too had been used to show the outside world that there was potential for openness and democracy in Syria. But many Syrians still believed that Assad was their best protection against the kind of chaos that had engulfed Iraq, next door, after the fall of Saddam. Christians and Alawites feared retribution if the Sunnis came to power.

In Washington, in opinion pieces in newspapers around the world, people kept saying that this was not 1982; the younger Assad would not be able to kill with impunity the way his father had done at the time in the northern town of Hama when he put down an Islamist rebellion. Some twenty thousand people were massacred then, their bodies bulldozed into the ground with whole buildings that had been brought down on top of people's heads. Today, there was television, Twitter, Facebook— the world would act in the face of such atrocities, just as it had in Libya to prevent the massacre that Gaddafi had threatened to carry out in Benghazi. But Bashar al-Assad knew this was the twenty-first century, and though he kept the international media mostly out of his country, he also did not appear on television to threaten that he would hunt down his people like rats in alleyways, the way Gaddafi had done. His forces were reportedly instructed to keep the daily death toll just below outrageous.

Every day brought another call for intervention, the same kind of "loose talk" that had infuriated Robert Gates during the Libya uprising. But

Syria was not Libya, and the cost of intervention was just too high for a president in an election year. Libya had lasted well beyond the "few weeks" that the Obama administration had insisted it would take to end the violent repression by Gaddafi of his people. Syrian armed forces were better armed and trained, with air defenses and jets bought from Russia. Syria also had the region's largest stockpile of chemical and biological weapons. Who knew how long an intervention would last or what it would lead to?

As the weeks went by, on trips with the secretary, over drinks in Washington, officials would ask me, "What do you think of the situation in Syria?" I had no particular wisdom or specific information, but in the search for a path forward in the face of such a cunning dictator, all ideas were welcome.

I told them, from experience, about Assad's expertise in sowing chaos, holding on to power, and outwitting everybody. I warned about a slow descent into civil war. Assad would burn the country before he handed it over to anyone else.

"But what good does that do anyone? That's just sandbox logic!" exclaimed one incredulous official. Perhaps, but it was Assad's logic, the kind that often escaped some American officials. They remained as result-driven as ever, often getting tangled up in their good intentions and unable to understand other governments' absolute indifference to their own people's welfare. But this administration seemed to be demonstrating an understanding that foreign interventions meant playing in someone else's stadium by someone else's rules and always remaining a stranger. Those advocating for action said Obama had swung to the other extreme of the Bush administration—so eager not to put a U.S. stamp on popular revolutions that he was overthinking the situation into paralysis.

America had interests to safeguard too, and in my life away from Lebanon I was becoming attuned to the thinking driving officials in D.C. I raised the prospect of months of protests, a simmering war, months of fighting.

"You don't want that, not in an election year. It's messy," I said. Our conversation was on background, so I couldn't identify the speaker by name.

"I'm not sure it has an impact on us. Don't get me wrong. I think it's terrible that people are dying, and I wish we could find a way to stop it, but if it continues to simmer like this, contained within Syria, it doesn't have a direct impact on our national security."

I had lived through war, I had felt abandoned by the world, I had clamored for help, and yet here I was sitting in Washington able to see why, from this official's perspective, America's national security was not affected by events in Syria, for now, and why intervention was still worse than nonintervention.

What had happened to me? Had I become insensitive to people's suffering? Forgotten my own past? Become too in tune with American political discourse? I hoped it was just my new appreciation of the complex role of a superpower and the shortcomings of other countries as well as my own. I also understood there were often deep connections between separate problems that constrained America's actions. How it handled Syria would influence its policy toward Iran, for example, which was much more of a strategic interest for America. This was the stuff of diplomacy for a superpower. Russia and China had their own considerations, their own interests to protect, when they vetoed resolutions on Syria at the UN. Comparisons are never straightforward but America vetoed plenty of resolutions at the UN that condemned Israeli military operations against the Palestinians or Lebanon. Everyone stood up for their buddies.

Washington, European capitals, and the Syrian opposition were perplexed by the position taken by Brazil, India, and South Africa. They had abstained from voting on one of the Syria resolutions. Their traditional nonaligned approach to solving the world's crises was not producing any results for the Syrians. Instead of supporting civilian protestors calling for democratic change, they were de facto supporting a repressive regime. These countries wanted a permanent seat at the UN Security Council, but their presence at the table didn't mean the oppressed people of this world were getting a new voice on the council defending their rights.

In Washington, every day my in-box filled up with e-mails in Arabic sent from somewhere in Syria, a basement, a safe house, someone's kitchen or living room. The Local Coordination Committees in Syria were grassroots activists who initially facilitated contact between protestors across Syria to help coordinate the movement. They also acted increasingly like

local government in areas that had fallen to the rebels. Slowly, their
e-mails started filling with more news of protestors being shot. Their
missives, in basic English or Arabic, continued to punctuate my days in
Washington. I woke up, made coffee.

Subject: Breaking from Homs.

Homs: 75 unidentified corpses were found in the refrigerator of the
National Hospital after the FSA captured it. Local Coordination
Committees of Syria.

Lunch break.

Subject: Syria 9PM.

Hama: Atshan. Violent shelling with tanks targeting the village leading
the damage of several houses and displacement of several residents.
Damascus suburbs: Hasya: Martyrs and wounded were reported after
the regime's army, backed with tanks, raided the town amid heavy and
random gunfire.

Afternoon coffee. More death.

There were long lists of links to online videos documenting the shelling, the dying, and the wounded. I had spent the first months of the Syrian
revolution watching them avidly, all day long. By the summer, they
became too violent, and I began to have vivid nightmares about the war
in Lebanon again. My feelings of fear and helplessness, carefully tucked
away and forgotten after four years in Washington, returned. So I took
the selfish and rather cowardly decision to stop watching the videos and
shield myself from the pain. But I didn't have the courage to ask the
LCCSyria e-mail senders to take me off their listserv.

Usually by the end of the day, all I wanted to do was cry. The e-mails
just kept coming, throughout the night. When I woke up, there would be
another five, ten, sometimes twenty of them in my in-box, staring at me
from my BlackBerry screen, a long litany of death, violence, and fear. I
had no right to cry: I was living in the United States, far from the chaos.
My family in Beirut was safe.

But my friends in Damascus were not. I was in touch with some of them and feared for their lives and their futures. And I was reliving the civil war in Lebanon, wondering why it was happening all over again right next door. Soon, the rebels themselves would be involved in atrocious acts of violence, torturing soldiers they caught, hanging informers. The lines between who was right and wrong, good or bad, blurred occasionally, just like they had in Lebanon over fifteen years of fighting. But in Syria there was still one ruthless president mowing down his people.

The e-mails from Syria were a silent version of the news flashes on Lebanese radio during the civil war that interrupted regular programming to tell us where shelling had erupted or which road crossings had snipers on them. A burst of music with a punchy beat would sound on the radio, followed by a phone ring, bringing dread to our hearts.

"News flash from our newsroom," a woman's velvety voice would then announce. Whenever my family was in the car, we kept the radio on to make sure we knew if we were driving into danger. At home, the moment we heard explosions, we turned on the radio to find out what was going on. We could tell from the sound that the shells were making whether they were incoming or outgoing, close or far, but the radio announcers would tell us who was fighting who, whether it was a minor eruption or something serious. All of the tidbits of information fed into our decision-making process—stay put or head down to the shelter? I've often wondered how the people who sat in those radio studios gathered the detailed information that kept so many of us alive for years. Not only were there no Internet, e-mail, or cell phones at the time, but landlines barely worked.

The Syrian e-mail authors showed the same ingenuity and determination. They even used some of the same language to describe the shelling: "intense" for sustained bombardment; "indiscriminate" for shelling not directed at a specific target but just aiming to destroy as much as possible in as wide an area as possible. Or both "intense" and "random."

I thought I had finally left fear behind when I had moved to the United States in 2008 for my BBC job. I had only spent holidays in the United States till then, a few weeks here and there over the course of fifteen years. Yet the feeling of familiarity and comfort was instantaneous after I arrived. I felt free of fear, the kind of fear that makes hundreds of thousands of people around the world seek a way out of the repression of their country, whether it's a new life abroad or a second passport that guarantees a way out to safety.

As I watched the images of children on the backs of pickup trucks fleeing their villages in Syria, I remembered the escape out of our neighborhood, under the cover of darkness during a lull in the shelling, my mother driving our old Mercedes, me in the backseat under a blanket, shivering from fever. My body reacted to every flare-up in the fighting with its own internal battles. This one happened early on February 4, 1984, when I was only seven, but snippets of the action are seared in my memory. Over the years, I've expanded the image by adding details from conversations with my family. After days of fighting, the Lebanese army had lost control of West Beirut, and Muslim militias had taken control of the territory. The president had the backing of the international community, and they weighed in, in their effort to shore up what they saw as the legitimate state and the national army. The marines had left Beirut after the 1983 truck bombing but were still off the coast of Lebanon. The USS *New Jersey* battleship fired three hundred shells onto the stronghold of the militias, south of Beirut and the hills southeast of the capital. But the president was a Christian, so "when the shells started falling on the Shiites, they assumed the American 'referee' had taken sides," wrote former secretary of state Colin Powell in his memoir, *My American Journey*.

The feeling that America was at war with Muslims was partly born and solidified in Lebanon.

My family was stuck in the middle, wondering why we were being attacked by the Americans. Every front line seemed to cross our neighborhood. We were right on the edge between East and West Beirut, in a no-man's-land; our building stood on the western side, but our front door opened on to the East. We were at the southern end of Beirut, beyond us the southern suburbs, stronghold of the nascent Hezbollah, and farther along other Muslim militias.

My father and eldest sister had stayed behind to look after the house and check on my father's office on the western side of town. A Lebanese army soldier at a checkpoint told my mother she was crazy to be on the road, but she insisted we had to leave. I was sick and had to be taken to a quieter environment. There was always someplace in the country where there was no fighting. The challenge was getting there. The soldier told my mom to turn off the headlights and drive slowly so as not to attract the attention of snipers. The city was in the dark. Streetlights were an exotic feature. We crossed the big intersection that I would later peer down while driving to the presidential palace with Clinton during that trip in the spring of 2009.

My mother drove as silently as possible, into the dark, holding on to the steering wheel, the windows cracked open so we could hear any movement outside. As long as we made it through the intersection, past the snipers, we would be fine. We were almost there when my mother started to make out an obstacle in front of her, a strange dark shape in the middle of the road, with spots of white. She turned on her headlights just in time to avert a crash: the biggest danger we faced at that moment was a stray cow taking a rest in the middle of the road.

With every week that passed, Syria looked to me more and more like the violent, fractured Lebanon I had grown up in. We didn't have one dictator facing down his people but a plethora of militias sowing fear. We had the same regional configuration of countries getting involved—Iran, Saudi Arabia, Israel, the United States, and Russia. China was not a factor back in the day, Lebanon didn't share a border with Turkey, and the Turks had not been a regional player at the time. But this felt like a replay of the bigger power game that opposed East and West in Lebanon: the United States with its friends Saudi Arabia and Israel pitted against Russia and its camp, including Iran and Hezbollah. Except that Syria was no longer one of the players and the persecutor of others, but its own victim. In Syria, more and more protestors were holding placards saying the world had abandoned them. As I had felt during the war in Lebanon, the Syrian people had no patience to understand what sort of geopolitical stars had to align before the violence stopped.

Just as in Lebanon, the national army was breaking up, militias were taking over, great powers were meeting in an effort to find a way forward that suited them all, but there was no obvious path. The diplomatic to-ing and fro-ing that took place at every turning point in Lebanon had looked to us like some nefarious plot was being discussed at our expense. Every time American officials visited Lebanon, or Russian emissaries visited Syria, or Russians and Americans met, we asked ourselves whether they would strike a deal—in our favor or at our expense. Now, sitting in Washington, in Tunis, or at the UN, watching from up close, I could see that it wasn't an evil conspiracy in which a country's people were cheap collateral damage; it was more benign—relentless work trying to bridge the gaps between two different worldviews with no clear path forward as long as all the players stuck stubbornly to their position and their interests. But that didn't make the pain any easier to bear.

The conflict in Syria dragged on, the death toll growing more rapidly as the rebels stepped up their attack and the regime's fight for survival became increasingly brutal. The United States, after holding out for months, stepped up its support for the rebels in the summer of 2012, helping to coordinate the supply of arms reaching them without actually supplying any weapons, and providing with them with communication equipment. Eager to avoid being dragged into another war or being associated too closely with the conflict, Obama tried as much as possible to avoid speaking about Syria during 2012. His political opponents were not wading into the Syrian debate either, a sign of just how intricate and complicated the conflict was—everybody understood that. The Obama administration was also wary about the growing number of radical Islamist Salafist fighters and worried that providing anything more than communications equipment or nonlethal assistance to the rebels could empower Salafists to take over Syria. But the radicals were getting weapons anyway, mainly from wealthy Gulf funders, and moderate rebels, frustrated by the lack of Western support, were joining their ranks. Clinton's hesitations stemmed from her desire to protect the country's minorities, namely the Christians, and ensure their survival in a post-Assad Syria, but the majority was paying the price. Many expected that Obama would take more decisive action if he were reelected, but even after November 6 there were still no good options, no clear vision for a post-Assad Syria. Unlike Libya, it was too big a minefield for other countries to take bold steps alone—without U.S. leadership there would be no decisive action. Frustration with the Syrian opposition was growing though, and in mid-November the United States finally banged heads together to help give birth to a more credible and representative opposition coalition. Administration officials admitted the push could have come earlier and that perhaps their eagerness not to put an American stamp on a popular movement had been taken to the extreme. Soon the United States and others would also recognize the Syrian opposition as *the* legitimate representative of the Syrian people, mirroring the Libya scenario. But the cost of direct military intervention remained too high and the onus was on the opposition outside and on the rebels and Local Coordination Committees inside Syria to unseat Assad with quiet American backing. At the time of writing, Assad remained in power.

Jake had a hard time living with the inconsistencies of U.S. foreign policy. He had a linear mind—the world had to make sense; everything had to fit. Why had they intervened in Libya but could not find the tools to do so in Syria? Why had the administration come out in support of protestors in Egypt but were cautious on Bahrain? Why was Pakistan getting U.S. aid when its intelligence agency was helping militants fighting U.S. soldiers in Afghanistan?

Hillary had lived a complex life with many inconsistencies—the details were sometimes jarring, but the overall picture made sense to her. She applied the same approach to her work as secretary of state.

She was deeply troubled by the violence in Syria. She felt she had failed the protestors in Bahrain. She wanted her country to do the right thing, but she was candid about the choices America had to make.

"Americans believe that the desire for dignity and self-determination is universal—and we do try to act on that belief around the world. Americans have fought and died for these ideals. And when freedom gains ground anywhere, Americans are inspired," she said in one of her speeches about changes in the Middle East. But America, she added, also had short-term interests that it had to pursue, not just values to defend.

"There will be times when not all of our interests align. We work to align them, but that is just reality."

I had never heard an American leader speak so candidly about the balancing act that was required in the exercise of American power. American leaders usually spoke publicly about higher ideals and the pursuit of more noble goals, keeping the discussion about special interests for private diplomacy, at the risk of making America look like a hypocrite whenever it failed or refused to help oppressed people anywhere. But there was no grandstanding here, just a simple and candid statement. People could be upset or feel disappointed, but it was hard to argue with such a statement. "I get that," I thought. I was slowly reaching the end of my own journey.

CONCLUSION

One thing worse than an America that is too
strong, the world will learn, is an America that is
too weak.

—Michael Mandelbaum, *Frugal Superpower*

When I came to this job in 2008 and when I decided to write this book, I never imagined how intense and emotional the journey would be. Up to that point, I had rarely, if ever, spoken, let alone written, about living through war in Lebanon, but it was a necessary journey back in time as I explored American power, looking for the answers to the questions that troubled me as a teenager and a young adult in Lebanon, while observing the exercise of American power today. Over the last few years, I have struggled often with my thoughts, questioned my conclusions, even my convictions, about what the United States represented or stood for, what I believed in, and what kind of world I wanted to live in.

I did not always settle on definitive answers because the world consists of shades of gray. But there was one event in my life that I could still only see in black and white. What had really happened on that October day in 1990, when Syrian troops invaded Lebanon? Was it true, as many Lebanese believed, that in exchange for contributing thousands of troops to the coalition to liberate Kuwait from Saddam Hussein's troops, Syria had been given the green light to occupy Lebanon?

Access to information was limited at the time; we relied mostly on local newspapers and local television and though Lebanon's media were the most open in the region, fear of the Syrian occupation prevented in-depth reporting of what had happened. I had also accepted the narrative of America selling us out for cheap to Syria and moving on. I found it hard to look back to a day that had been the scariest of my young life, even after years of war. But, mostly, it is often difficult to look at a painful event other than through the very narrow prism of personal experience. So for years I had neatly tucked away my memories, my pain and my anger, and hung on to the tidy explanation of a deal between Washington and Damascus.

But I had now looked as deeply as possible inside the American for-eign policy machine and had not found the plot; the closest thing was the Book, but its contents were wonky and benign. Now, for every fantastical scenario, for every irrational fear, I had an explanation to give to people who asked me what America was up to and why it acted this or that way. The time had come to unpack my own version of the plot.

I looked up old articles and found that most of the focus around that time was on Iraq's invasion and occupation of Kuwait, with very little written about my country. In fact, the narrative of a deal at the expense of Lebanon dominated most of the literature that I found. Many of the newspaper reports focused on efforts by then Secretary of State James Baker to get President Hafez al-Assad to sign up to the anti-Saddam coalition. Syria was designated as a state sponsor of terror by the United States, so Baker was heavily criticized when he decided to visit Damascus in September 1990 to discuss the coalition. As I prodded further, the out-lines of what had happened emerged.

The administration of George H. W. Bush had been working for some time to engage Assad, a cunning adversary. During his visit to Damas-cus, Baker was also hoping for a breakthrough in the hostage crisis in Lebanon, in which thirteen Western hostages were being held, including six Americans. President Assad had been a close ally of Iran since the Islamic revolution of 1979. Iran and Syria, thanks to the radical militant groups they promoted, such as Hezbollah and some Palestinian organi-zations, held the fate of the hostages in their hands. I was also reminded that Michel Aoun had asked the United States to recognize him as the legitimate government in Lebanon, but Washington had refused. A rival president, Elias Hrawi, had been elected in West Beirut, backed by the

Syrians, and Lebanon's already complex politics had become even more incomprehensible. Crucially, Aoun was receiving arms from Saddam Hussein, America's new enemy number one. Saddam was hoping to build his own front against the United States with the quixotic Aoun in Beirut and President Ali Abdullah Saleh in Yemen.

I went to see Brent Scowcroft, who was the national security advisor for George H. W. Bush at the time. I asked him how and why the United States had given away Lebanon to Syria. Scowcroft, now in his eighties but still as sharp as ever, looked at me in silence. I explained why I was asking and wondered whether he was perhaps feeling remorse at a decision made all these years ago or whether he just didn't want to tell me. But Scowcroft couldn't instantly remember the exact series of events that had led to the Syrian invasion. All his memories from that period were dominated by the efforts to oust Saddam from Kuwait and the White House's desire to build a broad, U.S.-led coalition that would signal a new kind of international cooperation in the post–Cold War world.

I was crestfallen. I could not fathom that a day that had left such an indelible mark on me and had been such a turning point for Lebanon was not a vivid memory for one of the men who had been at the heart of the decision making in the White House at the time. As a reporter in Beirut, I knew that Lebanon was not on the minds of all officials in Washington at all times. Since arriving in the United States I had written about countries being just a page in the Book and sat in the briefing room listening to a spokesperson answer questions about country after country, like a pop quiz. And yet I felt hurt. I knocked on more doors, asking former officials from the Bush administration, but no one remembered much.

I looked up old transcripts of the State Department's daily press briefing. Margaret Tutwiler, the State Department spokesperson at the time, was asked to comment on October 15, 1990. On the day of the invasion, a Saturday, the Bush administration had only issued a short statement. Tutwiler had nothing to add, so she just read out the statement.

"The United States government hopes that all the Lebanese people will support President Hrawi, the legitimate government, and the reunited army. . . . The United States regrets the loss of life in the October 13 event. We hope that this ends a sad chapter of Lebanon's history, and that the Lebanese people can now move toward reconciliation and the rebirth of a united, sovereign and independent Lebanon."

We really had been a blip on the radar. The ferocious assault by Syrian troops, the looting, raping, ransacking, and summary executions of soldiers and men of fighting age had all just been an "event." The United States had moved on while we found ourselves under the boots of our masters in Damascus. Baker, Tutwiler, and other American officials were questioned in public about why they had agreed to Syria's invasion. They insisted there hadn't been a green light.

I continued my search for answers and finally found someone with a vivid memory of that day. Edward Djerian, the U.S. ambassador to Syria at the time, explained in detail how and why the United States had been trying to engage Assad. There was the coalition against Saddam and the American hostages in Beirut, who were freed within a few years. Djerjian was also negotiating with Assad to allow Syria's four thousand Jews to travel out of the country. They faced severe restrictions and were often described as hostages. They were finally granted permission to leave in 1992. But the real prize was a Middle East peace conference. In 1991 in Madrid, Israeli and Arab leaders met for the first time in more than forty years of open conflict. Assad was there too, and his presence was key, because Israel occupied Syria's Golan Heights and the two countries were still at war. For the Bush administration, engaging Assad had been a success, Djerjian explained, and progress had been made on many fronts. The fighting had also ended in Lebanon, which, after fifteen years of strife, was a positive development. Reluctantly, I nodded that I understood. I could see Washington's rationale.

But had there been a green light? No, Djerjian said adamantly. Even when Baker had met Assad in September 1990, there had been no nods or winks to any invasion. But there had not been a red light either. Assad and Saddam were longtime foes, and Washington knew that the Syrian president would not tolerate the flow of weapons from Iraq to Aoun's Christian statelet for long. And because Aoun was Saddam's ally, no one in Washington felt the need to protect the rebel general. There were no attempts to preempt any move by Assad or inquire about exactly what he might do and when.

On October 13, 1990, Djerjian was woken around six in the morning in Damascus by two low-flying Syrian fighter jets, a very unusual occurrence. Startled, he turned to his wife and said, "He's going after Aoun." Moments later, the same jets woke me in Lebanon as they flew by our house and started their bombing campaign. Eight hours later, it was all over—and I was left feeling betrayed by the United States.

Two decades later, I found myself on the inside of the American foreign policy machine, or as close as an outsider can get. After traveling more than 300,000 miles with Clinton around the world and interviewing her more than fifteen times, I had a new understanding of the United States and of the woman who had given me a ride home on her plane in the spring of 2009. By now, America and Hillary Clinton had blended into one for me. No longer a politician, but the face—and the heart—of American power.

Clinton's willingness to answer any question, to explain what she was thinking and why the United States was doing what it was doing, whether on the record in front of the cameras or off the record in private, helped me as I matured and refined my analysis of the world and my views about America. Whether or not I disagreed with positions taken by Clinton or the administration, I was no longer mystified by the reasoning. Knowledge in this case truly was power.

I was also very much aware that my access to someone at the heart of American power put me in a unique position. On a quiet Friday morning in the summer of 2012, while I sat in the secretary's outer office on the seventh floor, I prodded her some about what she thought the United States stood for. Why should I believe in the United States as a benevolent force when it had also done much harm around the world, I asked.

"I see America as predominantly a force for good over the course of our history," she said without a hesitation. "But I'm also well aware of our flaws and shortcomings, of bad decisions, of misjudgments. We started off as a country that inspired more love of freedom and more opportunity for more people than any other human enterprise in the history of the world, but we still had slaves and we didn't let women vote. So in our own history, there is a continuing striving for that more perfect union."

I pressed further. How could the United States be a force for good when I had been shelled by a U.S. battleship, when the United States had been responsible for bloody coups in Latin America, for the debacle in Iraq? I expected her to say what she often said when confronted with the past: that instead of looking back at all the mistakes the United States had made, I should be willing to look forward and do my part, however small, in making sure it didn't happen again. But Clinton's answer startled me.

"Look at the way we rounded up Japanese Americans and put them in camps. It made sense to decision makers at the time, including one of our greatest presidents, but in retrospect it's something we are not proud of; in fact, we are ashamed of. . . . But we also make mistakes. And so I would ask that people look at us the way I look at us, which is that name any other society or nation that has done more to help lead the world toward the pursuit of happiness for every individual, for human freedom and dignity, but which, like all human enterprises, is flawed."

I had never looked at domestic U.S. history to put in context American excesses of power abroad. Knowing that American leaders looked back in horror at some of the decisions of their countrymen, as well as knowing that misguided, ill-advised decisions had caused harm to Americans at home, contributed further to dispelling my old belief that the United States was somehow intent on causing harm abroad to serve its wider goals. This did not, of course, absolve the United States of its mistakes, but it cast American power in a more benign light.

This White House did not flinch from using the darker tools of American power: the cold and calculated warfare of drone attacks with its chilling kill lists, unilateral military operations to catch America's most wanted on foreign soil, Internet worms that ate away at the computers at the heart of the Iranian nuclear program. But it did not pursue obscure objectives or a singular goal, or try to fix the facts around an ideology. Despite failures and unfinished business, the Obama foreign policy was seen by many as flexible and pragmatic and allowed the United States to reposition itself in a changing global landscape. And, of course, the United States will continue to weigh values and interests at every turn— but in a more transparent way, if only because of the spotlight of the media.

*   *   *

On the evening of April 25, 2012, Jake was halfway through dinner at his sister's house when his phone rang. Kurt Campbell, the Building's Asia hand, was on the other end, warning Jake he was going to speak in code—this was big, it was urgent, it couldn't wait until they were on a secure line or face-to-face. A very important man from the world's second biggest economy was seeking to come in, Kurt said. Jake tried to visualize the situation—come in to where? The United States? Kurt alluded to an incident two weeks prior when the vice mayor of Chongqing, in Sichuan Province, had sought refuge briefly in a local U.S. consulate. But that was an internal political scandal that the Obama administration had wanted nothing to do with and the official left the consulate after a day. So the man was seeking to get into a diplomatic mission. Jake prodded further. Was the mission in the same city? The capital, came the reply. He has won a prize, Kurt added. Jake was stunned. "THE prize?" He was thinking of the Nobel Prize winner Liu Xiaobo. Kurt suggested the image of Ray Charles.

Finally, the pieces of the puzzle were complete—it was Chinese dissident Chen Guangcheng, a blind civil rights activist known as the "barefoot lawyer," who campaigned against forced abortions by Chinese authorities trying to implement the one-child policy. The authorities had jailed him from 2006 to 2010 and had placed him under house arrest on and off since then. In 2007, Chen had won the Asian equivalent of the Nobel Prize—the Ramon Magsaysay Award—while still in detention for "his irrepressible passion for justice in leading ordinary Chinese citizens to assert their legitimate rights under the law."

Jake called Hillary. Boss, we have an issue, he told her. Stand by. When he updated her later on a secure line from the State Department, Hillary's first instinct was to say "Yes," we have to take this man in. But she wanted Jake and the rest of the team to look at all the legal and political implications first. No one knew exactly what Chen wanted and most assumed he was seeking asylum in the United States, a long and difficult process with many political ramifications for U.S.-Chinese relations. But the clock was ticking fast. Chen's situation was precarious. He was thirty minutes away from the embassy, a wanted man on the run who had escaped house arrest by jumping over the wall surrounding his house and had traveled four hundred miles, driving and walking for several days until he reached Beijing and met up with a contact. He was waiting on the outskirts of the capital in the car of another human rights activist. The Chinese police were in hot pursuit and would find him soon.

At the State Department, Jake and Kurt got on the phone to Beijing to get more details and spoke to the department's top officials, from the chief of staff and counselor Cheryl Mills to legal advisors and the career foreign service diplomat Bill Burns. The president was informed and the White House said it would go with Clinton's decision.

Soon, the choices in front of those meeting at the State Department became clear—not letting him into the embassy was just not an option. But how would he get there? If they told Chen to make his own way to the embassy, without help, he would never make it, and who knew what might happen to him. If the embassy staff picked him up, there was a 95 percent chance he would be able to enter the premises of the embassy, but the U.S. relationship with China might disintegrate. Clinton was getting on a plane in just a few days to participate in another long-planned round of the annual Strategic and Economic Dialogue.

For six intense hours, Jake and the others weighed American values and interests so they could give Hillary as clear a reading as possible of what was at stake and how it might play out. Much of their thinking was being done in a fog of incomplete information and emotions as the hours passed and dawn approached. They instructed embassy staffers in Beijing to start driving toward Chen so they would be ready to pick him up when a decision was reached in Washington. The relationship between the world's two biggest economies, the two biggest world powers, hung in the balance. Around three in the morning, when everybody had weighed in, some in favor, some against, Clinton and her team reached a final decision: the embassy staff should pick up Chen and bring him onto American territory.

On an emotional level, no one was ready to live with the stain of Chen's death or abuse on his or her conscience. On a policy level, the calculation was that the relationship with China would survive, but if Chen was to perish in China the damage to the Obama administration's human rights record would be irreparable. If the relationship with China was going to collapse over this, then it had been a house of cards and it was time to find out.

The saga continued as Clinton arrived in Beijing on May 2. She had said nothing in public about Chen yet and she avoided the traveling press corps while intense negotiations continued with the Chinese. Kurt and Jake, along with the new U.S. ambassador to China, Gary Locke, met with Chen for hours inside the embassy and hammered out details of a deal with Chinese officials. Clinton intervened with State Councilor Dai to seal the agreement. The Chinese promised that Chen and his family would be safe if he left the embassy and that he could pursue legal studies in China. Chen said he was ready to leave the embassy. He was taken to a hospital for treatment of the wounds he had sustained during his escape, but the deal fell through when the Chinese reneged on their promise to treat him and his family well. He was cut off from American officials and his relatives back in his village were harassed. Meanwhile, despite the tensions around Chen, the S&ED dialogue continued, unperturbed, as the two powers discussed the issues that remained key to the relationship. Finally, on May 4, Clinton's last day in Beijing, she negotiated with Dai to allow the barefoot lawyer to leave China. A few weeks later, he flew to New York City with his family.

For Clinton, the Chen Guangcheng affair and its resolution epitomized what she and Obama had set out to achieve at the start of the administration. They had methodically laid the groundwork for a solid, wide-ranging relationship with their rival, the kind that should be able to sustain the blow of a crisis—and it did. The S&ED concluded as planned and Beijing pursued its relationship with Washington almost as before, except for a few expected strident comments.

For Hillary, the denouement was a vindication of the comment she made in Asia, in February 2009, that had caused such consternation. Human rights were indeed one of many issues on the agenda of global cooperation with Beijing but they could still be forcefully defended, perhaps more so, because there was too much at stake for the Chinese to storm off in anger. The administration had replicated this style of engagement across the globe with all the big players on the global stage, from India to South Africa and Brazil, and with smaller countries, such as Vietnam. The stakes of walking away from a relationship with the United States were high for everyone; the damage often outweighed the benefits of a relationship with America. Clinton saw this as the real achievement of her years as secretary of state and of the Obama administration— working with the United States had once again become desirable. There would still be clashes of interest; Washington would continue to be criticized; its policies would still frustrate and anger many—it is after all the fate of every superpower. But America was once more a sought-after partner.

Clinton's record as secretary of state will be judged by many in narrow terms—she did not make peace in the Middle East, stop Iran from pursuing a nuclear program, or set Afghanistan on a certain path to prosperity. But while these failings have an impact on U.S. standing in the world and on American national interests, the narrow prism can miss the wider scope of American influence today.

Perceptions of American power in the United States and around the world are lagging behind the reality of the twenty-first century and the "rise of the rest" not because American power is diminishing but because the nature of power has changed. American power is bigger than the sum of the successes and setbacks on the issues that any administration tackles. While the war in Iraq seemed to send the United States hurtling down the road toward decline, it was indicative of a level of hubris that was out of step with the changing world. The United States can no longer decide what the goal is, how it will be achieved, and then take the lead and force others to follow. There is no "You are with us or against us" anymore.

Clinton's key contribution is therefore more intangible but, if pursued, longer lasting—repositioning America as a leader in a changed world, a palatable global chairman of the board who can help navigate the coming crises, from climate change, to further economic turmoil, to demographic explosions. As part of the Obama administration's effort to redefine American leadership, Clinton became the first secretary of state to methodically implement the concept of smart power. She institutionalized this approach in the Building: budgets now include funds for gender issues, foreign service officers are embedded at the Pentagon, economic statecraft is part of the diplomatic brief. Clinton was determined to make sure her work would not be undone after her departure and planned to invest a lot of her time following up and providing counsel to her successor.

Clinton was ready to glide out of her position as secretary of state with job approval ratings nearing 70 percent, with rumors rife about her potential run for president in 2016, despite her many denials. Then, on

September 11, 2012, militants attacked the U.S. consulate in Benghazi, killing Ambassador Chris Stevens and three other Americans. Clinton had nominated him for the post of ambassador to Libya and felt personally responsible for his death. The attack unleashed a fury of partisan criticism of Obama with Republicans predicting the unraveling of his foreign policy. But Obama stayed the course. Despite the shock and pain surrounding Chris's death and the clear security failure, the administration understood this was the price to pay for expeditionary diplomacy. Ever the politician, Clinton managed to dodge most of the acrimonious attacks.

By the time she left office, Clinton had traveled a million miles, rebuilding her country's image with her relentless public diplomacy and quietly reasserting American leadership.

Obama and Clinton believed that for America to continue to lead it had to rebuild a sound economic base at home, but early in their tenures the two former rivals differed in tone when they spoke about American leadership. Obama didn't fully embrace American exceptionalism and hesitated to speak forcefully about American power. Over the course of his presidency, he realized that he sounded too modest about what America was and what it wanted to do. He was signaling that America was going home, and this opened a gap that was now being filled by China or Turkey, countries that have a stake in running the world but are still too focused on their own narrow, domestic needs and problems to exercise global leadership.

By the time he gave his State of the Union address in 2012, Obama was on the same page as Clinton.

"From the coalitions we've built to secure nuclear materials, to the missions we've led against hunger and disease; from the blows we've dealt to our enemies, to the enduring power of our moral example, America is back," Obama said when he addressed Congress in January 2012.

"Anyone who tells you otherwise, anyone who tells you that America is in decline or that our influence has waned, doesn't know what they're talking about."

The Obama administration has laid the groundwork for continued American leadership into the twenty-first century. The foundations are still fragile and there are no guarantees of success. But Clinton and Obama strongly believed that smart power was the only way forward for America.

"This is truly the inflection point, because we now understand that

America, as powerful and strong as we are, cannot remake societies," Clinton told me. "We can help liberate them, like Libya, but we cannot remake them. That must come from within, and there needs to be a reformation in thinking amongst people in countries that have been downtrodden, oppressed, violence-ridden, and there needs to be higher expectations and demands placed on leaders who should be reconcilers, not dividers."

"The kind of help we need in the twenty-first century is for people themselves to overcome the differences that still divide them," Clinton told me during the interview for the book.

As a superpower, America has been more willing than past empires to share the world that it has made, and there's something there to hold on to. The difference between American power when I lived on the receiving end of it and today is that the gap between what America says it's doing and what it is doing is becoming narrower. The difference between now and then is Tahrir Square, Twitter, the Syrian rebels, Chen Guangcheng, Sherhbano Taseer, Mohamed Bouazizi, and all those who are no longer willing to be taken for granted, not by the United States and not by their own rulers. Knee-jerk reactions blaming every wrong on America are outdated and not very productive. There are too many ways to effect change without the United States, or harness American power to advance one's cause.

I had reached the end of my own journey too. I still struggle to accept that the Syrian invasion of Lebanon was one of those inconsistencies of American foreign policy. But I have met the human beings at the heart of the American foreign policy machine and I was willing to accept that they did not make decisions about war and peace blithely, at least not anymore. And while the anger and sense of betrayal I felt as a young teenager in Beirut are still with me, they are mitigated by my new understanding of American might and its limits. I can now see America for what it is, not what I want it to be or what was convenient for me to consider it. That perspective may be a more challenging one to hold, but I believe it is truer to the realities of today's world. There is greater strength in that and a wider horizon of possibility.

NOTES

This book is based almost entirely on firsthand reporting on the road with Hillary Clinton, as well as on hours of interviews in Washington and abroad that I conducted on deep background. Except for a couple of stops, I was on all the trips described on these pages. When I recount private meetings and conversations, I am relying on interviews with people who witnessed these events themselves or learned of their details from participants. Passages in which I describe a person's thoughts are based on interviews with either the person in question or people from his or her entourage with direct knowledge of that information. I did not source quotes from foreign officials that are in the public domain. All public statements by President Obama can be found on www.whitehouse .gov. The secretary of state's public statements are posted on www.state.gov.

1. "An Interview with Hillary Clinton," *Economist*, March 22, 2012, available at http:// www.economist.com/blogs/lexington/2012/03/foreign-policy.
2. See Associated Press, February 20, 2009.
3. "Confidence in Obama Lifts U.S. Image Around the World," Pew Research Center, July 23, 2009, available at http://pewresearch.org/pubs/1289/global-attitudes-survey -2009-obama-lifts-america-image.
4. Anne Marie Slaughter, "America's Edge: Power in the Networked Century," *Foreign Affairs*, January/February 2009, available at http://www.foreignaffairs.com/articles /63722/anne-marie-slaughter/americas-edge.
5. J. Bader, *Obama and China's Rise: An Insider's Account of America's Asia Strategy* (Washington: Brookings Institution Press, 2012).
6. H. Kissinger, *On China* (New York: Penguin Press, 2011), p. 501.
7. P. Beinart, *The Crisis of Zionism* (New York: Times Books, 2012).
8. A. D. Miller, *The Much Too Promised Land* (New York: Bantam Books, 2008).
9. M. Albright, *Madam Secretary* (New York: Hyperion, 2003).
10. Beinart, *The Crisis of Zionism*.

11. O. B. Jones, "How Punjab Governor's Killer Became a Hero," BBC News, 2012, available at http://www.bbc.co.uk/news/magazine-16443556.

12. Beinart, *The Crisis of Zionism.*

13. J. Klein, "Q&A: Obama on His First Year in Office," *Time*, January 21, 2010, available at http://www.time.com/time/politics/article/0,8599,1955072,00.html.

14. D. G. McCullough, *Truman* (New York: Simon and Schuster, 1992).

15. Ibid.

16. W. A. Eddy, *FDR Meets Ibn Saud* (New York: American Friends of the Middle East, 1954).

17. M. Hirsh, "Obama's Bad Cop," *Daily Beast*, April 22, 2010, available at http://www.thedailybeast.com/newsweek/2010/04/22/obama-s-bad-cop.html.

18. WikiLeaks cables.

19. M. Muasher, *The Arab Center: The Promise of Moderation* (New Haven, Conn.: Yale University Press, 2008), p. 190.

20. Eddy, *FDR Meets Ibn Saud.*

21. Ibid.

22. I. Malsang, "Arab Women Happier than US Thinks, Saudi Students Tell Bush Aide," AFP, September 29, 2005.

23. N. Kralev, "Hughes Asked to Correct Misperceptions in U.S.," *Washington Times*, September 28, 2005.

24. "China Seen Overtaking U.S. as Global Superpower," Pew Research Center, July 13, 2011, available at http://www.pewglobal.org/2011/07/13/china-seen-overtaking-us-as-global-superpower/.

25. Ibid.

26. Kissinger, *On China.*

27. S. Zhihua, trans. N. Silver, *Mao, Stalin and the Korean War* (New York: Routledge, 2012).

28. *Korea Herald*, July 22, 2010.

29. H. Kissinger, *Years of Upheaval* (New York: Little Brown, 1982).

30. O. A. Westad, *The Global Cold War: Third World Interventions and the Making of Our Times* (New York: Cambridge University Press, 2005).

31. D. Leigh and L. Harding, *WikiLeaks: Inside Julian Assange's War on Secrecy* (New York: PublicAffairs, 2011).

32. Verbatim quote from French official.

33. M. Calabresi, "Hillary Clinton and the Limits of Power," *Time*, October 27, 2011, available at http://swampland.time.com/2011/10/27/hillary-clinton-and-the-limits-of-power/.

34. Ibid.

35. Name has been changed for privacy.

36. Name has been changed for privacy.

37. Phrase inspired by W. R. Mead, "The Myth of America's Decline," *Wall Street Journal*, April 9, 2012.

BIBLIOGRAPHY

I have spent endless hours over the last few years pondering American power and America's place in the world. I referred extensively to these books to inspire my own analysis, understand the past, learn the context of certain events, or explore the possibilities of the future.

Albright, M. K. (2003). *Madame Secretary: A Memoir.* New York: Miramax.

Attali, J. (2011). *Demain, qui gouvernera le monde?* Paris: Fayard.

Baker III, J. A. (1995). *The Politics of Diplomacy: Revolution, War & Peace, 1989–1992.* New York: Putnam Adult.

Beinart, P. (2010). *The Icarus Syndrome: A History of American Hubris.* New York: Harper.

Ben Jelloun, T. (2011). *L'étincelle: Révoltes dans les pays arabes.* Paris: Gallimard.

Bernstein, C. (2007). *A Woman in Charge: The Life of Hillary Rodham Clinton.* New York: Knopf.

Bremmer, I. (2012). *Every Nation for Itself: Winners and Losers in a G-Zero World.* New York: Penguin.

Bush, G. W. (2010). *Decision Points.* New York: Crown.

Chandrasekaran, R. (2012). *Little America: The War Within the War for Afghanistan.* New York: Knopf.

Clinton, H. R. (2003). *Living History.* New York: Simon and Schuster.

Kagan, R. (2012). *The World America Made.* New York: Knopf.

Kennedy, P. (1987). *The Rise and Fall of Great Powers: Economic Change and Military Conflict from 1500 to 2000.* New York: Random House.

Kessler, G. (2007). *The Confidante: Condoleezza Rice and the Creation of the Bush Legacy.* New York: St. Martin's Press.

Kissinger, H. (1994). *Diplomacy.* New York: Simon & Schuster.

Kissinger, H. (2011). *On China.* New York: Penguin Press.

Kupchan, C. A. (2012). *No One's World: The West, the Rising Rest, and the Coming Global Turn*. New York: Oxford University Press.

Mandelbaum, M. (2010). *The Frugal Superpower: America's Global Leadership in a Cash-Strapped Era*. New York: PublicAffairs.

Mann, J. (2012). *The Obamians: The Struggle Inside the White House to Redefine American Power*. New York: Viking Books.

Nye, J. S. (2011). *The Future of Power*. New York: PublicAffairs.

Rachman, G. (2011). *Zero-Sum Future: American Power in an Age of Anxiety*. New York: Simon & Schuster.

Rice, C. (2011). *No Higher Honor: A Memoir of My Years in Washington*. New York: Crown.

Romney, M. (2010). *No Apology: The Case for American Greatness*. New York: St. Martin's Press.

Sanger, D. E. (2012). *Confront and Conceal: Obama's Secret Wars and Surprising Use of American Power*. New York: Crown.

Schaffer, T. C., and H. B. Schaffer. (2011). *How Pakistan Negotiates with the United States: Riding the Roller Coaster*. Washington, D.C.: The United States Institute of Peace.

Zakaria, F. (2008). *The Post-American World*. New York: W. W. Norton & Company.

ACKNOWLEDGMENTS

This book is truly the product of a long journey that started well before I put pen to paper and there are many people to thank.

I am forever indebted to the BBC's foreign news editor Jon Williams who has always believed in me and appointed me as State Department correspondent—I clearly could not have written this book from Beirut. BBC Washington Bureau chief Simon Wilson has supported my career at the BBC for over a decade and always encouraged me to reach higher. I am grateful to both for giving me the time and space to write this book. Thanks as well to Fran Unsworth for giving her backing to the project.

I am lucky to work for an organization like the BBC, which continues to invest in coverage of international news and the outstanding journalists who deliver it to audiences around the planet. I am grateful to all my BBC colleagues in all the countries I visited on my travels with Clinton. They welcomed me in their sometimes cramped offices and pulled off logistical miracles at short notice without ever complaining they were being big-footed. Specials thanks to Lyse Doucet, Orla Guerin, Aleem Maqbool, Jo Floto, Annie Phrommayon, Gidi Kleiman, Jon Leyne, Damian Grammaticas, Alan Quartly, Joe Phua, Ali Faisal Zadi, Bhas Solanki, Kevin Kim, Alan Quartly, Jimmy Michael, Rachel Thompson, and Ian Druce.

The BBC bureau in Washington cheered me on collectively. I am especially thankful to Paul Adams and Jonny Dymond for telling me to go home (and Jonny for reading my galleys as well), Adam Brookes for being my trusted soundboard for months on end, Christina Curtis for being so much more than an editor, and Ian and Lou Pannell for giving me sustenance on the last day with beer-butt chicken.

My colleagues from the State Department press corps are some of the smartest, kindest, and funniest journalists I have worked with. Thank you for making life on the road such an adventure. In particular, Glenn Kessler from the *Washington Post* told me everything I needed to know before applying for the job of State Department correspondent and has been a great friend and colleague during my time on the job. He read my draft and provided wise, detailed advice as only a master fact-checker can do. Helene Cooper cheered me on when the book was just a nascent idea and introduced me to my agent. Thanks as well to Joby Warrick, Mark Landler, Matthew Lee, Christophe Schmidt, Anne Gearan, Michel Ghandour, Samir Nader, and Sylvie Lanteaume.

Over the course of my career, I have worked for several great news organizations and have learned much from inspiring colleagues, including Roula Khalaf at the *Financial Times*, Lee Hockstader at the *Washington Post*, and Nicholas Blanford at the *Daily Star* who gave me my first break. I am also deeply grateful to David Ignatius for giving me the confidence to write my story and for understanding the world I come from.

When it came to the actual writing of the book I was lucky to find my inimitable agent Dorian Karchmar at William Morris Endeavor. She believed in this idea from the start and pushed me to dig deeper and deeper as I developed the concept of the book. She made me rewrite the proposal so many times that I was close to giving up, but during the arduous process I found my voice as an author and refined the thoughts that form the backbone of the book. Her energy is limitless and contagious.

The team at Holt embraced the project from the moment they read the first pages. My wonderful editor Serena Jones accompanied me on this journey and helped make the book better with tact and good humor. She made sure I reached the finish line while shielding me from the pressures of the publishing world. She never lost patience, even when I promised, repeatedly, that I was really almost there. Paul Golob improved the manuscript with his attention to detail. I could not have had a more dedicated team to promote the book than Maggie Richards, Melanie DeNardo, and Pat Eisemann. Thanks as well to Steve Rubin who told me only I could write this book. Designer David Shoemaker started with a few vague lines of guidance and created a striking cover that reflects the essence of the book and my journey better than I could have ever pictured. Jacquelyn Martin from the Associated Press was kind enough to work magic with her camera during a grueling trip and her photo makes the cover unique.

Although I was not counting on the cooperation of Hillary Clinton and her aides before I started this project, writing the book without their help would have been an even more arduous task. They never asked for the details of my project and they may disagree with my conclusions but I thank them for the access they provided. Philippe Reines and Caroline Adler gathered key information and answered endless questions in person and by e-mail. Victoria Nuland never tired of answering my relentless "But why?" Thanks to Nick Merrill and Ashley Yehl for their help on the road. Thanks as well to Huma Abedin and Cheryl Mills.

I wrote this book over the course of twelve very intense months during which I interviewed officials, former officials, junior officials, and their staff members, in Washington, Paris, Rome, Islamabad, Ankara, Tripoli, Cairo, and elsewhere, in person and over the phone. Several of them sat with me several times for hours on end, sharing their time, information, and insights. Several wished to remain anonymous but my writing and my analysis was enriched thanks to all of their generosity: P. J. Crowley, Jon Huntsman, Dennis Ross, Lissa Muscatine, Kurt Campbell, Karl Eikenberry, Jake Sullivan, Joe Macmanus, Jeffery Feltman, Brent Scowcroft, Eric Melby, Vali Nasr, Molly Montgomery, Fred Ketchem, Jeffrey Bader, Anne-Marie Slaughter, Lew Lukens, Edward Djerjian, Robert Wood, Husain Haqqani, Shehrbano Taseer, Aamna Taseer, Bernadette Meehan, Paul Narain, Ahmet Davutoğlu, Mahmoud Jibril, Ahmed Aboul Gheit, Osman Sert, Franco Frattini, Jean David Levitte, Maurizio Capra, Giuseppe Manzo, and Mirjam Krijnen.

Several people read the manuscript at different stages and helped greatly improve it. Special thanks go to Azadeh Moaveni, my longtime friend and intellectual partner and an accomplished author herself. She challenged me when needed and poured her soul into helping me refine my draft. This book would not be what it is without her. At WME, the gifted Simone Blaser went beyond the call of duty, tidied up my ramblings and my English, and asked unexpected questions. Andrew Small and Daniel Levy provided much needed expertise and made many corrections.

Jeremy Bowen has been an amazing colleague and true friend for years; his knowledge, reporting, and magical writing inspire me every day. Jad Salhab probably knows me better than anyone; he read my draft at short notice and reminded me of my roots. Marwan Muasher's enthusiasm after reading my proposal helped me believe I was on to something.

In my research I benefited from the help of four very bright recent university graduates who have great careers ahead of them. Eric Hoerger put in long hours of indispensable, sometimes tedious, research over many months and adopted the book as his own. The multiskilled Paul Blake helped me further understand the America outside of Washington and repeatedly tested some of my ideas among his friends. David Avalos and Ben Bulmer also pitched in at various early stages.

I am fortunate to have loving friends who stay close even when they are far away. They are my anchors and I am grateful that they didn't give up on me when I became a hermit. Michele and Karim Chaya have been a source of strength for years; Lamia Matta and Joe Newman were a second home right next door and endured endless moaning over good food and late-night drinks. Joe also took pictures and helped me create a website. The unflappable Joyce Karam saved the day multiple times. Karim Sadjadpour, aka D.C.'s handsome sheikh, has been my trusted guide to all things Washington. Tony Yazbek never doubted his high school classmate when she told him she was going be a journalist. Alexis Morel and Apolline de Malherbe continue to provide intellectual and culinary sustenance. Katie and Jonathan Whitney made a wonderful, indelible mark on Washington. Robin Shulman was the first to tell me I had to write a book; Carine Chebli and Baptiste Desplats gave me a place to write, twice. Kate Seelye has taught me a lot of what I know about how America sees the Middle East; Beirut and Washington would not be the same without her. Petra Stienen, Lubna Dimashki, and Josephine Frantzen were always a phone call away when I flagged. Elise Labott constantly made sure I was still alive. Nicole Gaouette listened to me go on about the book in Washington and on endless flights around the world. Thanks also to Kurt Hamrock, Ky Ta, and Anna Driggs for being on the eighth floor.

I would not have made it to the finish line without Marcel de Vink. He was there when the book was born; he inspired and nurtured my ideas with his rigor and brilliant mind. He kept me real, made me laugh, and helped me through the darkest moments with endless patience.

I would never have embarked on this journey without my parents, Raymond and Helen. Through fifteen years of war, my parents kept us safe and under one roof and did their best to provide us with normal lives. Living through war is nothing to be thankful for but it did push me to always seek meaning in life. Through shelling, water shortages, and near-death experiences at checkpoints, my parents taught me never to give up and to never blame anyone or anything else for what's going wrong in my life. I am in awe of their strength and grateful for their boundless love, and I hope that, after many rebellions, my choices make sense. My sisters, Ingrid and Audrey, their husbands, and my nieces and nephews bring joy to my life every day and have put up with many absences, real and virtual. My sisters are my best friends. They have been there for me every single day of my life. There are simply no words to describe my love for them.

INDEX

HRC = Hillary Rodham Clinton

ABOUT THE AUTHOR

KIM GHATTAS has been the BBC's State Department radio and TV correspondent since 2008. She traveled three hundred thousand miles around the world with Hillary Clinton and interviewed her more than fifteen times. Ghattas was previously a Middle East correspondent for the BBC and the *Financial Times*, based in Beirut. She was part of an Emmy Award–winning BBC team covering the Lebanon-Israel conflict in 2006. Her work has also appeared in *Time* magazine, the *Boston Globe*, and the *Washington Post* and on NPR radio. Ghattas was born and raised in Beirut during the Lebanese civil war. She currently lives in Washington, D.C.